The Nancy Tapes

Sidney Krome

AmErica House
Baltimore

Copyright 2000 by Sidney Krome

All rights reserved. No part of this book may be reproduced in any form without written permission from the publishers, except by a reviewer who may quote brief passages in a review to be printed in a newspaper or magazine.

First printing

ISBN 1-58851-504-4
PUBLISHED BY AMERICA HOUSE BOOK PUBLISHERS
www.publishamerica.com
Baltimore

Printed in the United States of America

ZICHRONAM LIVRACHA
MAY THEIR MEMORY BE A BLESSING

Nancy Kanow Simpson

Morris Kanow
Charles Krome
Sol Koren
Freda Herlich Bulmash
Eva Mae Hirsch Krome
Aaron Bulmash
Solomon B. Levin
Louis Rose
Esther Bitzeh Bineh Pineh Bessie Kolker
Perluk Herlich Kanow Koren Kaminsky

ACKNOWLEDGEMENTS

I would be remiss if I did not thank four people without whom my dream of publishing *The Nancy Tapes* could not have come to fruition: Willem Meiners, my publisher, for his belief in the book from the moment he read the manuscript; Christen Beckmann, my editor, for her commitment to putting the manuscript into publishable shape; Gary W. Kroeker, my friend and fellow writer, for his support for my writing through a decade of friendship, often through cyberspace; and most especially, Sophia Mastros Krome, my wife, for her belief in me, her commitment to me, and her support of me through 32 years of time and space.

To understand what really happened to us, imagine attempting to reverse the process. Imagine *wanting* to take a whole afternoon to prepare supper leisurely--without food processor, microwave oven, or cookbook. To live, after all, is to experience things, and every time we mince an onion, lower the flame under a simmering pot, shape the idea and substance of a meal, we actually gain rather than lose lived time. Anyone who has seriously attempted to do such cooking knows that it requires a kind of commitment that we are no longer able to give our quotidian lives, for this experience has become too dear for casual expenditure.

From "THE MACHINE IN THE KITCHEN" in *HARPER'S MAGAZINE*, November 1990, pp. 32-34, 36, 40; p. 36: "*From* 'Cuisine Mecanique,' by John Thorne, in the Spring 1990 issue of The Journal of Gastronomy, *published by the American Institute of Wine and Food in San Francisco. Thorne, who lives in Castine, Maine, is the author of a collection of essays,* Simple Cooking, *and a quarterly newsletter of the same name. His essay 'Vulgar Recipes' appeared in the November 1989 issue of* Harper's Magazine."

From Tape 951206A
Tuesday, December 31, 1995

On *NYPD Blue,* Zitowitz Zipowitz, the character Zipowitz [i.e., Sipowicz), after realizing that the murder of the older woman who ran the candy store was done by an old neighborhood kid, now a grown man, who was put up to the job by one of the two sons of the old lady and old man. And, of course, he didn't expect his mother to get killed, he thought the father would be there and give up the money, but she was there and apparently she tried to hold off and the guy shot her and killed her. And anyhow after they're all taken in custody, he goes back to the office, to the police department, and somebody says something to him. And he says something like, There are some things in life that you would like to be able to keep just the way they were, and that candy store was one of them. But unfortunately, it was not to be so, at least not in his life. So, it was not kept, but the point of the line was some things in life that you'd like to keep the way they were and one of them was the candy store. And there certainly are some things in life that you would like to keep, that we would like to keep, that I would like to keep the way they were, and that's very hard to do. That's actually, it's impossible to do. Over and out. Bye-bye.

Preface

In October 1990, my cousin, Nancy Kanow Simpson, went into The Johns Hopkins Hospital for her third--and last, but not the way we hoped--open-heart surgery. At the time of her first, in 1960, I was in the Army, at the US Army Language School. When her older sister Ruth told me that she needed a supply of blood to make up for whatever blood she would need for the heart-lung machine, I spread the word on the base asking that, at the Red Cross Blood Drive on the base, blood be donated in her name with her surgeon's name part of the destination. Within a day, Ruth called to tell me to tell the guys to stop: they had more than enough.

Between the first and the second in 1977, Nancy got married in 1964 to the legendary "boy-next-door" (but legends are often no match for reality, and that marriage eventually ended in divorce). On the morning of the wedding, Nancy asked me to take her to the cemetery so she could visit the grave of her father, Morris Kanow; she wanted us to go quietly, with no mention either to her mother, my Aunt Esther, or to our Uncle Layble from Montreal, who could have said prayers at Uncle Morris's grave. At the time of that second open-heart surgery, I asked Ruth if I should ask Nancy if she wanted me to visit her father's grave for her: I didn't know whether Nancy would think I was being gloomy and pessimistic or if she would really want me to go. Ruth thought about it, and then said that since Nancy and I had had our private trip to Uncle Morris's grave 13 years before, maybe it *would* be okay for me to ask Nancy. Nancy said yes, and I went on her behalf, alone.

So on the day of Nancy's third open-heart surgery, October 22, 1990, instead of being at the hospital to see Nancy with other members of the family, I went, alone, to Uncle Morris's grave, and I was there at 8:35 a.m., the time the surgery began.

And though I went alone, I didn't go alone: I carried with me a microcassette recorder. Sometime before, I had decided to carry one to record my thoughts and possible subjects for poems or stories, so that I would not have to worry about stopping to write things down. I began recording that morning at the cemetery. I don't really know why. Somehow, intuitively, I knew that soon I would need this recorder. And over the next nine days--as "the weather" and Nancy's condition "turned 'round," as she went into a coma before she even came down to the Coronary ICU, a coma from which she would not awaken--until her death on Tuesday, October 30, 1990, we gathered in the hospital waiting room and lounge, waiting and talking, waiting and praying, waiting and hoping. And as we waited and talked, I kept talking into my recorder, my thoughts and those of others in the family. And on the day of her funeral on November 1, 1990, I kept talking into my recorder. For days and weeks and months, I kept talking into my recorder. And I learned how much it became a life- and mind- and self-saving device in a way that I could not have imagined on that Monday morning when I went to see Uncle Morris in the cemetery.

At some point--I don't really remember when--I knew that some day I would transcribe what I had recorded, transcribe it and print it and make copies for everyone in the family who was there, who shared the time and the space and the anguish and the pain and the hope and the love of the waiting.

Then, in 1996 after I had finally begun the transcribing--that painful reliving of those days and nights--when I told my ophthalmologist what I was doing, he said something like, "That sounds like something a lot of people could identify with!" And so I began to think of trying to have what I now called *The Nancy Tapes* published.

In 1998, after a number of failed attempts to find a publisher, I reached Wim Meiners. When he read it, he responded with enthusiasm, but he also said that rather than *The Nancy Tapes*, the manuscript should be called *The Sidney Tapes* because it was as much or more about my finally coming to grips with the death of my father, Charles Krome, in 1954, and the deaths of so many others in the family, especially Uncle Morris Kanow in 1950, Aunt Freda Herlich Bulmash in 1954, Uncle Sol Koren in 1954, and Eva Mae Hirsch Krome in 1961.

And so the book now has, for me, a double focus, on Nancy and the terrible days in October 1990, and on my own grieving and grief, still sharp and painful after all these years.

There are two important epigraphs to this book. The first and original one-- about cooking slowly, being conscious of each step along the way, being aware of being alive at every moment; and the second one, newly added as I prepared the manuscript for publication--about wanting to be able to keep some things as they were and finally having to accept that that is not possible, except in our memories and in our hearts. As my wife Sophia said more than a year after the death of her mother, Maria Loizos Mastros, "I want her back."; "I know," I told her, "I want all of them back."

And so, too, this book has as its cover photograph a picture I took shortly after Nancy died, a picture of 2614 and 2616 Springhill Avenue, homes where Kromes and Kanows shared the 18 years of their lives that became memories for their lifetimes.

SIDNEY KROME

I wrote the following for the Herlich Family Newsletter issue of January 1991.

NANCY KANOW SIMPSON
OCTOBER 8, 1942 - OCTOBER 30, 1990

YIZKOR ... V'NIZKOR ...

"Earth's the right place for love."

"Birches"
Robert Frost

To Aunt Esther, she was daughter; to Joe, wife; to Allyson and Darren, as to Kim and Ken, mother; to Ruth, sister; to Dave, sister-in-law; to Mindy and Brian and Craig, aunt; to Aunt Lily and my mother, niece; to the rest of us, cousin. And more. To Ruth she was also best friend, in the way that people have only one. To Dave she was, as Rabbi Goren said, more sister than in-law; to my own sister Nancy she was, as Cheryl said to Darren, sister and friend more than cousin. And when she died in the evening of Tuesday, October 30, she left, as Jerry said, a deep and painful void in the hearts of all of us.

That Tuesday, at about 10:15 a.m., Ruth and I went down to the Johns Hopkins Hospital cafeteria to get a cup of coffee and talk. Among other things, we spoke about the existential attitude toward life: that each person must not be defined by others or by some generalization about his or her group but that he or she must find and set his or her own values and meaning within the context of his or her own life. After we came back up to the Cardiac Surgery Intensive Care Unit to await word about Nancy's condition and Dr. R told Ruth that he felt the time was right to disconnect the bi-ventricular pump which was pumping blood through Nancy's lungs and body, I said that Nancy's existential moment had come, the moment when a critical life-determining choice had to be made; and Ruth answered that in *this* case the choice was being made not by Nancy herself but by another. But we both knew that Nancy had indeed made the choice for her existential moment not just when she chose to go ahead with this surgery but in every moment of her life.

Although she had a congenital heart condition (an aortic valve problem), Nancy never let that condition determine her life for her. While there were some things she was not able to do, she did not dwell on those things; instead, she focused on-and chose always to do-the thing she could do: live. Twice before Nancy had chosen to have surgery for her heart condition: in 1960 and again in 1977. Each surgery was more complicated, more difficult than the one before, and the one she had this October was the most complicated of all, involving not only replacement of the artificial valve implanted in 1977 but also reconstruction of her aorta and left ventricle so that, for the first time in her life, she would have blood circulating through her body without being restricted. Nancy's decision each time to go ahead with surgery was based on a simple concept: it could enable her to go on living. When it came time for this operation, Nancy knew the risks, but she also knew clearly her options: not having the surgery meant passive acceptance of an inevitable end, the certainty of sudden or slow death; having the surgery meant active participation in the possibility of life. Nancy, being Nancy, could not have chosen other than she did.

There is a line in *STAR TREK: THE SEARCH FOR SPOCK* which fits Nancy and her life and her choice: as Kirk and McCoy stand on the Genesis planet and watch the self-destructed Enterprise streak like an enormous flaming meteorite through the atmosphere, Kirk asks, "My G-d, Bones, what have I done?" and McCoy answers, "What you always do, Jim, turn death into a fighting chance for life." Nancy's choices were always for life, not for herself alone but for her family and her friends as well, and thus her choice for life was also always a choice for love. And her life and her love were a gift to us all, a gift she gave not only of herself to us but also of us to her and of us to us.

In the nine days many of us spent in the family lounge of the CSICU, from the day of Nancy's surgery on Monday, October 22, to the day of her death on Tuesday, October 30, we shared not only the agony of waiting but also the hope, not only the pain of grief in our sorrow but also the comfort of love. Our being together was one last gift to us from Nancy: she knew that we were there, she knew that our love was directed toward her, and she knew that our being together would make what Kathie called the *"devastatingly* unbearable" pain of her loss as bearable as such pains can be. In Nancy's funeral service, Rabbi Goren spoke of that lounge, of being in that room with us on Monday night, after the news from the operating room had turned bad that afternoon and the news from the ICU ate away at our hope that evening; he spoke of the love which we shared and which would abide in that room long after we were gone. We will, all of us, remember that room for what Nancy enabled us to give to each other even as we strived so hard to give something to her: Brian focusing his energy on his Aunt Nancy; the group of us joining hands as Rabbi Goren led us in prayer; Mindy, Allyson, Kim, Ken, Cheryl, Jon, Craig, and Joel there with us every day-unwilling or unable to break away, wanting to add their youth and energy to try and help; Ronny being both very personal and professional-whatever we all needed; the incredibly supportive phone calls from so many family members; Darren sharing with us his poem about the sun in Nancy's eyes, in his mother's eyes.

As I offered a toast at Myron and Marilyn's wedding in Montreal last year, I said that I took inspiration where I found it, and for that occasion I took it from a gravestone in a cemetery: someone had engraved on the stone, *Le Coeur Qui A Profondement Aimé N'Oublie Jamais*, The Heart That Has Loved Deeply Never Forgets. That inscription needs to be changed now for Nancy: *Le Coeur Qui A Profondement Aimé Ne S'Oublie Jamais*, The Heart That Has Loved Deeply Is Never Forgotten.

Sid

THE NANCY TAPES

SIDNEY KROME

The first word goes to Ruth, Nancy's sister, what she wrote that Dave Weinstein read at Nancy's funeral on November 1, 1990.

Thoughts from Ruth:

I woke up very early this morning as I often do when I have too many things going on in my mind. It's an attempt on my part to try to get things organized and understood, a way of trying to make order out of chaos. This morning I was trying to make some sense out of today, some way of gaining strength just to get through today. These are some of my thoughts. They gave comfort to me - maybe they'll be helpful to you.

I am comforted by the fact that even though I don't know or understand much about a spiritual life after death, I have no doubt that if anyone could get that straightened out--and be a resource for strength, wisdom and support for us--it would be Nancy. In her own quiet way, her competence and determination to make things better and easier for those she loved and cared about will always be there.

Over these past months and especially these last weeks we were tied to Nancy in many special ways. All of us were there for her physically, emotionally, and spiritually. And she knew it!! She told me this before the operation. She felt so comforted by the out pouring of love and concern. Not only were we there for her, but we were there for each other. This experience has brought us closer and more loving than we've ever been. We said good-bye to Nancy two days ago. And her spirit and love will be with us forever.

And, even though we are all so terribly sad right now, and there may be times when we are so sad that we can't find her gift, her strength inside us, we can find that gift, Nancy's spirit, inside each other.

Today we are going through the FORMAL RITUAL of paying our respects and sharing our love. Today is really the opportunity for all the others who love Nancy and who love us to have the opportunity to do the same thing.

I love you Nancy, and I love you all.

THE NANCY TAPES

TAPE NUMBER 1B

MONDAY, OCTOBER 22, 1990
    Testing. Testing. 1, 2, 3. Okay, it's Monday, October the 22nd, 8:45 a.m. I'm just pulling out of the Hebrew Young Men's Association Cemetery where I've come from talking with Uncle Morris, and I'm on my way to pick up Mother and go to the hospital right now. Today's Nancy's surgery, and I came up here to talk with Uncle Morris. I talked with Nancy yesterday, and she said she would like me to go if I had the chance. I had come here with her when she asked me to on the day she and Dave got married. And I came the day of her second surgery in 1977.
    I got here about ten after eight, and I was leaving about 8:35, and something--actually, I was in the car and I was halfway down the roadway towards the exit to get out of the cemetery--and something told me to go back, so I went back. And I stood again at Uncle Morris's stone, leaning on his stone, and then just at 8:40 I said I had to stay for five more minutes. Then the haze of fog paled and cleared just a little bit, enough for me to see a very hazy pale sun, and as a matter of fact, now, I'm heading east towards the sun and the sky cleared and the sun, there was a bright white sun, kind of bright not normally bright but brighter than it had been. Now I have to go get my mother, and let's see trying to figure the best way--oh, well, I missed a turn, I guess I'll go back up Forest Park Avenue and cut across Forest Park Avenue to get her.
    I asked Uncle Morris to, well, among other things, I told him I was going up to be with the family, and I asked him to please be with Nancy in the operating room to hold her hand, to comfort her, to give her his father's love, to help her to live. And if he couldn't help her to live, to help her to die. To help make the passage easier. But that he should help her, he should be with her, he should be a good pleader for her, for her sake. So that she could live. He used to say, I remember the only one of the few things I remember him saying, "Hey, boy, get off the lawn!" Uncle Morris, I was on your grave, I said. To disturb your peace so that you could help give Nancy peace. To help her to live, help her to live.
    It's a very foggy day today. The fog has lifted, but the clouds are kinda thick, and it's very, very grey, and the sun keeps occasionally hazing, coming out of the haze and going back into it. Hazing in and out. But the fog has lifted quite a bit since I first got to the cemetery.

WEDNESDAY, OCTOBER 24, 1990
    Good morning, Mr. Phelps. This is Sidney Krome. It's now 8:08, Wednesday, October the 24th. I'm getting ready to pull out of the parking lot at Valley Village Center. And I'm on my way back to--I can't believe the traffic here. The way these people block the lanes so they can sit and wait for their lousy left-turn, and they block the light. Anyhow.

THE NANCY TAPES

I'm on my way back to the cemetery to see Uncle Morris. Before I go back down to the hospital to see Nancy, well, actually, to see Joe. I guess that's the trouble, I won't get to see Nancy, I don't get to see Nancy. Time out, gotta stop.

Okay, I'm on the road now. Down Reisterstown Road, heading back to the Hebrew Young Men's Association Cemetery where Uncle Morris is buried. To see him again. Before I go down to the hospital where Nancy still is. I don't know how she is this morning, I haven't called in.

But anyhow, to pick up. Sat, uh Monday, the day of the surgery, everybody was gathered at the hospital. I went out, I guess about a quarter to two, to call Sophie, just to let her know that there really wasn't much news again. Just to tell her again about the surgery. I had called her once earlier to tell her that at 10:30-- Nancy had been right on the money in terms of, I mean my sister Nancy had been right on target in terms of timing--that at 10:30 we got word that she was hooked up to the by-pass machine, and they were ready to begin the actual surgery itself on on uh No, no, wait, let me back up. Let me back up. Cheez! I should've done some of this before, but anyhow.

When I got down there, you may remember that Monday when I went to the cemetery at 8:30, I started to leave and something told me I should go back, and I went back and stayed another five minutes. Well, when I got down to the hospital, Joe told me that, well, they took Nancy up at 6:30 and while the surgery was supposed to begin at 8, the surgeon did not actually make the first incision until about 8:30. Which I thought was kind of weird in terms of how I had felt at 8:30 about having to go back to see Uncle Morris for at least another couple minutes, 'cause I had this really strong feeling to go back.

Well, anyhow, Nancy said that she expected that by 10:30, we would hear that the bypass machine was hooked up, but that the surgeon said he could begin the actual work on the heart at about 10:30 if she was okay.

Anyhow, I tried to call Sophie, and she was out at a meeting, I think, anyhow so I called her back about a quarter to--no, I called her then, and then I tried to call her after 12, but she was I guess at lunch. So I called her back about a quarter to two, ten of two, and when I came out from talking with her, I started to walk into the lounge area there. Joe had just gotten, had just been told to come up to the desk, and the woman at the desk was telling him, and he was, y'know, making a nice cheering sign that the, that Nancy had been disconnected from the bypass machine, that her heart was beating on its own, that, and over the next little bit we were told that in effect that they would be closing her up and the surgeon would probably be coming down, Dr. R would be coming down almost at any time because usually he let other people close.

Well, time passed, and time passed, and time passed. And a nurse came down and called Joe over, and I remember, I think later it was Ruthie who said that she knew something was going on, but that the nurse motioned to Joe, and Joe came over. And anyhow, we had all been standing out in the hall, waiting for the surgeon, there was a real line-up. And then all of a sudden I looked up, and the nurse was talking to Joe and to Ronny and to Ruthie. And apparently, what was that? What had gone wrong at that time? I don't ... something. Oh, I her her ... her blood pressure had begun to drop, she was not putting out, the cardiac output was not as great. So they were not gonna close, and they were gonna keep her on the machine, put the machine back on for a while. And so they did that. And that's when we all got kind of nervous.

So instead of the surgery being over at five or six hours, it really was much later. God, I can't even remember the time! It was probably about six, 5:30 or 6 or so that they brought her down. And the surgeon came in, and I remember thinking later, maybe it was, my feeling was colored by what had happened in between, but I remember thinking later that he looked like a surgeon who had to come in and tell the family that he had lost the patient. Now, that may be just my interpretation. But anyhow he came in, and he told Aunt Esther, he said to Aunt Esther that, when Aunt Esther asked him, he said it was very critical. Actually, at that point Joe, Joe got a little bit ... I mean, he could ... God, it was so difficult for him, for everybody, but especially for him. And he hugged the surgeon. He was talking about how, y'know, tell us whether she'll be jogging with me or whatever and stuff like that. Will she be able to uh ... is she ready to go jogging? And he was, he was trying to mask the terrible anxiety, the terrible anxiety that we all felt. That he felt. And the surgeon then said to Aunt Esther that she was very critical. And anyhow, he finally he walked out, and they brought Nancy by, and we went into this, we were in this side room actually, we didn't really see Nancy come by or it's I think we did, I can't even remember. She was very swollen, had all the tubes hooked up.

And Aunt Esther got hysterical because the people who were supposed to go meet with the surgeon were gonna be Ruthie, of course, and Joe. And they wanted Ronny there, and Allyson wanted to be there, and, of course, Aunt Esther wanted to be there, but that was a big problem. And so they finally agreed, and she wanted to go down, everybody was trying to keep her away, and my sister Nancy and Mindy and ... Y'know, people I thought were kind of hard on her, and at one point I said to Dave, I said, "Look, I don't want to interfere, but I mean, y'know, it's her daughter!" And so I went down to where they were to get some licorice, and, y'know, and then I said Ruth, I called Ruth, I said, "Somebody's got to talk to your mother," I said. What Dave and I said, y'know, "It's her daughter." So Ruthie finally, they thought, what they finally worked out, that Ruthie worked out, was that she would go down and talk to Aunt Esther and tell her that as soon as the surgeon had spoken with them, he would speak with Aunt Esther individually. That's what they finally worked out.

THE NANCY TAPES

Anyhow, that's when it turned out that they got the full story, as much of the story that, that things did not go as well. It also turned out that the, that the last artificial valve which had been put in thirteen years ago, because her aorta was too small for it even though she was by then obviously she was an adult, it was too small. That it pressured against the aorta and where one of the coronary arteries, the artery from the aorta to the heart itself, that when he tried to cut out the, well, what he said, what Ronny said he said was something about how the artery just kind of fell off. So he had to do a bypass. I mean, she was losing blood, and then he had to do a bypass, and he had to do a lot more cutting than he thought because her heart muscle was so thickened by the extra work it had to do all those years, 48 years. It was going with a lot more difficulty than he had thought, not as well. So, finally, he told and said in effect that the next twelve hours would be critical to see whether her heart would be able to start doing more and more on its own to be able to pump as much as it had to, but if it didn't, he would have to put in...

Sometime during the day or the evening, Ruthie gave me a diagram sketch, I got out one of the anatomy books that was on the shelf there in the room and I was able to figure out, she had been able to explain to me, and I was able to understand finally what was wrong with Nancy's heart. Time out.

Time in again. Okay, so essentially he said that it was gonna be, the next twelve hours were going to be really critical. And that if necessary he was gonna have to hook the ... he would ... at the end of twelve hours, he would decide whether he would have to hook up a ventricular, a ventricular assist machine. A ventricular assist machine to assist the left side of her heart which was having a problem, and also the right side of her heart was not working properly because with the new valve, it was not able to take all the pressure because it wasn't used to all the pressure. 'Cause it was used to the, I mean it could not take the normal pressure 'cause it was used to ... The problem with the excess pressure in the *?valves?*, and there was a problem with the right side.

Well, so we got, Aunt Esther and my mother went home, and the kids went home, and we settled down to try to sleep. The room that we were sleeping in ... Dave and Joe slept in the Garrett Room, they put mattresses and stuff that they found there, and, I don't know, and the rest of us were kind of sleeping on couches. Cheryl and Nancy, and Allyson and Ruth, and Ron and myself in that little lounge next to the ICU. And it was so warm in there, and Ronny turned down the thermostat. It got so cold at night that people really couldn't sleep so well, and Nancy was up and about 2 or 2:30. She noticed that there was activity going on, and I don't know ... The nurse this kind of frizzy red blondish-haired witch came out and gave her hell for standing out in the hall and looking in the window.

And that's when she also told Nancy that there were problems, that Nancy was having major problems inside, and they had to really work on her. Her blood pressure was falling. And that they had a call in for R, he was on his way, and they were probably gonna have to hook up that ventricular assist device. And we were up and then the chief resident, R's chief resident, a tall guy with a moustache, very tall guy. He came in, and he said that Mrs. Simpson was having great difficulty, that in fact her blood pressure had dropped, or maybe the nurse also told, I think the nurse also told us this, that her blood pressure dropped down virtually to nothing and her heart stopped, and they had to hook the machine, had to put her on the bypass machine, the portable one right there. And when the chief resident came in, he said it was grim, very grim, and that in fact they were not gonna just do a ventricular assist, they were gonna do a *bi-*ventricular assist, that is, a double thing, that her heart was not working at all. That it had stopped. They had gotten it everything hooked up, she had been less than a minute without oxygen. Which *devastated* everybody. And so he went out, and Ronny turned to Ruthie, and I remember at one point he started to cry and he looked at Ruthie and he said, "She's going to die." And when he said that, I know Ronny had been the one to be there, to be the surgeon, to help everybody understand, and here he understood obviously only too well what the resident meant when he said, "It's very grim."

There was a momentary pause there, when a surgeon said it was ... I just had a momentary pause. And they started deciding what to do and who to get, and so, however the decision was made that the kids had to be called, to be brought back from Rockville. Darren as upset as he was, and, you know, they looked at each other talking about Darren, and I said to Dave, "Dave, I don't know Darren, but you can't deny the kid the chance to be here, and if his mother is dying." And somebody said, "Well, we have to get Aunt Esther, because she would never forgive us if we didn't bring her, call her. I mean, after all, if something's gonna happen to her daughter."

So then the decision was made to get everybody back in as fast as possible. And this was about 3, little after 3. And Dave was gonna go with me to pick up Aunt Esther, and we decided Nancy would call Mother and tell Aunt Esther to get ready, give her fifteen minutes, and I would go. And I said to Dave, I said, "Do you really want ...?" Ruthie told Dave to come with me, and I said to Dave, I said, "Dave, you know, it's up to you. Would you rather be here?" And he said he'd rather be there at the hospital. So I told him, "Okay, you stay and I'll go." And Nancy said she couldn't deal with Mother and Aunt Esther, so I was off by myself to get them, and I took my bags with me, and I was off in the rain. Off in the rain to go get Mother and Aunt Esther, it was about 3:30-ish. I'm gonna stop this here 'cause the tape is about ready to run out.

Actually, I just checked the tape, it's not close to running out. So I've got lots more tape.

Anyhow, I went up to get them, and Aunt Esther was ...Y'know, as somebody asked me, Dave asked me when I got back, "How was the trip?" And I said, "Well, it was a trip, as a matter of fact." Aunt Esther was winding up hysterical, winding down unhysterical. Hysterical about God sparing her daughter, and why didn't God take her instead of her daughter? And then she said ... , this was, this one was one I just couldn't believe, it was a little bit much for me. I told Dave later that, and I said, "You can decide whether you wanta tell Ruthie what Esther said. She said, she was sitting in the back seat of the car, and she said, 'Morris, you failed in everything. I asked you to ...' She said this in Yiddish. She started it in English. She said, 'Morris, you failed in everything.' She said, 'I asked you to plead for your daughter, you should have gone and screamed to God! in front of God! Not to take her.' As if this was Morris's fault."

And she talked over and over again about all the charity she had given, all the rabbis she had praying, all the *tillim*, the Jewish prayers, the *tillim* that she was having said for her, the money and charity she had given, and how charity, according to the Jewish belief, charity can help put off the decree of death. And yet nothing seemed to be helping this. She, of course, was convinced that Nancy was dead. Had died. Actually, that reminds me, something happened in the afternoon, I have to, I'll go back to that. And all these things weren't working to help Nancy. And it was very interesting, she did say, and I told Dave about this also, it was very apropos. That when we got to the hospital, and Mother and Aunt Esther would not get out, they, y'know, told me to just, Mother said, "Just go ahead and park the car, and we'll walk with you." 'Cause it was, what? About 4:30 in the morning by then, and it was raining and dark, and I wanted to let them out in the driveway, and they, "No, no, no." So when we were walking, we found the crosswalk from the parking lot up on the second floor. And as we walked into the hospital, the electric doors opened, and Aunt Esther looked at the doors and said in Yiddish, and again I wish I could say this in Yiddish, she said, "Aaahhh, the doors open for me, *halevai*, they should only open for God to bring out my daughter." So that Nancy could live, and it was very very appropriate.

And here I am approaching I just passed the Beth Tfiloh Cemetery on the right, and now this one, the Shaarei Tfiloh Cemetery, so I'm coming up on the Hebrew Young Men's. So I'm gonna stop this for now while I go into the cemetery. Why is that car blocking that driveway? Anyhow, here I go to the cemetery.

Parked in my usual spot as you face the Hebrew Young Men's Association Building just to the left on this first intersection. And it's 8:30.

It's almost exactly 48 hours since I left. It was 8:35 when I was gonna leave on Monday. Well, here I go.

It's 8:41, and I'm getting ready to leave the cemetery. And there's a bird flying overhead. And the sky is blue, and the sun is shining. There are clouds in the sky. A breeze is blowing, and it's cool, and I can see the leaves of the trees blowing in the wind. It's more than a breeze, it's a wind. There's a big tree off there to the right behind some baseball batter's cage type thing behind the catcher's area. And I could see the trees actually the tree waving, the branches waving, that's going from side to side. The trees are flickering, the leaves are kind of flickering. The light of them is flickering. It's a different kind of day than Monday, with that grey overcast and that pale faded sun. Faded and wan sun. Thank you, Uncle Morris.

There was a car parked on Windsor Mill right by the entrance to the cemetery, and I pulled around him to get in, and then I pulled in and parked. And all of a sudden I looked up, and he had pulled in, and he kinda pulled up behind me. I didn't know who he was, so I went about my business. Went up to Uncle Morris's grave, and then when I looked back, I saw he was gone. And now when I'm leaving, I see he's out, parked, it's as though he's waiting for somebody.

Monday afternoon when the doctor was coming down, and everybody was waiting for the doctor, and we were trying to keep Aunt Esther from intervening and interfering, and going down, I didn't ... well, let me put it this way, they were, I didn't think, I thought she deserved to be there. And she was getting very very hysterical, and she thought that Nancy was dead already. And I think that the reason she felt that is because people were trying to keep her from seeing the doctor. And although they were trying to keep her from asking him what they thought were dumb questions and monopolizing his time, *et cetera*, she thought they were trying to keep her from learning that Nancy was dead. It was as though ... Oh, my goodness, where the heck am I?! It was as though she felt that because people were not letting her get there, that everybody was trying to hide from her the fact that Nancy was already dead.

And so I said to Dave, "Y'know, when we were kids, they tried to hide it from us, and I think she thinks we're trying to do the same thing to her, to hide the fact that her daughter is dead." And of course I couldn't help but think about how when T and I took Aunt Esther down to the hospital when my father was in, and she came down, just told me he was very sick, and that I could go home. Why didn't she tell me? It was what she did then, I mean, she hid it from me, my father was already dead. Instead of telling me to come upstairs, she told me, "No, you can go home." Uncle Aaron did the same thing when he took Ruthie down, and I was supposed to go down with them. They just left and left me.

Anyhow, Rabbi Goren, their rabbi from Rockville, Silver Spring, the *shule* that they go to, came 'bout 10:20 or 10:30 Monday night. And the nurse in the ICU would not let him come in to say a prayer because Nancy's condition she said was so unstable and there was so much going on. And there were doctors in there just about the whole time sitting with her. They would not let him go in to say a prayer in there, so we all kind of embraced and stood in a circle, and he said a prayer there. And I can't remember whether Bryan was still there at that point or not, but I know he, no, that was later, no, no, he came later, that's right. And we said prayers, and Ruthie gave him the collection of psalms that that Sonkie had sent. And he read one of them, the first one, then said another prayer, and we kind of were all arm in arm in a circle.

And then I remember saying to Ruthie, after I had read those psalms and read the notes, and I said, "You know, I said, did you read the notes?" And I said the interesting thing is that they had this feeling that sickness was form of punishment from God for sin, that if you got sick, it meant you had sinned against God, and somebody said that Nancy had not sinned. And Ruth said, "That's so strange." And I said, "It's worse than strange. That they would have that feeling." And we all tried so many different things, and then when the kids came from Washington, and Bryan sat there ... Oh, earlier, he had given to Ruthie an amethyst that he had gotten from an Indian Shaman in the southwest, in New Mexico, or wherever when he was down there with his group, his band, and Nancy took it and asked the nurse if she would, it was the charge nurse, asked her if she would put it in Nancy's hand, and she took it and she did and she put it in her left hand, the left hand, of course, being closer to God. And they kind of decided that this nurse must believe in New Age, the crystal, because she went, and she did it! And actually when Nancy was taken back up to surgery, at 3:30- quarter to four, she still had it in her hand.

I'd better stop and get gas, I just looked, I'm down below E. And here's an Amoco station. I'm gonna pull in here. Time out to stop.

So one of the things that I wanted to say in here. Of all the, the amethyst Bryan had given, I think I've already talked about, Bryan had given Ruthie. So Ruthie had given this amethyst, Ruthie gave the amethyst to Nancy who gave it to the nurse. She gave it to the charge nurse who put it in Nancy's hand. And so we understand it was still there in her hand when she went up, was taken up, and when she came back, as a matter of fact, from the surgery to hook her up to the bi-ventricular assist machine.

Ruthie also had two other stones of some kind that Bryan had given her. And in the morning when Bryan came back, came with, who was it? Bob and Shirley, Nancy and Joe's friends from their old Amesfield Court house, townhouse area days. And we were sitting there, and Bryan was sitting in his chair, he was holding one stone in his right hand. And one in his left hand. And the one in his left hand he was holding up to his heart, and his eyes were closed. And at one point, somebody said, "What's Bryan doing?" Ruthie said, "Bryan is focusing his energies." And, I don't think, I think it was in relation to the amethyst, but it may have been also in relation to this, somebody said, "Well, don't knock it, you try everything."

We were all trying somehow to channel our energies into Nancy. To help her. There I was, and here I am again today. Going to Uncle Morris's grave. And I went because originally she had asked me in 1964, when she and Dave got married, to take her, and I took her. I mentioned it to her her last surgery in '77, whether I should go, and she said, and I went for her then. And I said it to her on Sunday, and I went for her Monday.

Bryan with his amethyst. Aunt Esther with her *tillim*. Me with Uncle Morris. Last night when I talked to Raizel, she said that she would say her 20%, she called Uncle Label. "I asked him to get out his prayer books and say a *Mi-She-Berach* and anything else he could think of to say." And sometime, was it yesterday? Or Monday night? Or early Monday morning when we were waiting, and Aunt Esther was talking about all the rabbis who were praying, all the people who were praying, all the charity she had given, all the money, the charity boxes she had put money into.

And I thought, and I had said this also when Sophie's mother was dying, God could not stop everybody from dying. God could not stop everybody whose families prayed hard and focused their energies and did what they could and prayed and pleaded with Him. Everybody wants to be a *guteh bayteh* when someone has to die. But not everybody can be spared. And even those who are spared cannot be spared for ever. It's like I said to Nancy on Sunday when she was talking about that tube, and I said, "You know, Nancy, sometimes I'm able to think of that Beatles' song *Let It Be*. The tube has to be there, and you have to just let it be. So it can help you and do what it has to do."

That's the same thing about people dying. Sometimes, we just have to let it be. Sometimes, we cannot save them. Not the surgeons. Not the doctors. Not the nurses. Not our prayers. Not God. Yesterday afternoon, Rabbi Preis came, from the Suburban Orthodox. At least that Ms. G was so nice when I asked whether he could go in and say a prayer. She went in, and she asked the nurse and came out, said, "Sure, the nurse said just give her five minutes." And five minutes later, she asked him if he was ready and took him in. He was only in for a moment. Just for a minute. But they let him go in. And I remember thinking Monday night when they wouldn't let Rabbi Goren in, and afterwards I said something and maybe it was to Cheryl and Allyson, and I don't remember who it was to. But I thought that that was terrible. That as awful as Nancy's condition was, and I understood that, and I asked a question to myself, and I said it, Would they have denied a Catholic priest the opportunity to go in to give last rites? I don't think they would have denied that. I don't know. Maybe I'm mistaken.

Was there anything else I wanted to say at this point? I don't know.

When I picked up Aunt Esther, she practically fainted in my arms. Why are we in a traffic jam here all of a sudden? I don't know. Here it is, 8:58, we're at the Beltway coming up on Exit 20, the Reisterstown Road Exit, Route 140, on my way

THE NANCY TAPES

to get to 93 [*sic*] South so I can go to the hospital, and I'm in a traffic jam. I think that's it for now.

When I talked to Raizel, and she said how when she heard the 20%--I'm still in a traffic jam--she called Uncle Label and to get his prayer books out, and I told her, "Raizel," I said, "in the morning when they brought back down after they hooked her up, and Joe met with the surgeon and Joe told us that the surgeon said there was a 20% chance, Raizel," I said, "we practically cheered. When we heard there was 20%. We practically cheered." I said, "Ronny turned around and said, 'We hear 20% and we're happy, we're thrilled, we're ecstatic. To hear that there's 20%.'" I didn't tell Raizel that Ronny had turned to Ruthie and said, "She's going to die." I mean, Ronny's a surgeon, he knows what it means when a surgeon comes in and tells you it's very grim. It's very grim. And he said, the surgeon, the resident had said, we're gonna do our best to hook her up, to that bi-ventricular thing, and nobody knew whether she'd survive that. At that point. So when Joe came back in after talking with the surgeon and said he said 20%, and Joe said, "20% means that there's hope." That was like, like a blessing. The 20% meant that there was hope. It was so bad. 20%. It was like a sip of joy.

I've put back on, I've put back on, turned on, my Dylan Thomas tape. *Poem in October*, about his thirtieth year to heaven. I was listening to this on Monday, on my way to, on my to where? On my way to the cemetery to see Uncle Morris. Thinking about Nancy, and that's why I had to put it on today again. Nancy's birthday in October. And I know this is her 48th year, just finishing her 48th year, beginning her 49th year to heaven. But we're not ready for her to go to heaven yet. And thinking about Nancy's birthday and her years and the beauty of this poem. The beauty of her life.

That oversimplified it, it's not quite, the beauty of the poem, of her life, the richness of life, her surgery at this point, the possibility of death.

The ending of the poem, "Oh, may my heart's truth still be sung from this high height in a year's turning." Nancy, may yours be sung in a year's turning. "The weather turned 'round" this year, you should have been "marveling your birthday away," but the weather turned 'round. Maybe this will help us all "marvel our birthdays away." Craig's birthday was Monday. Craig's birthday was Monday. He spent it in the hospital with his aunt. With the rest of the family, with his aunt. Praying for her survival. Praying for her life.

"May it still be sung from this high *hill* in a year's turning." From this high hill in a year's turning. "May my heart's truth still be sung from this high hill in a year's turning."

"Oh, may my heart's truth ... still be sung ... on this high hill ... in a year's turning ..." May yours, Nancy ... Still be sung ... In a year's turning.

SIDNEY KROME

Thinking of my talking with Sophie this morning. I think I've decided I should, I'm not gonna go to Atlanta. The problem is, as I said to her, to Sophie, if something were to happen to Nancy, I would feel absolutely awful not being here. It's not that I expect something to happen, it's that as everybody knows, she's not, as the cliche goes, out of the woods yet. She is still very critical. If the odds were strongly in her favor, if there were, if she were out of the woods, if the surgery had gone as successfully as everybody hoped, expected, as originally to go, *we* did, maybe not the surgeon, but as we did. If she had been among the 90, 80-90% success rate from the beginning, and if she were simply recuperating, I'd go ahead and go. But today's only the second of the two to three days of critical turnaround on this bi-ventricular assist machine. **TAPE ENDS**

THE NANCY TAPES

TAPE NUMBER 2A

WEDNESDAY, OCTOBER 24, 1990

Okay, it's 1:07. I'm continuing on Wednesday, October 24th. On my way from the hospital up to school, going there to work, I don't know why, what I'm gonna do, but I'm gonna go in for a couple hours, and then probably go back to the hospital.

I just realized that the last tape ran out, I'm not sure exactly what else I said that didn't get put on there. But it ran out at the point where I was talking about Nancy being just on the second day of two-to-three days on the biventricular assist machine, and that therefore I probably was not gonna go to Atlanta. Better call and cancel my reservation.

What did I want to say today? It's a beautiful, beautiful, beautiful day. Beautiful sky now. There were some clouds this morning when I left the cemetery. Where Uncle Morris was, where I went to see Uncle Morris. And now I was just listening to *Poem in October*: "May my heart's truth still be sung on this high hill in a year's turning." That's how it ends.

Yeah, okay, there was some lunchtime conversation. Nancy was saying something about people praying for people to survive, and there has to be a kicker for God to choose, you know. I said a few minutes later, I didn't think there was any such thing as a kicker, I don't think God really chooses. Allyson talked about how much she loves Nancy, how much she loves her mother, and that maybe the difference would be loving, that that love would help the person live. And then she realized that two of her friends lost their mothers or their parents or at least one of the parents and that both of them, and that it couldn't be love, the love couldn't be what made the difference because they loved their parents and their parents died anyhow. She's right, I said. She was right. It doesn't, it's not that. It can't be that.

It's not like, you know, Samuel Beckett in *Waiting for Godot* used as the metaphor, as the image, the biblical story of the two thieves who were crucified at the same time as Christ, saying that he saved one, didn't save the other, all the stuff about that story. What that story omits, what that story omits in the play version at least is something that's in the biblical original. And that is, in the biblical original one thief taunts Jesus and says, "If you're the son of God, why don't you save yourself and save us all?" And the other thief says, "Leave him alone, he's an innocent man, we're being crucified, we're guilty, we're criminals, we've been tormented, we deserve our torment, in effect, we deserve to be punished because we're criminals. But Jesus," he says, "is not." And in the context of the biblical story, the one who is saved is the one who comes to Jesus' support, who speaks for him, who says he's an innocent man, and the one who is condemned is the one who has taunted, the one who is guilty of insensitivity, of a lack of compassion. And Beckett misses that point completely.

And the part of the point of reality, of life, is that we don't know why one is spared and one is not. The biblical story gives a reason, there is no reason! There is no reason! There is no reason! You may love someone and want the person to live, but the person dies!

Allyson's right, there is no kicker. And the thing in the psalms that I mentioned to Ruthie, that it's not a question of guilt or innocence. Somebody, Ruthie I think said it, "What did Nancy do to deserve this?" She didn't do anything to deserve this. It's not that she did anything wrong. She's alive! And part of life sometimes and unfortunately sometimes without reason, without cause, without justice, without justification, without motive, people suffer. Let it be! Let it be not in the sense of let people suffer, but you can't always find a reason for the suffering. You can't always find a way to stop the suffering. You can't always find a way to stop death. It's not always a matter of this person loves someone, and therefore the loved one is spared.

Joe, poor Joe, he sits there. He's been so good, and all he could do this morning was to try to talk to that woman whose husband was in there, try to give her some faith, some hope, some courage. Not glibly, but based on his own very, very painful experience, talking about what he went through with Nancy Monday morning, no, Tuesday morning. And how now this woman's husband is where Nancy was, what?, twenty-four hours ago at the time, twenty-seven hours ago. And that you have to have hope that something will turn around, but you don't know that it will, there are no guarantees that it will.

Joe sits there with Nancy's pajama top, and he holds it, and he keeps it in his pocket, and he takes it out. And he kisses it where her heart would be. Thinking that if he kisses her heart, it would help her. I don't know. Ruthie told Bryan that Nancy had given the amethyst to the nurse who put it in Nancy's hand then, and he wanted to know what time that was, and she said it was about 12:00. And so then he said that he thought so, it was just that he could feel it. And the point is like someone said, that one of the most touching things was watching Bryan sit there. It's not the stones, it's not the *tillim*. Maybe not even my going to see Uncle Morris, although Ruthie thanked me for going today, I told her I went again today. It's the energies, the focus of energies, our will, our putting ourselves with her to try to help her. There is no kicker.

Unless this is the kicker, that there is some way that we manage to focus and channel our energies to Nancy and that she can pull in our energy. I don't know. But there are others who try to do the same thing, and they don't succeed. Why should we feel that we will succeed more than they? I don't know. I don't know. It's not the stones. Ruthie said that Bryan really believes in that. Fine. If he believes in that, maybe that helps him channel the energy. But it's not the stones, it's not the amethyst. It's Bryan sitting there holding the stones and concentrating on Nancy. Ruthie talking about how with Rabbi Goren we all stood in a circle and prayed, and he led the prayer, and he talked the prayer and said the prayer, and we were there with our arms around each other. Maybe that would help.

FRIDAY, OCTOBER 26, 1990

Okay, it's Friday morning, the 26th of October, 8:37. Sunny. Windy. Kind of cold day. I'm on my way around the Beltway, on my way from the cemetery. To see Uncle Morris again. On my way on my way on my way from the cemetery, on my way to the hospital. And I woke up this morning and just a real bad feeling this morning. Shaving the song, *Teach me Tonight* the Maguire Sisters, "Did you, had you, did you, did you, did you say I've got a lot to learn?" That kept, I couldn't get it out of my mind. I don't know why, I don't know why. And it kept going in my mind, over and over and over again.

Anyhow, I don't even know what I want to talk about right now except that I'd forgot, let's see, on Monday, what happened? Monday afternoon about, was it 3:00 or 3:30? Whatever time it was, something like that, the nurse came down, she talked about Nancy's problem with her heart, blood pressure wasn't up as high as it should have been, it was down, and they were putting this balloon thing in to try to pump alternately with her heart. Ronny explained that it will kind of collapse as her heart pumps and then that would pump it back, and her heart would go down, and it would kind of alternate, fill-ins, and that would help. But obviously that didn't work.

What else? Yesterday I guess it was in the morning, yesterday, yesterday, okay, let's see, Wednesday and Thursday, they tried backing Nancy down, the machine, the artificial, the biventricular assist machine. They tried first on Wednesday, and at first R came out and told Joe that it was kind of encouraging and went back in, then came back and said that they were, they were gonna stop it because while it was encouraging that her, the parts of her heart were all working, they were not, they were not pumping strong enough. So they were gonna gonna stop the test. They would redo it again on Thursday.

And everybody was there on Thursday morning early. And they started about 10:20. And we all prayed, Ruthie read one of the psalms that Sonkie had sent down and then then just led us kind of in The Lord's Prayer. We all just thought about Nancy. And Ruthie said that there's one thing about that psalm, that it was as though the sick person somehow had done something, and she said we all know that in Nancy's case that it was not, that's not the case in Nancy's case. That the concept is in the notes to those psalms that that somehow that if you're really sick, sickness is the result of something that is some punishment that God is visiting upon you because you did something wrong, you did something to offend God. And that's just sheer unadulterated whatever garbage. No one's sick because of that.

Anyhow then C who was ... R had introduced Joe to C on Wednesday morning because R was going out of town Wednesday afternoon until Thursday afternoon, and so Thursday C came out, told Joe, and Ronny was listening, and I just had my ear set to the side. He said that it just wasn't working, Nancy's heart was not pumping strong enough. And he said something like, "You know, she's told us very clearly that, her heart has told us very clearly that without that machine she wouldn't last 10 minutes." The machine was pumping 4 liters a minute, and he said if it went down below 2, they slowed it down below 2, her heart couldn't take it, her heart would not, and the blood pressure would drop very quickly, and she would not be able to take it. But he thought there was one possible thing there, that there was some blood clotting around her heart from the surgery, and from the oozing, and that there was some, that the blood clot around the heart would be kind of wrapped around it almost and constricting it so that the heart muscle could not pump well. And what they were gonna try to do was to suction that clotting out and hope that that would free things up enough so that her heart could then go ahead and pump some more.

And I remember thinking that what was missing was Bryan sitting there with his stones, holding the one stone in his right hand, the one in the left one holding it to his heart and trying to focus his energy, but Bryan wasn't there. But Joe was sitting there holding Nancy's pajama top in his hand and just squeezing his hands together as though they were her heart and pumping, trying to to give motion and force to her heart. Nancy said that what she was thinking was that it was time for Nancy to get angry so her heart would pump. And Joe talked about how he had taken a shower at the hospital in the morning and he was thinking that Nancy's been so cooperative in listening to her doctors all along and now it was time for her to take over and that she had to do this on her own. But as he said earlier one day when I told him what Ronny had said about how Nancy was the kind of patient that he likes to have in surgery, a patient with the right, a very strong attitude, a very positive attitude, that attitude is very important.

And Joe said, and he's absolutely right, that sometimes attitude and positive will is not enough, there has to be something physical there for the attitude to work on. And that maybe in Nancy's case, there isn't enough there in her heart for her attitude, her spirit, her strength, her fighting will, to work on. And if there's no, if there's no muscle there, if the muscle doesn't have it, if the valve is not working enough, then all of her positive attitude and her will would do nothing. Could do nothing. Because there would be nothing there for them to work on. I don't know.

And anyhow, then later, they were talking about, sitting around, and Ruthie was talking about Aunt Esther and Ronny about Mother and Nancy about Mother and that they have to be, Ronny talked about how Mother has to always be the Queen Bee and know and have control over everything that goes on. Which, of course, is certainly part of what she is. Amazing different perspectives, of course, Ruthie does not feel that way about my mother, and Ronny does not feel that way, well, he does, a little bit, about Aunt Esther, he does. He certainly, the way, he pointed out, you know, for example, the way they can, Mother and Aunt Esther can, have almost bred into them as a reflex the guilt-tripping kind of thing. Pointing out about how, they asked Allyson to talk about how one time when she was going to go in to see Nancy, to see her own mother, and Aunt Esther was upset that she wasn't getting a chance to go in, that Allyson let Aunt Esther go in, gave up her turn so Aunt Esther could go in. And when Aunt Esther came out, she said, "Why don't you want to go in and see your mother?" And that as a reflex without even thinking about it, she turned it around and made it seem that Allyson had done something wrong again.

This also was, you know, in, and then, I think, it was, Ruth or Dave was talking about, I think it was Ruth, that they were making one of their trips to Montreal for something, and I guess Phil and Rose Weinstein were in the car with them. And they were talking about someone who had cancer and who had died, and there was some thought that maybe this person had committed suicide. And Ruthie said that at that point Aunt Esther's eyes kind of perked up, and she listened very carefully, and she asked, "What are you taking to commit suicide?" And Phil Weinstein said, "Mylanta." Of course, that cracked everybody up in the waiting room.

But perspectives are different. That's why I kept saying to people Monday afternoon, "After all, it's her daughter." Why I think Sophie helped the other day to get a chance for Aunt Esther to go in, talked to Ms. G. And Raizel last night on the phone, talking about how we have to understand, of course, that Esther is still part Kolki-al, Kolki-er, and that she's still Kolki-er, that it's still Kolki, that hysteria is Kolki, and said that kind of almost primitive emotionalism, that we have to put up with her hysteria and with the crying. And I, of course, but part of the problem though is that Ruthie seems to have a problem seeing that, and Raizel, of course, cannot see the extent, the extreme extremity of it that goes on in the hospital from Aunt Esther sometimes. I think that's it for now.

Last night, Thursday night, when Sophie and I got down to the hospital, nobody was in the room, and then Mindy called up, they were waiting at the front door. They were all going to dinner in Fells Point, and we just, Sophie and I just stayed. And she managed to talk to the nurse, and they let us go for a couple minutes. And it was kind of devastating to see Nancy like that. She had all the tubes, it was, the couple things that, the intubation, the respirator tube in her mouth pulled to the corner of her mouth. My mother-in-law, Sophie's mother, made me think of that, made me think also of Nancy and how much she said she didn't like that tube. There was blood under her right hand, it was on a gauze pad on something to hold her hand straight. But there was fresh blood under like she was leaking blood from someplace. And then I noticed around to the right that she had things in her neck. She had things in her neck, and her eyes were open, and she reacted to our voices, her eyes blinked. And her right hand moved, and it was, it was, but her eyes were, were open. It was as though if she was unseeing, it was like, I've seen those eyes before, from that poem, but I've seen those eyes before from my mother-in-law in the hospital. Those unfocusing open eyes. But I think that's simply from her sedation. That she's so sedated, or anaesthetized, whatever.

Afterwards I thought maybe I didn't say enough, maybe, I didn't know what to say. I was able to at least just stay in there and not get emotional inside there. And her. I also thought afterwards that maybe her hand motion, maybe she was trying to reach out to hold a hand, to take a hand, and maybe I should have tried to, but I don't remember where her left hand was, but her right hand, you couldn't touch it because there was, it was all wrapped up and it had needles and everything in it and the tubes and everything. But Sophie said her color was good, and her color was kind of good. And she didn't seem as swollen and puffy as I had thought she would be.

Her eyes. I didn't see any tears although Aunt Esther said that she had seen tears, but Mindy said that she was there and she could confirm that that's not what happened, that there were no tears. But I can confirm that my mother-in-law had a tear that rolled down from her eye when I asked her something about, when I said something to her about coming back, getting well and coming to Baltimore, we'd go to the Icaros and eat fish. And then Louise said, *Pothimises na fas ta psaria.* And there was a tear that rolled down, out of her right eye, along her temple. And then Sol's eyes, but I was afraid to say anything to him. And that poem about Sol and the wildebeest being killed by the wild dogs in Africa. That poem. And Nancy's eyes.

Alright, it's 9:52 Friday morning, I'm on my way up the Jones Falls Expressway to pick up Aunt Esther. Mindy was talking to her when I got to the hospital. Aunt Esther was insisting she was gonna take a cab down, so I talked to Ronny, and he's studying so I told her I would be up to get her. I had mentioned once before how on that Tuesday morning, 3:30-4:00 o'clock, when I was bringing Mother and Aunt Esther down, Aunt Esther said about Uncle Morris, "Morris, you failed in everything, I asked you to talk for Nancy, and you shoulda gone screaming, you shoulda screamed to God, for God to let our daughter go, to let her live." She said it again on the phone when I was talking to her I guess on Wednesday. She was at home, and I was at the hospital. She said it again on Thursday, she, not exactly the same thing. She then said it when she started screaming, crying and screaming, on the phone, "Morris, Morris. What's the matter with you? Where are you? Why aren't you doing anything? I told you you should go straight to God! He should let our daughter live! Why aren't you doing anything?" So, finally, I said to her, "Aunt Esther, you don't know what he's doing! And neither do I. So get off of him! Leave 'im alone!" I don't remember whether I said get off of him, but I said, "You don't know what he's doing and neither do I. Can't do it! Why, why do you blame him?" Gotta have somebody to blame.

Right. That's the family also. Rabbi Preis came yesterday again, and Aunt Esther was talking, and finally she got to talk to him, and we decided that was the right one for her to be talking to, Ruthie and I. She started talking about all the charity she had given, all the rabbis she had paid to pray for Nancy, and the only thing I heard him, really heard him say was, "You can't make a trade with God." Maybe she was talking about herself, give herself instead of, but she's ... And that's this whole thing, you give charity because you give charity, and you have prayers said because you have prayers said. Not because you expect that in return. But see, part of the problem is that Nanc, Ruthie and I were talking, that on Yom Kippur there's a constant refrain, Prayer, Repentance, and Charity can alter the severity of the decree. Well! No, I think what they do is they alter how we perceive the severity of the decree. How we react to it.

Which makes me think all of a sudden now this morning at 9:54 curving around on the Northern Parkway West exit ramp from the Jones Falls Expressway to pick up Aunt Esther, makes me think of Dr. K, L L K. Back when I was 13, that fall, and I was going to the Baltimore Hebrew College High School down on Eutaw Place and Dolphin, and we had a class in there. And I don't remember whether it was W's class or some class, and Dr. K looked out the window at the church, and there was a sign on the church that said, Prayer Changes Things. And K looked at it, and he said, Prayer does not really change things. He said, Prayer changes our attitude towards things, it changes how we feel about things ... *[traffic sounds]* But it doesn't really change the things. The *Tzedaka*, the *T'shuva*, the Charity, Repentance, and what was the other one? Huh! They can mitigate the severity of the decree. They can't mitigate the severity of the dec the decree.

If Nancy is beyond the help of the doctors, if she's beyond the help of us, if we cannot focus our energies into her to help her survive, God is not gonna reach down and help her survive, as opposed to a-l-l of those other people whose families are praying and wanting and wishing and focusing their energies as hard as we are. Maybe even harder. Allyson even realized it, even Allyson, 23-years-old with all her problems. She said the other day, she thought about how if we love her grandmother, it'll help her survive, and, not her grandmother, love her mother, it'll help her survive. And then she thought about her friends who also loved their mothers, and their mothers didn't survive. Their mothers died.

THE NANCY TAPES

It's not can love, it's not, God is not gonna respond to that and say that because you love, you're gonna, someone is gonna survive, or because someone else maybe doesn't express it the right way, they're not. It's out of our control sometimes. Things are out of our control sometimes. And so all those things cannot, they cannot really alter the severity. Maybe I'm growing up a little bit, finally. What they alter is how we perceive those things. Let it be. Not in the sense that you shouldn't rage against the dying of the light. But in the sense that you recognize that sooner or later the light must die, sooner or later, as I said to Dave, every child has to go through the loss of a parent. You always pray it will be later rather than sooner, but it comes! And sometimes you can help the person, sometimes you can help the person to live, sometimes you can't. Sometimes all you can do is help the person to die. Help the person through the transition, help the person through the pain and the anxiety and the agony and the suffering and the sorrow now. That's all you can do. It's all we can do for Nancy. It's all we can do for each other, it's all we can do for Allyson and Darren is simply to be there for them.

But we can't make Nancy survive! We can't make her heart beat for her. She may not even be able to make her heart beat for her. If the muscle is gone, if it won't work, it won't work! Sometimes the won't does not, sometimes is not real. Sometimes there are possibilities beyond our imagining. But sometimes also there is reality beyond our imagining. And we have to know the difference. We have to accept the difference.

I couldn't help Sol, but I could have helped Sol. I was so afraid with my father, and I was so afraid with Sol that I did nothing. Oh, Ruthie, you said you remembered my standing there when Uncle Aaron drove away, and you said, "What about Sonny?" And he said, "No, no, we have to go down to the hospital." And he drove away. And you said you've never forgotten that, you've always felt so bad about it. Ruthie, I told you how your mother told me just to go ahead and go home. Ruthie, deep down inside, I knew something was wrong. But I was so afraid, I was so afraid to stay. What I needed was someone to help me to stay. And nobody did. But it's as much me as it is anybody else. Darren and Allyson are so fortunate to have people to be where with them, be there with them to help support them. But they have to be there, and I couldn't be there. And even when Sol was dying, I was afraid to be there. Oh, I sat by him! But I saw the tear in his eyes, the tears in his eye, the tears in his eyes, and I couldn't say a thing.

A long time ago, I said to Raizel, or wrote her in a letter, that someone whose opinion I value very highly said that the problem with me, he said, that I don't have any guts. And you know something, that was Ronny. Raizel, I never told you who it was. And Raizel, you always thought that that was a silly thing for me to say, a little four-letter word like "guts!" And not understand what it meant. But I knew what it meant. I knew what he meant, and then what I meant. Guts may be an oversimplification, but it's the basic point of lacking courage and the will and the strength and the courage to do certain things. That's why you could not be a doctor. You were afraid to face blood. And you're afraid--afraid to face pain. You could have been ...

Alright, Friday afternoon now at 2:30 P.M. I'm on my way down Liberty Road. I'm on my way down Liberty Road heading in to work for an hour or so before I go pick up Charlie. Couple things about today basically in chronological order, two things.

First, in the car when I picked up, let's see, what happened? No, I went down to the hospital and ... They had not yet started that procedure, and Mindy was on the phone with Aunt Esther, so anyhow, the long and the short is I went up to pick up Aunt Esther and Mother and Lou, and brought them down.

And in the car on the way down, Aunt Esther said, "*Morris shweigt*, Morris is quiet, Morris is still." That is, again she's blaming him for not, he's not saying anything, he's not speaking up to God. And so I said to her, "Aunt Esther, Aunt Esther, don't say that, 'cause you don't know what the man is doing. You don't know what he is saying, you don't what he's doing, or what he's saying. So you can't say that he *shweigt,* that he's still."

Then we got down there, and Joe and Ruth and Dave and Allyson were in the little room with Dr. R. And anyhow when they came out, what happened was that they did the suctioning, they took the clot off of Nancy's heart, and they watched her heart, they could watch it from the outside. 'Cause they took the patch off and hadn't closed her up yet. And they put her, took, they turned that machine down, the biventricular assist machine down, and they actually turned it down as far as a one [1]. Yesterday, they c'd barely get it down as far as a two [2], then they had to move it back up again because her heart wouldn't take it then. Her heart could not assume the burden of the volume that the machine was giving up. And they really only had her beating, heart beating yesterday for two [2] minutes. Today they had her beating for 20 to 25 minutes, and they turned the volume of the machine down to one [1], y'know, much below two [2]. Which means that her heart was able, strong enough to pump for ten times as long as yesterday. And at the same time it was at, her heart was assuming a greater volume, not just two [2] liters a minute, but three [3] liters a minute, which is, which is a lot more. So that's a very positive sign.

Anyhow, what they did, what they're doing, Ruthie's suggestion that they're tissue-typing her. They're gonna get her on the list for a transplant, get the word out. Still gonna wait and see how her heart does, whether it comes back, and at the same time, they're gonna be looking for a heart-and-one-[1]-lung transplant. They're on the lookout for a donor. There's supposed to be a national list, but as

Ronny says, people cheat, they don't all put the donors on the list so he's gonna make some phone calls to call people that he knows, And the upshot is that people, we were feeling good today, the curve, as Dave Weinstein says, The curve had taken a turn up. Now, it's not, it's not hugely up, but it is up. After Tuesday, Wednesday, and Thursday, of no curve moving anyplace, the curve has finally turned up. We don't know how long it's gonna go up, but we're praying, of course, that it stays up and keeps moving up.

So what we did, went down and had a cup of coffee, and I had a piece of cake and some yoghurt on top as a, as a kind of a, we kind of celebrated, there was there was that good news. And Dave Weinstein was saying that his feeling was that had we not had this positive news today, had the doctor not been able to say that Nancy's curve went up even that little bit, he would have asked what they want to do, and I don't, Dave doesn't think he would even have mentioned the possibility of a transplant. So there is some more hope now. And the hope is a rational hope because there was a distinct turn, not a major turn, but at least a turn up. That's positive.

SUNDAY, OCTOBER 28, 1990

It's Sunday morning, 10:29, October 10/28. I'm on my way Forest Park, cough pardon me, Forest Park Avenue towards the cemetery to see Uncle Morris again. And I was listening to *Poem in October* as I usually do. And as I rewound, I rewound and it went just slightly too far, and I caught the last line of *Refusal to Mourn the Death by Fire of a Girl in London*. And the last line is, "After the first death, there is no other." But all I caught at this point was the line, "there is no other." And it suddenly made me think back, to thinking back to all the deaths in our family. And thinking what Ronny said, I guess it was Monday evening when I walked him out to the car to get his cigarettes, and he said something about how he had thought we had had such a happy childhood until he spoke with his therapist, then he realized it was just one tragedy after another. And so now my thinking is, After the first death, there was another, and another, and another.

But today there won't be any, not Nancy, not now. Uncle Morris is not keeping silent. Neither are we.

It's a beautiful, absolute beautiful Sunday in October with the sun shining. There are some clouds in the sky, but the sky is blue, the wind is blowing. And as I came down Forest Park Avenue, Hillsdale actually, the wind blew leaves in a rushing gush out of a side street, brown leaves swirling in the street. Here I am at the cemetery.

It's 10:44, I'm in the car, getting ready to leave the cemetery to go to the hospital. And I remembered while I was standing with Uncle Morris's stone and talking to him that Aunt Esther said, was it yesterday? or the day before? When she was talking about how he needed to scream for her, he [*sic*] said, "When she was born, when she was a baby, he used to sing for her all the time, sing to her all the time." And so what I said to him today was, "You used to sing to her, now sing for her. Let her hear your voice singing for her. Let her hear your voice singing for her." My hand on the top of the stone, and it was so rough. But I could run my hand, just slide my hand along it, and feel all the chips and chisels, the angles and the glitter, with the flesh of my hands. My hand, my fingers, my palm, my thumbs, my thumb. I could feel it all, even the grey, even the glitter. And the roughness of the sunlight. "Uncle Morris, let her hear your voice singing for her. Thank you for Tuesday, for helping her through that. Thank you for Wednesday and Thursday. Thank you for Friday. For letting her heart beat a little bit longer. And a little bit stronger. And thank you for Saturday, the left ventricle is working, it's the right one that's the problem. Help her, to strengthen her heart, Uncle Morris. Help her, to strengthen her heart. Let her hear your voice, singing for her."

There's a family here, conducting an unveiling. All dressed in black. The rabbi, there. I don't know who they are. I saw them from the distance. I see the rabbi now saying some prayers. I don't know if it's an unveiling or a year's *Yuhrzeit* or what. 'Cause the stone is already unveiled. There is someone there, a woman there also in a wheel chair.

And again I heard it, "After the first death, there is no other." No, the line should be, "After the first death, there came one after another."

Try it this way. Now 11:00 o'clock. Just coming up on Exit 20, Reisterstown Road, Pikesville, Garrison. Try it this way. After the first death, they came one after the other. After the first death, they came one after another.

Thinking now all of a sudden, coming down I-83, the Jones Falls, passing Exit 7, 28th Street, Druid Park Lake Drive. About the dinner last night, the toasts and how I had thought about making a toast, but I didn't. And now I'm making one in my mind, what it should have been, what I should have said, about how we were there to celebrate Ronny and Diane's anniversary, to celebrate life. And so we should also we were also celebrating Nancy's life. That poetry, poetry helps us to celebrate life, and that I wanted to, to quote or paraphrase lines from two poems that two poets, two poems by two different poets that help us to celebrate life. The first, Dylan Thomas's *Poem in October*, about the shower of his days, that ends, "Oh, may my heart's truth still be sung from this high hill in a year's turning." And the other, and may that be Nancy's heart's truth. And the other, a poem by a poet not yet quite so well known. Dylan Thomas was the first, Darren Via the second. And while I don't remember it all enough to quote lines from it, I do remember the title. And I know this, that the poem was a celebration not of the shower of life of his days, but of the sunshine, the life-giving warmth, the life-giving force of his mother's eyes. That he longed to see again, that he, that he sees now and will always see, the sun in her, in your eyes. Let us all pray that in a year's turning we will still be seeing the light of Nancy's eyes.

And now that I think of it, I think that, of what I thought about yesterday, about prayer changing things, and how it does not really change things, it changes our attitude, our attitude towards things, and how Repentance and Return and Charity can avert or alter the severity of the decree. And that they can't. What they alter is our attitude towards it, that's what poetry helps us to do. Alter our attitude towards life. To help us understand it and accept it.

Yes, poetry is a form of prayer. And I think of S saying that maybe instead of, instead of religion, instead of the formal kind of structured religion and prayer, maybe I would find my prayer in literature. Maybe that's what I have found, but I wouldn't be the first one to do that. And maybe now I understand what is meant by that. That I did not understand before.

MONDAY, OCTOBER 29, 1990

8:35, Monday, October 29th. One week since I had that feeling, that incredible urge to go back to Uncle Morris's grave before I left the cemetery. And here I am, I just pulled up in my spot. Going to see Uncle Morris again. One week later.

Okay, it's 8:53, I'm getting ready to leave the cemetery. I had a good cry, Uncle Morris, with Uncle Morris. Thank you, Uncle Morris. I forgot to mention yesterday, that I noticed yesterday morning, Sunday the 28th, that the two bottoms of broken bottles that I had found, one brown and one green, from when I had cleaned them up, I had put them on the curb beside the, along the driveway there near Uncle Morris's grave at the end of there. Heh, some traffic this morning. Someone had cleaned them up.

Anyhow, today, what I said to Uncle Morris, one of the things I said today that made me think of it, because when you say the *Yizker*, it says that you promise to do charity for the sake of the soul of the person. And I told Uncle Morris the charity I do is to come to him with new demands, to thank him each day. I thanked him today for Nancy's normal blood pressure for yesterday, and I told him that my *Tzedakah* is to come to him to ask him for more. To thank him for the last one and to make more demands on him. To thank him and to ask him, to thank him and to ask him.

I asked him again to sing for his daughter, to let her hear his voice singing for her, not just to her but for her now, to comfort her, to take her hand, to talk to her. To talk for her, to sing for her. To help her, give her strength. Give her strength. So that she can give her heart strength. And as I was, and I went and I took some pictures of his tombstone, of his grave today, as I did of some of the others. And I said to him, What did I say to him? I can't remember what I said.

I remembered what he used to say to the kids about, "Hey, boy, get off the lawn." And I told him again, I said, as I did I think the first day, that I would not get away from his grave, that I was going to stand near there and talk to him so that he could help Nancy.

I also told him that for the first time in the family, what did this, what does this is that for the first time in the family, there's a real chance, a real possibility, to save someone so the person will not die. A real chance. It may not be great, and the hope may not be great, but the hope is there. All those other deaths, they went so fast, they were so massive, that nothing could be done. This time there is a chance, there is some hope that something can be done. For the first time, somebody has a chance of living. The first time somebody who is near death has a possibility to still be alive, not to die. That's the possibility, that's the hope.

It's now 9:24, I'm on my way down to work. What I wanted to say also was about how yesterday afternoon Aunt Esther just very calmly and rationally yesterday morning, very early, Saturday night, Sunday morning, Nancy had a seizure, and everybody was very very worried, and they were supposed to do, they did an EEG in the afternoon. And when they took the EEG machine away, they, the word was that the surgeon wanted, R wanted to talk to Joe and Ruthie and Dave, and Allyson went with but. And the nurse took Aunt Esther in to see Nancy while they went. So anyhow, she came out and very calmly and rationally started telling us that the doctor had told her that there was no hope. That there was a very, very poor chance of survival, and there was no real hope, and she shouldn't be surprised if she got a phone call sometime. Well, we all got depressed. We all thought this was it. And she said the doctor was gonna meet with Joe and Ruthie and Dave and give them the details. But just wanted to let her know. Well, we were just so upset. And now I was out in the hall talking with Nancy. Nancy was just, almost lost, and I looked at Cheryl one point, and I said, "This is not, I don't think this is fantasy this time." 'Cause I felt Aunt Esther was really telling the, telling the truth.

And anyhow, then I went out, and I saw Cheryl out by the elevator and talking about how, and she started to, about how how could God let her live just a few days? and it was so unfair. And I started to say that God was not doing this to be unfair and it was, it was a good thing for the kids, her kids, at least to have all this support, that if you have to go through this, y' know, it's better to have this support, than to do it, to be all alone and not have anybody. And she said, "Oh, like you." And she started to cry and I started to cry, and I kept talking about the kids. And anyhow, when they all came out, when Ruthie and Joe and Dave now came out, we all went in the conference room, and it was good news. Not bad news.

The good news was that they had backed the machine down to one [1], and while it was only for ten minutes, that the doctor, surgeon, said this was the longest time. And that we must have misunderstood or someone must have misunderstood the other time. We thought it was 20 or 25 minutes on Friday, but that what was even more was that her blood pressure came up to normal, about a hundred and ten. Which was incredibly, very, very positive sign, incredibly good. And the other good sign was that her pulmonary pressure for the first time did not come up to match her blood pressure. It stayed down about 80, now 80 as Dave said, is course still very high. It's higher than it should be, but at least her blood pressure was higher than the pulmonary pressure which was a very very good sign.

So there's another, Nancy's taken another, another small step. And it's just marvelous. And that's why I had to go say thank you to Uncle Morris today and ask him to do some more. 'Cause it's not over yet.

9:33 down Reisterstown Road past Reisterstown Road Plaza. I've been saying something about Nancy taking a little step each day, and I said to Raizel the other night, after Friday. That it was like the saying of Chairman Mao, the journey of a thousand miles begins with one small one step. And Nancy had moved a half an inch and how she had taken another step yesterday, each day she takes another step. And it made me think now today of Neal Armstrong on the moon, a giant leap for manki, a small step for man, a giant leap for mankind. Nancy has been taking small steps, we're waiting for the giant leap to back into life. Not back into, but into full, recovered life. That's what we're waiting for and hoping for.

Thinking now again, it's, what's it? 9:36, of what R said to Joe and Dave and Ruthie and Allyson. One of them said that they had asked him point-blank on Saturday if he had a phone call that he had a heart and lung to transplant into Nancy, would he do it? And he said then that he would, because that was the last possible hope, and it was worth the risk. On the other hand, when they asked him yesterday about it, and he said he would have to think twice about it, because he thinks now that there's a real, very real possibility. After her heart came up to a normal blood pressure of a hundred and ten, there's a very real possibility that her heart will regain its strength and that she will be able to be taken off the machine. That that's a very real possibility.

The risk at this point is still infection. The infection which might be caused by the machine. But so far so good. There was the fact, they did say there was some small sign of infection the other day but that seems to have cleared up.

Ruthie yesterday was talking to I guess one of their friends, I can't remember his name. I don't think I've ever learned his name. But something about Tuesday morning, Monday night to Tuesday morning, bi-ventricular failure. Her heart actually did stop. But I think I said that before, I don't think it was quite called bi-ventricular failure, I heard it referred to as a bi-ventricular assist machine. So it must have been a bi-ventricular failure.

At the intersection of Keyworth and Reisterstown. Passing School Number 59, which has been cleaned up on the outside and they're converting it into apartments on the inside. And to the right here someplace was P's house in one of these white stucco houses. And now crossing Springhill Avenue now! And up there were our old houses and Jake the Tailor between Park Heights and Reisterstown.

Everybody yesterday was so startled by the striking, absolutely striking resemblance between me and my great-grandfather, Zalman Krome. I think it was D said that the picture was in the bag, and the top part was sticking out from the, let's say, roughly the middle of the nose, the bridge of the nose on up. And she thought it was just a strange picture of me. And just startling, everybody said that the resemblance was uncanny, including the, the woman who was working on the desk that day, yesterday. What I said before about how this is the first time we have someone who's got a who's close to death, we have a real chance of helping somehow to live who has a real chance to live. What I tried to say yesterday to them about Aunt Esther, was that she has no experience of people living. People die, that's all, people just die. They don't, there's no way to stop it. They had never stopped it before. No one has ever not died who was, except, now I think about *Bubbeh* in 1960 when they called Mother and Aunt Esther to come up there, but she didn't die until, I think, until '61. *[long silence]* **TAPE ENDS**

THE NANCY TAPES

TAPE NUMBER 2B

TUESDAY, OCTOBER 30, 1990
    It's Tuesday, October the 30th, 9:05 a.m. I just arrived at the cemetery. I decided to come again today. I don't, just don't feel comfortable missing a day.
    It's 9:21. I'm on Security Boulevard, heading up towards the Beltway to go to the hospital. I just finished talking with Uncle Morris again. Yesterday, Sunday, no, yesterday was Monday, I went to the hospital about a little before 1:00. Got there. Aunt Esther was so-so. We did get in to see Nancy a little before 2:00 for about ten minutes. Actually, we were having a little lunch out by the outer part, there by the elevators, and a woman came over and told Aunt Esther that by the time she finished her lunch it would be time for her to go in. So she, of course, thought that the sooner that she would hurry up and stop eating, she'd get in right away. As she interpreted it to mean what she wanted it to mean. We got in, and the nurse said that they had done the test on the heart machine and that Nancy had not done as well today as the doctors had expected. Which, that that, not done as well Monday as the doctors had expected that she would do after how well she had done, cough, pardon me, on Sunday. And that things were just so-so, and no real change, but that that was, could be considered sort of a step back, and, aahhhh, Aunt Esther managed to control herself, but she began to lose it a little bit after a while, so I, you know, just didn't think that she should be allowed to stay in that long. So I asked the woman later to tell her, not to tell her that she could stay ten or fifteen minutes.
    And anyhow, Joe came about four, and we went back in, it was Esther, and Joe had gone in with the flowers, and Esther and I went in. Che-che *[clearing throat]* Joe said at that point that he had talked to the doctor, one of the doctors, not R, and that the doctor had said that she had been on the machine all, they had backed the machine down, and she had been backed down for about about twenty minutes, her heart had been pumping on its own. But that he, he said that usually patients come back suddenly, almost kind of spontaneously, when their hearts are ready. But that that did not seem to be working with Nancy. So what they were gonna do was they were gonna just back it down somewhat and then let her heart pump with it, and see how she tolerated it. What happened was he noticed that the machine was set at 2.58 liters a minute instead of what he said was originally the 4.12. And that it had been on it since about two o'clock, so for about two hours her heart had been pumping. And to make up for the 1 point, I'd say roughly 1.5 liters that the machine was not pumping, and at that point her pressure was in the high 90, blood pressure was in the high 90's, and later when Ron called, told him about it. He said that that was good, since her normal was only about 110, so that the fact that it was in the high 90's was good. Also later on, Joe, I think it was, said something that her pulmonary pressure was, at one point I think he said 70, but he

said also that it was supposed to be about roughly two-thirds of what the blood pressure was. So while it was maybe a little bit high, it was low, it was going down, at least, which was good.

Ronny also said on the phone that he had seen Dr. T, and his cardiologist at the workshop, the seminar that he's at Towson, for the Emergency Medicine. He had talked with T and that T had said that he thought Nancy's chances right now, that as of yesterday when he talked to Ronny, were about 50-50. Which as he says is a significant improvement over the 20-80 that it was Tuesday morning after they hooked her up to the machine. So that seemed, things seemed to be getting better. He also said that he had some concerns about the transplant, that he thought that that might be more of a problem in her case, that they are trying to work towards getting her heart back rather than doing a transplant.

Incidentally, the family yesterday, there was another family in there, I don't know the name. The father had a transplant, and he came down at five o'clock on Sunday, and by yesterday he was sitting up and talking and joking, and feeling really very, very good. And they were saying, one of them, the daughters was saying something, there's somebody named D, and she was saying about how now he talks about how he's younger than D. I guess the heart he got must have been from someone significantly younger than he. What else about? And anyhow I was talking I think with Sophie about it, that the older of the two daughters who were there walked by, and I think she may have heard me on the phone, but later on in the waiting room, they were very, very nice, and the, the mother, I guess the wife of the guy who had the surgery, when I got there, she had gone down to get lunch, and she said she would bring back a sandwich for Aunt Esther. And anyhow, she did, cheese on lettuce and tomato on white bread. And she just, she wouldn't let Aunt Esther pay for it, and so I thanked her for being so kind to my aunt. And she, their family is just very very nice, and they were, the daughters wanted to know how Nancy was doing and everybody in the family and Nancy's kids, and they expressed genuine interest in ... My feeling is that, that we, we fear, we fear their joy, a little bit of envy, but we do fear their joy. He was the one who got the heart that came in, that, when we, I think we talked about it on Sunday, I guess he was the one, that R said was just too large, would have been much too large for Nancy, and they didn't even tissue match it because there was no reason to because they couldn't've used it anyhow.

I did manage to get Aunt Esther to come down for coffee yesterday. We went down from about, I guess, 2:30 till 3:15. And she told me the story about her and O W, U. The kind of the way it started, when she was still in Kolki. So in the paper, in the Yiddish paper there. She seemed a little bit confused at times about the name. That Srulick M, although at times she called him Srulick W, that was a cousin of Malka, *Bubbeh* Malka, put an ad in the paper saying something like

Srulick W, M kucked fur seine kusine Malka W, and gave his address. Anybody who knows her, anybody who sees her, knows anything about her, please write, gave his address. And anyhow, she clipped the article, and when she got to Montreal where *Bubbeh* was, let's see, *Zaydeh* had taken my mother and Aunt Lily and Aunt Freda first. And when she got there, she showed it to *Bubbeh*, and *Bubbeh* said that she wasn't interested, but somehow, oh, yeah, Aunt Esther wrote, and I think they were in Cinncinnati, this was confusing, at first she said Cincinnati, and then she said Detroit or Chicago. But anyhow, he sent her a ticket, and he bought her a dress, and somehow she met OW, W, I think from Chicago. And he really fell in love with her, wanted to marry her. And he came for *Peysach* to Montreal. And *Zaydeh* asks him what does he do in terms of work on *Peysach*, and he says, well, he's a doctor and if he has to see patients, he sees patients. *Zaydeh* was grilling him on how Orthodox he was, how religious, how *frum* he was. And asked him what he did about bread and about *matzuh* on *Peysach*, and he said, well, he said, when he's got *matzuh* there, he eats *matzuh*, when he doesn't, he has to eat bread. So obviously, he did not pass the test, and Aunt Esther said that *Zaydeh* grabbed him by the back of the neck and threw him down the stairs and then threw his suitcase after him. And kicked him out of the house. So Aunt Esther came to, sometime shortly thereafter Aunt Esther came to Baltimore, to visit Esther Dopseh's or Dopsuh. It was another cousin, and she didn't have money to go to Chicago, and just, she was ashamed to ask W for money. And anyhow, she met Uncle Morris, and she said either three days or a week she married him.

And when O W found out, she wrote to him, O found out, she wrote to him, and he cried on the phone when she talked to him. And he called Uncle Morris, and offered Uncle Morris a couple thousand dollars if Uncle Morris would let Aunt Esther go to him. And she said Uncle Morris said, Look, I don't need your money, I don't want your money. I love her, but you love her, too. If she loves you, if she wants to be with you, he says, I'll let her go to you, I mean it's up to her. Aunt Esther, however, decided that since Uncle Morris was so good about it, and that he was such a good man, that she was gonna stay with him, even though she didn't love him. So she stayed with him, she told U, OW, that she couldn't do it, she couldn't leave. And she said, U committed suicide. And he left a letter, a very beautiful but a very sad letter, that without Esther his life was nothing, meant nothing, and he committed suicide. He left the letter, his brother sent the letter to Aunt Esther, that's what she says, his brother sent the letter to her. And that the whole story about all this was written up in the Yiddish daily newspaper, the Yiddish newspaper, [??Might??]. Sometime, now, she married Uncle Morris sometime in 1933. Sometime in 1933.

She said Uncle Morris had two kids, he had Edwin, whom I had heard about. Edwin had leukemia and died on the before, according to Aunt Esther, he died on the day before his Bar Mitzvah. And he had another son named Dean, and that Dean apparently, according to Aunt Esther, is still alive someplace in a mental hospital, that he was severely not mental hospital, he's, but they put him away someplace. According to Aunt Esther he was severely retarded. And he was in Rosewood for a while. I guess that's why she volunteered and did so much work at Rosewood, but now she's, apparently, is not sure where he is. So she's not sure where he is. But apparently, she thinks he's still alive.

She also, then, you know, that's, you know, complaining about the quality of her life, what happened with her life, that she had no life, but it was misery. Because she didn't marry U, because he committed suicide, and she married Uncle Morris, and Edwin died before his, the day before his Bar Mitzvah, Dean was institutionalized. She said she introduced my mother to my father, my father was a friend of Uncle Morris's, and she also said that my mother never really loved my father. That's another one of her stories, and that ... Of course, then her, Morris's death, so Edwin died probably in 1934, and then, of course, Morris, her husband, died in 1946, he was only 50 years old, so she was a relatively young, 1946, she was a relatively young woman in her early 30's, or around 30. Early 30's. Something around that. And that, and then in 1950, she remarried. Married Uncle Sol, Sol Koren, 1954, he died. 1954, my father died, 1954, Aunt Freda died.

All along Aunt Esther, I mean, and Nancy has had this heart problem. And my mother says ... Boy, the stories on each other. My mother says that Dr. A knew from the beginning that Aunt Est, that Nancy had a very, very weak heart, that Aunt Esther would have a lot of trouble, a lot of problems, with Nancy, and that she would, eventually she would need major surgery. But that Dr. A didn't tell Aunt Esther this because he didn't know whether she could handle it at the time. *Ver vaisst?* One story leads to another.

So that's where it is right now. And it's now 9:34, I left the cemetery at 9:17, I was there for about twelve minutes. Took a few pictures at the end when I was leaving. Actually, I took some pictures yesterday. Anyhow, over and out. I'm going down the Jones Falls now on my way to the hospital.

I took a different way to the cemetery this morning. I went around the Beltway to Security, down Security, and I should've turned left at Curtin Avenue, and I thought that's what it was, but then when I looked at it, I thought maybe it wasn't. But it actually it was, and I went on down, and I had to take a left at Forest Park Avenue, and I really got, kind of almost lost control, yelling at myself there a little bit for having missed it. If I hadn't had to stay home a little bit this morning to do some paper work, for my Paragraph Writing class, class I'm teaching.

Last night, last night, I had trouble sleeping, I had a really headachey, just one of those miserable feelings. And that shirt, it was that white-collared shirt with the, kind of cream-colored but with red, blue, thin red and blue stripes on it, and it used to, and I think that maybe it was that shirt that bothered me, that wound up giving me that headache. I tried to go to bed early, but and there was that thing in, yes, and I forgot to bring it with, that column in *Harper's Magazine* about cooking. And one of the guys says something about, that the food processors, and they make for speed, but they take away from the time and would anyone really want it, to take the time and do it slowly, and they said, yes, because that's where you get the sense of life is from being involved in and doing things. And it was amazing because this is what I had been thinking about, this whole process of Nancy here that, and that, why this is so good, I mean not, don't misunderstand this.

Not that it's good that Nancy is so critical. But that, that there is something for her kids in this, in being alive and being aware of what it means to be alive, with the, not the anxiety but, I guess, not the anxiety but with the sorrows and the trials of life, that it's, this is, as Allyson said, this is the most, most difficult thing she lived through. Well, yes, it is. And someone had told Darren that this is real, yes, this is real. In ways that I hope he can learn to understand when Nancy gets better, that he'll be able to cope with this more. Being part of this, it's long, and it's extraordinarily painful. I don't know if it's really better for it to go quickly. I really don't, this may be too long. It's a week, today's Tuesday, it's a week today since in the morning that they finished the surgery on Nancy to hook her up to that machine, after the surgery on Monday didn't go so well.

It's a bright sunny day today whereas last Tuesday when Sophie and I went down, it was a miserable rainy day. And I don't know, there's a difference between the sun, excision of a person's life, this, this is slower, and it's more painful in drawn-out ways. But there's more of a sense of participating in it and not simply being a bystander in it.

And anyhow, when I did finally, then, of course, everyone, Sophie told me about the fact that the heat pump wasn't working, I went to check that, and I called in, left a call on the recorder. Anyway, I got back to bed and took a couple more Tylenol. And I was having that mucous congestion in my right maxillary sinus, and that was bothering me, that dripping feeling. And then it was as though I could see Nancy and in the room with her and was with her and was part of her and how awful for her to be too conscious about what's going on and just to have to lie there. Must be awful on her. I just hope she's not sensing or feeling too much of this or too aware of this.

When I was in the room with her and Aunt Esther yesterday and then later Joe, when Joe held the rose, that was something else, that Joe brought in a bunch of roses in a little vase with water, and he held one, I guess he asked a nurse if it would be okay, and he held one to her nose. He said she loved flowers so much and asked, he kept making, telling her to breathe it in, to breathe in the smell of the flower, trying to reach her consciousness with that. And she started trembling as she had when Aunt Esther and I earlier were in there with her at two o'clock, and the nurse said that she'd been having seizure activity. "Seizure activity," what a way to put it, "seizure activity." I'm not so sure that it was seizure activity, it seemed almost as much to be a reaction to our presence. To Aunt Esther's presence. To Aunt Esther talking to her. To Joe talking to her. To feeling extremely emotional, perhaps even wanting to cry and not being able to, and so her whole body shook. But maybe they're right, maybe it was seizure activity, I don't know. Seizure activity.

I tried to stroke her forehead. Cough cough. To stroke her forehead. Aunt Esther kissed her, Joe kissed her. And I talked to her. And I talked to her about, talked to her about, about Darren's poem, Darren's beautiful poem, *The Sun in Her Eyes, The Sun in Your Eyes*. Aunt Esther began to get emotional the longer she stayed in there. A little bit, she maintained pretty good control. She maintained pretty good control.

On Forest Park Avenue. No, not Forest Park, Windsor Mill Road, after turning right off of Forest Park Avenue towards the cemetery onto Windsor Mill Road. It's, at the corner of Kernan, Forest, Windsor Mill Road and I think it's Kernan Drive or Kernan Avenue, there's a big maple tree that's just a beautiful bright orange. In the, beautiful bright orange in the autumn colors.

Hi, this car, still, what day is this? Tuesday afternoon, 2:29, I'm on Mount Royal and St. Paul heading back to the hospital. This morning Ruthie and I had a nice talk over coffee, it was just very good. About this whole situation and about reality and about death and, not death but about the support and being alive and being alive to what reality is and what life is. And the support that Allyson and Darren are getting and the whole family being there. And how she felt that they would have had a real problem dealing with a sudden death, and I talked to Ruth about that article in *Harper's* about cooking and the food processor. And how one could wish to slow it down so that one could do all the cutting and commit one's time and energy, and that I felt that this is what was happening. We were all really very, very intensely alive. Even at this time.

Anyway, we went back up about eleven, and I went out to call Soph. And when I came back, Soph was in a meeting, and when I came back, Ruth was talking to R, and I waited. And then Ruth said that he had had Nancy on the machine on 1.5, down as far as 1.5, since eight o'clock, and that if, unless there was a, that if she remained stable, then he was gonna take her up between two and three. And disconnect that bi-ventricular assist machine, and close her up, that it was time, that they had to do it. And that he felt there was a, obviously he feels that there's a good chance that the, although he didn't say what the chance was, he felt that this was the time to do it, that the longer she was on the machine, the greater the risk that she would throw an embolism or get an infection. And they had to disconnect the machine, and that the fall-back would be that by-pass thing that they had before, last Monday, before they put her on this machine.

So, we started making phone calls, and she started calling her patients, and I called, she asked me to call Joe, and Joe was already on the phone with R, so I didn't talk to Joe. And I called Dave, and told Dave, and he had just gotten done talking to Joe. And I called and left word for Nancy, and I called and left word for Ronny, and I called and talked to Cheryl, and so people are gonna be gathering, and I decided I had to go see my class at least once, 'specially since they weren't gonna do anything till between two and three.

So I met my first class, there was only one student, and I met the second class at two, and kept them until about ten after, twelve after. I, fortunately, I had some assignments, some work prepared, for them to do.

And Ruth and I talked, and, you know, we had been talking about God and the role of God and attitude towards God, and I told her I thought that some people really do some good spiritual counseling. That it was good that Rabbi Preis had told Aunt Esther when she said she wanted to trade herself for Nancy, that Rabbi Preis had said, "You can't make trades, God does not make trades." And it's, you can't do that. And He doesn't do it. It's just not in the realm of possibility or of reality. And I even mentioned how Cheryl had said something yesterday about, Why would God let her live a few days, and it was, and then to take her and that it was so unfair? And I said, But God was not doing it to be unfair. And it was not God, He wasn't really doing it, and that she was keeping herself alive, and maybe we were helping with our prayers and with our, our focused energy. And I talked about how, thought about how, Aunt Esther saying, Why is God doing this to me? And that God is not doing it to anybody. Not even to Nancy. And that with some, y'know, we needed to have some, that I didn't know exactly what God was doing, and I wouldn't even try to ... And Ruthie said that she thought that, y'know, she kind of had the existentialist view that we have to find our own meaning and own values from within ourselves based on our own experience, and I agreed to that. I agreed with that.

And then later, that was while we were having coffee, and then later when we were talking about Nancy and this procedure, and we both were talking about how our hearts were, were beating and nervously for Nancy, and that this was really in one sense the moment of truth. And I said to Ruthie, "It's like Nancy is now having her existentialist moment." And Ruthie said, "Yes, but she's not making the choice." I said, "Well, she can't make the choice. But she can help to determine how strong her heart can be, at least, I, we think she can." She has been doing it all along on the basis of her determination, it's her, her will that has been doing a great, great deal of it. And we need to hope that her heart is strong enough for her will to work on and that her will is strong enough to work on her heart. That she has not been so depressed and defeated by all this, that she can't struggle any more.

Although I didn't tell Ruth how I had felt last night after going to bed with a headache and then having to get up about the heatpump not working and going back to bed, and how I, suddenly I didn't even consciously think about her, suddenly it was, Nancy was there, and I was part of her and just feeling how she would feel if, if she were conscious. And Ruthie asked how I thought she would, how I felt. And I said, I thought I felt terrified, just y'know, there's this all this going on. And actually, that's really what Ruthie had said about how, what she felt sorriest about was for Nancy that if Nancy is conscious and aware or when she is, that this total lack of control, this inability to, all these people were doing so many things to her and for her. And that she really couldn't do anything for herself. But actually, now that I think of it, there is something that she can do for herself, something that she has been doing for herself. I don't know whether it is enough. As Joe has said, She may have the will, but if there's nothing there for her will to work on, if her heart is simply not functional, not operable, if there's not any muscle, tissue, there to pump, then all of her will is not gonna be able to do anything.

Apparently, though, the other day, the left side was working all right. Whether the right side is now working well enough, we don't know. I don't know. When I talked to Dave about it, he said, I asked about the left and right side, I said, I don't know, I said, but apparently if the machine is down to 1.5, and she's able to maintain, as R said to Ruthie, a pressure of between 100 and 110, blood pressure, then that's a very good sign. And not a guarantee, but it's a very good sign. And that she has been doing something to keep herself going. And she needs to continue to do what she can do to keep herself going. And whether she'll be able to sustain it or not, we won't know until this afternoon when they do the surgery to disconnect that pump thing. And they said they would have as a fallback that bypass machine, I guess, that they hooked her up to Monday night after the surgery, before they took her up, took her back in to, after her heart surgery, before they took her up, like at 2:30 or 3:00 o'clock in the morning for the surgery to connect the bi-ventricular, bi-ventricular assist machine, assist pumps.

Now at the hospital. We're gonna go look around find a parking place. If I can.

It's 2:37 p.m.. And here I go.

When I talked to Sophie and told her that, about the 1.5, and the blood pressure of 100, the 110, she thought that was a very positive sign. And we all thought that was a very positive sign. But there's still nervousness about the actual disconnect, they have to take her up, take her into surgery to disconnect, and as Ruthie said, this is, R said, they have to close her back up. They have to close her back up. And they'll disconnect and close her back up. And it's 2:38.

SIDNEY KROME

    Well, it's 9:19. And it's over. And now I'm on my way to see my mother for a few minutes. And then to go home.

    When I got back to the hospital this afternoon, it's close to three, and they had already taken Nancy up, they took her up back to surgery at 2:20. I don't remember exactly what, we just kinda hung around for a while. Then later on, Dave and I went down for a cup of coffee, and we talked, we talked about Ruthie and I writing a book together, this book about friends. And Darren came down, and Aunt Esther came down, and Joe came down. And then Cheryl came by, and Riva and Al, and we were all feeling okay, and then, I guess it was when Cheryl came down, she said that they had called from the OR to say that they'd be bringing Nancy back in about a half an hour. And that the surgery was done. And the pump was disconnected. And they brought her back to the room after a while, a little while longer, maybe a little over a half an hour. We were waiting for the surgeon to come down. And I guess I went and called, or I don't know where I was. Then somebody came out and said they wanted us all to be in the room because she was very unstable, and they were having problems. And as I came down, I saw at one point that they had a machine, and I saw a guy running with some units of blood in the hall towards the ICU. And then I saw this machine outside, and I thought, and then Nancy went inside, and Nancy and Ruthie were talking about how they were putting her on the heart-lung machine, the bypass machine. Apparently something had happened. And then I went out I think to look for Darren, or, or I don't remember what it was. And when I came back, I noticed that someone had put blue parrots up over the windows so nobody could look in. And I went inside. Nancy said she thought it was that C one again. And it was just as well. Then Miss G came in and said that the surgeon would be in soon to talk with us. No, she came in at one point and looked at Joe and told him that his whole team, that R was in there, and his whole team was in there. And they were doing everything they could.

    And then she went out, and then she came back in. And I think I was sitting next to Nancy. She said something like, "We're losing her." And then G went out, and she came back in, and there were some other people there from another family, and she asked them if they were with our family, and they said no. And she said she wondered if she could ask them to leave for a few minutes. And at that point, those of us who saw what was happening knew what was happening. They left. Darren got up to walk out, and people tried to stop him, and he said, "Can't I go to the bathroom?" And I said, "All right." So he went out. He was gone for a while. And, let's see, it was Nancy's friend, no, Allyson's friend, Suzanne, and then Allyson, and then Cheryl, and Mindy. Then Ronny came over and sat between Cheryl and Allyson and Mindy, and Al, then Aunt Esther and Ruthie and Dave, and then Riva, and then Joe, and then a blank seat or two, and then Ken, Ken's girlfriend, and Ken, and then Riva. And, and me, and Nancy and Cheryl, and Ronny moved over from the end to sit between Allyson and Cheryl. And then R came in with, I can't remember her name, the blonde who was, who was charge nurse Monday night. He came in and said, I, he looked positively stricken. And he said, "I'm sorry to tell you that," I think he said, "she died." I know that she didn't make it, and that she passed, I can't remember even remember his exact words, I don't remember. There was a hushed silence. Some crying and Aunt Esther said, "What? What did you say?" Or something like that. She said, "Did you say my daughter died?" And he said, "Yes, she died." And then Joe got up and walked forward and said, "Doctor, could you please tell me what happened so I can tell everybody else?" And then he walked out. And then Ronny walked out with him. And then later Ruthie went out.

And Aunt Esther wanted to go out. But, we didn't let her. She kept talking about a rabbi who had told her that Nancy was going to live. And none of us could figure out who this rabbi was who had told her that Nancy was going to live. And we kept saying, there is no rabbi there. So I took her out, and it turned out that there was in the Pediatric Intensive Care ICU, there was a very, very Orthodox Jew, who was not a rabbi, however. And she sounded like she was going to accuse him, and I said, "Aunt Esther, don't accuse him." And she said, "I'm not accusing him, just talking to him." And she started talking to him, he started talking to her in Yiddish.

And while I can't remember exactly what he said, he said things like, "Now, I told you it would work out for the best. And it may be that it worked out good for her, that it was time that she had to go." And all this was in Yiddish. And he said, "I know it's painful, I know it hurts, I know it, it hurts so much you can't even talk about it. But are you smarter than God? That you know what should or shouldn't do, to tell Him what to do?" And he said, "You have another, ay?" He said, "Don't you have another daughter? A living daughter?" And she said, "I don't have any more children." I said, "Esther, yes, you do." I said, "You have another daughter." And he said, "You have to live for your other daughter. You have to stay alive and take, be part of that." And he was comforting her and giving her encouragement. So that was, that was all right.

And then G came out, and she wanted to know whether she was an Orthodox Jew, and I, because of preparation, I said, "Yes." And she came back and said she wanted to know something about having a rabbi present while they dressed her, and I said I didn't know, and I tried to find out, and anyhow, this guy, I asked this guy. And he said, "Well, somebody should be there who knows, but the sheets that she was wrapped in should go with her. And any blood that was in her body should go with her, that was in or out of the pump."

And then I guess people cried. And there was one point at which I had to knock on the door to ask about the rabbi, and then Ronny, they came out, Ronny came out, they came out. And I don't know, then I guess Joe went in to see her and to see Nancy, and then he told the nurse not to let anybody in until they had cleaned Nancy up a little bit. And then I guess they cleaned Nancy up, and then people could start going and start going in. Then Al asked if I wanted to go in, and I said I just hadn't decided, and he said, "I'll go in with you if you want to go." And I had to think about it. Then I told him that I would just ... And at that point, Nancy was in there, she had asked if she could have a couple minutes by herself with Nancy. And then Ruth and Dave went in. And then I decided to go in. And I went in by myself. And I said a *Kaddish* for Nancy. And Joe was in with Ken. And then Allyson went in, I think with Mindy and Ronny, I'm not sure whether Ronny went in with her. Although Ronny was in, I was in once with, Ronny was taking Aunt Esther, and Nancy went in and with her, and I went along and, and ??unclear?? was very good down there.

And it was, I guess this was probably about a little after seven, a quarter after seven, that the doctor actually came in to tell us that Nancy had died.

And I called Sophie and told her. And then she called back ten or fifteen minutes later, asked whether she should come down, and I had said something to Riva, and Riva said no, that she thought that people would be leaving by the time she got down. So I told her not to, called her back and told her not to bother. You know. And anyhow, at one point Nancy asked me to, oh, I had earlier, I had bought some M & M's, passed around some M & M's. And at one point Nancy asked me to go out and check on Cheryl and Darren. 'Cause they had been out for so long, and I went out. They were sitting outside and having a cigarette, and Cheryl was really giving him a lot of comfort and support. Talking about how Nancy and Nancy had been raised practically like sisters, living next door to each other. Next door to each other. And so they were obviously okay, and I came back up. And I went in to see Nancy again, and took Aunt Esther in to see Nancy again.

And then, oh, and this afternoon, Rabbi Goren was there again, and he talked about how he'd made *Mi She Berach's* for her, her name was always first, first thing in the morning.

And I went back in with Aunt Esther, and then I went in another time by myself, and I decided I would say an *El Molay Rachamim*, but I did it, but I couldn't read all the words, my glasses. Nancy was so cold to the touch already. Even the first time. After less than an hour. After less than, after about an hour. Or whatever it was, close to or less than an hour. Ronny called Diane, and she was gonna call, she was gonna call, she was gonna call Montreal. I tried to call Raizel, but there was no answer there.

And anyhow, Mother came back, and she called down the hospital, and Nancy answered the phone, and she said, Mother got very hysterical and said, "Let me know, tell me the truth, is she alive or dead?" And Nancy said, "You, she died, she's dead." So Mother was blaming Nancy for not, not bringing her, or for Nancy not bringing Mother home from Atlantic City. But Nancy had seen Mother, told her that she was leaving, and told her what was going on. And Mother decided to stay, or whatever. Of course, the way Nancy put it is that Mother said, "I'll go with you so you shouldn't have to drive alone." And Nancy said, "I don't you to go with me to drive, I can go by myself, I don't need you to drive with me. If you want to go, go, but, you know, you don't have to go with me to drive."

So I'm on my way now to see Mother. Ronny called the funeral home, Danzansky. And at one point they called, and I spoke with a woman there, and she said the concern about an autopsy, and I said, I don't think so, let me check. And I checked. And anyhow, I told the nurse to make sure that this Mrs. G, whoever she was, of the hospital admitting office or whatever, knew that there was not to be any autopsy, so there wouldn't be any problem when they come to get the body from the funeral home, when the funeral home came tomorrow to get the body. And Ruthie had, was writing down some phone numbers for me to call, but while she was writing them down, I went out for a minute when, anyhow, when I came back Nancy had already taken the list, and Nancy made the phone calls for her. So I don't know that I called anybody after that, I don't know what I did.

But it was strange that Ruthie and I were, both talked about how our hearts were fluttering at, at 11:15 when we were out trying to make phone calls about the fact that the surgeon was gonna do this procedure. Oohh, and Allyson cried.

And, oh, yes, later on Nancy, somebody said something about Darren, and and the question was whether he should be given a chance to go in and see Nancy, to see his mother if he wanted. And Joe and Dave both said that that he needed to be given a chance. And Joe was, he was just so concerned about Darren. He said he'd been to a couple of funerals and just had a really, had a bad, bad reaction. And he said, "You gotta make it like it's, don't put any pressure on him. You just, if he wants to, fine, if he doesn't want to, that's just as fine." So I went down, and he was still out there with Nancy [*sic*] and I talked to him, and Cheryl said to him, that, "You know, Darren, if you go, you have to understand, it's not to make your mother feel good, if you go, it's to make you, for yourself to feel better because she won't know, but if you want to go, you go." And he said, "Do I have to decide right away?" And I said, "No." And he said he wanted to think about it. And then he asked if something could be put in to go, like in the grave with her. And I said, "I'm sure that can be taken care of." And he said, "Well, let me see if I can find it." And he pulled out the Jewish star that he had shown me earlier; it was a Jewish star that I guess Aunt Esther had given him. And he said the chain had broken shortly after she gave it to him. And he had been carrying it around, he had wanted her to give it to Nancy, and he wanted to have it put in, so I took it and I said I would see that it got taken care of. And I took it upstairs, and I talked to Dave about it, and he said he'd be going to the funeral home tomorrow. So he said he would take care of it.

And he said, "Can they do it?" I said, "I don't know." I said, "But if they can't," I said, "I think that it might be treated as though it was taken care of." He said, "Do you think that's for the best?" I said, "Dave," I said, "I don't know," I said, "I don't know Darren," I said, "you all know him better. I mean, he's, somebody's got to decide whether ... But I don't see that it would be any real problem. I mean, I don't know, whether it would be a problem to put it in."

Jon was broken up pretty badly also about it. He was there. Ronny was just ... So I'm gonna call Ronny tonight and see if he wants to go out there tomorrow. Nancy's gonna pick up, Nancy and Cheryl are gonna go. They're going, they're going tonight. They're gonna pick up Aunt Esther tomorrow. And what? I'll pick up, I'll see about picking up Ronny, see if Ronny wants to go. And I told Nancy I would see about getting a tray, a deli tray of some kind, to take out tomorrow. Maybe cold cuts or lox and bagels and cream cheese and like that to take out. In the morning or sometime. And she said that she would like to pitch in too, and I said okay, that's fine, whatever. But she's going there now, and I'm gonna go see Mother, and then I'm gonna go home and maybe have a drink or something. I don't know what I'm gonna do.

What the supposed rabbi, what he said to Aunt Esther. First, what did he say first? Oh, that you don't know what's good for a person. It, maybe it's not good for you, but maybe it was good for Nancy, that she went now. And that, are you smarter than God? To know what to be able to tell God what He should or should not do. And that she has another daughter, and she has to live for the living. And that what can we do, as much as it hurts, this is part of life, that people die, and it's just like a part of life. It's part of a reality. That we have to understand. We don't understand, no. But to accept. To accept.

WEDNESDAY, OCTOBER 31, 1990

Okay, it's Wednesday morning, October 31st, 8:39. On my way down to meet my mother and Lou for breakfast. Something else the guy Aunt Esther called a rabbi, something else he said, last night. *Es tut vai, de velt geht veiter.* It hurts, and the world keeps going. He also talked, and this startled me at the time, about the six million Jews who died. And I think his point, although I didn't hear it all, was that if that could happen and the world goes on, then this can happen, and the world goes on.

Talked to Sonkie last night. Talked to Jerry and Kathie. Talked this morning to Raizel. It was hard to talk. All I wanted to do was cry. They're coming in. She said it's so cruel, so unfair. It is, unfair. And it's cruel except, except, except, except that implies that somebody is being cruel and unfair. That it's being done intentionally.

THE NANCY TAPES

And I talked to Aunt Esther this morning. And she said that she had called the doctor, and he called her back. And he told her that she, that basically, that if Nancy didn't have the surgery, she was gonna die, but if, and if she, since she did have the surgery, she did die. And I said to her, Aunt Esther, at least the surgery gave her a chance. It didn't work. It didn't work.

Raizel said that when she talked to Ruthie this morning, she said that Ruthie said they felt that they had been sitting *shiva* for a week, week and a half, ever since that Monday night-Tuesday morning. And that she had been on a roller coaster up and down, and up and down.

I have to see if there's some time today that I can get out to see Uncle Morris. I don't know when. But I have to see if I can get out there today, if not today, then maybe first thing tomorrow morning, early. I don't know. Sometime.

Just came from having a bagel and cream cheese and coffee with Mother and Lou at the Galley in the Alley. Now, Paul had called so I'm dropping, asked if I could drop off, I have to drop off his report poster and his lunch for him. Let me just pull in here and run this stuff in.

Was it yesterday morning, Tuesday? Or was it Monday morning? Not Tues, Monday afte, must have been yesterday morning 'cause Monday afternoon, I think it was, that Joe brought in the flowers. And yesterday morning they were open, the roses were open. And I think I took a picture of them, or tried to. They were in the waiting room. And yesterday Ruthie and I had a good, good, short, but good talk together over coffee.

She said how she couldn't believe that next summer would be thirty years that she and Dave are married. Thirty years.

I thought about but didn't mention to her the telephone call that I made to her from Germany when I was in the Army. It's something that my mother and Aunt Esther used to talk about a lot, that phone call. I'm thinking how, since then, how detached I've become from the family. Only on certain occasions have I gotten back. And I remember the toasts and the funerals and the weddings. But, but that's just on occasions. Just on occasions.

I'm driving down Park Heights Avenue this morning from Paul's school. I'm going down to Coppin on Park heights Avenue, and there's an ambulance, they're bringing somebody out or taking them in to bring them out, I think. Taking them into somebody's house. But I decided I have to go down Park Heights Avenue, and maybe I'll drive up Springhill and past the B'Nai Reuven again.

When Nancy was sitting out by the elevators, last night, and Cheryl was with her, and I went over to her, and she was crying. And then she started talking about D. And how she was gonna call him or something, and Cheryl and I both said to her, "Not now, Nancy, don't embitter it, don't get into that bitterness of that thing now." And she talked about how Nancy had written to him, written him a letter, when she was going in for the surgery, and how Nancy sued him, brought suit against him. But to dredge that up at that time, that bitterness at that time.

I've been thinking about the look on the eyes on the face, the eyes again. The look on Nancy's face that Sunday that Sophie and I went down, the day before her surgery. When we were getting ready to leave, I hugged her, and I said we'd see her like Wednesday or Thursday or Tuesday, whenever she got out of ICU, Wednesday or Thursday. And as we backed away ... Well, there goes a siren whooping up, coming out from someplace, an ambulance, here it comes, coming down Park Heights Avenue, better pull over. And that, and she had a look on her face of, of almost terror and fright, and her face and her lips almost trembling, as though she was getting ready to cry, and I suppose, I remember that at the time, and now that I think about it, it's as though, the look was as if to say, "Sid, I'm never gonna see you again." But this is my reading into it now. But it was a look at the time of being ready to cry, of fear. And then at that moment, R came in to talk to her and Dave and Aunt Esther and her and Joe and Aunt Esther. And Joe introduced us and then Sophie and I left, and that was it. And then later Sunday night, Nancy called, my sister Nancy called, to say that, and I had told Nancy that I would not see her first thing in the morning on Monday. That I would see her after she got out of ICU, after the surgery. And boy, did I see her! But then Sunday night, my sister Nancy, and Ronny *[glitch]* there at the hospital. And she said that Nancy couldn't remember whether I was gonna come down early in the morning or not, and she was just wondering whether I was gonna come down. And I said, No, I had told Nancy I was not gonna come down early in the morning. Cough. And of course, in retrospect, in retrospect, I sort of thought afterwards, it was as though she was asking me to come down, but I wasn't sure. And now in retrospect, I think that maybe she was asking me to come down and that I should have gone down. And I had been thinking of going down, and then Mother called and said she wanted a ride down, so I just went ahead and said I'd pick her up at 8:30 or nine o'clock and take her down.

And I guess what I should have done is that I should have gone down to the hospital first and seen Nancy and then gone back and gone to see Uncle Morris and picked up my mother. All these should have dones and should have dones. Things I didn't do.

Aunt Esther said it about Morris, but I wasn't sure about him. But I can say it about myself, and know that it is true about me. I failed in so many things. The human things. So afraid. Just so afraid.

I've never stopped being 16, I've never stopped being afraid, I've never stopped being afraid. Hearing my Aunt Esther scream, "Mo-ras! Mo-ras! Mo-ras!" When he died. Being afraid to go in my father when he died. I think that's why I had to go in to see Nancy last night, after she died. She was so cold to the touch.

THE NANCY TAPES

Just so cold. Worse than marble. Because you don't expect marble to be warm. But there's the shock of the cold of a human body.

I told Cheryl that Nancy was like a sister to her mother. And I told somebody, I think it was Sophie, that Ruthie had lost her best friend. Not just her sister, but her best friend. If and when Ruthie and I get together to work on her book, that has to be the dedication. To Nancy, Who Was Her Best Friend. She told me yesterday morning how they shared everything. There was nothing that they didn't share be, didn't tell each other.

I want to have a friend. To have a friend. All right, I'm coming up on Springhill Avenue here on Park Heights. And I'm turning left on Springhill Avenue. There's the Gs' old house. And there's ours, and the roofs are falling in. 2614. 2616. The still red porch of ours but it's faded. It's like it's a 30-year-old color, and the weeds. And we used to play stepball on the grass and 2612, the G's. And there's the old Talmudical Academy, now Springhill Elementary School. Turning left on Cottage Avenue now. On the left the houses where L S lived, on the right where T S and B S lived. Post-war houses. When I went with V to bury a turtle, turtle who had died. Coming up now on Keyworth Avenue. Looking down to the left, Enoch Pratt Library, Branch, was it 14 or 16? On Keyworth Avenue. Down the street, PS 59. And here's the empty lot where once stood B'Nai Reuben Shule. Mr. S, Rabbi B. And the houses across the street in utter decay. It's incredible. Garbage in the streets. And here we are at Shirley Avenue. The decay. The decay. This big *??deal??* of a house on the corner. I don't remember that it was yellow. And then to the right, it's gone now, was, used to be Beth Isaac Shule
TAPE ENDS

TAPE NUMBER 3A

WEDNESDAY, OCTOBER 31, 1990

Okay, it's 11:47, 11:47, it's 11:47. What day is today? Wednesday, October 31st. I just picked up some more tapes at Best and Company. Y'know, the last one ran out while I was talking about passing the old JEA Building, how the Beth Isaac *Shule* was still there, the *Shule* building was still there, but the JEA was missing, JEA Building. And then I, think that was around 9:30, I guess, and then I turned left off of Cottage onto Oswego and passed 2644, which was J A's old house. And here I am now, and I'm thinking, what I'm thinking, what I'm thinking.

Thinking. What did I think? How cold Nancy was to the touch. How cold the dead are. Not like stone, even, not like marble, not like granite, even the stone, the stone, the stone, Uncle Morris's stone, the top of it was warmer to the touch than Nancy's forehead was. At least that had the sun to warm it, inside she had nothing to warm her at that point.

She was so cold, and maybe her trembling, they said it was seizure, maybe it was, it was the seizure of crying, of emotion, of knowing she was caught, knowing she would not get out, knowing that there was no escape. Except death. The emotion, the trembling, and the fear, the trembling and the emotion of wanting to cry for Joe, for Aun, for Aunt Esther, I almost said Aunt Freda. The trembling of the fear of confrontation, confronting death, and knowing there was no escape at that point. The trembling of the cold, feeling that cold, the cold of death on her already. And knowing that as hard as she could struggle against the fear, against the terror, against the emotion, against the cold, that the struggling would not work.

And maybe there was this. Maybe what she gave us in staying alive. Imagine we had all gone our separate ways. Imagine if we were all off on our separate ways, and we heard suddenly that she had died suddenly, that she was alone or maybe just with Joe, but that we were all alone, each of us alone, individually alone, when we heard it. The pain would have been quicker, but it would have been almost unreal, an unlife pain, a non-life pain. How quickly it would have happened, surgically clean, as they say, surgical strike. There are no such surgical strikes, well, there are surgical strikes, but they leave their own kinds of wounds behind. They leave their own wounds behind. Oh, Dad! I cried at the cemetery, I was at the cemetery again to see Uncle Morris. And I cried in the stone. Did I cry into the stone? And I cried for Ruthie. She's lost her best friend. And she will never have Nancy to call again. For 20 or 30 years of her life, whatever she has left, Ruthie will never have Nancy to call again.

Oh, it's so cold, oh, the dead are so cold. I didn't know how cold they were. The dead are so cold.

THE NANCY TAPES

Thinking, too, though, I have to stop at a liquor store, and I'll get some Canadian Club. *Ah bissel brumf'n, brumf'n sollst de mitnehmn, brumf'n* is brandy, isn't it? *Shnapps.* So I guess what I'll be taking is *shnapps.* Canadian Club. The good stuff for you, Nancy. The good stuff. Canadian Club.

Y' gotta have a little *shnapps* there. For the *minyan.* In the morning and in the evening. *Va-y'hi erev, va-y'hi voker.* And it was evening, and it was morning. And that student on his paper or her paper who wrote morning meaning the time of day but who spelled it mourning, the grieving. In the mourning. In the m-o-u-r-n-i-n-g. And it was evening, and it was mourning time when it was evening time, last evening time, yesterday time, at the hospital. It was mourning, it was evening, and it was mourning. The first day. Evening and mourning of the first day in the same time.

I don't know if I said it on the tape before, but I need to say it now again anyhow, whether I did or didn't. If Ruthie and I do put her book together about friends, the dedication must be, To Ruthie and Nancy, Who Were the Best of Friends. Who Were the Best of Friends.

THURSDAY, NOVEMBER 1, 1990

It's Thursday, November 1st, at 8:23 AM. I'm getting ready to go pick up Charlie and go to the funeral, but I just needed to make a note of, this morning when I was shaving, the song *Red River Valley*, "Just remember the Red River Valley, and the sweetheart who's waiting for you." Kept going through my mind over and over, and I was singing it, and I don't know why. And just now, what was going through my mind was, cheez! another song, and I forgot, just, it's gone out of my mind again. Heh! Also have to remember to make a note about my kind of dream-vision of Nancy from Monday night. Like I was part of her and she was part of me. I could feel what it was like to be her in that bed with the tubes. And the fear. And that knowing. I remember that. I told Ruthie about it. The feeling of being terrified. I don't know if I made a note of this before or not. I think I did. But I'll check when I review this. Maybe I'll do it again later.

FRIDAY, NOVEMBER 2, 1990

Good morning, Mr.--ch-chem *[clearing throat],* pardon me. Good morning, Mr. Phelps, this is the Impossible Mission calling. It's 6:40 am, Friday, November the 2nd. I'm waiting at the corner of Village Queen Drive and Reisterstown Road for the light to change. I'm on my way out to Nancy and Joe's house, for the first morning *minyan* of the *shivah.* The funeral was yesterday. My notes and comments today will probably be kind of spotty because I haven't done this, actually, I guess, probably since late Tuesday night was the last time I did this consistently a little bit.

I don't know. Did I do it on Wednesday? I don't think so. Did I do it on Wednes? I don't know. Anyhow, I'll be picking up in a minute because the light is changing.

The notes will be random, of course. Tuesday night. How cold the dead are. I said that before. So I'm not gonna say it again. Monday night, I had this, I'm not sure if I put this in yet. But I had this kind of dream state, sort of, I had this headachey, just bad feeling, just worn out, tired, headachey feeling Monday evening. So I went to bed early, but then the heat pump stopped working, so I had to get up and check on that, and called in N's. When I got in back to bed, I took two more Tylenol. And having trouble sleeping still.

Traffic is heavy this morning. The sun's barely coming up over the oak trees on the horizon, on the left. Some clouds, a few light clouds in the sky, which otherwise, pale to slightly darker blue in the, in the *??unclear??*. Heading just past the Randallstown Exit of the Beltway and straight ahead, the horizon's a little bit, very light mauve, hazy mauve drifting up to kind of a pale grey and then a blue and then some light wispy clouds.

Anyhow, it was like I could see Nancy--oh, there's the sun, coming through the clouds. Bright orange. It was as though I could see Nancy and almost as though I was Nancy at the same time. In the ICU with the tubes, the needles. And as she, and her eyes that, oh, those opened eyes, just like my mother-in-law's, the unseeing eyes! Tears in her eyes, I think, at that point. As I told Ruthie on Tuesday morning, it was, it was as though she were terrified. Y' know, and not, as if she were, as though I were, if I, as I were she, I was terrified. Terrified. Lying there and being conscious of this and being unable to do anything. It was, that was the way Ruthie put it also, on Tuesday morning, the sense of being so out of control of your life.

Being out of control. Not being able to have any real control over what happens. Was it Joe or or Darren that I was talking to once, a couple times? About those inner resources that people have. And it must have been Joe, I think, and he said, "But what can your inner resources do, what can your strength, your will do, if your heart has nothing there for it to work on?" And that's basically what's happened in Nancy's case, her will, her determination were incredible. It's just that she lacked any, physically, she lacked any heart for her will to operate on.

I'd better stop this a minute. Traffic's getting real heavy here, coming down on the Interstate 70 Exit, on Security Exit and Interstate 70 Exit on the Beltway. Time out.

Getting off this Beltway at just the right time here, at Interstate 70 Exit, because it's backing up down on the Beltway itself, backed up to this exit. I don't know what's going oh, my goodness, look down there, the traffic is just loaded! The Beltway is just all bottled up down there. Past Interstate 70. But here it's so far reasonably clear. Your eye in the sky. Chopper six.

THE NANCY TAPES

This *??unclear??* note about ratches or watches, wrist watches. On many of the days since Nancy's operation, I've been wearing Sol's watch. And most of the days, a lot of problems with it, it wouldn't keep time right. Y' wind it up, and it would run for a while, stop running. And then I put it on again, Wednesday morning, the day after Nancy died, and it's been running perfectly ever since. It does wind down at night, it did wind down Wednesday night to Thursday morning, but it does that anyhow. But even last night, Thursday night to this morning, to Friday morning, it did not wind down, I mean, it was still ticking. Took a licking and was still ticking. Timex.

There's gonna be a fair amount of noise now because I'm driving at 65 miles an hour and the wheel, the tire sounds, the motor sound, the wind sound, all that seems to be providing some interference here. Background noise. The, the trees are leaved. Very pastelly, oh, what they call earth tones now, pastel oranges, yellows, browns. The trees yesterday were just beautiful, especially the maple trees, their leaves in many cases bright yellow, bright orange. Filtering from yellow to orange to brown, and very, very bright. Now passing some weeping willows and some, I don't know, small-leaved trees. Uh-oh, uh-oh, looks like some, there's something going on up ahead. Coming up on the Route 29 exit here at, on Interstate 70, I saw a flashing police light. But there's a police light. Okay. They got somebody pulled over for something right here. I'm getting off now on the Route 29 exit. Time to click off a second.

Going through my head this morning, a little bit now, but more while I was getting up and shaving, the old Mamas and Papas hit, *Dedicated to the One I Love*. "There's something I want you to do, especially for me, and it's something that everybody needs, Each night before you go to bed, my baby, Whisper a little prayer for me, my baby."

Merging now into Route 29, and the traffic coming off Route 40 and coming off of 70 is moderately heavyish in here, blending together on this road, at this morning time of 6:55 on our way to the morning *minyan*. Anyhow, that Tuesday morning that I got in, cheez! the traffic is just, the way these guys drive. That I got in, oh, I see why, there's this white pick-up right in this middle lane right in front of me who's not even moving at all, and everybody's passing on the right and passing on the left, and I see why. Time out.

Actually, there was also traffic in front of him, but now that the traffic has moved out in front of him, he's still moving slowly in the middle lane when he should be in the right lane.

Anyhow, Tuesday morning, October the 30th, I'm not sure if I had put this in before, but Ruth and I went down and had a cup of coffee and a sweet bun. We had a good talk, good talk. But she talked about Nancy's condition being that feeling of not being in control, that things were going on around her that she could do nothing about. Anyhow, then we went upstairs, and I stepped out for a minute, I don't know whether I went to the bathroom or went to call Soph or what, but anyhow, the next thing I knew when I came back, she was standing in the hall talking to R, and I just waited a little bit on the side. Although I probably could have gone and stood next to her, I don't know, I just felt that I really shouldn't. Part of me felt that I should be there, and the other part felt that I shouldn't be there. Anyhow what she said was that he had decided that Tuesday was the day to disconnect her from the pump. That he would have back-ups, that she had been on, had the machine cut down to 2.5, to 1.5, and she was still maintaining a good blood pressure. And he would have back-ups, he would have the balloon, he would have that by-pass machine, *et cetera*. But that was the appropriate day. That leaving her much longer on the pump had its own kinds of risks, potentially devastating risks.

So, what happened? So Ruth told me, and then we kind of, I guess, kind of hugged each other a moment, then it was time to make phone calls, and she was talking about how her heart, we talked, actually, she talked about how her heart was fluttering for Nancy in anticipation. And we had been talking over coffee about this existentialist feeling that she said she had, that you kind of define your own values through your own experience. And I said to her, Nancy's existential moment has come, and Ruthie said--I thought I had so recorded this before--Ruthie said that yes, that was true, but the problem was that Nancy was not making the choice to face her own existential moment.

And what I think about now is that maybe she was prepared to face her existential moment as far as her spirit is concerned. But that as far as her body is concerned, she was not. A bright reddish, reddish tree, a small tree with small leaves there, catching the sunlight and reflecting it off to the right. That her body was not prepared, that her heart simply was not going to, was not strong enough. And probably would never be strong enough for her to really have the existentialist choice. Except to make the choice to face the choice. To make the choice to face what would not be a choice.

So Ruth started calling patients, she asked me to call Joe to tell him that the doctor would be calling. By the time I got through to Joe, I didn't talk to Joe, I talked to one of his co-workers. The co-worker had taken the call and said that, told me that Joe was already on the phone with R. Then I called Dave, but by the time I got through to him, he had already spoken to Joe, and I told him that I had called Joe and *et cetera, et cetera*. And then I called Nancy in Atlantic City and left word for her to call, the message being that it's important but urgent and that it was not bad news. I called Ron at his hotel and left the same message. Then I called Soph, but she wasn't in, that's right, she was in and out at that, at meetings. R and D, A and R, or was she at screening? I can't remember what. Anyhow, she was out.

And then I had to go to class for a while. And by the time I came back--I think I recorded this--Nancy was already upstairs. They had taken her up at 2:20.

When I came back and, about 5, I guess, Dave and I went down for coffee. And then Joe came down to get something to eat. Darren came down to get something to eat. Aunt Esther came down. And then, a little bit later Cheryl came down to say that they had called and that they'd were giving her, bring Nancy back from the OR. Oh, and while Dave and I were down, we talked about this book, about writing the book that Ruth and I had talked about, her book on friends, her dissertation, about turning it into a book. I think Dave was trying to prepare, was trying to prepare the way for Ruth to have something constructive and positive to do, not simply work to divert her attention, but work on a project that Nancy had helped her on. Nancy had done the typing of her dissertation. That Nancy had done, had helped her on, and also that would have something to do with how she felt about Nancy, how she feels about Nancy. Nancy being her best friend. And the book about friends, about having friends and being a friend.

So we talked about that, and then when we went up, and then, of course, my sister was there, Nancy was there. And Riva and Al were there, they had brought-- who had they brought down? Riva and Al were there. Was my mother there? Now, my mother was in Atlantic City, that's right. That's right. My mother was in Atlantic City. She'd been out of. And at one point, anyhow, we were standing over there, and Darren had brought his poem back down, and he had drawn a bright sun in a corner, smiling sun, and then, To Mom, in red in the upper-right. And a rose alongside the poem typed, and down at the bottom green grass, and I told him that I only had an 8 by 10, that was 8-and-a-half by 11, and that he would either have to get a larger frame. There's that barn that I passed the other day where they're demolishing around it, and it's just, it's lost its walls and roof, all that's up are the frames on the right.

Anyhow that I would have to either trim it or get another frame. And he said that's okay to trim it, just not to trim the "To Mom." So I went, so Al said he had a friend who was a medical illustrator, and we went down to the guy's office. And what we had to trim away was on the right hand side pure white page, pardon me, and on the bottom we had to trim away, actually we wound up trimming away all the grass. All there was, part that indicated the green of the grass, and all that left sticking up from where we trimmed away were just a few little like sprigs of the grass, that's all. And in retrospect, I guess you could say that that which was cut off was the earth. From the earth where she lived, the earth where we live, the earth where she was part of our lives, physically. That, I guess, was kind of symbolic.

And anyhow, the medical illustrator, his daughter, I guess, is a neighbor of Ruth and Dave's. And he was familiar with the case from that, L S, I think, was his name, and he was also familiar because he knows R, the surgeon. And he kept saying that the case, that there was one for the books, it was one for the books, because Nancy had been on this time Tuesday, she'd been on this pump machine for 8, 9 days, this was actually, it was her eighth full day on the pump. And that she was still alive. But also that she was fortunate that she had R, that she had the best man to work on her. Time out to pass a truck.

What I need to try to do is, a note reminder to myself sometime, is to get a copy of Ruth's remarks that she gave to Dave that Dave read at the funeral yesterday. And if at all possible, a copy of the Rabbi's eulogy. And a copy of Darren's poem.

So at one point about 6 or a little after 6, the pump technician went by, and he had a smile on his face. And later Joe said that it was the first time he had seen anybody smiling about, at all when talking about Nancy's case. And the guy said that she was much better off the pump, and her heart seemed to be doing all right, for any details they'd have to wait and talk to Dr. R. Well, in a matter of moments, when we got, I got some M & M's, couple boxes of M & M's from the Pediatric Intensive Care Unit, and people would, and I had some and give some like to Joe and people sit around eating, munching M & M's in that little hallway. Time out for a stop here at Scaggsville, Route 216.

Whew, there's a lot of traffic! At the traffic light. And on the right is that Cherry Tree Center, that shopping center which was not there a number of years ago. Sophie and I had talked about how this road has changed and all these, in many places they have overpasses instead of the traffic lights. Scaggsville Road, Route 216, still has the traffic light though.

The sun is well up on the left now. And it's shining through some trees and casting a shadow of trees on the left on the trees on the right. But, oh, roughly the top half of some of the trees on the right are showing through and picking up the sunlight. There's pastel yellows, faded-out yellows, washed-out yellows and orange, the oranges are, and browns. To the left there, across the road, a bright clump of yellows crossing a river that is steaming. And the trees hang down just about to the shore line. And they're glowing orange in the sunlight. And in the steam rising the mist rising from the river. It's just a beautiful autumn day.

Last night at one point, Sophie was talking with Ruth. This was before the *minyan*, this must have been in the kitchen, and I had leaned against the little partition between the kitchen and the family room. And I looked up at the wall where there was a picture of Nancy and Joe, and the picture had been taken, it's a beautiful color portrait, the two of them dressed casually, informally, Nancy kind of leaning on Joe's shoulder, both of them looking off to their right, spectator's left. And stood there just thinking that it was just absolutely incredible that we were in a house where *shivah* was being sat for Nancy! of all people. I mean, I just, it was just, I know I haven't seen her very much in the last years, ten years, just occasionally, *Bar Mitzvahs*, reunions, and stuff like that. But this was someone from my childhood, this was a cousin from my childhood, this was a cousin of my generation. And she was gone. And she was Nancy, and she was gone.

There's an old, wooden house, with the windows boarded up in grey wood. Coming now to the Burtonsville Shopping Center, this is where 198 is. Where I make the right turn, head on over to their house. Time out, Jim.

So I guess Tuesday night again, it was, it was Nancy who noticed Tuesday evening that that heart-lung machine was out, that little corridor right outside of Nancy's room in the ICU. And that they were working on her. And then we were all asked to just kinda hang around the, be around the lounge. I went out, and when I came back one time, I noticed that the, the windows had been covered over and that blue paper, che *[cough]*, I guess, sort of like the pieces of protective paper hospital beds.

Now on 198 heading west towards New Hampshire Avenue, and there's a cemetery here on the left, and beyond it there's an open field with some steam rising from the field and the trees, in their autumn colors. The leaves in their autumn colors. The trees in their autumn leaves. The haze. Just above the ground. Just above the ground.

To the right now, che-che *[clearing throat]*, past the cemetery, there's a very large barn with a silo, but all the paint in the ceiling, the paint and the roof, shingles look like they need pou. There's a sign, it says Farm for Sale, a blue sign with, it's the Carr Farm C-a-r-r, it's for sale, and I was going to say that the house under the trees also looks as though it needs paint, but it looked all of the, better than that barn. There was no wall, che-che, pardon me, no wall and no ceiling, no roof. But I guess everything is along here. The idea of farm and rural areas is dissipating. There's a post office, Spencerville, Maryland. It's it's just a trailer of some kind. Painted red, white, and blue.

So we gathered in the lounge. And we knew something was happening. And it was very quiet in there. Then Miss G came in, and I think I did say this once before, I don't know. And she kind of pointed back to Joe, and she said, Dr. R was sitting there, che-che, pardon me, his whole team was in there. And they were doing, che-che, everything they could. And it was obvious that at this point that they were doing everything that they pos. What she meant was that she was, that she was going. That the her doctors were doing everything they could possibly do to try to stop her going, to keep her alive. But it was obvious also that there was not really a lot of hope. That this was a last-ditch effort. And then she went out, and then she came back. And there were four people from another family, and she went over to them and asked if they were with our family, and they said no, and she asked if they would mind leaving for a few minutes.

And I was sitting next to Nancy, and she clutched my arm. Oh, Nancy, I'm sorry. Last night on the way home from the *shivah* house, my mother said, Nancy will be lost without her. Sniffing. And she's right. Oh, she won't quite be lost. She'll go on.

But as Jerry said, Jerry Bulmash, when I talked with him, I guess Tuesday night, or Wednesday night. Sniff. Tuesday night, at Aunt Esther's house. There's such a void, there's such an empty spot, there's such a such a void, there's an emptiness there. Even though, he said, he had not seen her that much either, and I said I had not seen her. He said there was still that emptiness. Still that void. And for some, who were so close to Nancy, che-che *[trying to be able to speak]*, like Ruthie, like my sister, the emptiness will be even greater. I think I said this before. I told Cheryl, that Nancy was like a sister to her mother, they were like sisters. And for Ruthie, Nancy was her best friend. Time to stop a minute.

Last night, Sophie and Ruthie were talking about the book on friends, friendships, the ending of friendships, from Ruthie's dissertation, that we're, we might get work on. They talked about how, Ruthie talked about how after things calm down a little bit that maybe we could get together one Saturday and just spend a few hours talking about it. We talked about how she writes yellow legal pad, and I use the word-processor, and she was talking about how she couldn't use it. And then she said that, that she's not a rewrite person, she writes it all, and she writes it down. And she writes it out, and that's it. She doesn't do a lot of rewriting. On the other hand, I do a lot of rewriting. Get it all down, the way working on my papers, just get it all down, and then go back and re-structure, and re-organize afterwards. It's marvelous that she's able to do, do it that way, that's what Dave said. She works with the yellow legal pad. She writes straight through and fills it up, and he said you never see, there's never an erasure on it.

Okay, coming up now on to, down, I'm down New Hampshire Avenue and getting ready to turn right on, here it is, on Bonifant Road, right now. 7:20 by the clark car clock.

7:25 the car clock, 7:22 by Sol's watch on my left arm. So I'm pretty sure, obviously, that I'm gonna make it in time for the 7:30 *minyan*, though when I was getting my 6:38 start this morning, I wasn't too sure that I'd be able to make it. Fortunately, the traffic was not bad. And fortunately when there was that bottleneck, the bottleneck was on the Beltway, just past or leading up to, or up the Security, not the Security, the I-70 Exit, so I was able to get off without any problem there. I think I'm gonna stop this now and just enjoy this ride. Enjoy?!? Enjoy this ride down here, down Bonifant Road. Getting ready, coming up to and now passing Ruth and Dave's house. Closed up, I guess they're probably there already for the *minyan*.

THE NANCY TAPES

The sun is shining so brightly, and there's the occasional runner jogger out. Here's a guy in a red sweatsuit running in the direction of the traffic. He should be on the other side. Before, there was a guy in a dark blue one with a headset on, looked like one of those AM-FM radio headsets. Bright, beautiful trees and houses. Well-kept yards and things. Aunt Esther yesterday talking about, Wednesday and yesterday, talking about what a *goldeneh ballaboosteh* Nancy was to help, and everybody, Ruthie talking about proud she was of the house and how well she took care of care of everything.

Turning now up Corona. This is a beautiful suburban residential area. Large, beautiful homes. *??unclear??* big house. Like that area off of Garrison Forest Road up where J K lives. Turning left now on Jaystone. Getting ready to turn right now. On Silverstone. And there's the house on the corner. It says Halle Enterprises, Incorporated. H-a-l-l-e. The Laurelwood Model. There are people going, there's a guy walking up to the house for the *minyan*. And I guess now I can pull up right over here. Okay.

It's now 9:23, I'm heading back towards Baltimore to pick up Charlie to take him to school. There's a tree trunk standing, all the branches have been lopped off of it. But, Tuesday. I talked to Darren at one point. We talked again about how, sniff, well, they had kept Nancy alive. Oh, that cemetery is Union Cemetery. I missed the founded date. This is the cemetery on 198. About how what had kept his mother alive was her will, her inner strength, her desire to be alive, to live. That's what kept her going for so long. This was before she died. Talked about how people sometimes do not realize that they have this inner strength also. How, that they have more than they think they do. And I talked to him about, for example, the poem that he had written for Nancy. *The Sun in Your Eyes*. I said, "Now, y'know, I, you know, you told us you always read all this depress, listen to the depressing music of the heavy heavy metal or heavy metal rockers, and that's usually what you read and usually what you write, and then here, in at this time when your mother's in this condition, you can write that kind of poem to her and for her." And I said, "That that shows that you have, you have that strength within you. You have that strength within you, you just don't know it's there, and you're stronger inside than you think you are. Or than you, and." And then later what did I say?

Okay, Nancy saw the machine out in the, and I already, also about how I'd, yes, when I came back in later, and there was the, the blue paper was up, and that G first, G told Joe that the doctor was doing, right, and I talked about that already. And that they asked the other family to leave, and then another point she came in and very calmly and and kind of surreptitiously put three boxes of tissue on the desk behind some books and asked if everybody was there who was supposed to be there. And we said yes. We knew what that all meant, at that time.

And then the doctor came in--I talked about this, I think. And how Joe, after the doctor came in, there was this kind of silence, and Aunt Esther kind of gave a Whoop! and said, "What do you mean? You mean my my daughter is not alive, my daughter is not alive? Did you tell me my daughter is not alive?" And he said, "Yes, she died a few moments ago." People cried, and then Joe got up and walked towards the doctor and said, "Why don't we go out and you can tell me what happened, then I can tell everybody else?" Just that incredible strength of his at that point.

Now looking right ahead and at the meadows, farms, sign, and the incredibly beautiful yellow and orange of the trees there. There are two trees together, one yellow and one kind of a dark orange. Just the glow of them in the sunlight is incredibly beautiful. There's a flock of sheep to the right. Time to stop a minute.

Noticing as I record and play back, that one of the problems doing this in the car is that all the car sounds, the tires, the wind, especially when I had the roof open, but that all that sound is all picked up.

Anyhow Joe went in to see Nancy, and he came out, and he said he did not want anybody to go in to see her until, until they had, nurses had a chance to clean her up, and they did. Meanwhile, Aunt Esther wanted to go in, and they said she had to wait. And then she kept talking to that rabbi, another rabbi who had told her that her daughter was gonna live, and he lied. We kept saying there was no other rabbi there, so finally I said to her, "Let's go take a walk, Aunt Esther, while we're waiting." So we went out, and there was this--I talked about this, didn't I?--Jewish guy, a very Orthodox Jewish guy in black, black vest, black pants, and he talked to her about how, number 1--did I talk about this? That he said said it would be good, it would work out good, and maybe it's good for Nancy, and even though it's not good for Esther and not good for other people, it might be good for Nancy. And that who was she, was she smarter than God to challenge God? And that it's true it's a terrible pain, it hurts a lot, it, *es tut vaaiiy*, he said. But *de velt gehyt veiter*, and the world, the world goes on, life goes on. There is really no consolation, except this, that life goes on. And he even talked--I know he talked about this--about the six million who died in the Holocaust. That nothing could, y'know, life still has to go on, no matter what happens. And he asked her if she had another daughter and, a living daughter, and she kind of fudged on this. And I said, "Esther, what are you talking about? Course you do." And he said that, y'know, you have to live for the rest of the family that's alive. He said the kind of things that she needed to hear.

And anyhow, Nancy went in, she wanted to have a couple minutes by herself. Everybody, she went in, and she had her time by herself with Nancy. Then, I wasn't sure whether I wanted to go in or not. Al said that he would go in with me if I wanted to have somebody with me, and I said I just wasn't sure yet, and then

THE NANCY TAPES

finally, I decided that I would go in, but I wanted to go in, I would go in by myself. And I went in, actually, I wound up going in, I think, three times. Another time Ronny and Nancy were helping Aunt Esther in, and I went along to help. And told Aunt Esther that she had to be aware of the fact that in the next bed, in the same room with Nancy and just separated only by the curtain, was a living patient, a heart patient, that she could not get loud and hysterical. Because she couldn't disturb him, he still had a chance for life, and he didn't need to hear her. So she did extremely well.

Mile marker 15. Oh, the leaves and the trees. The colors of yellow and orange and green and greenish-yellow and greenish-orange and some reds and mauves and lavenders almost. Pastel, but glowing with the sunlight. Like the sun in your eyes. The sun in your eyes and the leaves and the trees and the colors and the trees and the leaves.

How cold the dead are. I know I said that before. She did have a slight smile on her face. I don't know if it was really a smile or just the way her lips were turned. On the right-hand corner of her mouth there was a red mark as from that tube, that, the inhala, in, an, intubation tube for the respirator. The tube that she had told us, told Sophie on Sunday in, the day before her surgery, that probably bothered her the most. And how we all realized that in all the problems that she was going through or the torment and everything, that probably the thing that bothered her the most in one way was the thing that should have, if there is a should have, bothered her the least, that is that inhalator tube, that intubation tube, for the respirator. And later, was it Wednesday or Thursday? I guess it was Thursday, at the, before the funeral, Ruth was saying to someone that she did have that smile on her face. That she did look peaceful and at ease. And she said-- this is when she started to cry--and she said, she said, "I saw how peaceful she looked, and that made it easier for me, to leave her." Aaawwhh, Ruth.

And Ruthie's comments read by Dave yesterday at the funeral, trying to make some order out of chaos, trying to find some meaning for all this. See, that's why I write the way I do, put it, draft it all down and then shape it all later. Give the order, the form to the chaos. After at least the chaos is created. She writes directly in form and order, it's wonderful if you can do it. I guess she can do it.

When I stopped on the way home Tuesday night, I got a couple more boxes of M & M's before I left, and I gave one to Cheryl, for her and Nancy to have on the trip 'cause they were going out to Joe's. Tuesday night. And I went and stopped, I was gonna stop and see my mother, but I stopped, Lou was downstairs with Aunt Esther, so I stopped in to see her and him, and Mother was upstairs on the phone with Ronny. Mother had stayed in Atlantic City. Nancy said that Mother called the hospital, screaming, kind of hysterically, "Just tell me this, is she dead or alive?" And Nancy said, "I told her, if you want to put it that way, then she's dead." And

Mother blamed Nancy for not taking her home from Atlantic City. And I asked Nancy, and she said she had talked to Mother, told Mother about the phone call, told Mother that she was leaving. And Mother said, "Then let me go with you, 'cause you can, you're in no condition to drive by yourself." And Nancy said that she told Mother that if Mother wanted to come, she should come, but that she didn't need to come just for the sake of Nancy's driving, that Nancy was very capable of going on by herself and driving herself. So Mother decided to stay. And so I said to Sophie, you know who's, exactly what tone each one spoke to the other. They do such battle, as Aunt Esther and my mother do such battle, as Aunt Esther and Ruthie do such battle.

So, did I call, I guess I called Jerry that night. Told him. And so I called Sonkie and talked with him. And Jerry talked about the void, the emptiness, inside. I think he had already gotten the word. He talked about the emptiness inside. Even though he had not seen her in a long time, even though I had not seen her. The emptiness--I've talked about this on the way down also. And how the real emptiness would be the emptiness that that Ruthie would feel. And at one point Sonkie said, "Aunt Esther, now you may not want to hear this, you may not like to hear it, but this is something I have to say to you." And she proceeded to talk over him, so she didn't hear him, but I heard him. And he said that Orthodox Jewish grieving, saying that you say to someone in mourning, the Rabbi said it again today, May you be comforted, among the, mourners, as the mourners at Zion are comforted, Zion in Jerusalem, may you be comforted among the mourners, of Zion in Zion in Jerusalem. And then also in Hebrew.

It's 12:13, Friday, November the 2nd. I just dropped Charlie off at his dorm. And now I'm going over to to Nancy and Joe's. I don't know how long I'll stay. What I was thinking before to myself was, I can't let go. I can't let go. *??Hey look??* I have to be there, every day or all day every day. I want to be there. I can't let go.

But also what I wanted to say was that, I really just don't feel like talking right now. So maybe on the way home, I can pick up with Wednesday and Thursday, this morning. *very long silence till* **TAPE ENDS**

THE NANCY TAPES

TAPE NUMBER 3B

SATURDAY, NOVEMBER 3, 1990
Okay. It's Okay, it's Saturday night, November 3rd, 11:02. On my way down to pick up Paul at his, che, at the Bar Mitzvah he went to. And I just wanted to record a couple of things so I don't forget them.

Wednesday, Soph and I took a tray out and the boxes of *rugelach*. Which turned out to be one of the big hits out there. And uh at one point, Sophie was sitting in the kitchen talking with Ruth, sniff, and I was leaning against the divider between the kitchen and the family room and looking at the picture of Joe and Nancy. Photograph taken sometime not too long before her surgery. Sometime after October of '89 when they discovered how severe the problem was and that Nancy would need surgery soon. And the surgery, Nancy and Joe both looking off to their right, to the left as you're facing the picture. And I stood there leaning against it, thinking this is something is wrong, something, I couldn't believe that we were there in a house of *shivah* for Nancy. It just, something was wrong and just sort of terribly wrong.

Thursday the funeral. Thursday the funeral. Couple of things. Sonkie told Nancy that she should shovel, that if, that they, if she was gonna shovel dirt, she should shovel it using the shovel upside down, blade turned upside down. Nancy did, and I didn't. Later discovered, Nancy told us why he said that. The reason for it is that he said Nancy died at a wrong time, she was too young, she shouldn't've died, she should've lived longer. That is, in, the lifespan is normally longer, but she didn't, and so the death was unusual, and so the shovel should've been turned upside down in a sign of recognition of the unusual quality of her death. Nancy pointed out that later the Rabbi himself, when he turned, when he shoveled dirt in, oh, he, he had the shovel turned upside down. When Joe was the first one to shovel dirt in, he took a large shovelful, and he kind of sprinkled and scattered the dirt the whole length of the coffin. So that it kind of, sort of, lightly drummed down onto the coffin, almost like a gentle rain. Did not make that heavy thudding noise. And then Ruthie threw some in, and Nancy, and then I did. And I resolved because it was so, there was not, the sound, so I filled the shovel with dirt and turned it over, high, kind of in the air so that it landed with a thunking chunking thunk. Loud enough to echo out of the the grave. And then others took their turn, and while the, it was being filled by others, I was talking with Raizel and Anne, Cookie, and Esther, and I said something how I'd never seen it this way, and done this way, and I think it was Raizel who said that it's supposed to be done so that you hear the sound though. So she said this after I said something about how gently Joe had sprinkled the dirt on the coffin, and Raizel said that you, it should be done so that you hear that sound that chunking sound, so you know the finality of the dead. That the person is dead, that the coffin is in the ground, that the coffin is being covered by it, by the earth. And so you should hear that thunking sound for the sake, sound of the finality. And I said, Well, that's what I tried to do. And Raizel said or Anne said, Yes, we know, we heard.

And then later at the end, sometime during that, Bryan had taken his shoes off and he walked into the woods in back of the grave. Then afterwards, after most, after, when I walked away and I I went up with Sophie and Charlie, and then Paul came up to join us. And I asked Raizel if she wanted to go up and see the *troika*, and at first she said no, and then she called to me, and they all came up. Raizel and Anne, and Esther and Cookie.

And then when we went back down, and I went back over, and there was Bryan on his knees on the cloth where the pile of dirt was, and the grave was almost, just about full. He was taking chunks of dirt, breaking them up, the clumps into smaller bits. Smoothing them out, very, very gently, on the top of the grave to make it smooth and soft and even, and filling in the corners of the grave itself so that they were even and smooth and doing it so gently, and breaking the clumps with his hands, and then Allyson, who had been crying standing near the head of the grave came over and kneeled down. She started running her hands over the dirt, breaking up the clumps also. The two of them there doing it so gently. And later that night at the house of, Joe and Nancy's house, and I saw Bryan in the kitchen, and I shook his hand and hugged him. We hugged, and I said to him, I thanked him for doing that, that it was such a gesture of love that we all needed that. I don't know how others might have reacted to that. I thought it was a beautiful, loving gesture. Coming at the end.

Other comments that I wanted to record right now before I forget them. Yesterday, Friday, coming home from the synagogue with Joe and Nancy in the car and Allyson, and Joe talking about how, how what? How nothing could be done. Prayers to God and all these things. And I said something about how everybody had done so much, the surgeons, and Nancy thought I meant just the surgeons, but I meant everybody, the prayers and love and thinking and Bryan focusing his energy with his stones. And I said it was like what Allyson had said about how maybe if everybody loved her more, expressed the love, they could save her. And then she thought about her friends who had lost their mothers and were not able to save their mothers, even though they, she realized that they loved them. We got out and walked up to the house, Joe and I started talking, and Joe was saying first something about how with all that love in that room and Nancy in that condition that nothing could save her, it was just the right time for a miracle. And God chose not to do it, perform the miracle, and so there was no miracle. And I wanted to say, but I didn't get to then, that you can't expect that miracle. So that did say to him I low, don't know if he heard me, I said earlier as we were getting out of the car, just a few moments earlier, that if everybody for whom people prayed and loved so hard were saved, that very few people would die.

And then it occurs to me now also, why should those people die who are not loved and not prayed for? But if the absence of love, the absence of prayers, diminishes their will somehow, or does not, not diminishes it but does not add to it. And anyhow, later also, Joe said, at, and I wanted to think about that thing, about miracle. I guess it's part of what I meant when I said to Nancy about let it be. And then Joe said that one of the things that he felt guilty about, not, felt bad, I y' I don't think he used the word "guilty," but he felt bad about not saying to Nancy that he wanted to say to Nancy was that all the time encouraging her to get well, that he felt that he should have said to her also that if it was too hard, too difficult, that if she couldn't make it, that it was okay for her to let go. And I told him that I was sure that she knew that, that she understood that, from him, even though he hadn't voiced it.

And when I talked to Ruthie later, Ruthie and I had a really good talk, sitting in the living room. I have to come back to the talk about religions, and religion in the Jewish religion and immortality and resurrection. And what Judaism believes and doesn't believe but what. So she said, when I told Ruth about what Joe said, she said that she tried never to say something to Nancy that would make her feel that she *had* to do that. Just to say that she was doing well. That's when I said to Ruth also, as we walked in, to get in the line to get something to eat, I said, told her that all those times I had gone to visit her father, and I told her I had only missed two days, what I had said to Uncle Morris, was that he should help Nancy to live if he could, but if that was not to be, he should please help her to die. Help her to make that passage across a little bit easier. And Ruthie understood and said that was, she felt that was right. No one would know, no one could have known then whether she was going to live or not going to live.

And yesterday, on Friday afternoon, at one point I was in the kitchen. Was I on the phone to call Soph? I can't remember what it was. But I think it was, Allyson was with Darren in the kitchen. And Darren was saying something about believing in God, but why does He have to make things so difficult? That's part of the nature of life. And that fits in with what Ruth and I were were talking about. I was talking about that friend of Nancy's who had called, and she said that well now she's in the arms of her Lord, and now she's with her Creator, and she didn't think Nancy would come back even if she had the chance. And I said to Ruth that offended my idea of of what human beings are like, and what the meaning of life was like. It is that struggle. It is that difficulty. It is that hardness in life. It ain't easy. And nobody ever said it was easy. And it's in the facing of that challenge that it also becomes worthwhile.

THE NANCY TAPES

And so it is also that I've I think I've come, Ruthie said something about my getting through my, making my own spiritual journey, and I said something about coming back now, and this, I said, maybe it's part of my age, it's my Jewishness. But it's also recognition, and I may have said this before, that prayer does not change things. It, as Dr. K said, God! almost 40 years ago, it changes our attitude towards things. It cannot alter the severity of the decree. But what we can alter is the way that we perceive and accept the severity of the decree.

Was it today, I think? When we were getting ready to go to the synagogue. Or yesterday? Ruthie thanked me for being there. And she said I've been really been a source of strength for her. And it kind of took me aback. And I said, Oh, Ruth, nooo. And she said, "Yes, Sid, you really have." And it reminded me how we had talked about the being there of the family together. And how I had said to her that I was glad that I could be with her, I was able to be with her Tuesday morning, first to talk and then, more important, to be there with her when she heard the news from R that they were gonna do that procedure to take Nancy off the pump. And to comfort her and give her a little bit of strength, maybe, help her just by being there and talking about it. While she went ahead, and then I went ahead and made the phone calls on Tuesday. Then today, this evening, coming back from the synagogue, she talked about how Rabbi Goren had made a tape, given Joe a tape of the eulogy, and that she would like to have it transcribed, and somebody said something about making copies, and who would do the transcription? And I volunteered to do the transcription. I would the, and they're going to let me do it. Joe's gonna make a copy of the tape, and I told Ruthie I'd make do the transcript on the word-processor, and we laughed. But I'm honored to be able to do that. Just as I don't think I need to say again, I said it to Joe that day he took the time, when he asked me about being a pallbearer on Wednesday, that I would like to be a pallbearer. And I thanked him for the honor of, for asking me to be a pallbearer. As I thanked the Rabbi today for giving me the honor of closing the *Aron Ha-Kodesh* after the prayers, after the reading of the *Torah*. I asked Dave in the car tonight about the Jewish star, about Darren's *Mogen Dovid* that Aunt Esther had given him, that he had wanted to put into the coffin, and he said, yes, it had been taken care of. He had given it to the guy at the funeral home and said Nancy had seen the guy open the coffin and, but that she got a little upset about somebody opening the coffin when it was supposed to have been closed. She asked Dave what was going on about the guy opening the coffin, and I asked him if he had told Darren, and he said he hadn't, and I said I thought it might be a good idea just to let him know that it had been done, as Darren had asked.

What I need also to say to Ruthie is thanks for letting me a pall, asking me to be a pallbearer. But also that I was glad to be able to be there to comfort the living. Since I could not comfort the dead. Be there to comfort the living and out of respect for the dead. I told her yesterday how the Rabbi had misinterpreted my saying what I said about, on Wednesday afternoon about the family not hearing the gift that Nancy had given the family. Not having died suddenly earlier, everybody would be separated. Each one in a different place, and be isolated of that immediacy of the knowledge of her death. But that we could all be together when we heard it, through the whole time period of suffering. Through her death, with her through her dying, and then her death.

So I said to Ruthie, ??unclear?? So I said to Ruthie, Nobody but ... People talked about the assassination of Kennedy, what they ask is, where were you when you heard? Not whom were you with when you heard? We all knew with whom we were when we heard because we were all together. That was the gift that she gave. As my mother-in-law, I said, another death-bed gift, had given her family the gift of having a chance to say goodbye to her and knowing that she knew that they were there to say goodbye to her. I told Ruth that I had told Eleni that her grandmother had given her one of the greatest gifts of all, to be aware that she had said goodbye. The chance to say goodbye and to know that she knew that Eleni was saying goodbye.

Ruth also asked this evening if I would be willing to write something for the family newsletter, something to send to Mindy to include in the family newsletter, for the family circle, the reunion newsletter. And I said I would. And again, I'm touched that she would ask me to do that. It's a moving thing to be asked to do something like that.

MONDAY, NOVEMBER 5, 1990

It's 9:33 Monday, November the 5th, passed just passed, passed Royce Avenue, passed Keyworth Avenue and PS 59, being made over into apartments with the sidewalks all torn up, so I turned up here, I didn't, not so, but I turned up here, Springhill Avenue and Park Heights, so I could look up the street. Later I'll have to come by and take some pictures. Ruthie, I had done that, taking pictures myself, and Ruthie felt, asked if someone would, said she would want someone to take pictures, so they could give them to Amy, Craig's girlfriend, so she could do some sketches or drawings or paintings of them.

What was? Yesterday was Sunday, November the 4th. At the *Shivah* House, watching *ET* and having an extremely difficult time with the scene in which ET dies, and remembering the scene in--what was that movie?--*Steel Magnolias*, when the daughter dies, and I said to Ruthie how I couldn't couldn't watch that, I had to get up and leave, and I said, "Whose big idea was it to watch this?" And it was Niles', and anyhow, then, Che *[cough]* Sniff. After ET has died, there's the point at which Elliot is talking to him, and the last thing Elliot says is "I love you, ET." And then he turns to walk out, and then he notices the flowers coming back to life,

THE NANCY TAPES

and then he runs back in, and ET's heart is glowing red and beating, and the, and Elliot says, "Does that mean that they're coming?" And then he says, *[in ET type voice]* "Go home, or Phone home, ET phone home." They're coming to get him. So he came back to life. That's a fantasy. They don't come back to life. At least not a physical life. Whatever life there is, for them, we really have no way of knowing. Of whatever life there is for us, we have no way of knowing.

And this morning, I was listening on the car on the way down to *Porgy and Bess*, and thinking about Aunt Freda. And yesterday in the car going back to Baltimore with Aunt Lily and Aunt Esther, I think it was Aunt Lily who said, "Now she is with with Freda. They're together, with God, with Freda. She's with Freda now." Now. I don't know.

Park Circle is not the Park Circle it used to be. I wonder if anybody even calls it Park Circle anymore.

Okay, it's, oh, there it goes, it's 11:01 on Monday, 11/5. Just picked up some more film, heading from Mondawmin, up to Springhill Avenue to take some pictures. I guess it was Thursday at the funeral, at the cemetery, Aunt Esther said something about Nancy her daughter with the *shayneh punim in dreyrd arein*, in the *kayvah*. That beautiful face being in hell. And later, I guess it was on ...

Later, I guess it was on Friday, talking with Ruthie about it, I said I interpreted that to mean the old Hebrew idea of like *Sheol*, like Hell is where all the dead went. So Ruthie said, no, she didn't think Aunt Esther meant it that way, just literally, in, under the ground, in the grave under the earth. And when I talked to Aunt Esther yesterday, I think it was Sunday, maybe it was Saturday, Saturday or Sunday, about, must have been yesterday, Sunday, about the poem R, Joe's niece had written, that poem, the card, about how much she loved her and missed her, and Aunt Esther said something about whether she would love it or feel it now that the worms are crawling, and I said, "Aunt Esther, I don't think, she doesn't feel that at all." It's incredibly morbid. Although ... Incredibly morbid. Just, just morbid, thinking about the worms crawling and ... Cough.

This morning I recorded the, or made a copy of the tape of the, the tape of what? The tape of the funeral service at the funeral home. Rabbi Goren, just moving, very very moving, again.

Heading up Park Heights Avenue now, coming up where Sussman's used to be, Sussman's Drugstore.

On Cottage Avenue now at 11:34. Approaching the spot where B K and I years ago saw what looked like a guy beating another guy up, pummeling him into the bushes, and we spent all evening looking for a cop, and never did find one. And here's where the JEA used to be.

Just came down Quantico to Park Heights, looking for Rabbi T's shule, but I'm not sure where it was. Up Park Heights now. Here's the firehouse to the left

-80-

and the, was it the *Chizuk Amuno*? there's the *Agudas Achim* on the right. And here's, on the left, the old Avalon Theater. How dare Barry Levinson take that name! The marquee is blackened now. Ah, hell! Can't get balanced. Can't quite get to it now 'cause of that truck. Maybe I can come back and take a picture later. Park Heights, Cold Spring Lane, Hoffman's Package Goods. Oh, and they have finally painted over or covered over the old EVERYBODY WELCOME sign that had like black and white for a reddish and white. When the Public Accommodations Bill was passed, they were the first one to welcome everybody and still got hit early, early on.

Park Lane to the left corner there. I remember coming up to the Hobby Shop and Read's Drugstore. It was a marvelous to walk up to then, in those days, for us kids. What else was up here? Oh, yes, there's Saint Ambrose Church. And what do we do? Turn left on Wylie Avenue. Turn left on Wylie Avenue to get to Royce Avenue. That's right. Left and then right. Here we go. Left onto Wylie Avenue. Left onto Wylie Avenue. And then right onto Homer. Left onto Wylie, right onto Homer. Here we go. Right onto Homer. Whoops! Is this one way? Oh, shit! Pardon me. I think this is one way. Do Not Enter. Do Not Enter Do Not Enter. Royce Avenue's one way up. Okay, well, I guess I have to go back out. Time out while I back around here.

Homer Avenue is one way heading south, so I can't do that. I started to, but I can't, I gotta go down now, go down, and Royce Avenue's one way heading up, so I've gotta go down Wylie to Reisterstown, then turn right because Garden Avenue is one way, can only take me around the corner to Sumter over there, so I think what I have to do now is go right here on Reisterstown Road. All right, let's try this.

Okay, so it's 11:58, just pulling away from the firehouse on Park Heights Avenue on, across from the--What was that? *Agudas Achim*? And my last picture was of the *shule*, but it was the last picture, so I don't know if it's gonna come out. I gotta get another roll of film so I can take some pictures there and of the, of the Avalon Theater. I get a little carried away with this picture-taking here, don't I? Well, what the heck? *Asha-i viatsa!*

Okay. Here comes a funeral up Park Heights Avenue. Grab a button. Although it's going in the opposite direction, it's going out Park Heights, and I'm heading down Park Heights. So. But what the heck? I'll grab a button anyhow. Lot of noise in the car. Long funeral! Long procession. Coming up now on Violet Avenue and where Kessler's used to be. Was that 1977 that I saw them remodeling Kessler's and turning it back into a house? Good old Kessler's, Sam and Barney. Would you believe that Paul is now friends with B? Who is Barney's grandson. Or is he Sam's grandson? I don't know, well, I think he's Barney's grandson, that's why his name is B, after Barney.

THE NANCY TAPES

Okay, headed around now, no, I'm just passed Ulman Avenue with Roland's Barber Shop, Roland, Roland, what was that guy's name? He used to cut my, Herman, I think. Roland and Herman. He used to be such a, I used to go to Greenberg's when I was a kid, go to Greenberg's with my father, and then somebody told me about Roland's. So I started going to Roland's, I really liked Roland's. Roland ga, they gave a better haircut there than Greenberg did. Hiya, Leah, how are ya? Hiya, Leah. The racetrack results. Do you, you got that at Greenberg's, did not get that, did not get that at Roland's. Roland's was a family place, Greenberg's, I guess, was like a bookie-joint type place. He was so thin! My God, now that I think about that man, Greenberg was so thin! The other day I saw S L up in the Hecht Company. Oh, the other day! It's probably been a month ago. Lozinsky's, on Park Heights Avenue. S L, the old neighborhood.

Some friends that I wanta have this, talking into it I feel like a character out of Beckett. *Krapp's Last Tape,* Krome's Last Tape. Except that Krome will probably go on making tapes until it's his last tape, but right now, he hopes it's not his last tape.

I need to find those earphones. I don't know where I put them, I thought they were right by the radio, down in my office, but they weren't there. I have to find a way to find them, because the ones that I got, the new ones, they're stereo, and so it only broadcasts into one ear. Where did I put them? Che [cough] I have to look around, maybe they're on the floor? I don't know, I'll have to look around for 'em though.

So I could transcribe Rabbi Goren's eulogy at the funeral service for Nancy. Incidentally, I have to call Rabbi Goren to find out what was the psalm that he opened with, the psalm that they use, that he spoke when we walked out, the pallbearers walked out with Nancy's casket. 'Cause you can barely hear it, I don't know which one it is, but there's a psalm there, you can hear the beginning of it.

TUESDAY, NOVEMBER 6, 1990

Okay, it's Tuesday, November the 6th. It's two weeks ago today, it was a rainy, miserable day. It's now 8:26 AM. Two weeks ago today it was a rainy, miserable day. About this time, I guess I was on my way home. We had gotten the news about, they had hooked up the pump, the bi-ventricular assist pump, on Nancy. And Joe had told us that R had said there was a 20% survival chance. Now, it was Ronny said, "We heard 20%, sniff, and we were delighted."

Today it's a beautiful, crisp and breezy November day. Last Wednesday, 'cause also today's also one week, sniff, since Nancy died, Tuesday evening. And it was probably close to, it was close to seven, 6:30, 6:45. Wednesday, I went to school for a couple hours. Then I went to the cemetery to see Uncle Morris again. I came back, picked up Sophie, and we went out to Nancy's house in Silver Spring.

And Wednesday afternoon, Rabbi Goren was there. And he sat for, oh, at least two two-and-a-half, maybe even three hours with the family. Talking about Nancy. We were ready talking about what they thought about her, and what they remembered about her, what was her spirit, her essence. And he captured it beautifully in in his eulogy, in the funeral service. At one point Nile told the Rabbi that he had called 911, or he wanted to call 911, to call the police to try to save Nancy's life.

And when we were talking at one point about the *minyan*, and somebody said something about women being part of the *minyan*. Aunt Lily was a little bit out of it, both her and Aunt Esther were ki, but mostly, I think, Aunt Lily taken aback by the fact that women could be part of the *minyan*. And, I think it was Ruthie, said, women are counted as, and then Mindy filled in, People. Or maybe it was Windy, Mindy said the whole sentence. Women are counted as people.

And everybody talks about what they remembered and thought about her. They talked about Darren's poem, and they gave the Rabbi a copy. He said that, of course, he would give anybody in the family who wanted to an opportunity to speak at the funeral service. But he also said that he felt it would be too emotional. It's usually too emotional a time, and family members usually can't speak because they're so overwhelmed emotionally by their grief.

And people talked about different things. Nancy's refusal to let her heart condition dominate her life. It was there, and it was simply a given of her condition, but it was not a given of her condition. It was not a given of her living, it was a given of her physical condition. Mindy talked about the determination that she got. Ruth talked about the love, the struggle. Joe talked about the love. I can't even remember all the details. After or when they were just about done, they asked if, Ruth asked if any of the, Oh, and they also somebody brought up the thing about the cheese platter that, as a sign of her humor, yes, they talked about her sense of humor. And they talked about her cheese platter that she said, I guess on Sunday, or maybe it was Monday morning *[sniff]* that everybody would be waiting and maybe they should order a cheese platter while they wait for, to hear about surgery. And somebody else pointed out, I think it was Ruthie, that I guess it was Sunday evening or sometime, and when they were all in the room, and the nurse came in and asked for Miss Simpson, and Nancy pointed to, was it Shirley B? And pointed to somebody else and said, That's her. Jokingly.

When they were done, Nance s, Ruthie asked if any of the cousins or anybody else had anything to say. I got up, I wanted to say something, I wanted to talk about the deathbed gifts my mother-in-law and Nancy. I broke down, and I I didn't break down, I just couldn't speak, and I ran out, sat in the living-room for a few minutes, and I composed myself, and Dave came in. Dave was fantastic, Dave Weinstein. He came out and, y'know, said, "It's it's hard, it's gonna be hard, the next couple days are gonna be the hardest." And it was incredible the way he got up at the funeral and read Ruthie's words. And managed to to do so quietly and with dignity and without breaking down, without losing control of his emotions. It was very, very important that he read Ruthie's words, it was very important that he do so clearly and carefully. That he keep to the dignity of the occasion, the dignity that Nancy would have wanted to the occasion.

And then I went back in and talked about, although I think the Rabbi at that point misinterpreted what I said. My point was that, what I was trying to tal, say was that the gift she gave was that had she died suddenly, we would've all been in our separate places, and we would not have been together. And we would not have had the comfort and consolation of being together, of sharing our love and our grief together. And that that was critical. And at some other time, I talked to Ruth about it, and said that she, sniff. It was like when the Kennedy was assassinated, people asked, the questions, Where were you when you heard? And no one asked With whom were you? or Whom were you with? There was a separation there.

That afternoon also, Wednesday, it was before that point, I think, Ruth and Sophie had a long conversation, and at one point I was leaning against the divider between the two, between the kitchen and, I--Did I say this before?--the kitchen and the family-room and looking at that marvelous picture of Nancy and Joe, the one that was taken sometime after they learned in October of last year how bad the situation was and between then and the time of the surgery. And thinking that it was, something was wrong, that that we were out of joint and would not, we couldn't possibly be in the house where they were getting ready to sit *shivah* for Nancy, it just didn't seem right that things really seemed just out of joint. It was just wrong, it was incorrect. It didn't belong.

And that reminds me of the dream I had now. It was early Sunday morning. I dreamed somehow that Nancy and I were kind of embracing, and when we separated, I didn't realize it was Nancy until we separated, and then I saw that the the creases on her cheek and on her neck, the right side of her neck. And I thought actually that was from my face pressing against her, but now that I think of it, that was the way her neck was kind of distorted by all the tubes and needles in her, on her neck when she was in ICU. And I remember I looked at her, and I thought, and she looked absolutely terrific otherwise, color was good, face bright and alive, with the sun in her eyes, as Darren put it, the sun in her eyes. And and in the dream, I thought to myself, Wait a second, Nancy's supposed to be dead. That can't be Nancy, this is, something's wrong here. And Nancy at that time said to me in the dream, I w "That was the wrong place, I shouldn't be here." And the next thing I knew, we were sitting out at a sidewalk cafe someplace, and, not cafe, a restaurant at a table outside. Ordering fish, some kind of fish, and and she was making some kind of a joke, or she made some kind of a joke about the fish. But I'm not sure what it was, I can't remember what it was. But there was some kind of joke about that that she made. And that was my dream Sunday morning, early Sunday morning. Well, actually, it was after sunrise, I think, I fell back to sleep.

I know that Ruth Wednesday afternoon, Ruth and Sophie had a really good talk together. I, y'know, I came into the kitchen at one point, and I was going to sit down and join them, but it was obvious that they were in a, that they were speaking together. And so I didn't want to interrupt, so I backed off and just walked on out someplace else. I think that was it for Wednesday.

It was really moving. Now passing Royce Avenue at 8:37 am. On, what's today? Tuesday, November the sixth.

Okay, it's nine o'clock, I just finished taking pictures up here of the Avalon. And the Avalon fire, the firehouse up here and the Avalon building. And the the little park here where Rovner's Avalon Hardware used to be. Yesterday I took pictures on Royce Avenue and Springhill. Did I record that? I don't know. Yesterday morning I went up and took pictures at, oh, about 10:30 or so, left school and went up and took pictures of Springhill Avenue houses, *B'Nai Reuven*, Pratt Library and Keyworth Avenue Branch 16, then Royce Avenue, 3316 Royce Avenue. Okay, where the *B'Nai Reuven* was, I took pictures also.

It was so cold and windy, my hands hurt now from the cold. Boy, are they cold! I tell ya, y' don't realize how cold it is 'till you get out there and stand around in it for 10 or 15 minutes. Mmm! My hands hurt! It is such a beautiful day! Driving down Park Heights Avenue, 3900 block. Ah, gettin' ready now, crossing Keyworth Avenue. And now the 3800 block. B E's house over there. Springhill Avenue, down to the right, Jake the Tailor, up to the left our house and the Gs' house there boarded up. Coming down on Violet Avenue, Kessler's, no longer Kessler's, about 1977 reconstructed back into a house. Place where about four three or four houses are missing and the block where Lozinsky's was is now gone, has been gone for a long time, and it's just kind of treed over and overgrown. I don't know if it was supposed to be made into a park or what, but it's just all, someday maybe I'll take a look down there. And the *shule* here, what *shule* was this? Y'know I have to come back and take pictures of these *shules* sometime also. Was this the *Shaarei Zion*? This was the *Shaarei Zion*.

Saturday night, November the third, coming back from *shule* with Dave, Ruthie, Joe, Allyson, and I, coming back from *shule* Saturday evening. Ruthie was talking about the tape that Rabbi Goren had made of the funeral service and given to Joe, and she said she would like to have a transcript of it, so I volunteered to do that, and I've gotten, and I've made so far three copies of the tape. Have to make a few more. But also uh thinking about the transcript, then she also said that, she asked, and I was touched that she would ask me to write a piece for the family circle newsletter to Amy to include in the family circle newsletter. 'Bout a page or so. About Nancy, little bit, she said, about her condition. But not so much that as what happened and the love and what Nancy was like. And what we all feared in this time.

Thinking about coming back sometime to take pictures of our Lower Judea area and thinking all of a sudden of the block in which Kessler's was, and there was also Larry's Beauty Parlor where Mother, it was Mother and Aunt Esther, where they all used to go. I don't think that's there, I think that's also been rebuilt into a house, now that I think of it. And was Greenberg's in that block? Or Greenberg's, Greenberg's was in, I think, Greenberg's Barber Shop was in the block after Sussman's, I think. And there was the Sherwin-Williams Paint Store and Hardware Store with Sherwin-Williams paint sign. And the *Shaarei Zion*. Maybe I'll do that sometime. Looking down now, from the Mondawmin intersection, Reisterstown and Liberty and Auchentoroly Terrace, you can see the silhouettes of the, silhouette of Bromo Seltzer Tower. And the USF&G, no, that's the World Trade Center or USF&G Building, I'm not sure. And you can see the sun glinting, shining off, reflecting off the water on the harbor. The wind is, it's windy, and the trees and the leaves blowing. Leaves rushing along the ground, sidewalk. And over here now at the, I can see the Auchentoroly Terrace *Shule* through the trees. This would be a good shot, too bad I don't have film left. Layin' down. Slope on my left, it's Reisterstown Road heading north on the right-hand side heading north is where A S and I, the summer I worked for the, we worked for the parks cutting stuff, and that's where there was poison ivy, and we didn't realize it, and we got a, I got a terrible case, we both got terrible cases of poison ivy. I think Nancy had that picture of me reading a comic with calamine lotion all over my arms. And I remember that one night that I fell asleep with my arms in the air. I had my arms raised up so they wouldn't touch, and I wouldn't scratch, and they wouldn't itch, and I woke up in the middle of the night, and my arms were in the air, my hands over my face, the moonlight shining in on the calamine lotion scared the hell outta me! Whooew!

Good afternoon, Mr. Phelps. Your mission, and it is an impossible one, is to try to record something of all the feelings and the events, the events of the feelings of the last couple weeks. And then to try to put it together into some kind of order. To take the chaos and turn it into order. As Ruthie said, I think it was Ruthie said, that she does, when she does her writing. Order out of chaos. There's oh, hell! There goes my coffee, almost.

THURSDAY, NOVEMBER 8, 1990

Today's, What is today? Thursday, November the eighth, it's now 8:11, I'm just coming from the Giant. Had to stop in and pick up a few things, like filters for the heat-pump, and I picked up some apples, and also I checked out, what I got was the slides were in there, some of the slides that I had taken, I looked at one roll, and what it was is the roll of slides I took Monday afternoon and evening, October the twenty-ninth, one week after Nancy's surgery. Today incidentally, in case you weren't aware of it, Sidney, today is one week since Nancy's funeral, and one week ago today Sophie and I were getting dressed and getting ready to leave to pick up Charlie to go to the funeral home for the funeral service. What did I just say? Uh, yeah, the funeral service day, one week from S.

What I was talking about before I interrupted myself with the fact that it's one week since the funeral service, is the fact that I stopped at the Giant and what I got was slides, and I looked at one roll of the slides, and they were slides taken Monday, October the twenty-ninth, one week after Nancy's surgery, and Tuesday, the thirtieth, the day that she died.

The first picture is a picture taken downstairs in the cafeteria when the mouse came out, poking its head around, under, crawling around under one of the tables, and, of course, I thought too late about trying to take a picture, and by the time I got the camera set and took a picture, the mouse was gone back in the radiator grillwork.

Anyhow, I'm about to go up on the 795, was gonna stop by and take pictures of PS 59 but I decided I really don't have time, I've gotta do some work! is what I've gotta do. And it's it's getting pretty tough to get back to do some work. In any case, I'm getting up on 795 now, on the ramp. And I wanted to record before I forgot, before I forget. Yesterday about, oh, I guess about a quarter after four, after I went to K-Mart, I stopped by to see Aunt Esther and Lily and Aunt Lily, and my mother was down there, and then my mother brought Lou down. But anyhow, went down, tried to see Aunt Esther, to see how she was doin'. It's amazing how the three of them just cannot get along, as I said to Sophie this morning, or was it last night? They can't stand each other's complaining. They can only stand their own complaining. But they don't like to listen to each other complain.

In any case, Aunt Lily was saying that, this was yesterday, which was Wednesday, November the seventh, that the night before, Tuesday night, November the sixth, she had had a dream about Nancy, and in her dream, Nancy looked, she said, beautiful, and she was beautifully dressed. Aunt Lily did not say what she was wearing. What kind of dress or what color dress.

That also reminds me that Saturday evening when we went to the synagogue, and I went to the synagogue with, let's see, it was Dave and Ruth, and Joe and Allyson and myself. Allyson was wearing a kind of purple and black striped dress, sort of striped, but they were wide bands actually, with a kind of waistband of black. And I said to her it was a beautiful dress, and she said that it was her mother's, that it was Nancy's, and I said, "Well, it's beautiful for two reasons, that's because it's a beautiful dress, because it's your mother's." And I thought it was marvelous that she was wearing Nancy's, Nancy's clothes. She had said something the night before in the car that she didn't have very many dresses and she was wearing her mother's dresses. And Nancy told her, my sister Nancy told her--why do I have to say my sister Nancy?! There's no other Nancy to talk about her right now--Nancy told her that it was--Oh God, there goes my coffee spilling!--that it was a *mitzvah* for her to wear her mother's dresses.

Okay, so in the dream, Aunt Lily did not say what Nancy was wearing, just that she looked beautiful, beautifully dressed. And that Aunt Lily smiled at her, and she smiled at Aunt Lily, and she called to Nancy and waved to her, and Nancy wouldn't answer, Nancy started to leave. I don't know if she was backing away or just leaving, and Aunt Lily started to go after her. And and Aunt Lily ran to catch her, and she kept moving farther and farther away, and Aunt Lily couldn't catch her. That's a truck going by, well, I'm going by a truck. I've got the thing open at the top here. Maybe I'd better close it while I record. And she just she couldn't catch her. She couldn't catch her. She just kept going and going, farther and farther away. And Aunt Lily couldn't catch her. Actually, she called out, she screamed out Nancy's name, and she woke herself up, woke Aunt Esther. But she couldn't catch her. Not one of us, none of us will be able to catch her again.

In *ET*, when Elliot looked at ET, apparently dead ET, and said "I love you, ET," and he started to leave, and as he was leaving, he saw the flowers and the plants come to life again, then he realized that ET was still alive, or was coming back to life. And ET came back to life, and I think I recorded some of this, it's a fantasy. We cannot make people come back to life, we cannot keep them alive with our love. We cannot keep them alive or make them come back to physical life. We can keep them alive in our hearts, but we cannot bring them back to life, back to physical life.

Allyson, I remember Allyson that one evening at the hospital, at the cafeteria, talking about her friends, and how she had thought if maybe, if they love Esther [*sic*] enough or expressed their love or transmit it strongly enough, it could help Nancy keep keep alive. But she realized that her friends loved their mothers as much as she did hers, or does hers. And that love is not enough, I mean, y', that will not keep a person alive.

Do we have a bottleneck here? We have a bottleneck here. I'm gonna get off on Reisterstown Road I think. Yeah, it's backed up to Reisterstown Road here on the Beltway, I'm gettin' off on Reisterstown Road here. I'm not gonna try to take this down. Was gonna take the Beltway around and go down the Jones Falls to give myself time to to drive and think and record, but I I'm not gonna try that with traff, not if it's backed up to here already.

It's moving a little bit, but I don't wanta be stuck in that. Anyhow here I go over to Reisterstown Road.

So that was Aunt Lily's dream. Trying to catch Nancy and not being able to. And then Aunt Lily also talked about the death, the dying and the death of Aunt

Menyeh. How on the night of, first night of *Shavuos*, she went to see Aunt Menyeh and Uncle Lable. And they were sitting out on the porch, and Aunt Menyeh didn't come out. And she, Aunt Lily, thought something was wrong, so she went in to see Aunt Menyeh. And Aunt Menyeh was lying in bed. And she went up to her and leaned down, and Aunt Menyeh said, *Oy, Leyeh, es ist schlecht,* oh, Lily, it's bad, it's *schlecht, es ist schlecht.* So Aunt Lily put her ear down to Aunt Menyeh's chest to listen to her heart and lungs, and what she heard, listen to her heart. She said was it she heard sounded like a kettle or a pot of boiling water bubbling and bubbling. And she knew that there was something wrong, and so she went to Uncle Lable, and she said she was gonna call 911. And Lable said, "Are you a doctor?" And she said, "No, but I can tell there's something wrong." And Uncle Lable said that she was not gonna let her drive, he was not gonna let her drive on *Rosh Hashanah*, on *Shavuos*, on *yontif*. And Aunt Lily said, y'know, she was gonna go ahead and call because anyhow. So she went ahead and called, and they came and they took her to the hospital and they, she wait s in and out at ICU for two weeks and in and out of consciousness, and then about two weeks later, I guess it was about two weeks later, Raizel called to say that she was dying, and Aunt Lily said she got excited, and she said, "She's dying, she's dying!" And Uncle Lable wanted to know why Aunt Lily was screaming so much and yelling, she should be a little bit more quiet. And I guess it was a *shabbas* or something, I think that's what she said, I'm not sure. And she ran outta the house with her coat, and she told, she told Raizel that she'd be right there, and she ran out without her, with her coat, but, of course, she didn't take her purse, she forgot and 'cause, she didn't have her purse with her because it was *shabbas*. And she ran out now, she said it took her the seven or eight minutes to run to the, I guess guess she ran all the way to the Jewish General Hospital, calling out and crying, "Menyeh's dying, Menyeh's dying." And people looked at her. 'Cause she was just saying it to the air, to the open. And people could hear her and listen to her. They looked at her, of course, as though she were crazy.

And Aunt Lily also said that when Aunt Freda died, in New York, she said that she just kind of fell to pieces.

Aunt Esther said, that when Aunt Freda died, *Baubbeh Malka* didn't even cry, and she said, "*Baubbeh*, Mother," she said, "how can you not cry, your daughter is dead?" And *Baubbeh* said something about how God has a garden of beautiful flowers, and He wanted another beautiful flower, and so He took Aunt Freda. And I said, "Esther, well, Esther, then why don't you just think the same thing about Nancy?" And that would help her. That would help her to think about Nancy. Because she talks, Aunt Lily said, she talks to Nancy all night long.

Aunt Lily said she hasn't slept two hours since Sunday night, Monday night. And last, and Tuesday night. In the three nights that she was there with Esther, she hadn't slept two hours. And when I came in yesterday, Aunt Lily hugged me and said, "Tomorrow's the big day." She was so happy, I think, to be going home.

So sad. You would think, as Sophie said, you would think they would cling to each other. They do cling, but their clinging is a form of fighting. Or it takes the form of fighting, bickering. I wonder why. They were always so close. Like I don't know why my mother does not take Aunt Esther in the car to do shopping once a week or once every other week and take her down to Reisterstown Road Plaza once in a while when they live right with each other. And I know my mother has Lou now. But even before she had Lou at home. Is that where I get it? I don't know.

Actually, maybe I will have a few minutes to take a couple pictures of PS 59 this morning. It's only 8:25, and I'm just coming up on Reisterstown Road Plaza. So in spite of all the shopping and the running around--and all the running around?! I just went to the Giant! But in spite of having to get off the Beltway to come right down Reisterstown Road, I'm not making such bad time. And I probably could take out about five or ten minutes to take some pictures down there of PS 59. My old elementary school.

But then I need also to take pictures of Isaac Davidson Hebrew School. To have some of those.

I think that's enough recording for right now, I'm gonna have to change the tape very soon. The tape is running pretty far down now.

What else I've been thinking of taking pictures of is some of the *shules*. I guess it was the *Agudas Achim* across from the Avalon, the *Shaarei Zion* down on Park Heights Avenue, near Lozinsky's. Taking pictures also of the Uptown Theater, taking pictures of the Crest **TAPE ENDS**

TAPE NUMBER 4A

THURSDAY, NOVEMBER 8, 1990

Okay, it's 8:30, Thursday morning, November the 8th, just starting a new tape. Putting the time and date in. Coming down Reisterstown Road, coming down towards Royce Avenue here. Just whoops! Coming down towards, just passing here, wait a second. Now where's? I guess that's where, this is where Maar Lesser used to live, I think, here on Reisterstown Road. This part.

Alright, passing Royce Avenue right now. And passing Royce Avenue right now, just passed Royce Avenue. Coming down to here, towards the old PARK LANE PARK AND SHOP. FREE PARKING. There's the sign. I need to try sometime to get a picture of that too.

Crossing Cold Spring Lane. Down to the right is where that guy used to live, the guy from the Penn Rock Hotel in Pen-Mar, Maryland. The guy that A waited on, big, robust guy. Very exuberant. Okay, I can see the, PS 59 now. In the distance. Oh, man, I can't stop, like there's no place to park on this street. Can't stop to take pictures. Because of the time.

Stopping now to take pictures at PS 59, it's 8:33, gotta move quickly 'cause of the time.

It's 8:50, just got done taking pictures at School 59, including the corner where Gleiman's used to be. Gleiman's where the Filipino yo-yo experts used to stand out and yo-yo for us as kids, and wondering now if I should go down to Towanda and take pictures of Towanda, where we used to play ball all the time, and where that kid burned himself to death. Aaoohh, man, why did you do that? Why did you do that? Actually, what I'd better do is turn around and go back home. Towanda Red Peace Around the World. Good grief, it looks different! That was never there before.

I'm gonna have to come back to do Towanda some other time.

What the hell? I'm gonna go ahead and take a few pictures here of Towanda real fast.

I just took about two or three quick pictures, I'm gonna have to come back sometime.

Pictures pictures pictures. It's like when they were tearing down Daddy's bar, the Sealunch Cafe, Charlie and Aaron's Sealunch Cafe, and I took, what? 21 rolls of film. Over 800 slides--oh, there's a car with his lights on. Oh, my goodness! Oh, well. I took all of those hundreds of pictures; sometime I have to sort through and pick out about 200 of them.

Here we are coming down here at uh to Park Circle in front of the new Parks Sausages. Park Circle. And there seems to be, I thought there was a traffic tie-up,

THE NANCY TAPES

and there is, there seems to be an accident down there, I see the lights of an ambulance. Or a police car or both. But traffic is moving slowly through.

Incredibly, what I forgot to say about Wednesday that I just remembered tonight--it is now 8:05 p.m., Thursday, November the 8th, just dropped off Lou from taking Aunt Lily to the Washington National Airport so she could catch her flight back to Montreal, the last one from out of town, from Montreal, here for the funeral, for Nancy's funeral, and she left tonight, took her to the airport, Lou came with. And incredibly, what I realized along the way is that when I recorded last Wednesday, which was the day after Nancy died and the day before the funeral, how Sophie and I went out to Nancy's house, and the rabbi ju, Sophie had a just long talk with Ruthie. And the Rabbi sat in the kitchen for a couple hours, the Rabbi sat in the kitchen for a couple hours--while I turn on and off the light in the car to make sure this thing is working. And the Rabbi sat in the kitchen for, to put the family, for two-three hours, talking about Nancy, listening to them talk about Nancy. What I forgot was that that was the first day, this is not what I forgot but which is *??unintelligible??* on my mind. We brought out a deli tray. I didn't realize that they kept kosher, so Dave Weinstein removed the cheese real quick. Cheryl gobbled up a lot of the cole slaw 'cause she loved it. We brought out two pou, I decided when I picked up the tray and got two pounds of the *rugelach* to take out. And it was such a big hit, I brought more out on Friday, I brought more out on Saturday, I brought more out on Sunday. Actually, I brought out about eight pounds of *rugelach* over Wednesday, Thursday, Friday, Saturday, and Sunday. Didn't bring any Thursday, the day of the funeral.

But what I forgot to talk about about Wednesday was that Wednesday evening, after we left, I told them, before we left, I told them that I would go to the airport, Washington National Airport, because Raizel and Chana and Cookie and Esther were coming in from Montreal, so I drove, Sophie and I went home. I don't remember what time it was, kind of early, about 5 or so. And had some something to eat at home, and then I left to go pick up, I left about eight o'clock to go pick them up at the Washington National Airport. Fortunately, Mindy gave me some pretty good directions which saved me some trouble, but it was tough on that 395 in DC until I spotted the, until I came to the exit for Washington National Airport, I thought I was on my way to Richmond.

And when I got to the airport, it was a little bit early so I called to see if they wanted to, first of all, to let 'em know that Mary Ellen, Ellie, Ellie and Sonny, had a baby girl that morning Sara, Sara Nicole, I think, at 2:30 Wednesday morning, someone had told me. Or was it Jerry who told me the night before? On Tuesday, that must have been Tuesday night, I don't, No! It couldn't have been Tuesday. I don't know. Anyhow, maybe it was Tuesday night.

And asked whether they wanted the Montrealers to stop by the house, and Mindy said, No, that's all right, just to, better just go home and go to sleep. So I picked them up and we drove around, and the first thing I told them was the good news that Mary Ellen, Ellie, had a baby. And then we just talked about Nancy's condition, and I talked about all the, all what had gone on for the week and the up and down. And I followed Mindy's directions BW Parkway around--Not BW Parkway! GW Park! George Washington Parkway around to 495 into Maryland, then took 29, Exit 29, Route 29 North, and I thought we had gone too far, got to Randolph Road and Cherry Hill, Randolph Road, and I thought, Is this where it is? And I made a left into the gas station, and then it was right near there, and I dropped them off. And I dropped them off. And the coffee shop was closed, everything was closed, they couldn't get a, couldn't get anything, and, God! almost bawled my eyes out when I left them there. Oh, my goodness!

And then tonight, Thursday, a week and a day later, Thursday, November the eighth, took Aunt Lil, picked up Aunt Lily at four, we left about ten after four for her flight, and Lou came along. And drove to Washington National Airport. She was the last one to head back. She spent Sunday night, Monday night, Tuesday night, and Wednesday night with Aunt Esther, and she said she didn't sleep two hours the whole time. 'Cause Aunt Esther cried and talked to Nancy all night long. I mentioned yesterday about the dream, 'cause I stopped over there yesterday, the dream that she had, or was that Tuesday that I stopped in there? I don't know what day it was. Monday, Tuesd, oh, it was yesterday I stopped over there. Ooookay. Oookay, that takes care of Wednesday then.

FRIDAY, NOVEMBER 9, 1990

Good morning, Mr. Phelps. Your mission is still impossible. But you must make the effort. Failure to make the effort guarantees failure of the mission. That guarantees impossibility. Unattainability. Attempts guarantee certainty of attempts. "Beauty is truth and truth beauty, that is a all ye know and all ye need to know."

It's Friday morning, November the ninth. 7:42. I've just come from the Diet Center, where I weighed in at one-hundred-and-sixty-nine pounds, I've lost six pounds since Tuesday. Three days of Tuesday, Wednesday, Thursday, of careful dieting. Ha! Ha! Ha! Of getting back to my exercise, I've lost six pounds. I had gained between Saturday the 27th when I was in the, weighed in at 170 and a quarter, and Tuesday November the, November the, November the sixth! I had gained four and three-quarters pounds. That represents the time period, the last weekend that Nancy was in the hospital, her death, the *shivah*, the funeral the *shivah* the funeral the funeral the *shivah*. And the *karidopita* that Sophie baked on Saturday and took down, had Saturday and Sunday at the hospital. And all the *rugelach* that I had brought down and the bagels and loxes and cream cheeses. And speaking of foods, well, I'm going to catch this reyd light here, and, oh, my God! look at the Beltway! Shit! Pardon me. How am I supposed to get to Towson now? Dammit!

Well, the nature of the traffic tie-up that I can see from here means that probably what I should do ... Now, it's moving a little bit. I don't know. Let me turn the radio on, see what's going on.

Well, I just changed my plans. The traffic was so tied up on the Beltway that I'm going down to school first. And I'll have to find time later to get up to Towson to go to the credit union.

But anyhow, speaking of food, Sophie made a *karidopita* that we took down to the hospital Saturday, the 27th, and Sunday, the 28th, for people to eat on, to eat. And one day Kim baked brownies. And every day I brought pieces of apples, red delicious and yellow delicious apples, and they were kind of a hit, people ate them, and people ate the brownies. Well, I'm gonna stop this for right now.

Somehow I'm having trouble getting myself started and talking again. Going down Reisterstown Road.

Turned it on. Actually, I thought the APR would shut it off, but I think unfortunately that there's too much noise for there to be silence for it to turn itself off. In any case, I've decided to try again. I'm here down at Falstaff Shopping Center. Down Reisterstown Road.

Anyhow, Thursday, the funeral day. November the first, a week ago yesterday. Curiously, curiously refreshing. On Monday, November the fifth, I woke up at 4:47. Now, had I gotten up on October 22nd, to go see Nancy before the surgery, that's probably about the time I would have gotten up, a quarter to five, to get up to get dressed, have a bite to eat or some coffee or something before going down to the hospital. I imagine I'll probably wake up at 4:47 on Monday for the rest of my life. Actually, I imagine that I won't. What I imagine is that I would like to imagine myself waking up at 4:47 every Monday morning, but I won't. Or at 8:35 Monday mornings, the day of the first in, surgical incision. But I won't.

On Tuesday, November the sixth, election night, I called Nancy, and it happened to be seven o'clock. Which was, I didn't do that intentionally, but maybe it was unintentional or unconscious, but that was just about the time that Dr. R came in to tell us that Nancy had died. Curiously refreshing.

Anyhow, the day of the funeral, Soph and I got up and got Paul up, we left early and went to pick up Charlie at the dorm. Unfortunately, he was feeling pretty lousy, he had some kind of a stomach virus, and he was feeling nauseous and just felt miserable all day. Fortunately he was able to bear up, but he was, felt awful. Went to the house, went to Nancy and Joe's house. Did I say that on Tuesday, the day Nancy died, I had, before she died, before we heard that she died, I had told Darren again, how good I thought his poem was. And we talked about inner resources, the inner strength, the power inside. That his mother has incre, has incredible, obviously was showing incredible power and strength. In her fight to live. And I said that many people do not realize what inner resources they have, and I talked about how if he could write, with all of his history of depression, his listening to heavy metal, and his, all that, that if he could write a poem like *The Sun in Your Eyes,* the poem that he wrote for Nancy, if he could write that kind of poem, while she was in the kind of condition that she's in, that it showed that he really had a lot of internal strength, more internal strength than he realized. Sniff.

The day of the funeral again. So we drove over over, and we went to the house. And we all kind of hung around. So then we drove to, drove to where? We drove to the funeral home. We were all in the family session section, and I went in at one point, Aunt Esther and Ronny and Joe, they'd all gone in to where the chapel where the coffin was, it was, it was a plain pine coffin, but it was, it was not a coffin. It was a casket. It had the form and shape of a casket, but it was that plain white pine, it was not a white box. And my father, I think, was buried in a box, Uncle Sol was buried in a box. Curiously refreshing. Now I remember what Uncle Sol, they had to open the box to put his *tallis* in, I think it was at the cemetery. And I remember I caught a glimpse of his body, that really bothered me. Disturbed me then.

First time I really looked at a body was my mother-in-law's, Sophie's mother's body. And then Nancy's. That close, touching her. The refrain, the dead are so cold.

Wednesday also, sitting at the kitchen table, with Ruth and Dave and my sister Nancy. Dave pulled out his list of, no, he pulled out, he asked, he had his list of people who would be asked to be pallbearers, and he asked me if I felt able to be a pallbearer, and I said, Yes. I almost cried, but I said yes. And I thanked him. And then he went through the list as he sat down, and Nancy got really upset. She said, as only she can, sniff, "I want to be a pallbearer! I'm going to be a pallbearer!" And, you know, Dave said, he hadn't thought of that, but, no, y'know, there was no problem, so anyhow, she was a pallbearer. And I said to Dave, that y' know, they had Ronny and then me and now Nancy and and Jerry Bulmash, and Craig, and I think Bryan was also a, and then there was Ioanna Iona Iona, a friend of Joe's and Nancy's--Royce Avenue, here we go! 3316. Hi, Aunt Freda.

When we, the pallbearers--see the things are coming in different order, kinds of order. When they called us up to be pallbearers, when they called the pallbearers to come forward, sniff, and Nancy was sitting in front of me, and sitting in back of me were Cookie and Esther, Raizel and Chana. Then when Nancy got up, Nancy and I got up, but Nancy especially, when Nancy got up, somebody, it I think was probably Cookie, but I'm not sure-- Whoooaawww! For the cars stopped here. Sniffing. Said, one of them said, Oh, look, Nancy's gonna be a pallbearer! Oohh, wee! I think it was actually the weee! which is the typical Montrealer expression. Like they couldn't believe that a woman would be a pallbearer. It was like, as Mindy had said the day before, women count as people. When Aunt Esther and Lily were expressed some surprise that they would be part of the count as part of the *minyan*.

As we were, we put our hands on the coffin, the wood felt soft and smooth, but there was a kind of a roughness to the texture. And I remember thinking at the time how Uncle Morris's stone, his tombstone, the gravestone, or that, that rough-hewn top of it felt, how did it, how to try to distinguish between the feeling on my hand, sniff, of the roughness of the top of Uncle Morris's gravestone, of the smoothish roughness or the roughly smoothness of the pine casket. Of Nancy's forehead when I would, the couple times I went in to see her while she was alive, just kind of tried to brush her hair back, smooth her forehead, soothe her forehead, caress her forehead. Then how it felt after she died. How cold it was. Even, even the gravestone of Uncle Morris felt warmer, 'course it had the sunlight shining on it. Sniff. Even the wood of the, of the casket felt warmer. Than her forehead did.

And as we walked out, they told us to put a hand on the coffin, it was on the roller arrangement thing. Sniff. Then we walked up the aisle, and I was in front of Nancy walking up, and she was behind me, and she reached her hand forward, and she grasped my forearm so tightly. And I think I said to her, "Hold on, Nance." It was so painful for her. It was so painful. She was better later, though. Sniff. She even introduced me to I W, W, whom I would not have recognized, in his beard, and his grey hair. And I think it was that night, after the funeral, Thursday night, I think it was then, that L B, or G, sniff, came to visit, she and her husband. And when she came in, and she went right up to Nancy even before being introduced, and thanked her for serving as pallbearer. I'm, there, she is not Jewish, but apparently either she knows about Orthodox Judaism or she simply recognized the generally conservative attitude of most formal religions towards women's roles. Sniff. And she realized that it was probably very unusual for Nancy to be serving as a pallbearer. Some of these drive like gazunks here. So she even said something about Nancy.

Okay, time out now, 'cause we're coming up to Mondawmin here and gotta go down to school. Just made a right turn off of Reisterstown Road around Mondawmin towards Coppin now.

MONDAY, NOVEMBER 12, 1990

It's Monday morning, November the 12th, 8:15 am. I'm on my way down Reisterstown Road to school. Eleni's following me down to print out a couple letters first. Today's uh three weeks since Nancy's surgery. It's amazing how things get measured. The weather turned around. The weather turned around. The day of her funeral. The day of Nancy's funeral, November the first, on Thursday, it was so foggy and misty and hazy I thought traffic was gonna be awful going down to Washington, going down to Silver Spring on 9, belt, the Baltimore Beltway and 95 to pick up Charlie at College Park. I thought it was just gonna be unbearable because at first they, it was an overcast day, people wouldn't be able to see. And while it was miserably grey and overcast, not overcast, it was a hazy fog, and it was all difficult visibility, it was terrible. The weather turned around, as Dylan Thomas said, and by the time, came time for the funeral service, and the burial service... , the afternoon at *Shaarei Zion* near *B'Nai Reuven*, back *B'Nai Reuven*, it was clear sunny day.

Okay, getting ready to, coming up here now onto Royce Avenue, just passing St. Ambrose, and evidently, here's the Royce Avenue sign now! Just broke the plane of the Royce Avenue sign.

The weather turned around. Talked to Ruthie last night. Talked about how, I said how it was just so impossible to believe. She said that she had spoken with Mindy, just ten minutes before, that ... How incredible was, she had told, said to Mindy, Nance Ruthie had said to Mindy that it was hard to believe that she would never see Nancy again. Never see her again. That's so hard to believe. At 8:17 on Friday, M, what Monday morning? *??unclear??* The twelfth. Whatever time it is or day it is, I don't know. Yes, I don't !

One other thing that keeps going through my mind from time to time, and has been for a while, especially since Nancy died, is the trip I took to Montreal with them, with her, on Myron and Marilyn's wedding. With Nancy and Joe in their white BMW last year. And Joe, Nancy sang, talking about the song *In the Living Years*. I can't remember who it was who made that song, but the point of the song is that you have to tell people you love them, you have to be with them, you have to help them. Not in some vague future time, but you must do it now while they're all still "in the living years." And here we're getting ready to go by PS 59. And I just pointed it out again to Eleni. I pointed it out to her last Wednesday when she came down to school, so I pointed it out again, and laughing and joking and joking and joking and laughing. In the living yea--Che! Che! *[coughs twice]*--In the living years. Do things now in the living years. Not when it's too late later on. Do it *now*, Sidney!

Good afternoon, Mr. Phelps. It's 3:37, Monday, November the 12th. Your assignment is to continue your assignment! What was I gonna talk about? Oh! Right!

It must have been Sunday, the last day of the *shivah* that I was talking with Al of Riva and Al, about Aunt Esther and the Orthodox Jew on Tuesday evening, October the, October the 30th, the day Nancy died. And I was telling them, Al and somebody else, I guess it was Ruthie, yes, about what the man was saying about how first of all, did she really consider that she was smarter than God? That she should know what to do or what to say or what tell God what to do or what to say or how to run His universe. And second of all, that he had not said that that Nancy would live, and what he said what he had said was that *es wird git zein* if he could, and did she know or that consider the possibility that maybe it is good *for Nancy*. While it may not be good for anybody else right now, it may have been good for Nancy that she died when she did. And that the world goes on, that as terrible as Aunt Esther's pain was, and it was a heavy pain, and he said he would not say it was not a heavy pain, but as terrible as the pain was, the world goes on. And he asked her if she had another living daughter, and I think she may have said, No, and I said, "Aunt Esther, what are you talking about?!" I said, "What about Ruthie?" And he said, You've got another daughter, you've got sons-in-law, and you've got children. And the guy said, Now you see, this is, you have people, you have family that is still living, you must take care of them.

Well, Al then asked, this was Sunday, the day of the getting up from *shivah*, which would have been the fourth of November at Nancy's house, Al then asked, Did you hear what else he finally said? And I said, No, I said, *[yaawwnn]*, I didn't hear, pardon me, the rest of it. And I didn't anything else. And he said, Well, what the guy finally said was that if you ask so many questions, *[??something in Yiddish, indecipherable??]* God might say to you, Well, if you have so many questions to ask, why don't you just come up here and ask the questions? Now, y'know, that kind of, that kind of stopped her. Okay, I'm gonna.

Now, to get back to Thursday, the funeral day, I I if I, Wednesday, the *rugelach*, Wednesday, back-track to the *rugelach*. On if, got the deli tray, and boy! the roast beef was so rare I couldn't believe it! The only one who could eat that that I know of out there was Cheryl, because she likes the rare roast beef, the rare meat. But it was incredible. I didn't realize that they kept kosher till I got it out there, and then Dave Weinstein took the cheese off and put it in separate plates, and I said, I'm sorry, I didn't realize you guys kept kosher, excuse me. Anyhow, but also got, decided to get two pounds of *rugelach*. And they were such a big that on Friday I brought out some more. And on Sa, Friday, *[yaaawwwnnn]*, Mother gave, pardon me, Mother gave me money for three pounds for her and Lou. And on Saturday I brought out two more pounds. And then on Sunday eve, I, two more pounds, so I brought out about eight pounds of *rugelach* 'cause they were such a tremendous hit, and everybody just loved the *rugelach*. Lenny's lovely *rugelach, lugelach*!

What of else am I gonna say? Gonna stop right now while I think about what else to say.

Actually, I would keep on, leave this machine on and let the automatic voice record take over, but the problem is that there's so much noise in the car that I don't think it would shut off. Let me try this. I'm gonna be quiet for about five or six seconds and see what happens. Well, it did not shut off, so I think the point is that the it's the noise in the car that would keep it going anyhow.

Now I'm on my way to Westminster to see about putting a couple ads in *The Community Times* for *The Life of a Star*. Okay. That's where I'm off to.

I think I'm losing it, in terms of these recordings.

Wednesday, that I talked about, did I talk about Wednesday when Dave asked, he had the list of, I don't even know what I've talked about in here any more. Dave had the list of pallbearers, and he asked how I felt, would, that, do I feel that I would be able to or want to be able, want to or be able to be a pallbearer? And I and I said, Yes, I thought I would. And I thanked him, and then Nancy very adamantly insisted that she was going to be a pallbearer. It wasn't necessary for her to be adamant and insistent the way she was. All that she had to do was to ask, just say, Look, I'd like to be a pallbearer. They let her, of course, and they would have let her either way. It's, and when we got up to bear palls, pallbearers, did I talk about this? I don't know. She was sitting in front of me, and she stood up, and I stood up, and behind me, *[yaaaawwwwnnn]*, I think, *[muffled in yawn]*, pardon me, I think it was Cookie saying, Wee! That famous Montreal wee! I think that's what I heard. When Nancy stood to be a pallbearer. They were stunned by it. And later that evening, when Ruthie's friend, when she met, saw Nancy and even before she was introduced to Nancy, she walked over and thanked her for being a pallbearer. Who was I telling about that? Oh, I was telling, I guess it was Eleni last night.

I, we put our hands on the casket. The feel of the wood, I said this, was warm. As warm as Uncle Morris's stone. Warmer than Nancy's skin or her forehead. And as we were walking up the aisle, the pallbearers, Bryan, Craig, Jerry Bulmash, Ronny, me, and Nancy, that's six. Iona was seven. Well, then who was the eighth? I'm not sure who the eighth was. Hmmm. But Nancy grabbed my right hand, and she clutched it so hard, and I tried to hold, she held, actually, not my hand, she clutched my forearm, and I held her hand, her forearm, and she dug her fingers into my forearm. It must have been so painful for her. So painful for her. To be Nancy's pallbearer. But I understood that she had to do it. And why she had to do it.

I have made six copies of the funeral service. One for me, I'll give one to Nancy, and the other four for whoever wants them there. Go back with Joe, with original. But in listening to it, as I did once, I was startled by ... Rabbi Goren's sighs. Those deep sighs. There are no answers to the questions, Ruth. At least not while we are alive. Maybe we'll get answers when we die. Maybe we won't. There are people now who believe they have the answers. And who insist on letting you know that they know that they have the answers. And who insist that their answers are the right ones. Rabbi's sighs, the rabbi's eulogy, the service was beautiful. He had taken all that was said to him, on Wednesday afternoon, and put it together into a beautiful whole.

Aunt Esther on Thursday, speaking of the, Nancy, of her *schaineh punim*, in the *kayvuh*, her *schaineh punim in dreyrd*. I think I said this. So I thought, I said to Ruthie that she meant the hell, the Jewish *sheol*, where the dead go. And Ruthie saying, No, she just thought she meant it literally, the ground, under the earth. And later, Aunt Esther, I mea, couldn't believe this one either. Whether I thought Nancy felt the worms, could feel the worms. And I said, No, Aunt Esther, she cannot feel the worms. She cannot feel the worms. She cannot feel the worms.

So on Friday morning I drove out, Friday morning, November the second. To be part of the *minyan* early in the morning. They were gonna start about 7:30, so I left about 6:30, by the time I got underway. And we were talking about what an incredibly beautiful morning it was. The steam, the mist rising on one of the rivers. The gold and orange of the leaves. The wind blowing through the leaves. The clear blue sky and the sun rising golden. The sun light golden. As it is now. Though hazed a little bit right now at 3:53 on Monday afternoon. By some light clouds in the west.

So it was three weeks ago that began we began to panic. Began to get scared. We began to get nervous. Three weeks ago. That the prognosis turned around, Dylan Thomas, from the two o'clock *Mazel Tov!* to the three or 3:30 Oh, shit! Though nobody said it quite like that. When I said *Mazel Tov!* to Joe, after he got the word at 2, that she was off the pump and her heart was beating on its own, and he kind of cheered, he cheered even before I said anything to him. Aunt Esther said, how right she was, Aunt Esther said, I'll listen to a *mazel tov* when I see her come down. Well, I think that was partly her tendency to see tragedy in everything. I don't think she was really prescient about it, I think she was just expecting the worst. That Monday afternoon, she got hysterical when they tried to keep her from seeing Dr. R. She was convinced that Nancy was dead already. And I said that the reason, that the reason I thought that she was so persuaded that she was dead, that Nancy was dead, was that people were trying to keep her from seeing the doctor, she thought people were trying to see her, keep her from seeing Nancy and learning that Nancy was dead. Because that's what they used to do, she and my mother. Like when my father died. They tried to hide everything until it was impossible not to hide it. So she expected that everybody was hiding this from her.

So on Friday, the second, I went out, and then, of course, I had to come back to pick up Charlie because he'd been sick and wasn't feeling well, and I had to take him back to the dorm. And I picked up some more *rugelach* to take with. And went back. And I guess that was the day that we talked about people's answers and certainties. Nancy was reading out of that book about the Jewish way of the dead, of death and dying, that Sonkie had sent or brought up. About how we believe or

Jews believe in resurrection, Jews believe in life after death. And everybody see, Gee, and I remember Mindy said, Gee, I didn't know we believed that. Nei, neither did I. Although I did by then.

And then going to the synagogue Friday evening, and I had forgotten to, or was it Dave asked whether they were supposed to continue to wear the little black ribbons? Sniff. And I said I really didn't know, I just couldn't remember, it had been too long, and course by the time we got to the, when we got to the synagogue, the rabbi at the door told them take them off, that you don't wear them on *shabbas*, you don't wear them in the synagogue. And Aunt Esther, Ruthie and Joe and Allyson could not come in until they were welcomed in as mourners. And Ruthie's comment, and Nancy agreed with her, who else was talking about it? That when, that Ken and Kim, in one sense, it was wrong, that Nancy would not have liked their being offered the black ribbons of mourning as children. Not because she didn't consider them her children. But because if they were going to do it, they should have done it the whole way and accepted the full meaning of Yi, of sitting *shivah*, and not just as a superficial, not just as an external gesture, but to accept also the public as well as the personal discipline of being a mourner for one's mother, for one's parent. Which they really didn't do. But then too, I don't think anybody, I don't think anybody sat on *shivah* chairs. They may have at first, but basically, they were sitting on regular chairs, most of the time.

The last night on the phone, which was Sunday, November the, November the eleventh, Ruthie told me that she had gone over to Joe's house. And that Joe had opened a letter and read a letter that Nancy had written the week before her surgery. Saying what she wanted done, that she had some money that she'd put away, it wasn't much, just a few hundred dollars. What she wanted from the kids, or what she expected from the kids. And Ruthie said how sad it was. How sad it was. To listen to the letter. How sad it was. To listen to the letter.

And Friday night, coming back from the synagogue, it, well, Friday night, was it Friday night or Saturday night? No, Saturday night, it was, I guess, after the *Torah* reading. And the rabbi called me and Dave up to close the Ark after the *Torah* was put in, and afterwards, I shook the rabbi's hand, and I thanked him for the honor. And he said, No, he said, it is our privilege to have you with us. If only he knew.

So it was Friday night on the way back from *shule*, from the synagogue, I was driving and it was Joe and Nancy and Allyson in the car. And we were talking about the love for Nancy and trying to help her, trying to save her, trying to give her courage, trying to give her strength. Trying to focus our energy for her, on her, with her. But Joe said, did I say this into this recorder before? I don't remember, I think so. We never did get to finish this conversation. The one thing that he had never said to her, that he felt guilty about not saying to her, that through all the times he had words of encouragement, he said that he had felt what he wanted also to say, what he should have said was, Nancy, if it's too tough, and if you have to let go, then just let go. When I told Ruthie about that, that I said to Da Joe that I thought that Nancy had heard him, that she understood him, that she knew it even though he didn't say it out loud. And when I told Ruthie about that on Sunday, she said that she tried in all of her talking with Nancy never to say anything that made her, would made her feel, would make her feel that she *had* to get well. That is, never to say anything that would make Nancy feel guilt on top of everything else for not being able to get well. So that's when I told Ruth about how when I would go to see Uncle Morris I'd ask him to help her to live, and I also said to him, If you can't help her to live, then help her to die. Make the passage easier. I think I've said this in here already.

Joe also was saying, we were talking in the car about what love could or couldn't do. And I talked about and I reminded brought up again what Allyson had said in the hospital before Nancy had died, and talking about how her love should help keep her alive, but that she knew that her friends had lost their mothers, that they loved their mothers. So Friday night, Joe was standing outside until he got called in, and he was talking about how those nights in the hospital room, and especially even that he said that Monday night when the rabbi was in and we all had our arms around each other in a circle praying for Nancy. That if there was any time that was right for a miracle, it was then. And then he got called in, but he said, But there was no miracle. What I wanted to say was, Joe, You can't have, we can't, you don't get a miracle when you expect one or when you want one. There's no telling when the miracles occur. There's no telling when people miraculously live even though each, every pain in, every body every sign is that they're going to die. Love is not always enough. As Joe himself said, oh, it must have been Monday or Tuesday or Wednesday, that all of her will to live, and all of our love for her to live might not be able to do anything if there was no heart, no heart muscle, if there was no heart in there that could beat, that could pick up that love, pick up that life, and help her to live.

It must have been Tuesday, must have been Wednesday, it must have been Thursday, after the surgery, 22nd, 23rd, 24th, 25th, that I had, went, dressed to go to school but didn't go. That Joe came out with me for a ride to pick up Aunt Esther and my mother. And I took my time going up there so he would have time to talk, and he talked. And he talked about his love for her, and he talked about not being able even to imagine what life would be like without her. What it would be like trying to do things without her, what it would be like not having her to talk to. He held her pajama top. That white pajama top.

And it must have been Friday, I think, although it might have also been Saturday, my mother said something to Nile about my sister, and she kept referring to my sister Nancy as Aunt Nancy and Aunt Nancy, and that Nile looked at her and said, That's not my Aunt Nancy. My Aunt Nancy is dead. And that's when Nancy realized why he wouldn't talk to her. 'Cause she was alive. And his Aunt Nancy was dead.

So, it's now 4:34, just come coming from *The Community Times* placing the ad. And I'm on my way back, I'm still in Westminster, but I'm on my way back now to pick up Paul.

Thinking about how I was there from early Friday morning 'till Friday evening. Except for the time to pick up, go back home, pick up Charlie, take him to College Park, and then come back. And on Saturday. Saturday. Did Sophie come out? Or not? No, I don't think so. No, 'cause that's right, 'cause Linda was there Saturday, Linda Weinstein and Walter. I remember how Mindy used to call him Woody! Vwoody Vwantan! Vwoody!

And then, so I took some more, I went out *??unclear??* in the afternoon, I took out a couple more pounds of *rugelach rugelach rugelach tugelach*. So I went to synagogue with them again. It was Dave and Ruth, and Joe and Allyson and me. And I asked if they minded *[??mishehbehyrach??]*. One time, I guess it was either Friday, must have been Saturday, maybe it was Saturday evening, Ruth thanked me for being there and said that I had been a real source of strength. And I said, Really? And she said, Yes, *really*. I could not believe, *cannot* believe that I am a source of strength. For anyone.

[??Broke us??] Most for Rail Fencing. That was a sign. So that was Saturday. Friday they brought the turkey dinner, L S. Mother thought they were gonna bring it on Thursday, but when I called Thursday, the woman finally got through, I called Friday morning I guess, finally got through Friday morning. Said that they had told Mother that they were not going to be able to do it for Thursday, and they would do it on Friday. So I apologized for the misunderstanding and I said, Thenkyouverrrymuch! And it was really very, very good. It was nice of L to pick the cost of at least half or more of it and throw some extra stuff in.

Saturday, last Saturday, was Saturday, going back, was it Friday? Yes, it was Friday that I said to Dave, who was also wearing grey slacks and a blue blazer, How come guys our age always wear grey slacks and blue blazers? And he said, Because uh back-ausuh, because we have no sense of color coordination, and this is the safe thing, we know that blue and grey go together. And so that was it. And then when we got to the synagogue Friday, there was the rabbi, Rabbi Goren, wearing the same out-fit. But Sat-ur-day, Dave did not wear the same outfit.

Sooo Saatuurrdaay *[yawning]* was the day that Allyson had on Nancy's dress. Actually, she had one on Friday night, but I didn't realize it Friday, I realized it Saturday only because I said something to her about what a beautiful dress she had

THE NANCY TAPES

on, and that's when she said that it was one of her mother's dresses. And then they had the Chinese kosher dinner Saturday.

Did I say before that Thursday, when we were in the car, in the Danzansky parking lot, waiting to go to the, after the funeral service, waiting to go to the cemetery, and I looked up and there was Shirley Bassin. Standing on the sidewalk outside the door of, outside the door of the funeral home. And as the hearse pulled away, she was looking at the hearse, and she was talking. And she was saying goodbye to Nancy, she said later.

And suddenly, and now, it made me think of Abe Kershman. When my father died, and I guess it was Marian who told us that when he heard he came in the door, and he stood there stunned. And he said, Charlie Krome died. And I didn't go to Abe's funeral. And I'm sorry, Abe. And I didn't go to Aunt Menyeh's funeral. And I'm sorry, Aunt Menyeh. Sniff. I should have gone to both. I can't remember now why I missed Abe's. I think I just couldn't, was concerned about getting away from school and work. But I should have gone, I should have missed it. And I know why I missed Aunt Menyeh's. Sniff. 'Cause I was afraid to fly. And Mother and Aunt Esther had gone up, and they didn't wait, let me know they were going, so I could have flown with them and had some company on the plane. And the next morning when I could have gone, there was a flight early in the morning. But I was too scared to fly up by myself. I'm sorry, Aunt Menyeh. Thus does conscience make cowards of us all. Baloney! Thus does cowardice make us miss life. Miss life when we're afraid.

When I was out jogging running walking, jogging, my last circle this morning, the last jogging part inwards, Craddock Lane and curving 'round there, thinking about A, J A, and thinking how I distanced myself from him. And suddenly, I realized, I don't know how true it was, but I had this insight, that I distance myself from people so that when they die, it wouldn't hurt so much. Then I started to cry while I was running, thinking about it. So that when they die, it won't hurt as much. *[??The diers??]*

By the time I got home in the morning, by the time I get home in the morning, Orion's belt has faded out in the lightening sky. This morning there was some white wisp of cloud passed over it that faded it out. It was so light. So faded. So pale. The sky.

Sunday, Soph and I went. The last day. November the fourth. Drove out. We drove out. And it was kind of hodge-podge for dinner. And on most days, except for Wednesday, and Thursday, bagels and cream cheese and lo **TAPE ENDS**

TAPE NUMBER 4B

MONDAY, NOVEMBER 12, 1990

Okay, it's 4:44. Side A just ran out, and I had to turn it over. It startled me, because I just I looked down and suddenly it was stopped. I didn't realize I had gone that far. I was hoping that much.

And I was saying about bagels and cream cheese and lox and *rugelach* and *tugelach*. Bagels and cream cheese and lox and *rugelach* and *tugelach* for lunch.

And Friday morning at the *minyan*, I had to borrow somebody's *t'fillin*, and get a quick lesson in how to put them on because I had forgotten. Then Sunday afternoon at the *minyan*, Sunday afternoon at the *minyan*, crowded into that study room, I guess it was a room also that Allyson used to make jewelry. *Rugelach* and *tugelach*. Sunday, Sunday afternoon *minyan*, Sunday afternoon at the *minyan*, and then a hodge-podge dinner. And then I said that we'd take Aunt Esther and Aunt Lily back to Baltimore with us if they'd be ready to leave fairly soon. 'Cause we didn't want to stay late. And Dave said that'll be one more area, that's eight, out of the, I said, Na, you don't owe me anything, I said, but then again, I'll collect some day. And then how, move over, buddy! Don't move over into my lane, buddy, that way.

Now wait a second, what else? And then it was time after the *minyan* to walk around, for them all to walk around, to do the ritual walking back into the world. They walked and laughed and joked a little bit. And I walked with Aunt Esther, and she cried. I could tell that Ruthie and, that they were, Ruthie was relieved to be able to get back to the world of the l living a little bit. And she was anxious to get home. Sniff. To get back to her life. Get back to her life. And I walked with Aunt Esther. We're so sorry, Uncle Albert.

But going through my mind, again today *The Red River Valley* song: "From this valley they say you are leaving. I shall miss your bright eyes and sweet smile. From this valley they say you are leaving. Do not hasten to bid me adieu."

I think I better turn this thing off, 'cause there's a lotta traffic here now on 795. And it's *peligrosso as-so-mar-seeeii. E peligrosso assomarse.* That was a sign on the train in Spain. The train in Spain from Barthelona, no! from Lerida to Barcelona when I was hitch-hiking. In 19-aught-and-62. 62. I think I'm gonna turn this off for now.

TUESDAY, NOVEMBER 13, 1990

I think I've discovered finally after, what? Three weeks now on this stuff? On this thing. One of the secrets of recording. I think the secret is going to be, at least recording in a car, keep the volume down a little bit, speak right into the mike, and that way if the volume is down, it will not pick up the other sounds of the car.

THE NANCY TAPES

How 'bout if we try this, Sidney? Good morning. Today is Tuesday, November the 13th, it's 7:54 am in the morning. And I'm on my way to Annapolis for a meeting.

And the traffic is now coming to a complete halt right here by the Security Boulevard Exit, and I am stuck on the Belt-way. Now. Good morning, Beltway.

Of course, an idea for something to put up in that coronary surgery ICU. A maybe that rainbow photograph with the quotation from from Dylan Thomas. "Oh, may my heart's truth still be sung ... from this high hill in a year's turning." With the rainbow.

Continuing now while the Beltway traffic begins to move. I think I talked about, but I'm not sure that I did, how Sonkie had told Nancy to turn the shovel over. She did it. I didn't, because I didn't know why, you see. I think I talked about this. How Joe, lovingly and very gently, spread the, spread the, spread the dirt over the coffin. Over the casket. Nancy shoveled some ov, shovel upside down. I shoveled a big heavy clump, and turned it over so it clatters loudly. And just a little bit later Raizel saying that, I said that Ruth was talking about, we had never seen it done like this, and I talked about how Joe had spread it gently and that Raizel said something about how it's supposed to be loud, so that you hear the sound, and you suffer the finality of it. And I said that I tried to do it like that, and she said, I didn't say it quite like that, but she said, Yes, we heard, I don't know whether you *[??but they?? the dirt??]*. And then later I shoveled some more. I guess Craig and, Craig and Bryan? Craig and Joe did most of the shoveling, and later Bryan was down on his, Bryan had, at one point he had taken his shoes off and gone into the woods. And then he kneeled down, and that like hover barefoot and with his hands he was smoothing, breaking the clumps apart and smoothing them around. And I guess Joe did some of that also, I didn't, don't remember seeing Joe do it. And then, and Allyson got down on her knees and near Bryan. She spread some clumps around. And she spread some around. And later, was it Ruthie? said, somebody said that Bryan had said that he knew that Aunt Nancy would want it to be spread around neatly. She wouldn't want those big messy clumps. And so they tried to smooth it out for her. Sniff. That's un-be-liev-able! That's unbelievable! It's unbelievable!

See, it's not simply being Krapp recording your last tape. It's the one who has to edit Krapp's last tape. It's the one who has to take all of this, that'd be Mr. Phelps, and bring some order to all of this chaos.

I think it was to Joe Friday evening in that conversation we didn't get to finish. When we were walking up to the house after coming back from the synagogue. I think it was to Joe, I think it was to Joe, but it may not have been, it might been to Dave, that I said, the line from *Zorba*. That Zorba says to What's-his-name, Do all your books tell me why people die? Can you tell me why people die? Can you tell me why people die?! The answer is, no. The answer is no. It's like that woman who called, I was talking told Ruthie about. Who said that Nancy was now in the arms of her Lord, in the arms of her Creator. And that she was better off. And she wouldn't come back even if she had the chance to. Well, I don't know, maybe the last part might be true. As to the letting go, we have to let go, but sometimes we can't! And I wonder if they have to let go on the other side. I don't know. If so, I hope Uncle Morris was able to help out.

Aunt Esther talked about the smile on Nancy's face, afterwards. Ruthie, at the doorway to the family room in the funeral home. Ruthie at the doorway, talking to one of her friends, about how peaceful Nancy looked. And she said, that that made it easier for her to leave Nancy. Sniff. Oh, the dead are so cold! Oh, the dead are so cold! Why does He make it hard, Darren? So hard? I don't know, I don't think He makes it so hard. I don't think it's that intentional. Sniff. Aunt Esther kept saying, Oh, Gott, why did you do this to me? Why did you do this to my Nancy? God didn't do it to you, Aunt Esther. I don't know that God even did it. And if He did do it, I don't know that there's any real answer that we would have as to why He did it. We can find rationalizations. We can find words about death-bed gifts. But wouldn't it have been better, wouldn't it have been better to have realized this without that kind of a price to pay? And why should she have to pay that price so that we can learn something, so that I can learn something, we can learn something?

At one point Ruthie said maybe it was the last thirteen years that were the gift. The last thirteen years since her last surgery. Maybe they were the answer to the prayers, already. Maybe, Joe, that was the miracle. Joe. Maybe. That you did have those six and a half years of married life with Nancy. That you did have that life with her. The life that you would not have had had she died thirteen years ago. A life that the two of you would never have known. Had she died thirteen years ago.

The traffic is moving, speeding up and slowing, and speeding up and slowing, and speeding up and slowing. It is now 8:07. Sniff. I've been on the road again for about eighteen or nineteen minutes. Honk yer hern, honk yer hern, honk yer hern.

So on Sunday, Sophie and I in the evening drove Aunt Esther home, and Aunt Lily back to Baltimore. And they all seemed, in Washington, Silver Spring, they all seemed relieved that the *shivah* was officially over. It was, it was a beautiful clear night. And they walked arm in arm. And I could hear them laughing and joking a little bit and talking. And you could tell it was good to be alive. There was a relief a bit. And Aunt Esther and Aunt Lily sitting in the back of the car. And then Aunt Esther talking about what God had done to her, to her daughter and the *shaineh punim.* I don't know what else to say right now. I'm gonna click this off.

Cheryl kept calling Aunt Esther all week long, "*Shaineh.*" *Shaineh.* And on that Monday, that first Monday, she sat with Aunt Esther and talked to her, and she

THE NANCY TAPES

just did absolutely beautifully. As did Joel. He has a way of sitting and looking someone right in the eyes, right in the face, while they talk.

Just passed a uh Mitsubishi a white Mitsubishi, Galaxy or whatever. Just going by on the road, and the license plate made me think of the old song: "Old dog Trey ever faaaaiiiithful, Grief cannot drive him awaaayyy. He is gentle, he is kind, and I'll never never find a better friend than ooolld dooogg Treeeyyyy." Ooohh, my goodnessss! Ooohhh my gooodnessss! Ooohh my goodnessss!

Yesterday evening after dinner, I went down to turn off the water. But this is still, what's today? Today is still Tuesday, so it was yesterday, Monday, the twelfth, I went down to turn off the outside water because of the freeze warnings. And uuhh when I did so, I found these old tapes. And I brought two of them up and played them. One of Sophie and me tickling Charlie, it was, played on, said on the tape it was October 25th, 1974, when he was just like two-and-a-half, laughing and having so much fun. And he kept saying, Sickening! What's your name, Mom? What's your name, Dad? What's your name, Ma? What's your name, Dad? Sickening! And I thought, How things change! How things have changed!

We also listened to the tape of us with Paul on his second birthday. Actually, it was August 10th, 1979, the day we were gonna have his second birthday party! in Steubenville. Quit that! He kept saying, Quit that! Quit that! He changed. Things changed. *I* changed! I guess.

Langweilige soldaten diese menschen. That was that thing on the latrine wall in, not Herzo Base but Bad Aibling base. Mietraching. *Langweilige menschen diese soldaten.* Boring people, these soldiers.

And of course there's the *??unclear??* then of course the experience on Thursday, November the eighth, of taking Aunt Lily to the airport. Now that wasn't bad, I was kind of looking forward to it, but Lou went along, I didn't realize, when she said Lou was gonna be going along. And I was kind of upset with the fact that I had to take him along, not because of him so much as because, you know, Mother kind of just, that was it! He was going along. And I had been looking forward to a chance for a little visit with Aunt Lily, which of course I didn't really get so much. Because Lou sat in the front and Aunt Lily sat in the back.

And at one point she was talking, and he got all upset and he said, Well, hey, can I talk here? She would talk from the back, and he would talk from the front. And neither one of them was listen--There's a rattle in that passenger side something. And, and so it was difficult to hold a conversation with either one of them. Although I kept trying to hold one with Aunt Lily, and on the way it back it was, he talked almost non-stop talk. It was, it was, and he talked about all of his experiences, how much he had done. I'm not even sure what he talked about, he talked about the judge, talked about when he was petty officer in the Shore Patrol. When he was a Marine. How his family didn't have any money, and that's why he went in the Marines, and that that was one of the best things he had ever done was to have gone into the Marines.

They even have some signs up here in the area. Navy Football Use 70 Rowe Boulevard 3 Miles. That's the one I wanta take. In three miles. Notice Congested Area Prepare to Stop. Well. Notice New Traffic Patterns Next 5 Miles. Well, I guess I'll just get over here in the right lane, since all these others are moving. Why is that rattling like that over there on the right?!

It's now 11:06 am, I'm on my way Caton Avenue, coming back into Baltimore, coming back from Annapolis this morning, what's this morning? Tuesday, November 13th, two weeks ago today, yes, and just happened to, switching the radio around to 92.3. Caught, oh, maybe half, little over half of Beatles song, *Let It Be*: "Let it be, let it be, whisper words of wisdom, let it be, let it be." It was just about two weeks ago today at about this time that at eleven o'clock that R came out, and I came back and saw Ruthie talking to R and R talking to Ruthie and vice versa and vers vicea. And he was, that's when, and she told told me that he had decided they were gonna go ahead and try to disconnect the pump. The bi-ventricular assist pump. It was just about this time two weeks ago today! And hearing the song made me think that on that Sunday, the 21st of October, the day before Nancy's surgery, when Sophie and I went to see her, and we were getting ready to leave, and she was talking about how she couldn't stand that that respirator tube the intubation tube for the respiration for the breathing. It just really bothered her so much. At first we thought she was talking about a GI tube, NG tube NG tube, but she was, no good, no, not talking about an NG tube. She was talking about the intubation tube for the respirator. To help her with her breathing, and how much it bothered her. And I remember I kind of hugged her, and I said, Nance, I said, when, you know, things like that bother me, what I try to do, I try to think of that Beatles song, *Let It Be, Let It Be. Let It Be. Let It Be.* There *won't* come an answer, let it be. Sniff. There will come an answer, let it be. Oh, let it be! If you can't help her live, help her to die. Sniff. If it was too hard, she had to let go. There wasn't enough heart there to work with. It just had to go. Let it be. Let it be. Whisper words of wisdom, let it be.

Song on the radio, *We're Gonna Get Married*. "And we're gonna love until the end of time and we'll never be lonely." That's it just. Loneliness comes. Time ends for one if not the other. Time eventually ends for both. And when it ends for one but not for the other, you will be lonely. When it ends for one but not for the other, the one will be lonely. The *other* will be lonely. The one time ends for, we don't know what will be. Or what is. But the one, the other who is left with time, in time, is the one who will be lonely. Old age, singeth Porgie, what is you but nothin' but bein' lonely. You can be old when you're young if you're lonely.

THE NANCY TAPES

Well, it's Tuesday evening at 5:25. I guess it's kind of getting close now, actually, now that I think of it, to the time at which Nancy died two weeks ago today. And the song that I was just listening to, that just came on the radio was Patti Paige. *Tennessee Waltz*, "I was dancin' with my darlin' to the beautiful Tennessee Waltz," and I began to think about that time approximately ff, no, thirty-eight years ago? was I fourteen? Or was it before I was fourteen? When that song was popular, and I was singing it on the piano, singing it leaning on the piano while Ruth was playing it. I remember that. Do you? Of course, I did!

"I was dancin'" There it is. "With my darlin' to the Tennessee waltz, when an [singing along] old friend" Well, fadeout. Beautiful purple-clouded skies "and while they were a-dancin'" over there in the western horizon. "My friend stole" Mauve, dark mauve. "my sweet"

"Now I know just how much I have lost, yes I lost my little darlin' the night they were playin' the beautiful Tennessee Waltz."

WEDNESDAY, NOVEMBER 14, 1990

Good morning, Mr. Phelps. It's Wednesday, November the 14th, 7:53 am according to the clock in the car. Car in the clock. On my way down Reisterstown Road to go Pikesville Middle School. For American Education Week. Last night I went and spent about an hour and a half with Aunt Esther, ate a little of her *khumash broit*. Not burned. Actually, that's an in-joke, because I guess Ruthie tried to make some *khumash broit*, sniff, and burned it or something. And Nile said, something like, it's, Grandma, ya burned the *khumash*, ya burned the *khumash*, Grandma.

Let's see, so I went to visit Aunt Esther. A couple things that she said. First of all, her face is just incredibly lined. It's the most awesome thing. I wouldn't believe that a human face could have so many wrinkles on it. Creases and wrinkles and nooks and crannies and crevices in the skin and the flesh and the folds. Not so much flesh and folds as in nooks and crannies and creases and wrinkles and lines. And Aunt Lily's face around her right eye, there are a lot of wrinkles and creases, but around the left on the left side, there're relatively few, especially in comparison with the right side. Course my mother had her face lifted. I, it was, I don't remember what year it was, but I remember going to the hospital, and they advised me not to go in because her face was so blown up and swollen, and purple from the trauma of the surgery that she was, her face was hideous to look at. Y'know, this was the day of the surgery. I don't ever want to do anything quite like that, like go through all that, that, not that cosmetic surgery. There's something about the wrinkles in Aunt Esther's face that give, that gives her face some real character. It's just an incredible number of wrinkles. It looks like, looks like the earth from high up in the sky. High up in the sky. From like 30,000 feet in an airplane or even from up in one of the satellites, the way those wrinkles look. Or there was something in that poem by Tennyson about the, about the eagle. The wrinkled sea. The wrinkled sea and the wrinkled land. That's, okay, that's it.

Now also, what was I gonna say? Oh, yes. Couple things that she had talked about last night. First, at one point, she was looking at all the pictures of Allyson and Nancy, and she said, *A pin a pindike kinder*. And I had a feeling that I could figure out what it meant. But, wha, but then she said, y'know, It means paper children. That is, they they're in the photographs, especially Nancy, Nancy there *only* in the photographs. Nancy no longer there in the flesh. And then, y'know, periodically she would really start crying and get just, but she'd, then she said to me a couple times, she was in control, she was okay, and she was. She was okay. But periodically she would break down and cry and. Sniff. She again about Uncle Morris. Talked about how, Oy, how he should've, he should've screamed *Gevalt!* to God that God should let Nancy live. And again I said to her, Aunt Esther, you don't know what he did, you don't know what anybody did, you don't even know if what he did could have done any good, I mean, y'know, who knows what could've done good. Who knows if *anything* could've done anything? Other than, other what? Other than the medicine? Medical science? Surgery? But even, but that could only be certain, a certain amount. And so she talked about Uncle Morris, about that, and then later on she talked about how much he loved her, he just was so devoted to her and loved her so much.

And then a little bit of time passed, and then she looked up, and I, but she talked about other things in between, and she talked, looked up and said that he loved her so much he wanted to have her with him, and and how selfish he was to do something like that. Incredible how out of the mouths of babes as they say come who knows what? Interestingly though also, she talked to me in Yiddish the whole time. But it was a very clear distinct, unslurred, carefully spoken Yiddish. A carefully enunciated, very, very easy to understand the way she was speaking. And then, normally she doesn't speak that much Yiddish, but just once in a while she'd drop in a word or two, but last night it was as though she reverted to all Yiddish. It was just, it's very striking. Very striking. Uncle Morris, so selfish. He had to take Nancy to be with him. Incrediburgable!

Thank you, Mr. Phelps. Add that to your mission impossible!

Okay, it's 10:31, Wednesday, November 14th, leaving Pikesville Middle School after American Education Week visit. I was in Paul's English class this morning. They had some of the posters up from the Book Report Projects that the kids had done. And someone had done a project on a book called, and this poster was up and in red, all caps in red. On three lines:

THE NANCY TAPES

SOMETIMES
NIGHTMARES ARE
REAL

And the book was by

LISA
ORGAN

I didn't get to see what it was about, there was something about, there was a list of detectives names there, but the title was intriguing, *SOMETIMES NIGHTMARES ARE REAL*.

And I'm on my way now to Duron Office Supplies in OM, real fast to see if they have a dictaphone-type machine, and then if I can, I wanta get over to K-Mart, I need to get over to K-Mart to see what they have in the way of those little, not of cassette recorders, something that I can play back the tape of the funeral. Okay, here I go.

I think I'm gonna go straight on up to Greenspring Valley Road to Park Heights to get to Duron.

"Love you." Listening to *Hawaiian Sunset* in the background by Andy Williams, that old song. "to yooourrr" There was a line in there about how "now that we are one, clouds will not hide the sun." Actually, that's not quite what love, I don't eas I don't think that's quite what love should be about, that you say the clouds will not hide the sun. Clouds still *do* hide the sun. There is a reality out there. But one is better able to live with and to cope with clouds hiding the sun when one has someone that one loves. *That's* the difference. It's not that the clouds don't hide the sun. It's not that that ceases to exist or ceases to happen. People get sick, people suffer pain, and people die! Clouds--hide--the sun! Love--helps one, love helps one live, live with, love helps one live with and cope with the clouds hiding the sun. That's the difference.

No, Duron did not have one. So they referred me to, what's the name of that place? Radio Shack. And, of course, Radio Shack did not have one. So I'm off to, it's a long way around, off to K-Mart, over on Liberty Road to see what they've got.

Owings Mills Boulevard here by Painter's Mill Shopping Center cuts all the way through now. I don't know wonder where it goes to. Goodbye.

THURSDAY, NOVEMBER 15, 1990

Hello. Yes, standing out now on the corner of, Good Grief, it's noisy out here! Reisterstown Road and Village Queen Drive and Crossroads Drive waiting to be picked up to go to work. Beautiful sunny day. I think I better put this thing away, there's too much noise out here.

SIDNEY KROME

It's 8:20 am, it's Thursday, November the 15th. Two weeks ago today was Nancy's funeral, that was a big truck roaring by. I better shut this off. I don't know if anybody's gonna be able to hear this, including me.

Okay, Mr. Phelps. It's now 4:41, Thursday, July the 15th. It's Cheez! What a slip of the tongue! July the, July the 15th was the day my father died. This is November the 15th, and this is two weeks since Nancy's funeral. Just picking up the Beretta, heading on. Wanted to put down, put in a couple comments. First of all, Tuesday evening when I was with Aunt Esther, something I forgot to say was that when I talked about that, was that she did, she told me about a conversation about how Nancy was mad at her, what my sister Nancy--What am I? What do I mean my sister Nancy??!! What other Nancy now is there now to be mad at her?-- But Nancy was mad at her because she, Aunt Esther, Nancy called her one day. And Aunt Esther said, Who is it? And Nancy said, It's Nancy. And Aunt, Nan, Aunt Esther said, she said something like, Oy, tanks God, you're back! Like, like she was alive again, like she hadn't, came back from death or something. And and she said that Nancy got real upset. And I said, Well, Aunt Esther, I said, What do you think? And she says, But you know sometimes I just don't know where I am. So there was that. And it reminded me of how, one time my mother called Nancy Eva shortly after Eva had died.

And what else? Oh, yes. Early morning morning walks Monday and Wednesday and today, morning walk-jogs, today I got out there a few minutes early. Got there a few minutes early. And anyhow, it's been, it's a waning moon, and it's just been absolutely beautiful, clear and crisp and cold. And the crescent moon, the crescent of the moon has gotten smaller and smaller, sl I shouldn't say s, I should say slimmer and slimmer. Each day I've been able to see that, the crescent and the ball of the dark side of the moon is just that beautiful grey with a glow around it, be. And today the crescent was so tiny, so slim slo so such a slim slender crescent of the moon. Pointing up. I was right when I told the class when the crescent points are pointing to the right, it's a waning moon, not a waxing moon. But I told them, the crescent points pointing to the right, it's a waning moon. And today it was clearly waning. It was just down very low on the horizon, very low. The rising moon is falling down the sky. The rising moon is setting in the sky. The rising moon is the ri as it r it rises lower, it rises lower, it rises lower.

Incidentally, I am shortly, when this tape runs out, I'm gonna stop using this cassette recorder, the microcassette recorder, and instead I'm goin'--Look at the new Toys-R-Us! Instead of using the microcassette recorder, I'm gonna use that new GE mini-cassette recorder that I have in my briefcase. I need to try that out for a while. I have yet to be able to find, maybe I'll try in in, oh, and there's the big sign Hardee's sign on what used to be this Roy Rogers here. Try the that office supply place in Pikesville. Lucas Brothers, is it? See if they have anything. I'll have to give them a call. Or go down sometime.

Maybe I'll go by tomorrow and see if they've got anything. I also need to go by Ames or someplace to see about picking up that Panasonic cassette recorder. They had them in the window at Best, but they were out of stock. Guy said it would be four to six weeks which is pretty ridiculous. At Bell W. Bell they had just a GE, but it didn't have a counter, and I don't know, I think I'd like to have the counter in it.

Over and out. Roger wilco, Mr. Phelps. Your mission, should you choose to accept it, Mr. Phelps, is to make order out of chaos. Communicate a meaning. Communicate a meaning. That's what I said to the students. When you write, you're trying to communicate a meaning. Your own, your meaning, whatever it is.

FRIDAY, NOVEMBER 16, 1990

Good morning, Mr. Phelps. It's 8:02 on uh Friday, November the 16th. On my way to do some more errands, and your mission, should you decide to accept it, is to continue to try to make sense out of chaos or disorder. Actually, one might say, Good morning, Captain James T. Kirk of the Starship Enterprise. Your five-year mission is to explore new worlds, to boldly go where no man has gone before. Or Captain Jean-Luc Picard! *Your* mission, should you choose to accept it, is to have the ongoing mission of exploring bra bold new worlds exploring new worlds, to boldly go where no *one* has gone before. Actually, though, in a sense, every one has gone this way before because everyone, we, ma, I shouldn't say that, *many* people have tried to make sense out of this chaosly disorder. Some have found their own, and some have found group orders. And and some have found nothing, and some have not even bothered to, not even bothered to look. Now where was, Don's?, where was that place? Was it this first one? Or the second one? I think it was in the first one. So let's turn in here, in Greenspring Valley Road, and then go into this parking lot right here. Okay, one feels that one is in an obstacle course right here, isn't one? Okay. Here I am trying to get uh the, oh, look at that, oh, there's a driveway back there. Oh, okay. Well, that's interesting.

Okay, it's 8:14. I've just dropped off my jackets and my trench coat. The jacket. Boy, to replace the lining would have been 50 bucks! 50 bucks it would've been. But to fix it only 15, but obviously, it's not gonna look quite as good.

Anyhow, what I also wanted to say is the other day when I was talking I forgo, I think I forgot to mention something that--Wait a second, I gotta stop, I gotta get out onto Reisterstown Road so

Okay, I'm back in the saddle again. It's 8:21, Jean-Luc Picard! Captain James T. Kirk. What was it he said in *The Search for Spock*? "What have I done, Scotty? My God, Scotty, what have I done?" As the Enterprise was blowing up.

"What you always do, Jim," said Bones, "turn death into a chance for life." Turn death into a chance for life. Like Joe said to Sophie last night was that in some ways this was like a best thing that could happen for Darren. Because he's coping. And if, as he said in the hospital one day, this is the realest, is the hardest thing he's ever had to deal with. And somebody else said, it was reality. Had to deal with reality. And he faced reality, that he is facing reality. He's, he's really doing well. Nancy would be proud of him.

In any case also, let me move on. What I wanted to say the other day, and I think I forgot to say in here was about the games we used to play on Springhill Avenue. I think I thought of this the other day, and I know I did because, let's see, today's Friday, Thursday, I guess Wednesday night when I was putting some of the slides away, slides of Springhill Avenue, thinking about the games we used to play. Wire ball. And throwing the wire up out in front of B G's garage across Springhill Avenue. Wire ball. Sniff. Wire ball. And Step ball. And Stick, where you use a sharp pointed stick to be the thing that you played, it was like a form of Tag. And then Redline, 1-2-3-Redline and Free-da-Base. Grab someone, you have to say, 1-2-3-Redline. And the time that H K, I think it was H, ran down the lawn from, I guess it would'ave been the Gs' lawn right next door to us, towards that lamp-post, and he went to Free-da-Base, and his arms went, his hands and arms went on either side of it, and he hit face first into it, actually with his teeth and broke off the front tooth. And now H is a, what's he, a triathlon athlete? Saw him up at the JCC, Pro-fitness. And I never went to Abe Kershman's funeral.

I'm on my way down into Pikesville now. It's 8:24, but I want to see if Lucas Brothers opens at nine, I'll stay and see if they have a dictaphone type machine that I can use for transcribing these tapes. I mentioned it the other day. I guess it was Wednesday afternoon to, what's his name? To M. He said that Lanier made about the best, if you can afford it. And when he was down in Texas they could afford the best of everything down in Texas. So we'll see what Lucas Brothers has to say.

Last night when I talked to Aunt Esther, she had the chills, aches, I think she was coming down with the flu. I was gonna go down to see her, but she was in bed, and she talked about how she had talked with, I guess with Joe. And she talked about how *finster* it was in the house, and she has talked, mentioned several times how *finster* it was in her *oygen*. How dark it was in her eyes with Nancy gone and now talking about how *finster* it is must be in the house with Nancy gone and as though the family's falling apart. But actually, Joe told Sophie last night that they're doing pretty well. Allyson got a promotion at work and a raise, and Darren is coping well, and he's getting into his group, into his therapy, and Joe is, Joe is getting by, he's cleaning out Nancy's stuff, going through her papers, going through her clothes and packing up for the dead. Packing up for the dead. Packing up for the dead.

THE NANCY TAPES

Today will probably be my last day for a while on this machine. I want to try to use the mini-cassette recorder. That I got, see how that one works. So I may stop this one for a while and go to that one. Over and out. Roger wilco. Captain James T. Kirk, Starship Enterprise. Captain Jean-Luc Picard of the Starship Enterprise. And there's an unmarked, I thought that was an unmarked state police car. Now I can see the siren, the light flashing thing up in the, it's not flashing. But it's up on his ca, up on his dashboard.

I just turned the radio on, going in here in Pikesville. Just passing the Shapiro's which is now closed. And on the radio 1010 WYST, *"Don't Step on My Blue Suede Shoes."* And suddenly it flashed back to, I guess when I was in speech class at College Park, and let me pull over here and park if I can. Wait a second. In my speech class, and we had to do something, I guess, in front of a tv was it? And I read the lines or kind of declaimed the lines of *Don't Step on My Blue Suede Shoes.*

Well, Mr. Phelps. What you just learned can really make your mission more impossible. The cost of a transcriber machine is 260 dollars minimum here at Lucas Brothers in their catalogue. The guy suggested I try Radio Shack. But I did try one. They didn't even look in their catalogue. Maybe I should go back there and ask them to look in their catalogue.

In any case, in any case maybe I could try a Radio Shack and go to their catalogue. Exit only. Why don't you wait a second? Oh, Jesus! What is this guy doin'?! Chinchillas.

In any case, Holy Cow! Holy Cow! 260 dollars is the cheapest one. I thought 50, 60, a hundred bucks, maybe, but 260! Whoooaawww, bayby!

Well, I've got about 7 or 8 pictures left on this roll of film. I'll go down, take a few of the *Agudas Achim* across from the Avalon. This may be the last recording on this machine. It certainly will be for now. Because very soon, as soon as this tape is done, I'm gonna switch to the other, the mini-cassette recorder.

Driving down Reisterstown Road, just crossing Garrison Boulevard, Garrison Avenue. Coming down towards Royce Avenue, towards it, I'm not there yet. And thinking about Towanda, Towanda, the day I took pictures of PS 59 I also took pictures of Towanda. Which made me think of the Towanda Reunion that was held in September that I didn't get to. When I saw M B, at our, City's 35th Reunion, September also, 'bout two weeks later, he talked about how I had missed it and D C was there. But I remember what I wanted to say here was that when I saw B, I was startled, it was so good to see that he was alive! Because about a year ago or sometime, Ron called, when I talked to Ron, he said he thought he saw something in *The Jewish Times*, an obit notice, he thought it was M B, he said it would be about his right age. When I saw M W at the Rally for Soviet Jews in May, Operation Exodus, I asked him about the reunion, he said he didn't know about it.

Oh, I've just passed Royce Avenue. And then he also said, I asked about M B, and he said, 'cause I s, B used to handle it, and he said, Well, he said, he heard that B had a heart attack or something, and they had to bring him back from--Oh, well, No Left Turn 7 - 9 AM, 6 - 9 AM. Son of a gun, I guess I'll have to go around the block or something here. At Cold Spring Lane. PARK LANE PARK AND SHOP PARK LANE FREE PARKING sign. That goes back probably 35, no, 40 years. But, what was I saying? Yeah! And he said he heard that B had been brought back from Florida, had a heart attack or a stroke or something, and I told him that I, you know, I thought I heard, told him what Ronny had said, and so I thought, what I heard from M, what M had to say, that maybe he had died. But he hadn't! And it was wonderful to hear that the news was wrong. Or that the stories were wrong.

Stopping now to take pictures of the *Agudas Achim shule*, the Avalon *shule* on Park Heights Avenue.

I'm on my way again down Park Heights at 8:55, 8:56, after having taken pictures. And what passed me and is now to my right is a roofing contractor's truck, and towing behind it what he has is one of those small black, the tar makers, the tar heaters. Thinking back to the Springhill Avenue days, in the alley and finding and picking up, picking up pieces of that tar and chewing on it. I remember chewing on tar. Strange, the things that kids try. Some days over at B E's house, passing that A W's house. The Fs' house, second from the corner 3736. And going past, coming up now on Violet Avenue. Where Kessler's used to be, it's now a house. Was it back in the, roughly in '77, when I drove by they were reconverting it back into a house. Sam and Barney Kessler, and now my son Paul, our son Paul, is good friends with Barney's grandson. Strange-uh. I'll have to stop at that food place and get a can of coffee to take with to school. Over and out. Coming down now to Park Circle. Coming down now to Park Ciirrrcle, aannd here weee g aarrrre. Park Cirrclle. Where Parks Sausage is now is is now Parks Sausage. Ay-round the bend.

Missing is, now I seem to be missing an empty case for this microca microcassette tape. I don't know where it is. Because what I've been doing is putting the completed one in the case of the new one, but now I've got a complete, almost complete one, I've got the new one in my pocket. But if I'm not gonna start that one, I'm gonna start the other cassette recorder that I have, the mini-cassette recorder I have in my pocket. Over and out.

Mr. Phelps, this tape will not self-destruct within five seconds or four seconds or whatever it was. *You* may self-destruct! Ha-ha-ha-ha! But the tape won't. Coming over Mondawmin now looking down at the city, the skyline, which is usually beautiful when it's clear, but there's a real pall, a real haze now over the city. Look at it hanging there. God, I wish now I'd, now I wish I had film. There's a plane pulling a banner down there. Boy, I wish I had film in the camera to take a picture of that. Oh, well, *asha-i viatsa*.

Background is that song about the living years. Sniff. That was on the radio
TAPE ENDS

TAPE NUMBER 5A

FRIDAY, NOVEMBER 16, 1990 (CONT.)
I'm continuing my Nancy tapes on this; instead of switching right now, I'll switch later.

It just came on the radio, that *In the Living Years*, that song that we heard on the way up to Montreal that Nancy talked about. Oh, God, it's so sad. "It's too late when we die to admit we don't see eye to eye." And then something about his father dying, and he wished he had told him in the living years all the things he had t' say. Oh, how true that is. It's time for me to start saying some of those things now, while people are still alive.

And I'm gonna start saying some of them by getting some of these slides made into prints: Springhill Avenue, for Ruth to give to Amy, Craig's girlfriend, to do some sketches and stuff for her. And maybe some of the rainbow pictures and some pictures of Charlie and Pete, and of the family, our group, okay, I'm going in now.

SATURDAY, NOVEMBER 17, 1990
Okay. It's now Saturday, November the 17th, at 10:06, I'm on my way to College Park to pick up Charlie. It's a gray, rainy-ish day. And that previous bit was recorded on Friday morning, November the 16th, that was approximately noon, when I got to the--Che-che, pardon me--to the Shutterbug. So what I'm gonna do now is I'm going to repeat that into the mini-cassette recorder. And I'm gonna hold off on using this machine any more at least until I can maybe in January when I get some of my money, buy one of those dictaphone transcribers; there is one that can handle both kinds of tapes that's well over three-hundred dollars, I think. But I'm gonna have to wait to buy that. So for now, I think what I'll probably do is, I'll probably go into. I think I should really stop doing this and talk into the other one so I don't have that much to transfer. Over and out, it's now 10:07, and I'm on the Beltway heading towards College Park.

TUESDAY, NOVEMBER 20, 1990
Good morning, Mr. Phelps, Captain Kirk, and Captain Picard. It's now 8:10 am on Tuesday, November the 20th. I'm sitting here in the car on my way down to school, I'm gonna go right down Reisterstown Road, I think. And I think I've decided, given the quality of the recording or the lack of quality on the other recorder, the mini-cassette recorder, I think what I'm gonna do is keep using this. And then in January, I'm just gonna have to go get, get one of those machines that can do both micro-cassette and the regular cassette tapes. What I've tried doing right now is I've backed down the volume to about halfway, in the hope that this will not pick up all the outside noises, the rattle, banging, and the uh the sounds of

the tires and the, the humming and drumming of the car driving. So now I'm gonna see how this records here.

Now I've got this one on. And I've got it on the AVR. No, I don't. I can't tell, 'cause I can't see 'cause the print is too small. I can't tell. Now it's on AVR. Okay. It's now 8:18, and I've just passed uh Reisterstown Road Plaza, coming up on the Reisterstown Road branch of the Library. Whoops! Whoops, whoops, whoops! Watch it there, Sidney! Better pay attention to the road, here, for a few minutes.

Now, what I'm gonna do, Mr. Phelps, Captain Kirk, and Captain Picard, I'm gonna stop talking for a few seconds and see if this one cuts off as well as the other one cuts off. Actually, apparently, the AVR on the other one seems to work better than this one does. No, the AVR's not working right on this one.

Uuuhhh Good afternoon, Mr. Phelps. Here I am on Dukeland Street and Liberty Heights, on my way home. It's 5:04 p.m. on Tuesday, November 20th, and I as I was coming along Dukeland Street with "Twilight Time" by the Platters playing in the background, I looked up to my left and what to my wondering eyes should appear but the waxing crescent moon! The first sliver of moon, of the new growing moon, waxing, with the crescent corners pointing to the left, just as I had told the students it would. Deep in the dark your kiss will thrill me, like days of old. Ah, twilight time, twilight time! It is a beautiful twilight! "for evening, just to be with you" Sky slight, oh, there's a contrail of a jet. "at last at twilight time" Kind of an orange orange glowing orange, few color. Twilight time. Wonderful, that crescent moon. Absolutely beautiful. Thin, thin sliver. Not quite as thin as the last sliver of the waning moon that I saw last week. Or whenever it was, yes, last week. Let me hear how this sounds now.

Okay, I'm, just uh got home, it's 5:30, now 5:31. And looking up at the crescent moon, and the sky has darkened considerably, but it's still lightish over there, but I can see now that the crescent moon is brighter. And you can see the dark of the moon around to the left of it with a kind of a dark glow around it. A beautiful evening. "Heavenly shades of night are falling, it's twilight time."

I was waiting to see if the AVR would work, but it's not, so I'm gonna talk. It's 8:46, Tuesday evening, November the 20th. Just coming upstairs to change, but I got home from work this afternoon about 5:30, little after 5:30, and when I saw the crescent moon. Ruthie's letter had come, her card, with copy of Kathie's letter, and a card from her friend Beth, I think her name is Beth, and the poem that Ron and D had sent, and her card for us, maybe primarily for me, I think, for all the time that I spent with them. And I read the poem out loud, the poem from the, anonymous but attributed to the Native American. And I kinda broke down and cried, and Soph came over, and we hugged, and I kinda cried.

Then I said that when I was at Paul's school, I had seen that sign about, in the English class, about the reports, that the one that said one that said what? The one that said the one that said the one that said, "SOMETIMES NIGHTMARES ARE REAL." And I said to Soph, "And sometimes reality is a nightmare." And I said, "The only difference is that fortunately, when you have a nightmare, you wake up for it when you wake up from it, you wake up from it, when you wake up from it, it's over. But reality you don't wake up from. This nightmare that is reality, this reality that is a nightmare, we don't wake up from." And now I think of the line, I guess it's from Joyce, *Ulysses*, when Stephen Dedalus in the classroom with the headmaster, and he, he says something about, that is God, that, that shout in the street. And then I think he says at one point that that God history! history is the nightmare from which he's trying to awaken. History is the nightmare from which he's trying to awaken.

Interesting now, the quiet of the bedroom, that when I played back what I just said, I could hear the buzzing, the same kind of buzz that I heard on the mini-cassette recorder.

WEDNESDAY, NOVEMBER 21, 1990

Good morning. It's 6:59 by the car clock. Actually, it's probably 7 o'clock because it's one minute slow. In the morning of Wednesday, November the 21st. We're getting ready to go to Steubenville. It's gonna be a little bit yet, I had hoped to be on the road by 7, it'll probably be a good 7:30 or so before we get on the road.

But anyhow, I forgot to mention yesterday that yesterday morning while I was out walking, taking my morning walk from approximately 5:37 till 6:05 I looked up in the sky and saw a actually, I was looking, it was just a beautiful sky. Clear, crisp day, morning, before dawn. And I saw a shooting star, it came dropping straight down. And I was walking up Wimbledon Lane to the right, 'round by the pool, past there and on the straight side down, sort of in the direction of Reisterstown Road, and and there it was straight ahead of me. Just, absolutely beautiful.

THURSDAY, NOVEMBER 22, 1990

Okay, what I've done now is I've put it on the normal speed, I wanta record normal speed to see what the quality of the reproduction is. *[reading from newspaper]* Bush confident. Leaders of a 34-nation summit unexpectedly pushed the Persian Gulf crisis to the top of their agenda today as President Bush expressed confidence that Mikhail Gorbachev will support a United Nations resolution on using military force against Iraq. Period. That's from *The Evening Sun* of Tuesday, November 20th. Che-che. It's now Thursday, November 22nd, 10:45 am, here in Steubenville.

THE NANCY TAPES

FRIDAY, NOVEMBER 23, 1990

Good morning, Mr. Phelps. It's Friday, November the 23rd, 10:45. I'm beginning to put a few things back in the car for the trip back to Baltimore. And a couple things I wanted to say.

Just about fifteen minutes ago, I was upstairs in the dining room area. *[sounds as of carrying or shifting suitcases]* Soph was looking at Mods' plants, coulis, I guess, but they were in the window, facing sort of east, southeast, I guess, southeast. And all of them had died. And she looked at them, and she said, "They all died." And she said, "No one had taken the time to water them." And then she went over and looked at the picture of Theo Mike, Thea Angela, Mother, and Theo Nick. *[progressively softer]* She kind of wiped off the area where Mother's face was, and went back over to the window, and I went and hugged her, and she cried and picked up a tissue. The plants died. Because nobody took the time to water them here. Neither John nor Dad nor anybody else who came by. Nor anybody who came by. Sniff. How sad. That her plants would die, in less than a year, simply because nobody took care of them.

And yesterday at 2 o'clock, I happened to look up, and I said to John, "Well, 27 years ago today just about at this time it was all over." Two o'clock Eastern Standard Time was 1:00 p.m. Central Standard Time. And that was just about the time that Kennedy was pronounced dead. November 22nd, 1963.

MONDAY, NOVEMBER 26, 1990

Good morning, Mr. Phelps. It's been several days. This is Monday, November the 26th. Five weeks ago today that Nancy had her surgery. It's now 7:57. It's a bright, clear moderately crisp November morning. I'm on my way down first to stop at Pikesville Middle School to drop off Paul's gym suit which he forgot to take with him. Time out for a stop for a cup of coffee and a *??move??* Traffic.

7:59 by the clock, 8 o'clock by the uh radio time. But, now WYST, *I Saw the Harbor Lights.* "I watched the harbor lights, how could I know." Bring back the memories, memories of PS 49 Robert E. Lee Junior High School, and A G and listening to WCBM radio in the afternoon on Saturday afternoon. Jo Stafford, *You Belong to Me,* dedicated dedications dedicated dedicated to the one I love, which was not even a song then. Dedicated to me by A G, to A G by me, and I never did take her out. Whooaa! Anyhow, whoops! Getting ready to make the left turn here on Hooks Lane. I'd better shut this thing off while I make the turn here. Time out.

Well, actually, I didn't get to make the turn because the guy in front of me was too slow and the light changed. But anyhow, went to visit Aunt Esther yesterday afternoon, and several things that she said that I would like to record here for a matter of record on *the Nancy Tapes*. For Phelps, Kirk, and Picard. And the click click click of the light.

Okay, here we go down Hooks Lane now. One thing, she looked at the, at the picture of *Zaydeh* and *Bubbeh*, and Aunt Freda and Aunt Lily and my mother when the three of them were kids in the 1920's shortly after they all came to this country. And she looked at it, and she said, "How could they be quiet? How could they be quiet?" Speaking of her, her mother and father, my *Zaydeh* and *Bubbeh*. "Eh, how could they be quiet?" she said. "And let Nancy die. They let Nancy die 'cause they were quiet." And I tried to tell her, it's not up to them, really, whether Nancy lives or dies, it's up to God. And who knows was what they did or didn't do, what they said or didn't say, or if they said or didn't say anything or if they care or don't care. Who knows what the condition is? She also said something about, and pointing to all the plaques on the wall and about all the charities she had given to, and she said, "I I gave so much to charity, I thought I could buy it, buy her out, buy Nancy's life out." And, and she said, "But I couldn't." And I said, "You're right, Aunt Esther," I said, "You can't buy her life out," I said. Later, when she looked up again and said the same kind of thing, said that I could tell that she said that she thought she could buy her back. Well, you can never buy her back once they're gone. And, hey, you can't buy people's lives that way. And then also she kept referring to the hospital, Johns Hopkins, as the slaughterhouse. As the slaughterhouse. Several times she referred to Hopkins, the hospital, as the slaughterhouse.

Actually, something else I forgot to mention is the fact that yesterday I finally sat down to write the piece for the family newsletter about Nancy, and, it took a while, and I'm not sure. Sophie liked it, che-che, pardon me. She liked the first version I gave her, she hasn't seen the second version yet. But I'm not sure how much I like it. I have to see how I look at it and send it off to Ruth and Ruth to look at before I send it off to, to Amy.

Good morning again. Still Monday. Having dropped off Paul's stuff, I'm now heading down Seven Mile Lane to where it will cut into Park Heights Avenue if I can ever get through this traffic light here at Smith because everybody's turning left. And, okay, now, che-che, pardon me. Here I go.

I was just thinking of something but I forgot oh, yes, I know. On, was it Thanksgiving Day? Or the day before, the day after? What day was it? Anyhow, John and I, I remember we were watching this movie, *Running Against Time*. Have to see if I have the book, I think the book, they said the book was called *A Time to Remember*, I think that's the book I picked up in Steubenville a year or so ago, paperback book. 'Bout a guy who tries to go back in the past to prevent the assassination of Kennedy in order, in order to prevent the massive build-up in Vietnam, the Vietnam War, so that he could save his brother's life, his brother died in Vietnam. And as, as we got into it, and they realized that, or the scientist who was, had developed the time travel machine realized that you couldn't go back and you couldn't change anything, and he said something about haven't been able to change even a blade of grass. It reminded me of *The Rubaiyat of Omar Khayyam*. Che-che. And, of course, the very next thing that he said to the female lead was the line from *The Rubaiyat of Omar Khayyam*, about the moving finger. The lines, not the line, "The moving finger writes,/And having written [*sic*], moves on/Nor all they piety nor wit/Can call it back/Nor cancel half a line." Yes. Thinking also about Nancy. Thinking about Soph's mother. The inexorability. Once things begin to move, they move, and there's nothing you can do to stop it. It's as the liver specialist said about the medication that Mods was taking. That in the first dose was itself was enough, was so toxic, and there was such a massive reaction to the medication that, that even stopping it right after would not have helped. That one dose was enough. Once is enough. All it takes is one one little bit. That's all it takes sometimes. To start that wheel, that ball rolling down the hill. And once it starts, you can't stop it. It becomes a nightmare, nightmare from which there is no awakening.

Blue Monday. Just listened to *Blue Monday* on WYST. Remembering, something about *You Belong to Me* and WCBM and listening to WCBM Saturday afternoon and standing on the porch at 2614 Springhill Avenue. Standing on the porch and listening to the radio. What was I doing? Just kind of hanging around sometimes. There I was, thirteen going on fourteen, I remember that letter from A G. That I carried folded up in my wallet for so many years. Until it finally fell apart. And I don't know whatever happened to it, though I had meant to keep it forever. My first love letter. I love how your face gets red when you get mad. What else? I love everything about you, love how your face gets red when, when you get mad, even love how your face gets red when you get mad. Don't never change. Don't never change, A G. Don't never change.

But things do change. For example, now, coming up coming down here now on Park Heights, I'm on Park Heights coming down on Hayward Avenue, and che-che, pardon me, there is no more Pimlico Hotel here! There is, however, a McDonald's. But the Pimlico Hotel is gone. Don't never change. It's gone from here, it's now at the CommerCentre on Reisterstown Road. And Hooks Lane. But don't never change, man, don't never change. And coming down now to Belvedere, there's the Pimlico Race Track on the left. Coming down now towards Belvedere. To what used to be the Pimlico Movie Theater. Which closed yeeeaars ago and became a Read's Drugstore, I think, and now it's, what's, it's Goldenberg's Bargain Outlet, which it became also years ago.

And coming up now, coming down now to what used to be the Uptown Theater but is now Kingdom Hall of Jehovah's Witnesses. The Pimlico Hotel, the, not Pimlico Hotel, Pimlico Theater, less classy. The Uptown a more classy type neighborhood theater. The Pimlico Hotel [*sic*], I think, was where I went that time that Daddy was talking about going to the circus, and for some reason I thought they weren't gonna go, we weren't gonna go, and I wanted to go to the movies, so I went to the movies, and when I came back, I found out that Daddy had taken Ron, *[voice quavers]* and they had gone to the circus. *[crying]* I didn't know they were gonna go! Sniffling. Sniff. I didn't know they were gonna go. Sniff. I didn't know they were gonna go! Sniff. Ooooohhhh! Just passing St. Ambrose, in front of St. Ambrose now. And coming down on right, there to the right that is Park Lane. Oohh, I remember Park Lane. Used to walk up, to the Hobby Shoppe. Used to walk up here to the Hobby Shoppe. Who would let a kid now walk that far? Sniff. I don't know. *[quavering]* I didn't know they were going to the circus. I didn't know they were going to the circus.

Now at the intersection of Park Heights and Cold Spring Lane. And then down to the front, the old Avalon Theater. The old Avalon. Barry Levinson stole the title. 'Course he used it in a more erudite, exotic sense. But the Avalon, the Avalon Theater, and the marquee is blackened. But the facade of the building is still beautiful. Can't imagine what it's like inside there now. Sniff. *[whispered]* Oh, God! The shops boarded up and decaying. The old *Agudas Achim* Synagogue on the left. And which **shule** was this down here a little bit farther down on the right, the one that always looked like a church? Oh, not today! But someday I have to stop and take pictures of it. Well, maybe I should, nah. Which one was it? What was the name of this church? What was the name of this **shule** when it was a *shule*? Not the, no, I don't know what it was. And then down here around to the right would be.

Now, we're down here at the traffic light at Shirley Avenue. Sniff. Down to the right, now the Shirley Avenue Street Park which has been here for years. Down to what used to be Isaac Davidson Hebrew School. I Do Hate School. And to the left, that flying peace dove with the lights on it. How many years ago did they tear down that gas station? And on the left hand corner also, different corner, Al's Cutrate Liquors, which used to be SIDLEN's Pharmacy. Sniff. Different Sussman's. Traveling down now through the 3900 block of Park Heights Avenue. There's is Park Heights Street Academy, and here's Keyworth Avenue, down to the right PS 59, I need to take pictures of the east and north side of PS 59. And now crossing Springhill Avenue, the famous Springhill Avenue. There it is. And the Gs' house over there, and the Fs' and what used to be, what used to be Kessler's on the left. Which reminds me this morning when I was in, oh, when I was in where? Oohh, when I was in Pikesville Middle School, when I went in to drop off Paul's. There's, there's a liquor, Robinson's Variety Store which used to be Sussman's down at the corner of Ulman Avenue and just passing Roland's Barber Shop there on the right. And then on the left that *shule*, what was that *shule*? I gotta take pictures of that one too. So I've got two *shules* there. And then the Auchentoroly Terrace *shule*.

Anyhow, when I went into, sniff, into Pikesville Middle School, there was B K. I heard someone calling, B, and then I recognized him, from having been over his house one time, a couple times, actually. The grandson of Barney Kessler. Isn't it a small world? Isn't it amazing?

TUESDAY, NOVEMBER 27, 1990
Hello? Hello. Yes. It's 8:02, Tuesday, November the 27th. It's four weeks today since Nancy died. And I'm just passing through Park Circle. I came down Reisterstown Road again today, and came past the. And thinking about Maar Lesser, Mr. Lesser's house where I took my *Bar Mitzvah* lessons, and anyhow also thinking about that and thinking about how coming down now, coming down, coming down into Park Circle, and I looked up, and there was a sign. Reisterstown Road and Park Heights Avenue. The street signs, but then there was also the sign, the street sign that said Henry G. Parks Jr. Cir. C-i-r-period. Henry G. Parks Jr. Circle. It's no longer Park Circle, it's Henry G. Parks Jr. Circle. And I went past also the Reptile House, and the old Reservoir and now going past the old Park Superintendent's House here on, in the Druid Hill Park. And there's the slope, where the, the bus stop used to be, that slope where A S and I cut grass, and sat down on the hill with the little sickles in our hands, cutting the grass, and didn't realize that we were cutting the grass, but we were cutting also poison ivy. And that's when I got that incredible case of poison ivy on my forearms. A case so bad that I rem I had that big blister the size of a silver dollar. And also went to, went to sleep with my arms in the air, sleeping on my back, arms in the air up over my head, and the sunlight the sunlight the moonlight coming in the open window on Springhill Avenue, and then the moonlight glowing on the calamine lotion on my arms and scared the crap outa myself. And sitting also on the couch on Springhill Avenue reading a comic book and in a undershirt and shorts. And reading a comic book. And I guess it was Nancy took the picture of me sitting there with this intense look of concentration on my face reading the comic book.

And I wonder what ever happened to that picture. I carried it around for years. But that picture is gone, gone with the wind, gone with A G's letter, love letter to me when I was fourteen.

A S. Used to pick me up at Park Heights and Springhill on the way down into the park to go to work. And I was supposed to go to his wedding, he invited me to his wedding, and I didn't go, and I don't know why the hell I didn't go, some idiotic no-count no good reason. And I remember afterwards, at College Park, he said that he was disappointed that I hadn't come. Disappointed a lot of people, A. Not just you.

SIDNEY KROME

Passing the old Western now, the Douglass High School. I remember coming by it yesterday, noticing the sunlight on the that would be on the east side of it and the, the brick and the sunlight on the wall.

A photo essay of walls? With Robert Frost's poem *Mending Walls?* Anyhow. It's 8:05 now and I'm into here in the Mondawmin parking lot waiting to go left here, to go left, to go go into campus, to go to work. Mondawmin, Mon-daw-min. When they used to have their Saturday night concerts there, when it was open air, before it was a closed-in mall, and D R, G, walked around barefoot in a suit.

Okay. It's Tuesday evening, November 27th. It's 7:07 p.m.. I'm at the corner of Falstaff and Park Heights. Just left Aunt Esther's house. It's four weeks ago this evening that Nancy died. Four weeks ago roughly this time, about sevenish that we learned that she had died. And I stopped at Aunt Esther's to pick up some *mandle* bread, and then Joe came in. And so I stayed, and we visited for a while, and he's having some soup, chicken soup, and eating there now, and ts he had an appointment today with R and talked about things that R said, questions, he had a yellow legal sheet of legal pad paper. With questions that he had asked R and, and answers that R had given. And he also read the two paragraphs of a letter that Nancy had written on October the 16th. Two weeks before she died. A week before the surgery. Two weeks exactly to the day Tuesday to Tuesday.

And he read two paragraphs of it, the opening and closing paragraphs, the rest he had, uh, he just put those two together and xeroxed them together on one single page. The rest were special instructions that she wanted, for him, for the kids. And he had a very difficult time reading, but he wanted to go through it. Also he gave an article from some uh seniors magazine about, about facing grief and going through grief. He talked about how he today when he was at the hospital, he went to into the ICU, and he stood in the hall, looking at Nancy's, the bed, well, it wasn't really *the* bed but might have been, a bed. A bed that was in the place where Nancy's bed was, where she h'd lain for a week, and where she died, and, and that one of the nurses had said something about how he was strong to be able to uh to do that, and he said, simply, that this was something that he felt he had to do, he had to face things. And and so he had to face it.

I'm trying to remember as much of the stuff as I can remember of what he asked R. The first question about about the heart-lung transplant, ts and that R said that he felt that that she was really not a good candidate for it, a for it, after the three surgeries and that that she pro she would not, they just didn't feel she could have survived it, and that she would as good candidate [*sic*]. And then I said, this, like what was in the uh the consultant's reports that Joe had shown to me in the hospital. ts And so he asked R why he had even suggested it, and J and he said it's because he was so emotionally involved with the family, just wanted to give some hope to the family. And and Joe asked what would have happened if if they had not done any surgery at all. And he said she just simply would have deteriorated. And she would have died. There was, no hope for her. That, that quite possibly she would have died anytime, and that quite possibly it could have been very sudden. That Joe could have been sitting in the family room watching TV with her and then simply stepped out of the room, and then come to have found her dead. Or her condition could've deteriorated so badly that she would have become invalided, and and simply wasted away and died as an invalid.

And and Joe asked about one second. And Joe asked about *[heavy sigh]* the decision to take her off the machine that day. Oh, and he also said that that bi-ventricular assist machine has only been in use for about a year or a little over a year, a couple years. And and that he made the decision to take her off the machine because he just felt it was time, all the signs were pointing towards it, and that it is possible that had they waited another day, her heart *might* have gotten stronger. But he didn't know that it would have, and and he was also concerned about possible brain damage, because of, as one of the ef side effects of of being like this. And that he felt that while she was fairly aware of things the first few days, after a while he felt that basically she was unconscious the last four or five days. And and basically unaware of things at all and. He just he just was not sure whether or not there was any brain damage. And Joe agreed that, had she survived the surgery but suffered uh major brain damage, that her condition would have been worse and that she would never have wanted to do that, knowing the condition of two of Joe's aunts who suffered severe strokes and and major major problems of of that kind. And R also said that a he asked about her living this way, and and R said that he knew many patients, there are other people whose conditions were not as bad as Nancy's who *died.* Who never got to surgery. And he felt the thing that kept her alive was just her incredible, indomitable spirit. Her will to live, her desire to live. And that this was what kept her alive. *[goes silent]*

I had pushed the speed up so I'm gonna have to push the speed back. There's a little part there, that was at normal speed, and this is back on the half-speed. It's-ick.

And that she, there were pa and that that there were patients who had far not nearly as bad as her condition, but who who died. And what kept her alive was, was her determination.

He said also, what else did he say? What am I thinking about? Oh, that he told Joe that he felt that almost that every decision he made was the wrong decision, because no matter what he did *[sigh]*, things went wrong, and things couldn't work out, and nothing he did worked out right. And that's, I said something to Joe about that movie *Running Against Time* about the Kennedy assassination, this guy who went back in the past to try to prevent it. And I said that no matter what they did, every time they went back things got worse and got worse, and so, what they finally had to realize that some things could not be changed. And that no matter what you do, no matter what he had done, no matter what decision he made, it would have been a wrong decision because there was nothing he could do to to fix her to to bring her to to to hel to make her be healthy enough, her heart be healthy enough to live. And tha and that no matter what he had done, nothing he could have done would have saved her. And that he i in a response to a question of Joe's, that that he didn't realize, that there was no way he could know how bad her heart actually was until he actually got in on the surgery and opened her up and saw what kind of condition her heart was really in, that it was, it was just incredibly weaker than he had thought. And all the time on the heart-lung machine had, of course, it not given the heart sufficient oxygen, not even given the brain sufficient ox it it not nothing was sufficient while it was on the heart-lung machine. And while at first they disconnected her at 2 o'clock, the day of the surgery, they found when her start heart started to fail they had to hook her back up again, so she was back on the machine for again for another three or four hours. And so that made, like a total of about of about ten hours that she was on the machine and not simply not simply six. Okay. Time to pull in at home.

WEDNESDAY, NOVEMBER 28, 1990

Hello? Why is the light not on? Why is the power light not on? Hello. Good morning, Mr. Phelps. What is going on here? The power light is not on. Is this thing working or not? Let me stop and check.

Well, it's working. E e even though the power light is not on. And I don't understand that, but I can see the tape is turning and my voice was recording.

Good morning, Mr. Phelps, Captain Kirk, and Captain Picard. It's now 8:34 by the car clock on the morning of Wednesday, October [*sic*] the 28th. I have just gone through some slides of Sonny and Ellie and the kids, picked them out, now that's from January of 1988, I have finally gotten around to picking them out, to have prints made to send up to them. I also picked out slides of Rosie's and Wolf's and Mushe's gravestones to make prints for prints for Ronny and Nancy and maybe even for myself, I don't know. In any case, that's what I've done.

I'm I'm I am I am finally uh trying to get started telling people things by doing things like this. Okay, where was I?

Now last night, ye I went to see Aunt Esther, and I mentioned this and Joe came over, and and he went through his yellow sheet of questions, and I he he had, there were two questions which he said were Nancy Belle's and I'm not sure which ones they were. The basic point though was ... What? What?

Okay, two questions that he said were Nancy Belle's, but I'm not sure which ones they were. He said that R gave him about an hour and a half; he spent that, a good hour and a half. I mentioned that, I mentioned that he went into the ICU. Essentially, I mentioned about the wrong decisions thing, what R said about every decision seemed to be a wrong decision. Clearly there were no right decisions to be made. He did talk about how Nancy's heart muscle was so incredibly thickened from the extra work that it h'd had to do all of her life for 48 years, that so thickened that the ar the two ventricles were were narrowed down, the the volume of blood they were able to pump was reduced incredibly because of the space taken up by the by the by the expanded muscle. Just incredible.

And that the thing he felt that had kept, yes, I said this, about how he had othe seen other patients whose heart conditions were *less* severe than Nancy's and who had died. What had kept her alive was her incredible will and spirit. And that had no surgery been done, she would have died sooner rather than later. That it would have been likely that or possible either that she would have died suddenly and unexpectedly. For example, while Joe and she were watching TV, Joe might have gotten up to go to the bathroom, come back and found her dead. Or she might have slowly, not necessarily slowly, but over an extended period uuhh deteriorated just just become incredibly debilitated and bed-ridden. Sniff.

At one point Aunt Esther said, "If they hadn't done the surgery." And and of cour she kept referring to the hospital, the seventh floor, as "The Slaughterhouse." And I said, "It's not a slaughterhouse, they save more people than they lose." And she said, "But that's where they do all the surgery." I said, "Yes, but the surgery most of the time they're able to help people." Oh, and she said so *There's* Chili's with the with the ribs. Tha it's raining! It's drizzling. What is this?! It's not supposed to come until tomorrow! Or tonight.

Anyhow. That still have to check it a minute. Okay, it's working all right.

That Aunt Esther said, "Well, if they hadn't done the surgery." And then Joe got, y'know, he was, he got a little frustrated with her, that, What would she rather do? Sit at home and listen and wait for a phone call that said, Nancy couldn't go to work. Then a phone call that Nancy couldn't come to visit her. Then a phone call that Nancy was in bed. Then a phone call that that that she was dead. I mean, that's what it would have been. A sl Where did this car come from? Close up behind me. Oh, no, we're not gonna play this game. Okay. There's a bus stopped here in front of McDonald's, why's he stopped with his four-way blinkers on? I don't know. Oohh, son-of-a-gun! The rain the rain the rain. Anyhow.

And I mentioned to Joe about the, I think I talked about this. The Kennedy movie *Running Against Time*, that the guy who went back in time, trying to stop the assassination, no matter what they did, things simply got worse. And Joe asked about asked R also so that there was nothing that anybody could do, there are some things that simply happen, and and you can't do anything about them, as much as you try, they're beyond human control. For example, Aunt Esther at one point said that if S was alive, Nancy wouldn't've died, and I said, Aunt Esther, S is not God either. She doesn't want to accept it in many ways herself. When I talked to. Wait a second. The point was clear that all Joe's "if" questions. For example, if when when when R called him on Tuesday to say he was gonna disconnect her from the machine, incidentally, he also said the machine, this bi-ventricular pump, is relatively new, it's only been in use a year, a couple years. He did also say that what? There was the other thing I was gonna say.

What he said was when when R called him on Tuesday about disconnecting the machine, the ventricular pump, and Joe said did he, really think it was time, that maybe he he could wait one more day. And R said, Well, y'know in retrospect it is possible that one more day might have made a difference, but he really couldn't be sure about that and the thing that he was really concerned about was the possibility of brain damage. That this, this machine, that Nancy had been on now for nine days does not work as efficiently as the heart, is not as good as getting the oxygen to the brain *et cetera*, and there is some possibility of brain damage. And then he said that it was feared that while Nancy was very responsive the first two or three days after surgery, after that she was not so responsive, and he felt that eventually she was unconscious. Now he was not saying that she was brain dead, she was not brain dead, but that she was unconscious, and that that her she was not responding as well as she had been. And that there was potential for brain damage. And Joe said, to us at that point that he, that had the surgery been successful but had Nancy been revived and and found to have severe brain damage, as a result of being on *??garbled unclear??* that that would have been worse, that Nancy had spoken with Joe about the fact that two of Joe's aunts had had severe strokes and were severely debilitated mentally, just terrible. Their mental faculties were were terribly lost. And that Nancy had said that she never wanted to have to live like that, like in in effect like a vegetable. So that Joe felt that that had that happened, that would have been that would have been worse, to have Nancy living as a as a vegetable with with no mental awareness, no consciousness, no ability to function intellectually.

Incidentally, that reminds me that yesterday I got a call from G C, that the about the woman who had been found murdered in that school on Monday afternoon, that her daughter was a student at Coppin, and as a matter of fact was was G's student worker, and that not only did that happen, but that in, yesterday morning, on Tuesday, the girl's grandfather had died of Alzheimer's, and anyhow, G was asking if something could be done, and I said something about how, well, maybe I could draft a letter of sympathy from the president, and she said that's basically that's what she meant, that's what she would like to have seen. So we were able to help this student get in, talk G was able to talk to the instructors and work out for her to get an Incomplete so that she could at least stay in school and not not have to withdraw from school because all she could think about in her grief was that she had to withdraw. So we were able to stop that and and help her out. G basically did it, I made a couple phone calls. G made the rest. But that devastation of her mother was only 44 years old, to hear of her being murdered one day and then the next morning to hear of her grandfather dying of Alzheimer's was just absolutely incredible. Absolutely incredible.

Let's see. Joe also got on Aunt Esther as as did Mother about the fact that Aunt Esther simply does not pay enough attention to Ruth, that all she talks about is, is Nancy's gone. She sits there all day long, and all she can think about is Nancy and, and just as I kept telling her about how she has another daughter, just as that that very Orthodox Jew at the hospital reminded her that she had another daughter and that she has a family. Joe got very very upset and tried to get her to recognize that and to pay attention to Ruthie before she loses Ruthie, not to death, but to, just to, loses her for not paying attention to her. Anyway, I think that's about it.

Oh, he also, Joe also read two paragraphs from a letter that Nancy had left behind. It was dated October the 16th, which was the Tuesday before her surgery, but she had written it on the wordprocessor at work. And Joe said that at the funeral or at the house a couple people that she worked with came up to him and talked to him about how they had seen Nancy crying at her desk and they thought it was about the surgery but Joe now thinks that what it was is that she was crying as she was writing this letter. It's beautiful J Joe only had xeroxed the first paragraph and the last paragraph. The rest of it which had to do with instructions for what they should do for the kids. The letter was to Joe and Ruth and Dave. Interestingly, she put Weinstein in parenthesis after Dave's name. It was a beautiful letter. Very very loving. With some of Nancy's humor in it. And Joe read that he he he broke down and cried which is natural, is normal, I mean, his wife just died a month ago and here he's reading her her kind of her her her her her will letter sort of emotional will letter just beautiful. So I got a copy, and he he gave me a copy, he gave Mother a copy, and he gave Aunt Esther a copy. I want to type all these things in and and consolidate them and and do. Here we go past Royce Avenue. Hi, Aunt Freda. Aunt Freda and Royce Avenue. That reminds me that that at one point, I guess it was Saturday night after the funeral, coming back from the synagogue, from *kaddish*, talking about how the house was re would be referred to, and by her kids, and Ruthie said, pointed out that when Aunt Freda died, even though Uncle Aaron was still alive and the kids were still there, that we still referred to it as Aunt Freda's house, not Uncle Aaron's.

And here's another broken down bus apparently and cars trying to get around. Okay, we'll just pull over here, it's very simple.

SIDNEY KROME

That that we still refer to it always as Aunt Freda's house not Uncle Aaron's, and that probably, you know, her kids would continue to call it Aunt Nancy's house. And I said they probably would.

And what pops into my mind, last night also thinking about, about Joe and and his questions for R and that. And Joe was saying two things. Number one that thing that popped into my mind was that, that as I mentioned to Joe that Saturday night though we didn't get to finish the conversation, coming back from the synagogue, how in in *Zorba the Greek* Zorba asks the young Greek guy, Do all your books, can all your books tell you why people die? And he says, No. And and there is no answer why people die. And what I think what made me think of that was at that all of Joe's, as Joe kept trying to explain to us what the doctor had said, Aunt Esther kept saying, Why did God do this to me? Why did Go, and Joe said, He didn't do it to you, He did it to your daughter. Why did God do it to my daughter? Why did she have to die? Why did He take?

There goes Springhill Avenue. Down the street there to the right was there that seventeen or nineteen year old kid was shot last night and murdered. Two guys just broke into the house and blew him away, it's just incredible!

And and Aunt Esther would keep saying, Why this? And why that? But, and Joe said, I'm trying to tell you why, I'm trying to explain the the answer the questions I asked the doctor, and the answers he gave me. And you're not listening, you're not paying attention, you don't want to hear that. And uh what I didn't say, maybe I should've, but, I, just anyhow *[silence]* **TAPE ENDS**

THE NANCY TAPES

TAPE NUMBER 5B

WEDNESDAY, NOVEMBER 28, 1990 (CONT.)

Starting SIDE B, the light is still not on. But anyhow, as I was saying, what I should have said but I didn't, maybe I shouldn't have anyhow, but I didn't say it anyhow, is that anyway, short story, *Snows of Kilimanjaro*, the hunter, the gigolo, kept by this rich woman. Sniff. He is dying of gangrene, and she keeps in her boozy sentimentality, her her grief at this impending death, keeps saying, Why did this happen? Why did this happen? He says, Well, I suppose it's, obviously, it's because, y'know, when I went out, I wore shorts, went out hunting, I wore shorts instead of long pants. And that's when I got scratched. And she says, Oh, why did this happened? And he says, Well. That was just a momentary pause for a sneeze.

And she says again, Why did this happen? And he says, Because of the we didn't have the sulfa powder, and I couldn't disinfect it, and it's so infected. And she said, Oh, why did this happen? ts And he said, Well, because the truck couldn't get through, and this and that, and we couldn't transport me to the hospital. And here's this guy spinning wheels ahead of me. Sniff. Skidding. In other words, every time she asked for, but what she was asking for was the same thing that Aunt Esther was asking for, was the same thing that Zorba was asking for. Not the mechanical explanation of the biological breakdown that was, that caused death, but Why? Why do people die? What does it mean? Why? Why did God do this to me? as Aunt Esther said. That, but that's not, why does God? Why does it happen that people, why does it happen? That a 48-year-old woman like Nancy dies? *[voice cracking]* Well, she had a heart condition all her life that eventually killed her. But that's not sufficient for most people. It may be sufficient for someone like S who has talked about that's the reason that people die. But it's not sufficient for most people. They need a reason, they need an explanation.

And what else was I thinking of? There was another thing before.

Actually, I went back and listened to the other side and this side. There was no other thing. That was, that was the two things. The Kazantzakis *Zorba* and the Hemingway *Kilimanjaro*. But just as a reminder for me possibly for later. Something else that I have to talk about is the conversation with Ruthie last night, when I called Ruth, and about her letter to R, and my telling her about Joe and and that I thought it was a good thing that he had been to see R because now I th I said I think for Joe there are no more ifs. I think Joe now understands, that there was simply nothing else that could have been done to save Nancy's life. Nothing, else, nothing. There were no right decisions. There were no right decisions, for R to make. And the question of why doesn't satisfy most people, the answer of her heart condition.

THE NANCY TAPES

It doesn't satisfy me, never has. But for 36 years I have pretty much suppressed the question, or I let it out in strange ways. Anyhow. I have refused to really face it. Joe said you had to face it head on, he had to face it head on. That's why he had to go in to the ICU and see Nancy's bed and see where she lay for a week and see where she died. And that's funny, I remember smiling at the time and thinking, or smiling to myself and thinking, how much I had wanted to go back there, not so much to see that room that place where she died, as to sit in that lounge, that waiting area, where we all were for nine days. To see that, that place where love was.

Okay, I wanta talk about the also wanta talk about, I wanta take just a quick moment while I've got, although I don't have a lot of moments, but anyhow very quickly. When I went to see G yesterday afternoon, she talked about the terrible juxtaposition on the tv news, the night before, on Monday night, Monday evening, how they had talked about that student's mother, the one tha the housekeeper was found murdered, and they talked about it very very matter-of-factly, and then the next news story was about the whale, and they used the word, they spoke of that as a "tragedy," about the whale, but they did not speak of the murder of this woman as a tragedy. They spoke of it simply as, matter-of-factly, as another murder. That's what I said to G. You see, G, people are murdered every day in this city, but whales don't die every day, whales don't swim in or come into harbors, dead, or come into harbors and die.

Okay, I have to remember to talk about the conversation with Ruthie last night. Over and out. And, Soph's comment, was it afterwards? After I had talked to her? Or before? I think maybe it was right before, maybe it was right after. She was sitting at the diningroom table, and she started to cry, and I put my arms around her, and she said, she was so tired of so many deaths. And that she wanted things to be the way they used to be. Over and out. Phelps, Kirk, and Picard, where are you now that we need you? Now that *I* need you, at least.

Good morning, again, Mr. Phelps. Good morning again, Mr. Phelps. The power light, the red power light, is still off on this AVR hand-held microcassette recorder. Hello, again. Hello, again.

Okay. It's now forgot to reset the forgot to reset the the counter when I turned the tape over. It's now, what time is it now? It's now 10 I it's 10:54 according to the car clock, I left, leaving campus on my way up to up to up to up to going up to the Shutterbug out there at Chartley, to save some money by having copies made there. I guess it'll save some money al y'know but anyhow. Anyhow. It'll be cheaper there. So here I go, I'm on my way, round again, singing the song about Molly B.

Last night when I got home, and and after I had dinner, I was stuffed. I was stuffed. And Soph said something about, I've mentioned this, how she was tired of all this death, that she wanted things to be the way they were and, thinking of, the deaths this year. Last year was F F's father, but then was Mods and Mrs. Yalanis, and O's father, and Nancy, and now P's uncle is dying, his whole, all his all of his systems are breaking down. And as, aft contrary to Dylan Thomas, after the first death there is no other, theologically speaking, I suppose that's true, from a Christian point of view, theologically speaking after the death of Jesus there is no other because all are saved in Jesus, according to Christianity.

So last night also called Ruthie, and we had a nice talk, talking among other things about Joe's conversation with R. He he was supposed to see R on Friday, but then he went to the hospital, but R had two emergency surgeries to perform on newborns. Incredible newborns have to have heart surgery. Of course, then there are the surgeries that are performed on the fetuses in the womb. With any luck and good skill, and and his art as well as his science as a surgeon, those two newborns will live long and full lives, although I don't know what was wrong with them, what he had to do, but hopefully, they'll be all right.

And Ruth was saying that he was sup originally supposed to take Aunt Esther, but they missed their cues or something and anyhow, oh, Aunt Esther, because she came home last week instead of, she was supposed to spend the weekend there with Ruth, Thanksgiving weekend, but she didn't bring her clothes out, and when Ruth asked her why not, she said because Ruthie had told her that Ruthie was going out of town. Actually, Ruthie was not going out of town last weekend, she's going out of town this weekend, but Aunt Esther, either deliberately or unconsciously, confused things. So Joe and and Joe said he had wanted to pick Aunt Esther this time to go, and Ruthie told him that that he shouldn't do that. And he she said, You're gonna waste your time with with R, the time that you have you need the answers. She said, My mother will not pay any attention, she'll simply say the same thing, ask the same questions, that she asked every person who had a uniform while we were in the hospital: why? why? why? But her whys are not directed at information. And so it would be a waste of time to take her along.

And we talked about Joe's conversation, and she asked how I, how I saw Joe, and I said I think he's well. I said, He's grieving, he's crying, I said, but that's normal, I said, he he broke down a couple times while he was reading Nancy's letter, but I said, That's normal. I, you know, I said, it's he's not, I don't think he's, y'know, pathologically depressed, he's not, obsessed, I think he's a man who's grieving for his wife, and I said I think he's well. And he's going to be well. And and she asked what I thought about his conversation. She said that she thought that he really needed to see R. And I agreed with her. I said he really did need to see R. I said because now, he knows, that there are no more ifs to be talked about. And that really any of the ifs that he had or that Aunt Esther had or that anybody had, the ifs, could not have changed things. Nothing could have changed anything, given

Nancy's condition. And I said, And I think Joe now accepts that, he now sees that, that there was nothing that could have been done. A And he now sees that the situation is, as he had said, as Joe had said to me that Saturday when we got back from *shule*, that was the time for a miracle, that that nothing else, nothing human, could have saved Nancy's life. In effect that a a and in effect from the moment she was born with this, she was going to die from this, and she was going to die earlier than a normal life span. My mother said that that she knew when, when Nancy was born, that A and Doctorrr G, I think, who was the obstetrician who delivered her, both told her that they could not tell Aunt Esther the truth because Aunt Esther was hysterical and she couldn't accept or listen to or talk about the truth, that Nancy had major heart problems and that she would need a lot of special care as she grew up. That she would need a lot of special care as she grew up.

There was something else that just flitted through my mind, but I can't remember exactly what it was. Oh, Aunt Esther said frequently that Nancy should not have had the house with the two stories. And Joe talked about how when they used to go to the hospital *[something goes haywire with the speed; speeds up to be unintelligible for a time-maybe just completion of the previous sentence]*

Okay, I put in one new battery. It just happens that the batteries went, the batteries are dead. The batteries went dead. I put in one new battery I had in my pocket, but I can see it's really not working well. I'm gonna have to stop and get some more batteries.

And Joe said that when they--this is still with the one battery, one new battery, I have to get some more batteries--when they went up the this two stories in in the hospital, Nancy could not make it all the way up. And he would have to help her, push her, and they would go half-way up, to one half-way up one landing, to, after about one set of stairs, and she would have to stop and rest. Then another half-way up the rest of that landing and stop, and then another half and stop. And and Aunt Esther said that, y'know, she had always told her not to do two stories and Joe said, Maybe she shouldn't've done that. It may be that Nancy's desire to live, fully, and not to let herself be too severely limited by her heart condition, maybe that's what, maybe, that's what contributed to her death at this point, to making her heart so weakened that that there was nothing that anybody could do. Her her desire for life, her participation in life, maybe was what weakened her so much her heart so much, put so much stress on her heart, caused it to beat so hard, to pump so hard, caused the muscle to thicken so much. There's no way to tell, I mean, I don't know, the doctors don't know, but but that occurs to me now, that that might have been part of what it was, that had she permitted herself to live an invalided life, had she let the symptoms come out, and lived according to the symptoms, then maybe the symptoms would have come out sooner, maybe the surgery would have done sooner, maybe maybe maybe maybe. Ifs and maybes, ifs and maybes, Sidney, there are no more ifs and maybes. But that's a distinct maybe. That's an if or maybe.

And Ruth also talked about the letter that she wrote to R. Let me stop and check this. She sent him, the letter she read, it was a beautiful letter, I'm gonna have to ask her for a copy of it. She thanked for him for his skill, she thanked him for his compassion, and she said that they were grateful that Nancy's life was in the hands of such a a skilled and passionate, and compassionate and caring surgeon. And they wanted to thank him and all the doctors on his team and all the nurses on the ICU. And that this was the most intense time of her life, the eight, nine, or ten, nine days in ICU with Nancy, the most intense time of her life. When we talked, when she and I talked, I guess it, I don't know if it was about Darren or Allyson or even about herself or about Joe, she again mentioned how real this was, that this was reality. This was reality. And very intense reality. And she said that Thanksgiving Day, they had, Darren wrote another poem which she said was a beautiful poem, and Joe read another of open letter to Nancy. And Dave Dave gave some concluding remarks, and I said, it was, I thought that it was good they had some kind of a ceremony, a ritual, and she said that she felt that they needed, they couldn't simply go ahead, as though it were a normal Thanksgiving. But they didn't want to get into such depressed and gloomy and sad and grieving state, but they felt they had to acknowledge that this Thanksgiving was different from other Thanksgivings, from other Thanksgivings.

And incidentally also Aunt Esther has decided to go ahead and have her Chanukah party. At first she was not going to have it, but apparently, I don't remember who told me this, but maybe it was Ruth told me that my sister Nancy had said something to her about why she should go ahead. And so she, that's all the encouragement as Ruth said, that's all the provocation or actually all the encouragement that Aunt Esther needed, to go ahead with her Chanukah party was simply the fact that Nancy said that, and I told Ruth that I felt that, that going ahead with the Chanukah party was something that she should do, that Nancy would have wanted it to go ahead. And Ruth said that she felt exactly the same way, that that the party should go ahead.

At high volume this thing picks up all of all of the sounds outside, the rushing noise, it makes it very very di high volume of this machine and of the high speed of the car it picks up all of those noises. I'm trying it now at a much lower to see what happens. And the light's on now, I guess because of that, that no, it's fading out. It's that one good battery I put in with the bad one.

Anyhow, it's 11:42, I've just picked up the prints from the slides of the rainbows, and the houses on Springhill Avenue to pass on to Ruth for Amy to use, Craig's girlfriend, and the rainbows to be used by me perhaps as a donation to the hospital to that lounge, a rainbow, a rainbow, a rainbow with calligraphy underneath, not Dylan Thomas maybe but the line from Robert Frost, "Earth's the right place for life for love Earth's the right place, for love."

That's better now, Mr. Phelps and Captain Kirk and Captain Picard. Thank you very much for the new batteries.

Better also get out a new tape to carry around, because this one is over halfway down. The next one I'll have to use I think I'll use on the normal normal speed.

THURSDAY, NOVEMBER 29, 1990

Good morning, Mr. Phelps, Captain Kirk, Captain Picard. It's 8:22 by the car clock. It's Thursday, November the 29th, am. It is overcast, bit of drizzle has fallen on occasion, it's windy and turning colder.

What I wanted to say this morning was simply that this morning, this morning while I was out doing my walk on this morning, I heard the leaves blowing and scraping along the asphalt and the sidewalk, leaves rustling the trees, the leaves rustling among the leaves on the lawns, the leaves on the lawns rustling among the leaves on the lawns, among the leaves on the trees and the leaves on the street and the sidewalk, rustling and scraping, not just rustling but scraping along the sidewalk. And thinking of the line from *Waiting for Godot* about how people *ils sussurrent*, they murmur and they speak and they murmur, they rustle people rustle like leaves, like leaves they rustle like rustle, and thinking about that, I thought about the leaves blowing before the wind, scraping the blowing and rustling before the wind in the wind with the wind, and I thought in French, *ils sont ils tipauent ils sont des feuilles, ils sont des feuilles qui courent devant le vent* they are leaves, which run before the wind. And then *ils sont des feuilles qui dansent devant le vent* they are leaves which dance before the wind.

And they also made me think of A, JA, LN, LN, JA. Remember that time he talked about how, seeing the leaves rustle, the wind, leaves blowing across the street. We were in the car, *[sound fuzzy, blurry]* was it at Springhill and Cottage Avenue? Somehow that's what sticks in my mind, but I'm not sure that's exactly where we are, and he talked about that. And how he thought sometimes of writing something, writing a poem about the leaves, blowing in the wind, the leaves blowing on the street. *Ils dansent, ils courent, ils sont des, ils sont des feuilles qui courent, ils sont des feuilles qui dansent, devant le vent, devant le vent* before the wind before the wind *m'sieur. Devant le vent le vent devant.* Overrr and out. For now.

And it was Hermann Hesse who wrote, about his age, about our age, the 20th century, the 1920s, that it was a *"feuilletonistische Zeitalter,"* a a *feuilleton* being not the leaf but the leaf a page a leaf of a newspaper, that this was the depth of consideration given to serious matters, as they write in the newspaper article, like my OP-ED page pieces. Aren't they deep and philosophical? Whooeeww! All right! All right! Oh, well, *asha-i-viatsa! Asha-i viatsa! Viatsa asha-i!*

Hello again! Mr. Phelps, Captain Kirk, Captain Picard. *[sound very poor]* It's now 8:34, and I'm coming down Reisterstown Road towards Royce Avenue, Royce Avenue, Royce Avenue. And thinking also about what Ruthie said, did I mention this? I already mentioned this, in the car, on that Saturday after the funeral coming back from the synagogue, that they still, we always refer to Aunt Freda's house as Aunt Freda's house, even after Aunt Freda was no longer physically in the house, that is, after she had died. And that she expected that the kids would still refer to Nancy's house as Aunt Nancy's house.

Okay. So what else was I gonna say? Here we go passing Royce Avenue. And Aunt Freda's house. And there was something else I wanted to say. Not that. But Hmmm! There was something else I was going to say. And I have forgotten, *in toto*, what it was. So I'll just stop here at Park Heights, not Park Heights, at Reisterstown and Cold Spring Lane. I'm at McDonald's and the Payless Shoe Source and Barry's Video and this what used to be a gas station here, near Park Lane. And think about, what else it was? Something about Aunt Freda? Not just about the house being Aunt Freda's house.

Oh, yes! In December of nineteen hundred and fifty four, after Aunt Freda died, after the funeralll, sitting on the couch, and I think it was H K came to the door about going to schooooll, and then I sat there crying about having to go to school, not about having to go to school, crying about Aunt Freda's death, and and not really wanting feeling up to going to school. And Uncle Laybel was there. And my mother said to Uncle Laybel, something like--Oh, there's a dead cat in the road!--my mother said to Uncle Laybel, something like, *Zaisst.* And I I don't, I think it was, I don't remember if it was in Yiddish or in English, my feeling is more it was in in English rather than Yiddish. Do you see? Freda was not just an aunt like you say an aunt, Aunt Freda. She was, *[voice breaking]* she was Aunt Freda. *[crying]* She was Aunt Freda! And here's PS 59. PS 59 . PS 59. She was Aunt Freda! Oohhh, God! December, December, 1954. 36 years agooo. *[voice breaking]* And in October of 1954, it was 36 years agoo, that Uncle Sol died. It was 36 years ago in Julyyy, that my father died. It will be 36 years ago in just a couple weeks that Aunt Freda died. And it is, four weeks and two days since Nancy diiieed. Four weeks ago today was the funeral. Over and out. I guess.

Now in what's now Henry G. Parks, Jr. Circle, at the traffic light. Parks Sausage building to the right. Where Carlin's Park used to be. And to the left across the Circle where the old reservoir used to be, with the softball fields and Reptile House, and I read recently in an article about a tip teenager, nineteen-year-old or twenty-year-old, convicted of murder in the murder of a homosexual there, that that area around the Reptile House has become a hangout for homosexuals.

But thinking about winter, and how we used to come down, when it snooowed, and we would, we would, we would come down when it snowed, and we would sled ride down the slopes of the old reservoir, down the hill onto that road, there, which is now blocked off, and has been blocked off over for years, and the time Ronny came down and we thought, Oh, my God! here comes a car and for-tu-nate-ly, fort-u-nate-ly, he got across the street before the car got there. Hoooh! And then playing softball, after the reservoir was chopped off! and smooothed down. Have to get pictures of that. And on the other side, that field where we used to play football that is now overgrown with thistles and weeds and weeds and thistles and all kinds of stuff, and they're not supposed to mow it. They're not supposed to mow it, there was a sign there the last time I was there. There's an Eagle Talon like Niko got. There was a sign there that said something about not mowing, and I'll have to go take a picture there, and it's across the street from Three Sisters where als where also we used to play ball. And coming up now on Reisterstown and Liberty Heights, and around the corner a-round the corner where was was where MF, M, and his sister, D, and their brother B, where the Fs used to live. The Fs used to live, around the corner on Liberty Heights, and how we came down, and we played pitch and poker or pitch one day in the snow when there was no school. *[sound still blurred]* Haaaahhh And then we walked on up, walked on up Reisterstown Road, walked on up towards Park Circle, 'cause we didn't have a caaarr. Oh, my goodness, I remember that. I remember that weelll.

See, I'm doing just well enough to function. But I won't crack up. Noooeewww. Not I. I will maintain the control essential to an outward appearance of clarity and sanity, and understanding of the situation. When in reality, *[whispered]* I don't know anything. People think I'm sooo calm and think I'm sooo worldly wise and think I'm sooo intelligent and I'm just so solid and substantial. Weell?

FRIDAY, NOVEMBER 30, 1990

So, it's 8:05, in the morning. Mr. Phelps, Captain Kirk, Captain Picard. On the morning of Friday, November the 30th. A clear sunny day. When I was out walking this morning, it was clear and not yet sunny because the sun had not yet arisen. So here I am in the car driving down Reisterstown Road, drinking a cup of coffee out of a Mr. Goodwrench, one of those plastic car cups, and suddenly I've got something in my mouth. Well, I pull it out as soon as I can, and lo and behol-- incidentally, just passing within s sight of what used to be the Boxwood Motel, which is now simply just a vacant lot. Anyhow and I pull this piece of plastic out of my mouth, and when I finally do get a chance stopping at a traf light to traffic light to look at it, it turns out that it's from a Sunkist orange or a Sunkist grapefruit or a Sunkist something, one of those little plastic circular things, round plastic things that fits on a piece of fruit from Sunkist, and it must have gotten in there, I guess in the uh dishwasher, washing machine. Isn't that an interesting piece of something to add to your mission, Phelps? Wonka, Wonka!

Sarah Vaughan, *Unforgettable*, from W-Y-S-T, at 8:15 in the AM. And as we move on down Reisterstown Road, towards toward untoward toward Royce Avenue. Park Lane coming up shortly on the left. Shortly after we shortly after we shortly. Royce Avenue passing, Rrroyce Avenue right now! 3316 Royce Avenue Mohawk 4-2448. Aaand there's the sign, PARK AND SHOP/PARK LANE/FREE PARKING. Is that sign, what? More than 35 years old? 40 years old. Cold Spring Lane, down the street there was that guy, from the Penn-Rock Hotel in Penn-Mar, Maryland. Wackow!

Coming down now from Shirley Avenue. The Lower Park Heights Multipurpose Center. And here we are at PS 59, Louisa May Alcott School, crossing Keyworth Avenue nnaow! Go, Sulu! Here I am now on Springhill Avenue, here we are, at Springhill Avenuuue. Jake the Tailor. Jake the Tailor. Or.

Here at Liberty Heights and Reisterstown, actually I'm on Reisterstown and Liberty Heights. It's 8:21, and it's very curious, there's a police car with the lights flashing, now the lights are not flashing, there's a little red car behind it, a little red car, uh looks like it says Colt on it, license plate. There's a guy sitting in the car, light-skinned black guy with a beard, and another guy came outta the house. Black guy, also black guy w light skin, also with a beard. They just pulled around the corner and turned up turned up Reister Liberty Road Liberty Heights Avenue, what it is here now. And when I looked in the mirror, the the police car, the lights were not flashing, but he did have his four-way blinkers on. But I didn't see any officer in the police car at all.

SUNDAY, DECEMBER 2, 1990

Good morning, Mr. Phelps, Captain Kirk, and Captain Picard. Actually, it's, yes, it is still morning, 11:52 but, surprise, this is Sunday, aaaaannndd what else? Another surprise! I'm in a Ford Escort, not in a Beretta. Aaaanndd I'm not on my way to work, I'm on my way up to TOYS-R-US. Whoops! If I'm not careful, I'll be on my way to having an accident. TOYS-R-US. And then to Weis. And where am I going? I'm going to get Paul a com a Nintendo game for his pre-Christmas, and I'm going to Weis to get some napkins and some tisss-ues. And what I just finished doing for about the last hour and fifteen minutes is typing into the computerrr on a on Nancy's d the N Nancy d Nancy's Directory under Family under Skrome, What did I type in? I typed in Nancy's letter to Joe and Ruth and Dave. And I typed in Kathie's letter to Ruth, and Beth's card to Ruth, and the poem that Ronny sent. Maybe I need to work some of that because I think maybe I think I need to work some of that, I think I might might need to work some of that into the

the thing I did for the newsletter, for the family newsletter, for the family newsletter. To send to Amy for inclusion in the family newsletter. Over aanndd oooouuutt!

Actually, there was something else I wanted to mention in here, on this Sunday. It's now Sunday afternoon, I've just finished at at TOYS-R-UUUS. But there was something else I wanted to talk about, and I forgot all about talking about, till just now. And that is, that on the day of the funeral, when Joe and Allyson and Darren and Kim and Ken were standing there waiting for the rabbi to the rabbi was pinning, and Ruth and Aunt Esther, getting ready to pin on the black ribbons to be cut, the black ribbons, the official sign of mourning, of grief, of death, of mourning grief and death, death grief and mourning, Ron walked up behind Darren and put his hands on his shoulders and kind of leaned his head against Darren's back--What has gone wrong? What is with this car?--Leaned his head against Darren and, rubbed his back of his neck and his shoulders. Do you remember that? I remember that, now.

MONDAY, DECEMBER 3, 1990

"Up in Paradise up above, if you would tell me I'm the only one" It's Monday morning, December the 3rd, it's 7:58, chem, pardon me, it's 7:58. It's a rainy cold morning, December morning. And W-Y-S-T is playing *Sh-Boom! [very blurred]* Is there any wonder I listen to this station? "Sh-Boom, Sh-Boom, da-yadadada dada Sh-Boom Sh-Boom! Every time I look at you, something is on my mind, Sh-Boom Sh-Boom, If I could take you up to Paradise up above, Life could be a dream, Sweetheart, Sh-Boom Sh-Boom!"

Excuse me here, it's 8:08, just passed the Town House Motel here on Reisterstown Road. 32 years ago. August of, August? From 1958, when Ronny and Eva got married, that's where family from Montreal stayed. At the Town House Motel. *[voice cracking].* At the Town House Motel. At the Town House Motel *[on the very edge of crying].*

Okay, just passing where I think Maar Lesser's house used to be, just below the church here on Reisterstown Road, I don't even know the hundred block, what's the hundred block? 47-hundred block or so, 40 48-hundred block about. And moving down, moving down now toward toward toward Royce Avenue. Toward Royce Avenue. Moving down now toward Royce Avenue. And here we are passing Royce Avenue right nnaaoooww! Royce Avenue! Royce Avenue. That's the windshield wiper, that noise you hear in the background. And there's the PARK SHOP PARK LANE/FREE PARKING sign as we come up here on Cold Spring Lane. Get a job! Get a job! Get a job! How did I do that? Thinking about the fact that symbolic reference. The objective correlative. The *shivah* house, talking with Craig and he played soccer at Hopkins. And he played at Coppin twice I think he said, two or three times, at least twice, on our campus. And not only did I not go out to see our team play, which is as it is or whatever it might be, but I didn't realize that that they were playing Hopkins, I didn't realize that he was playing, I didn't realize that I could have gone out and seen Craig play soccer a couple times on our campus, I mean that's the kind of family contact, some people are able to keep up. I didn't keep up anything. Almost nothing. Last night, Riva and Al were over with my mother and Lou, over for dinner. Talking about Penny. Penny's in her second year, I think, of University of Pennsylvania, a three-year MFA program, and her significant other as they say, is Henry is at Arizona State, she'll probably be going down there when she gets done, but what do I know about her? Thinking about, ah just crossing just crossed Violet Avenue. I missed Springhill. Thinking about how in 1970 when we got back from from Greece, saw Barry and saw Penny, and she had had an exhibition up at up at up at Reisterstown Road Plaza, but she had a couple paintings in an exhibition there. I had talked to her, I said something about giving her one of the, one of my pictures of Sophie and asking her to paint a portrait of it, but I never did, of course. Never did a lot of things.

Some people are has-beens. I guess I'm just a never-was in a whole lot of ways. A never-was. Family-wise. Professionally-wiiise. Oh, I'm, I'm Executive Assistant to the President, but I'll never be a Vice President for Academic Affairs, I don't have the wherewithal to kill. Creative, my poetry, my novels. Unwritten. Barely started a few of them. What a waste. It was JAP, JAP who said it to me in the senior year at City when I'd asked him about writing a letter of reference for me. All that potential, never lived up to it. Watch this traffic here, coming through Henry G. Parks, Jr. Circle. Not Park Circle but Henry G. Parks, Jr. Circle. Whoops! Watch this traffic here, Sidney! In the rain. Watch. Except those meatballs! Including yourself.

Boy, it's raining a lot harder now! Aren't you glaaad you left your trenchcoat in the cleaneerrrs?! Whooaw! Smooooth move, Sidney!

DAY??, DECEMBER ??, 1990

Good Morning. Good Morning. Good morning, Mr. Phelps, Captain Kirk, Captain Picard. It is eight o'clock, or it was eight o'clock when I got in the car, it is now 8:01. It's pouring rain. It's pouring rain and cold, and where am I going? Okay. I'm on my way down to school. I'm still in the development right now though, I've been to get weighed this morning and came back picked up some tapes to take down to this conference, I think I'm gonna try to record a little bit while I'm, anyhow while I'm taking notes. And I was gonna go up to OM, Owings Mills Mall and catch the subway from there, but it's pouring so hard that I think what I'll do is I'll go down to drive down to Coppin, and and then drive up to Mondawmin Mall, and take the subway down to to where? take the subway down to to go to that conference. Sniff. In any case, here I am, in any case. What am I doing? Oh, yes, now, la this morning, I got up and did not run, I knew I wasn't gonna run 'cause the rain was so gonna be so bad, but what I did was, oh, man, I listened to the tape of the funeral service, of Nancy's funeral service. Rabbi Goren, I have to call him to get two things: the Hebrew the Psalm that he opened with, and the Psalm that is read when the pallbearers walk out with the coffin, with the body on that, the body in the coffin, on that that roller, take it out to the hearse. 'Cause I don't know what the Hebrew was, in both cases. And also in the middle was the *El Molay Rachamim*. All right, I'm gonna stop this now 'cause the light has changed, gettin' ready to go out on Reisterstown Road, here we go! Yo, Rinty!

What I realized what I realized what I realized while I was listening to the funeral service. What I realized was that there were two things that I had needed to transcribe, Darren's poem and the little thing from thing I don't know what to call it, the talk, Ruthie's thoughts that Dave read at the funeral service. I know it's part of the funeral service. I know both of them are, but I wanted to type both in separately, from the paper that each had given me. And I didn't do that so I have to do that as soon as I can. *[very blurred]* And maybe I need to talk with Ruth about maybe revising that piece, I I'm no I'm I'm not quite satisfied with it, maybe there's something I need to include from Ruth's not from Ruth's, from Kathie's and from Ruth's, and and from Darren's and from that, Beth's, Ruth's friend. I have to think about that. Don't rush it, I should not rush it. I need to make it what it needs to be. And do it soon.

Sunday evening, December the 2nd when Mother and Lou, Riva and Al were over for dinner, we had the radio on 92.3 92 STAR, and all of a sudden what came on was that song, *In The Living Years*. That song, that Nancy talked about, when we were driving up to uh to Montreal that time. Oh, dear! Incredible!

One of the things that occurred to me this morning, it occurred to me Sunday as I was typing in Nancy's letter and occurred to me again this morning as I was listening to the rabbi's sermon, the same thing had occurred to me last December, at the 50th birthday party, Ruthie's 50th birthday party. Thinking about how the the the kids, thinking about how Nancy's kids said to Ruthie that what they appreciated was her unconditional, unconditional love, unconditional, non-judgemental unjudgemental I think was the word, unconditional, love and commitment that she had shown to them. And thinking about this also with at the Nancy's letter and the funeral service, at, in terms of Ruthie's kids towards Nancy, their aunt. She their aunt, they her nieces and nephews. And how close they were and how much she had given to them also. And thinking about the line that in the rabbi's sermon about how, y'know Joel came along, Mindy's boyfriend, in time to to partake of Nancy's love.

SIDNEY KROME

I think about how I know nothing about Cheryl, or even really about Scot, or Chuck or Jon or Amy. Wonder what contact do I have, with my brother's kids, with my sister's kids. What contact do I have with my brother or my sister? Yesterday, we received I received the the lapboard computer that Ron sent down, he had said that he would, when he that he'd be getting a new one, and that he would send it down with Jon some time when Jon came up and, but instead, he Whoa! Whoa! Whoa! Whoa! Whoa! Car a car in front of me skidded in the wet. As this guy down on the sidewalk flagged somebody down and the guy stopped unexpectedly. And instead of waiting for Jon, he D had it had D, the aide who takes care of Amy, take it down, and they packed it up a and take it down to a ship-out place, they packed it up, and sent it out and I received it yesterday.

Thinking also about the line in Nancy's letter, how she wished that she were a millionaire so that she could leave behind something that was really of value of hers for the kids. She left behind something that's of far greater value, herself, her love. That Darren was able to write that kind of a poem is just incredible. He doesn't realize, I tried to tell him, he doesn't realize, how strong is his life force, his desire for life, how strong is his inner strength. But isn't that the way it always is, that people don't realize? And that there's always an up and a down, always going from depths to heights, heights. Maybe it's out of his torment that his strength grows. Would that I could have written a poem like that for my father, then? But it was years before I could. Years and years. *[whispered]*. And years.

Coming down Reisterstown Road now toward just crossed Northern Parkway, did that exist? *In illo timpo? Ston kairo ekino? Se afta ta chronia?* In those days? Anyhow, now here's Rogers Avenue. And there's a beer, wine, liquor, numbers game store on the corner where Weiner's Pharmacy used to be. In the background, Elvis Presley *Blue Christmas,* and to the r to the right there little bit to the right on the other corner, what used to be the Hilltop Diner. I never really hung that much at the Diner, now Brice's Lounge Brice's Hilltop, but to the left, the old what used to be the Crest Theatre and Sid Mandell's, where we used to go on Friday nights and Saturday nights sometimes. Crest Theatre's now the Stardom. Stardom. Old Crest Theatre, Friday nights I used to take the bus up Reisterstown Road when there was a movie I wanted to see, and I remember Ruth said to me something about how, I was just independent. I was just independent. *[very loud and like crying]* Ho-ho-ho-ho-ho-ho-ho-ho-ho!! Oh, my goodness gracious sakes alive!

Coming down now to Reisterstown and Belvedere. Sniff. And on the left corner, I guess that would be the northeast corner is now a place called the Tax Corner. At what used to be upstairs was at Benny's Benny's Poolroom. I only went there a few times, I didn't really hang there the way other guys did like K and a bunch of others, a whole bunch of guys, I mean, a lot of people, hung there at Benny's and over on Liberty Heights at Knocko's. At Knocko's they used to have a guy called J. I think J was at Knocko's, or was J at Benny's? I can't remember. J was I guess a black kid who worked there, a black guy, I don't know how old he was. Reminds me of M who used to work at the what was Burke's grocery store and then it became Schwartz's, the alley store on Springhill Avenue in the alley, under under that corner house. Sniff. M. Sometimes on Saturday evenings he would, after work he'd kind of play with us guys, and I remember one night we were out there wrestling around, horsing around, and he said he wanted to wrestle, he said he wanted to Jane Wrestle. And we thought that was so funny.

The Magic Touch on the radio and just crossed Royce Avenue. Do-do-do PARK AND SHOP/PARK LANE, PARK & SHOP, across the top the ampersand sign white letters on blue background and in the center PARK LANE yellow letters on a red background horizontal then below that also horizontal FREE PARKING white letters on a blue background.

Again, just passed Keyworth Avenue and PS 59. PO's house to the right. Where was DR's house? Coming up here on Springhill Avenue, all these cops out on the corner, I wonder what's goin' on? Oh, my goodness! Two cop cars and cops out there. Wonder what's happening. At Springhill Avenue where that was murdered the other night.

THURSDAY?, DECEMBER 6?, 1990

Good morning, Mr. Phelps. It's 7:43 am according to the clock radio the car clock. I'm sitting out here in front of the response machine, here Mr. Phelps, Captain Kirk, and Captain Picard. Pardon me, gentlemen. No offense intended. Sitting out here in front of the, anyhow I just. Anyhow, last night we went to the f Hubbard Funeral Home, C and L, C's father had died, RM, and while we were there, it's been a bad year. And while we were there, some woman started talking to Sophie, apparently she's somehow related to the M family or somehow there. And Sophie said, Did you hear what she said? And I said, No, what did she say? Did you hear how she put it? I said, No, I didn't. What did she say? And she said, *O Thanatos inei poli pikros.* Death is very bitter. No matter how old or how young. *[last whispered]* C's father was about 80, but the onset of illness was very very sudden. And his whole bodily system failed, just deteriorated incredibly rapidly, and and he was gone.

Anyhow I spoke with Joe and Dave last night and they both said they had they had read the piece. Joe said he thought it was very good, he had a few corrections, few additions, though mostly he said typographical, and Dave said that he thought it was beautiful but Ruth also had a coupla corrections. And I said, Well, fine, I'll just get them on Saturday, and I'll send the disk out to Mindy [*sic*] as soon as possible.

SIDNEY KROME

Okay, I'm gonna cut this now, I'm heading for the credit union in Towson first and then down to school. Bye-bye.

Yesterday afternoon, at the close of the small group session, I went up over and talked to AS. I wanted to talk to her about the piece on Sam Jones, I did talk to her about the piece on Sam Jones, I want to send her and T a copy, because of the Michelangelo story that T talld tall told about the kid who watched Michelangelo sculpt the David, and Michelangelo asked him how would he, how, what he thought of it, the kid said it was beautiful but then he said, How did you know it was i he was in there? And, of course, that's what Michelangelo always said, that he simply helped bring out what was already in the marble, that he could already, he could visualize it just by looking at it. And I said to A I said something about Sam being someone who teaches English in our department, and I said, It's incredible *[voice soft]* after five years, I still talk in the present tense about him sometimes. It's still Aunt Nancy's house, it's still Aunt Freda's house. On Royce Avenue 3316 Mohawk 4-2448. Mohawk 4-24448 2448. 3316 Rooce, Royce Avenue. And I'm outta here!

Hiya, guys, whaddaya say? Graves, Phelps, Picard. It's 4:18 P.m., Thursday, December the 6th, just passed the old *shule* and where Lozinsky's used to be. Comin' up now on Robinson's Variety Store which used to be Sussman's, I already passed Roland's Barber Shop, coming up now on Violet Avenue, the corner *de la coin de la rue*, where Kessler's used to be, and now where Trenton Democratic Club used to be and across the street there on Park Heights that other side of Park Heights where Fs used to live and there the G and P and RG and up there Springhill Avenue just passed Springhill Avenue. And s **TAPE ENDS**

THE NANCY TAPES

TAPE NUMBER 6A

THURSDAY, DECEMBER 6, 1990

Good afternoon, gentlemen. It's now 4:20. This is a new tape. I'm gonna try this new tape on the normal speed to see whether the quality of reproduction is or is not significantly better. I did find by using the GE minicassette recorder at the conference that it really did a pretty good job. It really did. Actually, it did a very good job as a matter of fact. And the quality of the recording on this normal speed is really fine, really outstanding quality.

Anyhow, what it is is I'm on my way up to the JCC; I agreed to serve at least a little bit on their film committee. Okay, over and out. Watch out! Park Heights and Belved, just passing, already passed the Uptown Theatre and just now passed Belvedere. Oh, I just passed what used to be the old Pimlico movie theatre.

It's 5:23 now, I'm on my way home. Up Park Heights Avenue, coming up here where the Beltway Exit is, Beltway entrance and exit are. And I just saw the flickering light of an airplane, and it reminded me that this morning while I was on my walk-jog, I saw a bright blue-white star, not just twinkling but actually flickering brightly even behind a cloud. Just very very str it was kind of in the northwest, west northwest corner side of the sky.

FRIDAY, DECEMBER 7, 1990

Gentlemen, good morning again. It is Friday, December the 7th, Pearl Harbor Day. It's now 7:06 in the Escort clock. Bill Docket's, Bill Doggett's I think it is, *For Forty Miles of Bad Road* playing in the background. And to the east southeast or south southeast or east eastsouth or something like that, there are layers of lavender and mauve and beautiful, the sun is behind the clouds, but the color is flaring through beautifully. When I was out walking this morning, there was an enormous halo around the moon. And around the halo and in the center was the half or quarter moon, I guess. With the points, they were not yet points 'cause it was halved really, facing east or north or right, right, and to the north side of the sky of the moon inside the halo was a bright white planet still inside the halo which was enormous. It was a little over halfway through the halo, over halfway through. Over and out.

Sky colors pasteling out, actually, I was gonna say slowly but rapidly. It's now 7:11, they're very faded and faint now, very faded.

On Reisterstown Road crossing Menlo Drive, Menlo Drive on the other side of Park Heights where M lived. And coming up on the Town House Motor Hotel. 1958. Ronny and Eva Marriage. Whacka-whacka!

Remember Beryl, remember sitting around the pool, remember remember remember!

THE NANCY TAPES

SATURDAY, DECEMBER 8, 1990

Good afternoon, Mr. Phelps, Captain Kirk, Captain Picard. Surprise, surprise. It's Saturday, December the 8th, it's 12:36 p.m.. I'm on my way back to EVT to pick up Paul from the basketball tournament of the GOYA. And I've been thinking about whether I put something down.

Yesterday evening I typed into the computer, the wordprocessor, Ruth's words, some thoughts from Ruth that Dave read out the day of the funeral. I know it's part of the funeral tape, but I wanted to type it in separately, and I typed in Darren's poem. And I typed in Ruth's letter, not Ruth's letter, Ruth's card, the card that Ruth wrote to us, received December, November the 20th, when she sent a copy of Kathie's letter and Beth's card, and the poem that Ronny sent down, the American the Native American poem. And her lines in there about how important it was for her to have us to commiserate with her, to laugh with her, to be with her, to lean on, for her to lean on. I'm not sure exactly how that was directed, other than that I know that on Monday, October the 22nd, when the news began to go bad, when things turned around, when the weather turned around, and Ruth, we knew that that things were not going so well for Nancy, we first heard. Ruth was saying that at at one point, people walked out, and and I was there with her, Dave and Sophie, and she said something about how she couldn't even be sad.

The problem was, of course, that everybody was looking to her for strength, Aunt Esther, everybody, and and she could not allow herself to to cry like she did. Everybody else went out, was out of the lounge for a little bit, and Sophie sat with her, and I kind of, I remember I stood at the door trying to shield them. And she cried sitting with Sophie, and I said to Sophie later it was good that Sophie was there because I'm sure that Ruth probably felt that she could not could not let go at that point, that she needed to be the one to be strong even with everything going on. And it was good for her to have Sophie there to cry with, to cry to.

12:40 on the Beltway. All of a sudden I started thinking about WCBM radio, AM radio, 'cause I had 1010 on, WYST. And WCBM, 680 on your dial, was the station I used to listen to in the 8th, 9th grade, when I was at Robert E. Lee PS 49, Robert E. Lee Junior High School. Che-che. AG. That was the station that we all used to call in our dedications on on Saturday afternoon, and I used to stand around on the porch, hang around on the porch, and listen to WCBM and all the dedications.

SUNDAY, DECEMBER 9, 1990

Good morning, Mr. Phelps, Captain Kirk, Captain Picard. It's 10:10 on Sunday, December the 9th. I have to go out pick up Charlie. And all of a sudden on the radio, WQSR 105.7, came Acker Bilk. Y' hear this song? I can't remember what year it was popular, and I can't remember the title, I'm sure they'll give it.

Sniff. But it made me cry. All the years, made me think of all the years that I've been detaching myself and have detached myself from the family. Sniff. Oh, my Lordy. Acker Bilk. "Big number one hit for Mr. Acker Bilk, *Stranger on the Shore*." *Stranger on the Shore*. Didn't say what year. *Stranger on the Shore*. Acker Bilk, *Stranger on the Shore.* Yes, that was a good one, I rememb that title is a good one too for that song and for how I feel right now, I'm a stranger on the shore of the family.

And thinking about how I said last night to Joe, and then at the table, Soph talked about or raised her glass of wine how she would miss Nancy and miss her mother. Sniff. And I said at the table as I had said to Joe earlier, it should have been four there not the three. That we were missing Nancy. And Ruth started to cry a little bit as did Joe. And then later I thought, at night I thought, in bed I thought, or was it this? in bed going to sleep. That actually, I could not think of the last time, if ever, how long it had been, if ever, since we had invited Nancy and Joe and Ruth and Dave over for dinner just to have dinner and sit and visit. If ever we had done that. And that probably had Nancy not died, we would not even have Joe and Ruth and Dave over at this point. Sniff. We would not have them over. And I thought also last night, Ruth talked about, I mentioned to Ruth about Craig playing soccer for Hopkins and how they played Coppin a couple times. And she said, Oh, yeah, she said, she and Dave came over one time for the game, and couple of Coppin's African players got real angry with the ref, and he red-carded one of them which meant not only was the kid out of the game but he couldn't play in the next game. Sniff. And they had to call the police because they were threatening the ref. And I thought to myself, how sad that our relationship was such, as I've said before, that I didn't know that Craig was coming to Coppin to play soccer for Hopkins against Coppin or I'd've gone out. Sniff.

And not only was it that point, but they didn't call, Hey, Sid, we're coming over to campus, Craig's playing, why don't you come by? I don't remember if I've said this before, I don't think I have. But I don't remember, I don't think they invited me or Soph to say anything on the tape they made for Ruth's 50th birthday last year. I know I wasn't on it. I don't remember if they invited me and I couldn't make it or or what. But I didn't participate. And that made me so sad at the time. And it still makes me so sad. That the relationship was so awful, so non-existent, I was such a stranger on the shore. That I didn't even participate in Ruth's 50th Birthday Tape. Either because they didn't ask me or I didn't accept or whatever the reason, I don't think they asked me even. They asked my mother. Sally Krome Levin. Sniff. Who proceeded to talk not about Ruthie, but how when I was a kid I found rubbers and played with them and filled them with water and used them as balloons or something. What the hell did that have to do with Ruth's birthday??!! Not a thing. Not a thing.

THE NANCY TAPES

MONDAY, DECEMBER 10, 1990

Good morning, gentlemen. It's 8:05, Monday, December the 10th. Mr. Phelps, Captain Kirk, Captain Picard, it will be your ongoing mission to explore new worlds, to make order out of chaos. Regardless of the worlds or the chaos or the nature of the order or the chaos, actually, that you meet or see or come across. But your methods, your methods, your methods, the means do not justify the ends. Einstein would not sell his soul for the Unified Field Equation in that teevee play, *Mr. Einstein for Lunch.* Because he knew, because he knew, because it's the challange, the schallange, as Inspector Clouseau would say. It's the schallange that makes life, not the surrender of the schallange for the end itself. But in any case, as I was saying. Where was I? You were asking us all why you wanted us to be here. Yes, Inspector Clouseau, in any case, I have to add you, Inspector Clouseau, to my Mission Team in the morning and any time of the day when I give a mission to my Mission Team.

In any case, the tapes originally, well, actually, the tapes originally started as notes and then they became the Nancy Tapes. Now I guess they're gonna become simply The Tapes again because I can't keep switching tapes and tapes. So, a multitude of things will then go into the tapes as they, as was my wont before. Sniff.

I had to call Ruthie yesterday about another change in the thing about Nancy because I noticed Saturday night that when she gave the list of additional things to go in, that she listed all the kids' names but she left out Ken Kim and I didn't know whether she wanted that left out or what. So I called, and she said that actually Ken wasn't there that much, she what she had forgotten about Kim, but she said I should go ahead and put them in. Che! So I did. And I have to get that off to Amy today.

In any case, did I talk about Saturday? I think I did. I think I did, talk about Ruth and Joe and Dave, Ruth and Dave and Joe being over.

But also at this point, and I need to say something about something else. Oh, right, yesterday. Yesterday was, we went for our tree and we did things differently this year. That's gonna be maybe the first line of the poem, "We did things differently this year."

But now back to the Nancy Tapes cut. Now. Okay, now why were things different? Things were different also because this is the first year really that *Giagia*, Mods, is gone. Sniff. The first year in Christmas preparation that Soph's mother is gone, my mother-in-law is gone, that the boys' *Giagia* is gone.

But thinking also now, also something reminded me, oh, yes, I thought something yesterday I guess, or or maybe it was Friday, I don't remember which day, or Saturday. About Nancy's dying. Sniff. Switching gears here, gentlemen. Are you gentlemen aware of more information here coming up. Thinking of of what? Of what was I thinking of? I was thinking of what? Whoops! Watch out for this bus stopped here. Thinking of. In her own way, Aunt Esther was right. With her expectations of doom. On that Monday of Nancy's surgery, when everybody was waiting for Dr. R to come down to explain what had happened. And she insisted, she said, Nancy is dead, why are you hiding it from me? And I remember I said at the time--sniff sniff--to Dave and to Ruth, that that was the way they were, they always hid death from us, and so she expected that if we were hiding something from her, we were trying to keep her from seeing the doctor, what it meant that we were really hiding from her was that Nancy was dead. Hup! Here we come onto Royce Avenue. Good morning, Royce Avenue, 3316, Aunt Freda's house. Sniff. And that she expected that we were hiding from her, what we were hiding from her was that was that Nancy was dead. And actually her anticipation of doom, her expectation of doom, was more on the mark than anybody else's expectation or hope even. Hope cannot always give life or sustain life. It can't do that.

As we were talking at the dinner table on Saturday. Che-he-heeeeh! Sniff. Talking about how--sniff sniff--the mind-body connection, and how the will to live and the the expectation to live and how this just--sniff--in Nancy's case it couldn't work. And I said, y'know, as Joe and I had talked about, sometimes the physical the body is so far gone that the mind that the will the spirit cannot help it, cannot make it live.

Oh, look at PS 59, they've finished some of the landscaping around the front, and they've got some grass--Che-che-heeeehhhh! Pardon me.--and sidewalks--sniff--around it. Che-heh-cheh-heh!

Talking about Norman Cousins. Sniff. Soph talked about how he had, when he had that debilitative degenerative disease, set himself his own prescription in conjunction with his doctor. Watched Laurel and Hardy and Charlie Chaplin and all kinds of comedies to make himself laugh on a regular basis because he felt that laughter, laughter had a healing effect, laughter stimulated-- sniff--certain maybe certain chemicals within the body or whatever to help to help the healing process. It made me think, of course, also about the thing in *Readers' Digest*, "Laughter, the Best Medicine." But also he died recently.

And it made me think very cynically of the line from the old crime or mystery stories, "Laugh yer way outta this one, Buddy!" But he couldn't laugh himself outta that one. There comes a time, as with Nancy, and this is important, that all the hope and all the faith and all the power of positive thinking, as they say, can't do anything! Sniff. There comes a time when there is only the miracle. And as Ruth said, and as she and I discussed, talked about on Saturday, maybe the mir, she had said it at the hospital or she had said it after Nancy died, maybe the real miracle was that Nancy was able to keep herself alive for 13 years after her second heart surgery. That when they examined her and tested her, they had expected her this past year,

89 to 90, they expected her to be showing more severe debilitated symptoms, but she showed none! I mean they, chemical symptoms, the heart symptoms were negative. But in terms of how she acted and how she lived, there were no negative symptoms, she was a-symptomatic. She would not let herself live a life of death and doom. She lived a life of life. And that's the, maybe that's the miracle, that she was able, that she lived for 13 years after that last surgery.

TUESDAY, DECEMBER 11, 1990

Good morning, Che-heh! Pardon me. Mr. Phelps, Captain Kirk, Captain Picard. It's 9:24 on Monday, no Tuesday, December the 11th. Tuesday, December the 11th. I'm on my way down Reisterstown Road and guess what just came on the radio? Listen to this one. Add this to the information. "Oooh, yeah, Gonna find her, Because I knooooow she loves me so. I knooooww she loves me sooo. So fine, so fine, so fine yeah" Carry on your mission, gentlemen.

So fine Now, we are coming down Reisterstown Road, approaching Royce Avenue. Lucille Avenue. Woodland Avenue. "She loves me soooo. Doodle doo doodle doo Well I knooooow." Bleeb-bleeup. 'Cause my baby tells me sooooo" Soo-woo-woo so fine. St. Ambrooose. And *??umatilo? a new martillo??* on the right. And here we goooo Rrroyce Avenue, December, December the 9th. Was it December the 9th? Or December the 10th? *So fine* Hmmm! I can't even remember the exact date that Aunt Freda died. But I do remember Royce Avenue, 3316 Royce Avenue, Mohawk 4-2448. "Gonna find her" So fine.

Just passed Boarman Avenue on the right. Mac's *C'Est Bon* Cafe which used to be the Boarman for pizzaaahh many many many many many many many many many many years ago.

The newly beautified PS 59 on the left with its all nice new landscaping. "If you don't know me by now, you will never never never really"

One of those cherry-pickers holding somebody up. Good grief! One of those cherry-pickers holding somebody up. And the guy in the second floor window washing the windows inside PS 59. Crossing Springhill Avenuuue!

Ruth was delighted to get those pictures of Springhill Avenue that I gave her. 8 by 12s and some 5 by 7s. I was touched by how touched she was. Touched by how touched. Stopped for the school bus.

How's this one??!! *Petit Fleur* Graves, not Graves, Phelps, Kirk, and Picard. *Petit Fleur*!! Remember walking into the Lola Montez in Munich. Back in Aught-61. And this guy looking up as I, was it Ed and I walked in? And he said, Kasavubu! Lumumba! The time of the Congo! Crisis. Kasavubu! The Lola Montez and *Petit Fleur*. Lumumba! Fade out and end.

SIDNEY KROME

WEDNESDAY, DECEMBER 12, 1990

Good morning, Gentlemen. Mr. Phelps, Captain Kirk, Captain Picard. It's now 8:07 am on the Escort clock. Heading down Reisterstown Road towards Royce Avenue. And I just heard on the radio, and this is something you really must add. Ray Charles singing, *I Can't Stop Loving You*. Something something something, "So I'll just live my life on dreams of yesterday." On dreams of yesterday. Cheeeehhhh! Sometimes, sometimes it's tough here, man, I wanta tell you somepin, this is not Krome's last tape. Sniff. It may be last tapes, plural, but it's not. That song on the radio yesterday, was it either on the way to or coming back from-- Here's Royce Avenue, Ladies and Gentlemen! Royce Avenue, 3316, Mohawk 4-2448. Aunt Freda's house, as Ruthie said.

Listening on the radio either taking Paul to WMIX or coming back from WMIX where he did his interview with the DJ the song, the song "Gimme the beat, Boy to Heal My Soul Wanta get lost in your rock and roll. Wanta get lost in your rock and roll to ease some of the ease my soul." That's it, that's it, that's it, get lost in your rock and roll! Ease my soul! Fade out! Fade out! And disappear! Oh, that this too too solid flesh would melt, thaw, and resolve itself into a dew! A dew! A dieu, kind hearts, a dieu! Say a dieu! Remember me! Che-heh! Pardon me while I wheeze in my coffee here. Somebody's stuff being evicted out there on the street in the gutter. Their furniture.

Ten minutes past eight o'clock, and now here we are down at Keyworth Avenue, at PS 59, guy out there fixing or cleaning the windows. Yes, they're cleaning the windows, spraying them. Sniff. And there's some grass now and trees.

Coming down here on Rockrose, just passed Rockrose, and here's Ulman Avenue. Ulman Avenue. Ulman Avenue. And what's that next one? That's it Norfolk, Norfolk Avenue. He doesn't drink, smoke, nor folk. And what is this one? Hilldale, the one that led down to the old one that led down to no, Suffolk? The one that Che-heh! led down to Carlin's pool, I think it was Hilldale. Or was it this one, Suffolk? Where there was a drugstore on the corner. Remember that drugstore on the corner? I remember that drugstore on the corner! Walking back from Carlin's pool. Yup, used to get some stuff there. Can't remember the name of it, but I remember it.

"Gimme the beat, boy, to ease my soul, gonna get lost in your rock and roll!" "I can't stop lovin' you." Whoops! Stop at the reyed light here in the new Henry G. Parks, Jr., Circle, not Park Circle, but Henry G. Parks, Jr., Circle.

FRIDAY, DECEMBER 14, 1990

All right, it's, geez, what time is it?! 2:59, Friday, December the 14th, 1990. Captain, Mr. Phelps, Captain Kirk, Captain Picard. Just passed 4216 Liberty Heights Avenue. The home of former home of MLL. Remembering standing out

THE NANCY TAPES

on the street on Liberty Heights, not Liberty Road Liberty Heights, after playing basketball one night and wearing my, must have been while I was a freshman or sophomore in college 'cause I had that black hat, a black cowboy hat, and that M-1 Deck Jacket, Navy N-1 Deck Ja M or N 1 Deck Jacket, N-1. And it was snowing, and I was out here trying to hitch a ride, and some guy stopped and gave me a ride. And when he finally stopped and I got in, and he said to me, "Sorry, buddy, don't mean to offend you, but at first I thought you was a nigger." Never forget that. Never forget that. Good Lord! Here's everybody stopped in the middle of the intersection of Liberty Heights and Garrison. Well, I'll wait and get around here. Oh, there we go.

How's this for a couple names for a couple characters? Ian I-a-n **TAPE ENDS**

TAPE NUMBER 6B

FRIDAY, DECEMBER 14, 1990
Raight. Raight, Phelps, Kirk, and Picard. That where continue before I was so rudely interrupted. It's now 5:12, before when I came to the end of my tether at least the end of my tape. Names of two characters for novellas or novels or works of fiction if ever I write ever anything again. One, Mr. Ian Naow, I-a-n N-a-o-w, Ian Naow! From the play of Shakespeare by the same name. The other Perry P-e-r-r-y Neam! N-e-a-m Perry Ne-am Ne-am. Because you know why! 'Cause that's what he called himself. Got that?! Got it!

Of course, the day is still Friday, December the 14th. Yesss! Still the same day! I wouldn't kid you guys.

MONDAY, DECEMBER 17, 1990
Che-heh! Pardon me. Good morning, Mr. Phelps, Captain Kirk, Captain Picard. It's now 8:10. Sniff. According to the car clock in the Beretta. Monday, December the 17th. I'm on my way down Reisterstown Road to go to work this morning.

And I just was thinking about Aunt Esther's Chanukah party yesterday at which Nancy wasn't. I mean, maybe she was, but if she was, she was there in spirit. She was not there in the flesh. At which Nancy wasn't. Sniff. At which Nancy wasn't! And I've been crying this morning. We were looking at the pictures I had given to Ruthie of Springhill Avenue. And at one point Jerry asked if he could have a copy of the picture of 2614 and 2616, and he said he would. I asked him, Well, what about Royce Avenue? He said, Well, yeah, that ok, but he really wanted Springhill Avenue 'cause he had spent more time there. Oh dear, oh dear, oh dear.

And there were some pictures of me that Ruthie looked at. One of me in that M-1 Deck Jacket with the black hat. Sniff. The black cowboy hat. And Ruthie saying, This is the Sid that I knew. This is the Sid that I knew! And where is the Sid that *I* knew?! And a couple pictures at College Park by the back door of Calvert Hall. One, actually one, I don't know whether it was the back door, but one in my R-O-T-C uniform and one in a pair of--sniff---a pair of Bermudas and one of those shirts that I got at Waynesboro, P-A, at the--Che-heh!--in that summer that A and H K, G M, and I worked at the Penn-Rock Hotel in Penn-Mar, Maryland. And I had my R-O-T-C ribbon pinned to my fly. Sniff. And showed it to Ruth and Soph, and I said something about having that award pin someplace, R-O-T-C award pin someplace, I've seen it, and Dave Weinstein looked at it and he laughed. At that point that's when they realized where it was, and I think it was Ruth or Soph, I think it was Ruth who said something about my being a rebel even then. Sniff. Oh, God!

And thinking about making copies of the 2614-2616 picture. Sniff. To give to, Nancy said she wasn't sure and then finally she said, Okay, one for Nancy, one

THE NANCY TAPES

for Jerry, one for Ronny, one for me, and gonna have some 8 by 12s made and have them mounted, I think I'll have them mounted. I don't know where I'll display them, but I think I'll have them mounted. Sniff. And then what? And then what?

I think about all the places that I want to take pictures of the old neighborhood. And I said something about the *B'Nai Reuven* not being there any more, the *B'Nai Reuven* not being there any more, it was just a field, and somebody said, Did you drive by? And I said, Of course. And Phil Weinstein saying that he knew my father when they were kids, I mean, little kids, and that they used to deliver newspapers together, and I never knew that, I never knew that! I never knew he knew my father then. Sniff.

And because of the question of whether or not there are pillars or columns holding up the roof at our house in the middle, right on either side of the stairs. Sniff. The steps right there by the, where you go up and down to the porch. Nancy went upstairs to look for pictures, to look for pictures that were old pictures, that might show it, and she came down with a bunch of pictures.

And there were a whole bunch, there was a picture of Eva by herself, there was a picture couple pictures of my mother with Sol. Eva and Ronny together, picture of Ronny alone. Sniff. Picture of our family in 1959. Our family which included, Why was that in 1959? Who would've taken that in 1959? Anyhow, it was me and Eva and Nancy and Ronny, and Aunt Gussie? I think it was, or Aunt Ida. And Aunt Kitty and Mother. I wonder what was the occasion for that? In that living room on Springhill Avenue. And there was a picture from dated 1933 of my father and mother before they were married, and Aunt Esther and Uncle Morris. And how incredibly much Ronny looks like my father, looks like Daddy. Sniff.

And I said something to Jerry about his father's old Buick and how my father used to take us down when we were kids to the bar on Saturday and take us out to a restaurant and then his father would bring us home. And I asked Nancy again, told Nancy, talked to Nancy again, I'll have to get her a tape recorder. Sniff. Tape recorder. To use. And to record her memories give her tapes. And I have to work on that slide thing, that slide thing of my father's bar, Daddy's bar on Pratt Street. The slide thing. Okay, I think it's time.

Well, here I am! All of a sudden I'm here at Rogers Avenue. The diner used to be on the right. What was it, Nate's and Leon's on the left? Or Sid Mandell's. The left. The Crest Theatre on Friday nights, and Ruthie saying one time, and I think I've said this before, Ruthie saying one time about how independent I was, not independent, and how I just, you know, if I wanted to go someplace, I did, and Fridays I would go up sometimes take a bus up by myself when nobody else wanted to go, and I would just go up and go to the movies on Friday evening, on Friday at the Crest. Just go to the movies.

Pictures to be taken. Crest Theatre. Uptown. Pimlico. Avalon. Yes. Okay, over and out.

And I said something yesterday evening to Jerry. Yesterday afternoon about the pictures for Sonny of him and Ellie and the kids at Aunt Esther's house in January of '87. How it had taken four years, and I was finally getting around and that I need to get at his, he said if I didn't have a Kansas address for Sonny to let him know, he'd give me the address. And I said something how it had taken me four years, and Jerry said, Well, but at least you do 'em, at least you do 'em, at least you do 'em.

Watch it here, Sidney. *Traffico mundi.* Sniff. Sniff. Coming down now, Woodland Avenue, coming down Reisterstown. I have to take pictures also of Park Lane. Right! Remember Park Lane and that parking sign. But of Park Lane. Sniff. And maybe of the Boarman Cafe and this block down here where Dominick's used to be. And here we go crossing Royce Avenue now. Get ready, Royce Avenue! Royce Avenue! 3316 Mohawk 4-2448. What was Aunt Esther's phone number? I don't remember. And we were talking about sitting, about sitting on the climbing over the steps and in the the bush the snowball bush in front of Aunt Esther's house and the rose bush in front of ours.

And somebody that's sitting on the wall between the two houses. And sitting on the wall between the two houses and how I was standing out there when, on September 6, 1946, when I heard Aunt Esther scream, Mor-ras! Mor-ras! Mor-ras! Oh, God! And I was so terrified! And Florence Winakur said, I don't know, but her father's lying on lying there on the floor. And it wasn't it strange that when I talked about the houses, I guess to Soph, and I mentioned the Fs living next door to Aunt Esther, I had forgotten completely, completely forgotten that D V and the Gs, M G, and that they lived right there. Right next door. I had forgotten all about that, and last night we were talking about it, living like that, and I said y'know that her mom and dad were literally the boy and girl next door, and she said that it was just incredible, that she couldn't imagine anything like that. Because they weren't they had nothing like that in their own experience. Sniff. And when I think about 2614 and 2616, and writing a poem called *Symbiosis*. Sniff. Symbiosis, symbiosis.

A picture also of Sussman's and Sidlen's and Kessler's and the block where Lozinsky's used to be and the block where Greenberg's Barber Shop used to be and Roland's Barber Shop and the *shule* down there.

I'm writing a poem about that, *Symbiosis*. A poem called *Symbiosis*. 2614 and 2616. And here we are at Henry G. Parks, Jr. Circle, instead of Park Circle. Over and out.

The tape really goes fast at this normal speed which is a half an hour on each side. That's all it is is a half an hour on each side instead of the hour at the half-speed. I may have to go back to the half-hour on each side. I have to go buy anyway, okay, yeah, okay, over and out.

TUESDAY, DECEMBER 18, 1990

Good morning, Mr. Phelps, Captain Kirk, and Captain Picard. It's 7:58, Tuesday, December the 18th. On my way down to school, decided to go down the Liberty Road way and now and on 105.7 the Beatles, "Let It Be, Let It Be!" Made me think of that Sunday when Sophie and I went down to the hospital. And Nancy was telling about how much she couldn't stand that, yeah, let it be. *[me also]* "Let it be. Whisper words of wisdom, Let it beeeeee! And when the night is cloudy, there is still a light that shines on me, Shine until tomorrow, let it beeeeeee." And Nancy was talking about how much she couldn't stand that intubation tube in her throat. I told her how he had, y'know, sometimes when I have things that I can't stand, I try to think of that Beatles' song, *Let It Be*, just let it be. And thinking about how when we were leaving "Let it beee" And Dr. R came in. And I know Nancy looked "There will be" devastated. "an answer, Let it be" I remember that look on her face. Like she was ready to cry. "Let it be," And when I told Sophie about that, she said, No "Let it be" she just, she just saw someone who was anxious to speak with the doctor and "There will be an answer," and that was it. "Let it beee." But I know what I saw. "Let it be" Unless I was projecting, and I don't think I was at that point. *[Closing chords—"Let it be."]* That devastated look. A look of wanting to cry. I remember that. I remember that! Sniff.

And the phone call Sunday night from Nancy, my sister Nancy. That Nancy wanted to know if I were coming down. I shoulda known, that was a call, she wanted me to come down! Sniff. But I didn't.

I'm on Gwynns Falls Parkway now. It's 8:04. Towards Coppin. I just, a guy on the grassy boulevard in the middle running with his dog, a husky, a white black white-faced husky. Sniff. And the dog had the leash in his mouth, the end of it, and they were running together, and I thought, how beautiful, the way they're running together, and it made me think of of our Collie Lady. Sniff. And how beautiful she was. And how they came to take her away because she had bitten somebody who teased her into biting. Don't take her away! Sniff. And I was out on the street again, on Springhill Avenue. And then we were inside the house. Don't take her away! Down in the basement in that little front room under the porch. Don't take her away! Don't take her away! And Kicky the cat. Kicky? Who disappeared. Or was she hit by a car? But she disappeared out the back. My father used to put his shoes out at night, to air out. Sniff.

WEDNESDAY, DECEMBER 19, 1990

Time out here. Good morning. Good morning, Captain, Mr. Phelps, Captain Kirk, Captain Picard. It is Wednesday, December the 19th. Time is 7:34 by the clock on the car. Course my hands are freezing because I didn't bring I didn't bring gloves today, thinking Ha! Ha! thinking Ha! Ha! This morning. All of a sudden I thought something about Ruth. I was thinking about telling her about how I had felt about, y'know, not knowing that Craig was at Coppin for a soccer game and not knowing that they were at Coppin for a soccer game and how I felt that it was so awful that we had lost such contact. And thinking back to the phone call in June of '61 when she and, right before she and Dave got married, when I couldn't come back for the wedding and thinking about what good friends we were in high school and in college. And remembering one of our trips to Montreal together. Was that in J? Over the break of 1957, January '57, December of '56 and January of '57. I think that's when that was. Sniff.

And thinking how when I talked to her when she was, right before that day be, when on the phone from Germany when she was marrying David. She, I remember her saying that one of the reasons, she said something like, I think one of the reasons I love him so much is that he reminds me of you. Meaning that he reminds her of me. And anyhow this morning while I was very early this morning after I got the newspaper and all, came back up to wash up and I was thinking of that. And thinking about that really just, I mean I just, I was really just kinda crying there. Silently, softly, quietly, but the tears were running down. Not really running down! They were brimming up! We won't be together again, at least not like that. Not the way we were. Remembering how Ruthie said about the pictures, That's the Sid I know, the picture of me at Maryland. Picture of me with that cowboy hat on. Picture of me at College Park in the back door of Calvert Hall with that ribbon on my fly. And Ruth saying, Even back then you were a rebel. Ha-Ha! Re-*bel*! Re-*bel*! Re-*bel*! Question, ant! That's what that's what R R used to say. Question, ant! Ant, question!

SUNDAY, DECEMBER 23, 1990

Good morning, Mr. Phelps, Captain Kirk, Captain Picard. It's 9:17, Sunday, December 23rd. We're in Steubenville. This will be a test for you because partly me, at least this part will be. Because I'm not gonna tell you how we got here. Or When we got here or what! What?! Woke up this morning about 8:30-ish from a dream. Ah-ha! Let me put the top back on the coffee.

In the dream, I was someplace. People were talking about what the Chinese had done, that they had massacred, murdered, slaughtered twenty-nine million of their own people. There were a man and a woman talking about it. And I couldn't believe it. And the woman said something like, They had sent them to the horrors.

THE NANCY TAPES

Then I thought, they let somebody kill them, they had sent them to the horrors. And I think now in my mind that at least I thought afterwards that that had to do with when the Nazis killed the Jews. In the horrors. To the horror! Not the horrors! I'm not sure if it was plural or singular. To the horror! Maybe it was singular. They sent them to the horror. And the next thing I knew, I was an American GI. And I was someplace where people were trying to escape from the Chinese or Chinese people were trying to escape from the Chinese army. And there was a woman crawling on the grass, she was flat on the grass. Wasn't much taller than her body was though. Sniff! And she had somehow gotten across this deep ravine. Sniff. And on the other side of the ravine were the Chinese soldiers. And they raised their weapons. And they began to fire. No! Before they raised their weapons and began to fire, she wanted to get up to start running. And we, the Americans American GIs, we told her, No, no, no, no. We screamed, Don't get up! Sniff. Stay down! Stay down! And the next thing we knew, the Chinese were firing, the soldiers were firing. And actually, no, I would assume that they were firing up at a positive angle. What made me think of that was Paul's word from his game Silent Service Submarine Service. The angle, the negative angle, firing at a negative angle. They were firing up a little bit. And yet still they killed her. They shot her. Stand there and watch bullet after bullet after bullet go into her body. There was nothing that we could do. Nothing that we could do. And the next thing I knew--sniff--I was reading about it. About the survival. 'Cause the woman was pregnant. But somehow, somehow the fetus she was carrying lived. Or someone was able to rescue it from her dead body, her dying body. And it lived. Sniff. And years later I was reading about her child who was a boy. And the book I was reading was a dual-language French and English, and the book was by Albert Camus. The book was by Camus. And the boy was in the, was it Tuileries Garden? No, there's another *jardins*, oh the *Luxembourg Jardins*.

Some other kids, and he was kind of brown-skinned kid. Almost like a little J B, only darker, darker, darker brown. More brown rather than that goldenish Asian color, more of a brownish color. Sniff. And he was with other kids. And I was reading the last lines of the book. The last short paragraph in French and in English and struck by the difference. How many extra words they had put in in English. And thinking, reading about the kid, and it said something like: "The brown-skinned boy. The brown-skinned boy moved slowly through his life ever after." And I remember I was starting to wake up from the dream crying reading that. Sniff. About this boy. Had that crying feeling, like I was going to cry.

I wish I could remember all that was written on that last page of that book by Albert Camus. And I remember waking up thinking, God, but it was so beautiful! The way, the way he expressed the sadness and the sorrow of it and and the continuing living of this boy. And thinking later when I was thinking about the dream, thinking: He could never have felt the feeling of seeing what happened to his mother and of how he survived, but maybe later someone told him that he would know intellectually. Sniff. And he might be able to feel the feeling of imagining himself feeling it. But he could never feel the feeling of actually seeing it. But maybe he did, maybe somehow he was able to feel the feeling of it and that that's why he was always moving slowly throughout his life. He moved slowly through the years of his life. Moving slowly through the years of his life. He moved slowly, through the years of his life. Maybe that's why he moved that way, because he could feel that feeling of being there and seeing it, being part of what was that was happening.

Anyhow I told Soph about the dream. I woke up, told Soph that I had this strange dream. Sniff. I just stopped and lay there. Thinking about that boy and the difference between his feeling of being, his feeling, knowing 'tuitively, imagining the feeling. Sniff. The broadened imagin, run deep in the imagination to be able to imagine one's self in someone else's situation, to be able to imagine *him*self in his own situation, to be able to imagine himself in his mother's situation. The feeling of experiencing, the feeling of imagining, and the separation between feeling and simply being *told*, intellectually knowing but not really feeling.

Is that me? Intellectually knowing and not really feeling? Am I the brown-skinned boy?

MONDAY, DECEMBER 24, 1990

o, Mr. Phelps. It's just about 7:30, Monday, December 24th, 1990. I'm sitting in 2810 Sunset Boulevard. Soph and Charlie and Paul have gone to church, Dad's in the bathroom.

Thinking about being in Kroger's today with Sophia and seeing M M, who said that she and her mother had been thinking about Mods. And Sophie said to her, Tell N we're sorry, but there's nobody to make him *xerotigana*. And then later we were at the dairy thing, and Sophie said something about egg-nog. And I said I thought we should get some. And then she started to cry. And I know exactly why. 'Cause Mods always liked to keep egg-nog in the house.

And then Charlie's been talking about liver, getting the liver that *Gia-gia* used to make. And we remembered how when we came up here last year on Friday the 20th, no, that would have been Friday, the 22nd. Mother was sick and in bed, and she called out for Sophie, and basically what she wanted to remind Sophie was to get the liver out for me. And tonight Sophie fried *calamari* and *smarides* and made *rovithia* and *pilafi* and fried fish, and John said something about how Mother was surprised one time when she realized that he liked *calamari*. He talked about how much he liked *rovithia*. What else about the food? The *smarides*, one night we she brought out the *smarides*. I said to her later it reminded me how last year when

THE NANCY TAPES

Mother was in the hospital still here and she was in her coma, and Father Jim went up to her and whispered something in her ear, and they all wondered what he had whispered. And Paul said, oh, he knew what she [sic] had whispered, she *[he]* had whispered, "*Smarides*, Maria." And Pana this year made *kourambiedes* using Thea Angela's recipe and I think Desi's recipe, and it was they were almost as good as *Gia* Mother's. Thinking how much everything revolves around food. And that's worth a poem. Liver. Egg-nog. *Calamari. Smarides, rovithia,* and *kourambiedes.*

This afternoon when Dad was throwing, when was it? last night? throwing his tissues around, and they were talking about how Mother was, put up with him, and why she couldn't stand it, how she was, Paul said something about how the last **TAPE ENDS**

TAPE NUMBER 7A

MONDAY, DECEMBER 24, 1990 (CONT.)

Okay, it's 8:05 S Monday, December 24th in Steubenville. Anyhow, continuing the last one, somebody'd said something about whoops ps how the last thing she could do was to die. And she did that. And they all said how happy he was that she was at peace now. At peace. Someone was saying this afternoon how he depressed he is when he comes in this house. He can't stand, all he can do is just sit there, and he can't wait to leave. That must be why he was so closed in on himself yesterday evening when he came over and just sat and read the newspaper and didn't say anything until it was time to leave. 'nd Sophie was saying they were talking about who had seen and how in in dreams she always appeared she was always smiling. In Eleni's dreams. And Sophie said even Eleni V had seen her in a dream and she was smiling.

But she wasn't smiling in my dreams. Her eyes, it was those eyes, just like Nancy's eyes. Those eyes. Poem about eyes. Sol's eyes. The eyes of the wildebeest. The eyes of Mods, the eyes of Nancy. The poem about food food. Everything centering around food. The egg nog, *xerotigana*, the liver, *sikoti* and onions, the *kalamari*, the *smarides*, the *rovithia*. No broccoli today, but broccoli *mprocola*. Talking to Soph about how we used to sit here after they'd come back from church, watching the midnight liturgy from Rome, the midnight mass from Rome, Christmas mass, wrapping the boys' presents, then getting out the cookies and milk and the sugar for the reindeer, for Santa, first for Charlie, and then for Paul, here.

THURSDAY, DECEMBER 27, 1990

Good afternoon, Mr. Phelps, Captain Kirk, Captain Picard. It's 4:33 Thursday, December the 27th. Ah, turning left from Linduff Avenue up Iva Way going back to the house on Sunset Boulevard, just coming back from getting a pint of Canadian Club for *Papou*. And thinking now about the poem about food and remembering that I think it was yesterday that Sophie spoke with Uncle Mike and Thea Nina about coming to the *mnimosino*, the one-year memorial service, coming up on Sunday, December the 30th, which will, actually two weeks under a little bit over two weeks under. Over Under Under Over A little bit over two weeks under a year, actually. And Uncle Mike is going to bring *pichti pichti*, another food of Mother's, one which I didn't eat. But one which for Sophie and for Paul and for others will be sorely and sadly missed. *Pichti. Pichti.*

But no one has yet said anything again, about trying her *xerotigana*. I shall miss the melting crunch of fried dough, crushed walnuts, deep fried. I shall miss the melting crunch of dough, deep fried, and folded over on itself, *siropi*-poured, *siropi*-soaked, and crushed walnuts sprinkled on top. I could eat them and I never felt sick. My stomach never bothered me. And I never felt full. I was always satisfied with what I had, always full, always comfortable. But also, always hungry. For more. The hunger and the taste for the sweet melting crunch of dough, deep fried, soaked in syrup. Not soaked, moistened with syrup. And sprinkled with crushed nuts.

And the trio of heroes for my work, not just a duet, of Ian Now and Perry Neam, but I forgot all about Peter Burns. Peter Burns, also.

SUNDAY, DECEMBER 30, 1990

Ah, good afternoon, Mr. Phelps, Captain Kirk, Captain Picard. It's 2:35, Sunday, December the, Sunday December the 30th, 1990. I'm on Wilma Avenue. Heading up towards the Fort Steuben Mall after dropping Paul off at Weezie's and Charlie off at Yula's.

Today was the one-year *mnimosino* for for Mother for E Mods, *Gia-gia*. Here in Steubenville, it's it's really, it's like nine days short of short of a year, but this was the only Sunday they could really have it. And yes, some stuff that I read in the in the liturgy, moth rust and thieves. Lay up your treasures in Heaven where neither moth nor rust can corrupt them nor thieves break in and steal them. For there where your treasures are so wh is your heart, too. And thinking of Mod's and thinking of her making *xerotigana*, and I wonder if I could have that, that one frame made into a photograph of the last *xerotigana* in the in the skillet with her hands hovering over it. I wonder if I could do that, I'd like to see if I can, I'll have to try if I can do that. And also at the cemet it's pouring down rain I pouring d just pouring down just pouring down rain today. Kind of windy, but not as windy as it was at the funeral, but it's like. The funeral was windy and cold and snowing li almost like a blizzard, there was the snow was not that deep, but it was just blowing very hard and very cold, freezing cold. Today at one point during the service, I guess it was when when Father Andrew, the new priest, called people to come for communion, the wind started blowing over the dome it was just incredible wind. And thinking how Mother's just incredible the bad weather, her funeral and today at the first year *mnimosino*. *Eonia i mnimi* went first from the priest to the *psalti* to the choir and then a few people the in the congregation picked it up. Since it was also for Kiki Bellas, it was the last one was *Eonia ton i mnimi, eonia ton afton i mnimi*, I think at one point they said and and at the cemetery, at the gravesite, it was *eonia tis aftis i mnimi*. And then at the end Father Andrew put some of the emptied the incense out near the head of the grave, and and I don't know why he stamped, I guess he felt he was afraid it might catch fire, but he stamped it out. And he told Pana that it was a Greek custom, he didn't know whether people followed it here, but it was a custom to empty the the incense into the grave so he did that. *[very heavy rain]*

SIDNEY KROME

And Mrs. Vogagis had made *finikia*, and while I wanted to try one, I couldn't bring myself to try one, so I didn't try any *finikia* of hers 'cause they weren't Mother's.

I'd like to get that that that one frame made into a picture *to televtaio finiki to televtaio xerotigana, xerotigano*? *tigani*? Whatever the singular would be. That might be even better for the for the quotation from Frost. Even better almost than the rainbow the Earth the best place t for love, I don't know where it's likely to go better. "Earth's the right place for love."

I would like to say something today but I don't know if I will. I did say *kaddish* when I got out and people were not, were waiting for Uncle Mike, I found they were waiting for Uncle Mike, and I walked up myself to the grave and tore up some grass, put it there and and said said a *kaddish* for her. And stood for a moment afterwards was standing there in the rain, and John didn't come up 'cause he didn't want to get wet. Dad didn't come up, and they kind of joked about the fact that he wasn't there, but, I don't know, he should have been at his wife's first year and that woman, what was the name? AC, I guess, said that Well, and his age and all this stuff, and I know he's up in that age. But he's letting his depression get a hold of him or it has gotten hold of him much worse than it should have. *[rain sound]*

But there was something else I was thinking of about about a poem about something, but I don't even remember what it was right now, so I'm gonna shut this off and see if I can find a parking place here at the mall.

Right, I remember now what it was. Talking with T T who's in her third year medical school, and we were talking about how how she was glad to see that in one way it was it was good that the the memorial service for the two, they did a *Trisagion* a pri memorial prayer for her grandmother today also, and and she said it was like, it was fitting that it be together since they were such good friends. And I talking about how difficult it was at Christmas time and remembering Christmas and all, how difficult it was on everybody. The sadness coming together with the joy of Christmas. Well, there he goes, somebody pulled in, no nobody pulled in but yes they did, no, they didn't, there's the parking space. And she said that you know, it had been two or three years, and now it kind of blended together and gave a different feel to the holiday. I mean, the sadness with it. And I said something about the different, gave it maybe gave it different perspective. And then I, we were talking about the she was talking about how our kids had grown, and I said something about N, N and how her brother and how he was standing, near the first pew in the center section of the church, and how tall he was, and somebody was standing in the first pew, and at the first pew it's it's actually lower than floor level, so it made N look even taller than he was. And I said it was a different perspective, and then I said, You know, maybe that's it also with the with the Christmas and

THE NANCY TAPES

New Year holidays 'cause her grandmother died on New Year's Eve, that the death of the person and the memory of the grief gives a different perspective to the different perspective to the holiday. Yes, a different perspective. That's worth a poem. I think. The perspective. I didn't tell her that I'd been thinking for a couple years of writing a poem about her grandmother's death. *Zalistica*, that's what she said to D, right before she died, *zalistica. Zalades. Zalistica.* I was gonna write that poem *Zalades* about her.

An' I also have to say something in here about the idea of looking up and seeing the prophets and thinking about Jesus as human and not the Son of God and how different things would have been and what what, in what way he might have revitalized Judaism had it been seen from that light and had he not been treated as God because at one point during the prayer service they refer to him as the Lord God Jesus Christ. Over and out.

Actually, not over and out. While I was standing at the grave and and they were chanting the *Eonia i mnim mnimi*, I couldn't help think of Nancy and think of Ruthie on that Monday after we heard the bad news and things had turned around, how the weather had turned around in the surgery, and Ruthie saying how she, she didn't even have time to be sad, she couldn't be by herself and be sad and cry. *[rain]* But she did have Sophie was there to be with her, was able to be with her. And she could cry then, I remember I stood kind of by the doorway as a kind of a watchman, to let her cry with Sophie. Over and out, now over and out.

Oh, not quite over and out. Ruthie had said something about me having my religious quest, and I said something about how now I was turning back towards Judaism. And I was thinking in a way about being Jewishness, but now I'm thinking not about the Jewish customs and traditions, I'm thinking about the Jewish attitude toward life in terms of, that's also what I meant when I was thinking about Jesus. Not not as the begotten son of God, not as the Lord God Jesus Christ, but is as a human being, to make life and living better, to summon us to a sense of living to a sense of the ethics of living, of the spirituality of living. So that we think more about *that* and do that more, rather than the material things. In that sense, Mother and the *xerotigana*, that's what I was thinking about also, Mother and her *xerotigana*, her hunched back that I noticed, how difficult it was for her to stand and to spend all the time, the joke I made about her slaving over the hot skillet while her daughters read the catalogue, but the joy and the pleasure that she got from bringing the sweetness of the *xerotigana* to our lives. That's what it is. And thinking also of Nancy saying how she wished she had a million dollars to leave something really of herself. What she doesn't realize is that she left something of far more value than that million dollars. Okay, over and out, *now*!

SIDNEY KROME

WEDNESDAY, JANUARY 2, 1991

[long silence] It's Not for Me to Say Good morning, Mr. Phelps, Captain Kirk, Captain Picard. Happy New Year, Gentlemen. It's 8:02 am, Wednesday, January the second, 1991. I'm sitting in front of the Giant where I've just dropped off newspapers and bought some stamps. And I turned on the radio, it's in the car, "It's not for me to say," Johnny Mathis. Listen to these words, gentlemen. "Perhaps the glow of love will grow with every passing day, Or we may never meet again" *[me with Mathis]* Or we may never meet again. May never meet again *[my voice crying]*. "never meet again." We may never meet again. "But then, it's not *[both voices]* for me to" To to to to to "say." Thank you, Johnny Mathis, for that wonderful bit of chaotic information to make our order out of. Got that, Kirk? Got that, Picard? Got that, Phelps? Your mission impossible. I have to look at the rest of the words of that song, too. Over and out.

I was going to listen to Robert Frost this morning, but I think I'll just listen to WYST, Great Songs of the Fifties. Amen, brother. Hot Rod! For the greatest people in the world, ladies and gentlemen, my listeners. Mozahhh. Actually, some of the other words to that song, "It's Not for Me to Say, you'll always care, But then it's not for me to say," for just for the something about for the moment. I can't remember the rest of the words. Oh, well, I thought I thought of something, but I didn't.

Put this one in your pipe and smoke it, gentlemen. *The Old Lamplighter.* "The old lamplighter of long, long ago" Wacka-wacka! 8:19 am, coming down Reisterstown Road, and there's the Town House Motel *[voice breaking, sob]* "for he" August 1958 *[crying]* "someone who watched him" Or was it June? I don't know, I think it was August "he makes the night a little brighter" Ronny and Eva "wherever he" *[crying]* Taking Raizel to the cemetery "may go, the old lamplighter" I live in the cemetery *[crying]* "of long, long." *[my voice over radio]* "He made the world a little brighter wherever he would go, The old lamplight lighter of long long ago." It's long long ago *[sobbing]* long long long long long ago.

Actually, the Marlene Dietrich song, *Ich bin von Kopf bis Fuss auf Liebe aufgestelt und das ist meine Welt und sonst Garnichts*, which was translated in English as *Falling in Love Again.* I'm I had my own version of that song, it is *Falling Apart Again.* Falling apart again, I have lost my brain, there is nawt no gain, all I feel is pain, *und sonst* **gar nichts**.

I remember I remember at Aunt Esther's Chanukah party this year, in December, December the December the, what was it? the 16th? Sunday, when I showed the pictures of Springhill Avenue, Jerry Bulmash said he wanted a picture of Springhill Avenue houses, even over and above Royce Avenue, although he wouldn't mind Royce Avenue also, but he really wanted the Springhill Avenue 'cause that's the one he remembered the most.

And I remember Jerry standing out in the alley, screaming and cursing. I was supposed to be going out someplace with M, and we were standing on the stairs, and I couldn't help bring him in because we had to go out, 'cause I was an *asshole then*, even then, and I remember M saying, You hear him, he's crying for his mother. Although Royce Avenue, here we go, just passing Royce Avenue, 3315 [*sic*] Royce Avenue. Sophie said last night my mother doesn't appreciate me, and I said, Nobody appreciates me, gesturing and joshing and apparently, for what I really am. Nobody really does. *Schmageggi.* A *schmageggi.* A do nuttin'. "What about me?" What about me? That song going on. Who's that? I don't know what his name is. Joel, Billy Joel, I don't know. What about me? What about me? "What about meee?" What a dipstick. *Que sais-je faire-je?* What have I done? What have I done? What have I ever done? What have I *ever* done?

Cold Spring Lane, actually, right now, Reisterstown and Cold Spring is where I've been saying this stopped at the traffic light, Reisterstown and Cold Spring. By a Park Lane Shopping Center. Remember Park Lane? Remember Park Lane. *Que sais-je faire-je?*

Ha, what a song that is now I'm hearing. "Don't ever let anyone step all over you." "No one can change your life except for you." Whoa! Watch out, gang. Coming up down here on Reisterstown Road, coming down to PS 59, Louisa May Alcott School on the left. And wasn't that interesting that the people who, Strover Farmen and Garten, whatever they were, Alcott Place, is that what they called it? It was a picture on on on what? "Chuck-a-change-ch-ch-change" on the file cabinet "ch-ch-change-you can go your way" in the president's office, G's office, that they had sent B a Christmas card, a picture, the side picture School 59 on Keyworth Avenue, picture of that side entrance 's what it was. PO, how y' doin', P?

Coming up now on Springhill Avenue, up to the left, Jake's the Tailor, Jake the Tailor's, and beyond that 2614 2616 Springhill Avenue. Abe Kershman walked into his house, I never saw it, but I imagined it, I have a picture of Abe Kershman walking into his house, hitching up his belt and saying, Charlie Krome's dead. Can you believe it? Charlie Krome's dead? *[louder with sob/crying]* Can you believe it? Charlie Krome's dead.

5:04 p.m., Wednesday, January the 2nd, I'm on turning into home, here's Connie Francis and "There's Nothing Left for Me, the way Nothing what it used to be" amon I'm am in a "among my souvenirs" or something like that. "A photograph or two among my–*[me also]*--souvenirs" Connie Francis, the Great Whine. "A few more t"

SIDNEY KROME

FRIDAY, JANUARY 4, 1991

Good evening, Mr. Phelps, Captain Kirk, Captain Picard. It is now 11:00 p.m., Friday, January the 4th, 1991, up at the St. Basil's Academy in Garrison, New York. Earlier this evening heard someone, I don't know if it was the priest or someone talking about hugging, kids needing hugs, and kids needing to be loved, and be hugged. And I wondered now, how many times I had hugged my kids. Charlie, occasionally, Paul, almost never. When was the last time I just hugged him? Spontaneously. Just hugged him just hugged 'im hugged'im hugged'im hug hug hug'im. Time passes. How did he get to be 13 and a half already? How did that happen? And then remembering all the times I took Charlie to Wabash Avenue and picked him up at his day care centers, day schools, took him to Wabash Avenue, and to Patterson Avenue to see the Liberty Train in 1976. And it scared him, 'cause it went by close. How much of their childhoods have I missed? But I wasn't away, I didn't work late. I can remember for years lying and watch just years recent last years watching tv home on Wimbledon Lane. Most evenings, most evenings, most evenings, but where did it all go?

SUNDAY, JANUARY 6, 1991

Good afternoon, gentlemen. Sunday, January 6th, 1941, 1991, it's 4:00 p.m.. Why 1941? What happened in that year? In any case, just finished watching a movie on channel 21 channel 20 DC WDC Sun DC 20 Sunday Afternoon Theatre Matinee Theatre called uh "Merlin and the S Merlin and the Sword" 1983 Malcolm McDowell and Candace Bergen. But the other female lead looked like Dyan Cannon, I'm not sure if that's who it was though. Anyhow, at the end she's inst in a cave with Merlin, and another medieval woman and as they manage to get back to Camelot, she says, Don't leave me behind. I started crying almost uncontrollable, thinking of my father and saying, Daddy, don't leave me behind, don't leave me behind, Daddy. *[almost crying]* But he couldn't help it. Think of the time going to the circus. Thinking also of his dying, more of his dying, dying, he died. But thinking also of the movie, Mordred, gotta get that movie, Mordred evil like Mordred and Iago, vicious and evil, spiteful, hating the good, and that's why and that's just the way they were, hating the good, Mordred, Mordred and Iago. Get that movie. And Merlin cast the monster brought up by Morgan La Fey and he said, Get back to the slime pit of Morgan's mind. What a great line--Back to the slime pit of Morgan's mind!

MONDAY, JANUARY 7, 1991

Good morning, gentlemen. It is 7:58, Monday, January the 7th, 1991. Snowing rather heavily, we've already had ab I would estimate about 2 to 3 inches on the cars here, Baltimore County Schools are closed, Paul's in bed, glorying in his day off. And I just thought of a little rhyme when I got in the car: *Peftoon ta chionia, kai pernoon ta chronia,* the snows are falling and the years are passing. *Peftoon ta chro chionia, kai pernoon ta chronia. Asha-i viatsa.* Over and out for now.

Ho-ho-ho, it is to laugh. It's now 7:59, I've just turned right onto Reisterstown Road, going up to pick up S's secretary, and I had said to her--ha-ha- Reisterstown Road shouldn't be too bad at this time. Well, ho-ho-ho, I wonder if they've done anything to this, except let cars drive on it. Good grief! Well, that passing lane isn't too bad, but this lane isn't too good, isn't too good here. I better be careful, better be real careful going up and down this way. And going down this slope down here down to uh Greenspring Valley Road. Over and out.

Uh oh Up by Owings Mills Elementary School, parts of Reisterstown Road are looking as though they have been plowed or something, they're not as bad as they were down around Queen Anne Village.

WEDNESDAY, JANUARY 9, 1991

Good morning, gentlemen. Mr. Phelps, Captain Kirk, Captain Picard. Just ah come on, buddy, will you do something?! Look at these guys. Just getting on the Jones on the Beltway here leaving home. What the heck is it? What the heck is it? It's 8:33 by the clock in the car. Wednesday, January the 9th, 1991. Yesterday marked the first year, the one year since Mother died Mother-in-law, Soph's mother died, one year ago yesterday, 52 weeks ago Monday. Intresting eluff interestingly enough, on Monday the 7th of January, it snowed here s very very heavily. 52 weeks ago on January the 8th, 1991, the day my mother-in-law died, it also snowed, real heavily. Because when I called from school and found out that she had died, and I came home, and it was snowing real hard here, so I couldn't no I couldn't take the boys and drive up. And so we left on Tuesday the 9th which would be a year ago today.

Soph talking to Louise yesterday afternoon around 5 and talking about the year had passed, and Soph talking about how what a fast year it was, it was incredibly fast, I it was like I was just, it wa yesterday like the day before yesterday was just Sunday the 7th of January 1990, and I was just coming back from Columbus, and I remember leaving Soph and Paul in the parking lot outside Ohio State OSU Medical Center January 7 1991 [*sic*]. Yesterday kind of stressful but, and and Monday night, January the 7th this year it was terrible, gall bladder type pain again, and again as a year ago Soph had to take me to Baltimore County General. They this year they gave me a shot of bentyl that really really helped. And so today I have an appointment to check with see if the gastro-enterologist to see what's going on, but to try to see what's going on. Over and out for now though.

SIDNEY KROME

Here it is snowing again. No, it's it's drizzling freezing drizzling rain. Frizzling frizzling dreezy rain. **TAPE ENDS**

THE NANCY TAPES

TAPE NUMBER 7B

WEDNESDAY, JANUARY 9, 1991 (CONT.)
Good morning again, gentlemen, it's 8:40. I've turned the tape over. Whoops! Better watch where I'm driving here. I've turned the tape over, it's 8:40 am, same day, Wednesday, July January the 9th, 1-9-9-1, 1-9-9-1. Oh, maybe that's the number to play today. Anyhow, I forgot what I said at the end, except about frizzling dreezy rain. Frizzling dreezy rain and about how I went to the gall bladder thing Monday night, I think that's already on there. That's already on there. About my pain Monday night, January the 7th, Soph had to take me to Baltimore County General again. They gave me the bentyl, and that was a lot better, gall bladder. And we thought, it was Mod's gall bladder at first, but it turned out it was much more serious than that. All right, I'm gonna over and out this for now. Over and out this for now.

FRIDAY, JANUARY 11, 1991
Good morning good morning, gentlemen. It's 8:39, Friday, January 11th, 1991, I'm just coming in to what is now Henry G. Parks, Jr., Circle, instead of Park Circle. And that's wh the sound you hear in the background is the windshield wipers scraping. It's snowing. Here comes a snowplow moving rather m more rapidly than he should, the dipstick. And today's exactly one year since the funeral of my mother-in-law, Mother's funeral a year ago today. Snowing here in Baltimore, it was snowing furiously and cold and windy almost like a blizzard in Steubenville a year ago cheh up on this hill, in the cemetery took took her to bury her. Just passing now the old reservoir which now the ball fields and thinking about Ronny coming down the slope on a sled and just missing or being missed just missing that car coming up that street which is now marked as a waxing area for cars.

And I guess that's what I wanted to talk about was the funeral a year ago, the snow oh, yes, and here I am coming down Reisterstown Road, I'm passing Druid Hill Park, on the left, coming up on the Park Department Superintendent's house *[wiper scraping throughout]* on the left. Which I think is abandoned, not in use now. And thinking about and there at the intersection where it's now been fixed, the intersection near Liberty Heights and Reisterstown Road, where AS and I cut weeds and stuff and where I got that really devastating case of poison ivy of poison ivy. Thinking about the time when we were in high school, we came down, we played cards at MF's house, M's house, which was around the corner on Liberty Heights. It was a snow day, we were off from school and and I said something about, I had won a lot swadn a f lot not a lot some money playing pitch, and we talked about going back up, and I said something about walking, and somebody said something, MB, I think, Cheeks, said something about my being a little bit tight with that money, not wanting to part with any of that money I had just made playing pitch. But it would be nice to walk in the snow. Would have been nice.

MONDAY, JANUARY 21, 1991

Aahh. Good morning, gen cheh. Good morning, gentlemen. It's 7:56, Monday Monday, January the 21st. We uh oh, look at that coffee splashed all over the. Oh, well. Monday, the 21st of January. We took we took we took.

Good morning, Mr. Phelps, Captain Kirk, Captain Picard. Smoke this in your pipe and put it. Last night we took Charlie back to the University of Maryland for his second semester at College Park, University of Maryland. Watch it, Jack! Turmoil! Lots of emotional turmoil, there. Supposed to take him to Annapolis Hall, he said, but Annapolis Hall turned out to be all locked up, and Soph persuaded him to ask somebody, and this student said, do have to go to Harford Hall. And anyhow, he we took him up to Calvert Hall A, room 2103 is his new room, Calvert Hall A. Oh, damn it! Pardon me. Anyhow, we took him up there, and lots of emotional turmoil. First of all, of course, there's simply the fact of taking him back, and again as the last time, chem, more I think this time, because of where we're taking to, I had been in Calvert Hall D. And Annapolis Hall Harford Hall areas near Charles Hall, and I remember that's when we took Ronny out years ago, and he was in Charles Hall, I remember we took him to Charles Hall, and I remember my mother saying to someone, You can't get away from it, because that was just like a year after my father died. No, wait a second, it was, it was the year my father died, '54 because he graduated in '53, went to Western Maryland for a year, and so we were taking him to Charles Hall to Charles Hall to Charles Hall. And anyhow the emotional turmoil, not only, combination of things, the fact of taking Charlie back. Put that in your pipe and smoke it.

Add that to the chaos theory, it's chaos theory, as M D says, the HVAC man. Chaos theory chaos theory. We took him back and make sense out of chaos. Chaos is chaos. You can't make sense out of chaos, or else it's not chaos. But part of the point of chaos theory is that there is a an order to chaos, even. To chaos there is an order, and that's what your mission is, gentlemen. To find the order in chaos.

But I was, the room was so miserable, I mean, it was like a 3 it was like a 3-room suite there on the side but it's a suite, Good Lord! You walk in the main door, and there's like the living room area, and all there was was a couch in there and a garbage can. Not a small waste basket, but a big metal garbage can. And and Charlie's room C, there was A to the left, the living room area straight ahead, and to the right a little hallway with B which was a single room and C which was Charlie's room with a guy named G K. C was smaller than B, and and there was a 2-man room, it was just incred so narrow. There was a li one electrical outlet, there probably was a second one behind the bed that we simply couldn't find it. It *[stifled laughter]* it was so dirty! The guy had left his dirty underwear on the floor and dirty socks and empty bags of like potato chips or whatever. I'm telling you! It was miserable! It was depressing to look at. It was it was a, it was, of course, emotionally upsetting to be taking him back, at that time. I mean taking him back at any time, because, of course, it means that he is, of course, he's getting older, and, so are we, and he's growing up and he's 18, he's gonna be 19 in, let's see, February March, two and a half months, what's this? this is January the 21st. Just about two and a half months, he's gonna be 19.

When I was 19, when I was going on 19 19 going on 19, that was the end of my sophomore year. That was the year that the end of my sophomore year, would have been 55 57 going on 19, and that was the time when M'sieur A and the French class, pardon me while I sip my coffee. M'sieur A M'sieur A asked the class do, he had to get the names of the seniors so he could get senior grades in. And and when I didn't raise my hand as a senior, he said, Well, M'sieur Krome, he said, you're not a senior? I said, No, sir, no, M'sieur A. He said, Then, he said, you are a junior? I said, No, M'sieur A. He said, You are a sophomore? I said, Yes, I am only a sophomore. And, I can't remember the name of that girl who was sitting behind me, used to sit behind me, and she tapped me on the shoulder, and she said, It's that receding hairline, that does it, Sid! Wha-ha-ha! And everybody laughed, as did I. To think that I was, oh, dear, well, I'd better go through this yellow light ah turned red. Uh oh That car behind the car behind went through also! Anyhow, it was to laugh. That people would think that I was a senior when I was only a sophomore, and as it was, I was a year ahead of myself, because of 49. So instead of being 20 at the end of my sophomore year, I was only 19. So I was even a year younger.

And that is the reminiscence of of what was about a week ago or two weeks ago, we took the kids, so Sophie and I took the boys, Charlie and Paul, we went to Bob's Big Boy for dinner, and when I went to pay when I went to pay, the guy took off, he says, Of course, well, there's the discount, sir. And he took off like 10% from the bill. And I said to him, Well, what what's the discount for? And he looked me, he looked at me, and even though I had not asked for it, he looked at me and he said, he said, The Senior Citizen discount, sir. Now, the Big Boy policy that they have posted is that if you're 55 or older and you request, and show ID, you can get a 10% discount as a senior citizen, but by, Hey, man, I didn't request anything, I didn't ask for it because I ain't 55, I'm only 52, man, only 52! And everybody said, well, it's the grey hair, it's the grey hair, maybe I should try Grecian Formula Number 16. I ain't gonna try no Grecian Formulas Num 1, 2, 3, 4, 5, or 6! And here I am going down Reisterstown Road.

And pretty soon and I've decided I think that I'm gonna go, I have, I called Amy yesterday, and I have to call her travel agency today the 800 number back-

causa because I've decided that, passing Sol Levinson Funeral Home, I've decided to go up I think on Thursday night to Montreal, take the Montrealer, I guess I'll go with everybody else, but I'm not going on the sleeper, I'm going on my coach. Going on the coach. Going on the coach, going on the coach. Up to Chaim and Lorna's their kids' Bar/Bat Mitzvah, their twins Bar/Bat Mitzvah for the twins. Bar/Bat Mitzvah and everybody's just, this is going to be the first major thing after Nancy's death *[crying]*.

Town House Motor Hotel August 1958 *[voice breaking]*, Ronny and Eva's Wedding, sniff. That's where they all stayed 1958, thirty-two years ago 32-and-a-half years ago. Oh, my goodness! And suddenly it becomes incredibly important for me to go and to go the day earlier, to be on the train with them even though I'm not gonna be in the sleeper car. As I told Cookie years ago, I go on the train, and it's a nostalgia trip and for a few hours I'm traveling back into my childhood, and it's okay because then I come back, and it doesn't bother anyone. But I can feel like I'm a kid again. And everybody was alive *[voice breaking-crying]*. And everybody was alive! Sniff. Isn't it incredible, one of Paul's best buddies at Pikesville Middle School is the grandson of Barney Kessler. Isn't it amazing the way things go around, and they come around. Sniff. Wheoaw! Watch this traffic here, Sidney. Coming down to Reisterstown and Belvedere. Where was Benny's Poolroom, upstairs, I only went up once or twice. It was Knocko's over at Liberty Heights and Garrison, Knocko's with J! Rack 'em up, J! J 'em up, Racky!

And I remember saying to PMN the other day, as we saw BB, about how, how I used to work at the one of my part-time jobs in school was at Northwestern Loan, the pawnshop on Pennsylvania Avenue. And that BB's sniff father was the tailor there and how he had invited me to his house for egg nog and some Christmas cheer and listen to some of his jazz records and how honored I felt that the Book! they used to call him the Book! the Book! Coming down Reisterstown Road now getting, closer to Royce Avenue, sniff. Whoops! Watch this traffic, Sidney, and watch these cars in the right lane getting ready to pull out, Gaw head, gaw head, lady! Or mister, whatever you are. Past now this is the block Manchester here, I think this is the block near the church where Maar Lesser used to live, the guy who, bu not Frank Loesser, Maar Lesser, who gave me my lessons for my Bar Mitzvah. Oh dear, oh dear, oh dear, oh dear, oh dear, oh dear, oh dear *[singing-like to tune of Ghost Riders in the Sky]*, Oh dear oh dear oh dear oh dear oh dear oh dear oh dear, Da-da da-da da-da-da da da-da-da-da-da-dummm Coming down this Reisterstown and Reisterstowning Road. And on the left there is Royce Avenue, RRRoyce Avenue! 3316. And to the right, was the little block of shops where used to be used to be Domenick's Pizza! Back when we was in high school. And in college. Domenick's. And here's the Park Lane Park and Shop Free Parking. I need to take some pictures of this. I need to take some pictures of this. I need to come out with my camera. With a bunch of film some time. And take pictures of all these places and areas.

Roight! I had stopped, now moving down Cold Spring Lane, down past Cold Spring Lane, that guy used to live down there, that guy from that the family that A waited on, and there's Mack's *C'est Bon* Cocktail Lounge, which used to be Boarman Cafe Pizza and Boarman's. The family that A waited on at the Penn-Rock Hotel in Penn-Mar, Maryland. Now I can see Francis, not Francis Scott Key, what's it? Louisa May Alcott School, PS 59. Converted into senior citizen housing, residences, apartments. Ah, yes, I remember it well *[imitating Clouseau]*. Car wash here on the right. Shirley Avenue which is has been now b blocked off, Isaac Davidson Hebrew School I Do Hate School. There's the Shirley Avenue Street Park, and there's the Isaac Davidson down to the right past there's the Towanda where that kid set himself afire! Oh, man! *[almost whispered]* And this is PS 59 on the left now. And on the right this block of Reisterstown Road where PO used to live. And now coming up here on Springhill Avenue. Everybody ready, set, S-p-r-i-n-g-h-i-l-l-A-v-e-n-u-e! There we go, passing it now, the famous Springhill Avenue.

And coming up now on Violet Avenue, Violet Avenue, famous Violet Avenue, where used to be used to be the famous Kessler's Deli up there at Kessler's Deli, which has been reconverted back into a house, that was back in what was that? '77, I remember, seeing that being done as I was driving down to school back in like '77, I think it was '77. Coming down now, that as Ullman Avenue where where Sussman's Drugstore used to be down on the corner of Park Heights. And what is that street? Hilldale down which was Roland's Barber Shop, coming, now down in to Park Circle, what used to be Park Circle, now is Henry G. Parks, Junior, Circle.

Henry G. Parks, Junior, Circle, and here Parks Sausage where used to be Parks Carlin's Park with the swimming pool and the rides and everything, and I remember how I used to lie in bed with the window open at 2614 Springhill Avenue, my head down at the foot of the bed so that the air coming in, what little air there was coming in over the window, would come over my body, and I could hear the Ho-Ho-Ho! of one of the of the Funhouse. And I could also hear the sounds of the rides and the music and the calliopes. And the the shots in the shooting gallery, I could hear it all. And here to the left now is where used to be the reservoir, where they, course they took the reservoir down years ago, even when we were kids. And we used to go sled riding down the side of the reservoir. And the time Ronny almost got hit by a car. And we used to play ball there, the Cavaliers. And around on the other side of the Reservoir, the other side of the Reptile House. Where there used to be that little flat field where we'd play football where we'd play football where we'd play football. And then Three Sisters where we would also play football across the street from that. And that hill that road s s side road hill which is now blocked off. Where where when I worked in the park that summer, Hogback Hill. Hogback Hill. Remember Hogback Hill.

Uhoh my. Ts oh, my. Coming now here and down to the right where Liberty Heights, where they fixed up this intersection, Liberty Heights and Reisterstown, and to the right, Mon-daw-min. G, DR coming one Saturday evening concert, barefoot and in a suit. G. Remember him? I remember him. And R at College Park, Question, ant. I wonder what R is doing now.

TUESDAY, JANUARY 22, 1991

Good morning, gentlemen. It's now 8:05 am, Tuesday, January the 2-what?- 22nd, I'm heading east on the Baltimore Beltway. Mist mist misterrr Mr. Phelps, Captain Kirk, Captain Picard. It's a bright sunny but very cold morning. Somebody said something about 8 at the Inner Harbor, I don't think it's quite that cold, they said it was 17 this morning at WJZzzz. Last night I called Ruthie, and we talked about getting together, and it'll probably be the either 8th or the 15th of February to talk about working on her book. And also talked about, she asked me if I had been out to the cemetery to see Nancy, and I said, no, I hadn't. And she said, 'cause Joe had been out there, and he was there for 2 or 3 hours, took some flowers, took a blanket, sat on the blanket. She said he gets very emotional and very dramatic. And that there were some stones on on Nancy's grave, and she thought maybe I had been out there, and I said, No, I had not been able to be up to get out there yet. And she said that Joe had taken flowers, he had asked Ruth if he could bring roses, and she said, Of course, if you wanted to. And she said talked about the the Jewish prohibition against flowers. And I said, I don't know why, I said, but I did hear years ago that Jews do not are not supposed to take flowers out to uh to a cemetery. And she said she had seen out where Uncle Morris' grave was, people planted ivy and and flowering plants and bushes.

And I said, I didn't know and it called to mind August of 1958 August of 1958! *[voice almost breaking]* when I took, when Raizel came down for Ronny and Eva's wedding and I took Raizel, she wanted to go to the cemetery, and I took her, and we stopped. And she got flowers *[voice like crying]* to put on Aunt Freda's grave. Sniffling. It was just yesterdaayyy! It was just yesterday! *[voice breaking-crying]* And Ruth and I talked about how fast, I said, You know, I said, it's like a cliche, I said, but the older I get, the faster time goooes. And she said, Yes, but the cliche is true, it's a true cliche. Sniffing. And I told her, about, about my mother-in-law, about Mother's Mods'. It's been a year, I said, and it's gone so fast. I said, It's like we just got back from Columbus.

And she said the time had gone so fast. She said tomorrow, that is, today, January 22nd, it'll be three months. And I said it was three months since Nancy's surgery. And she said, but she considered that it's like Nancy was gone as of that day. Sniff. And she said it had gone so fast, but also that it seemed so distant in the past. And I said, maybe that's because it's gone so fast, it seems like yesterday, but the time has gone by so fast, that that time has now gone farther back into the past, it has receded with that speed and speed recedes. Speed makes time recede. Even though it's short, it seems long, and it recedes distantly, ever so distantly. Sniff.

[voice crying] And she started crying on the phone. *[clicking signal throughout]* And I held back. Sniff. And I remember now how she cried that Monday afternoon. And said, said that she couldn't even be sad because she had to be strong for everybody, for her kids, for Nancy's kids, for Aunt Esther. She had to hold things together. Sniff. And and when she talked about the flowers, it made me think of t my taking Raizel out, what was that? 32 years ago? *[voice crying]* Little over 32 years ago. Sniff. And how Allyson poor Allyson and Darren, they had gone down, Allyson was supposed to stay a week, and Darren was going to stay for a while. But it was so bad that though they went down on a Saturday by Tuesday Darren was calling Ruth and saying that he didn't think he could live there. And she said she knew just what he meant. That was just just not the figurative but quite literally, that he didn't think he could *live* there. And she s told me then about Nancy's letter, the parts that she had not read to us, not let us read, not even let the kids read. That Nancy was afraid that if Darren went, did go down to live, that he would get so depressed. Sniff.

Ruthie talking about how Allyson wanted to go out to Montana to Helena, Montana, where she had this friend Tim, this guy she knew from Charleston, and that at the time Ruth told her that she felt that she was just running away. And now she wants to go, and Ruth had said if she could make it something positive for herself, that maybe i it would be all right to go, and Allyson said that that she had talked it over with Joe and talked it over with someone else but that she really valued Ruth's opinion. And she wanted to know what Ruth th thought. And so Ruth told her that she felt that at this point it might not be a bad idea. Allyson is planning to go to to George Mason University for her master's degree in the fall, so it wouldn't be for that long. And Ruth said that she told Allyson that she felt that Allyson was her connection to Nancy and that she was Allyson's connection to Nancy. And I think that's what they are, each other's connection to Nancy.

There was something else, but I've forgotten what it was. Not just the connection to Nancy. Sniff. Maybe it was just the connection to Nancy. The connection to Nancy. I have to stop this for a moment here, while I get my thoughts together.

The construction now on Fairmount Avenue has proceeded so that now. Good grief! We're on the new part of the constructed road curving around to to where are we going here? Going down towards towards the credit union State

THE NANCY TAPES

Employees Credit Union, towards SECO. Holy cow! Boy, they're really doing work here!

What else was there about Allyson? Oh! Oh, I know what it was! That Allyson had said, Oh, Ruthie was talking about how, for Darren, down in Charleston, he wouldn't have anyone to reach out to to hold onto. But that here at home, in Silver Spring he had everybody, he had Ruth, he had Dave Weinstein, he had his cousins. And she said that Allyson said that that as devastating as this experience was, that through through everybody's being at the hospital that week that Nancy was in there, that she now felt that she had so many more people to reach out to, like me and Sophie and and my sister Nancy, that gave her many more people to reach out to, that she had that many more family contacts to call on if she needed some help. That's what that experience gave everybody.

Remember that article about kitchen and cooking, and everybody was in the kitchen, everybody was cooking Nancy's last meal, or she was cooking the last meal for everybody.

That click-click noise you hear in the background and heard in the background, that's the left-turn signal here in Towson, getting ready to turn left on uh Joppa Road.

Just turned the radio back on after recording and sitting here waiting for the light to change and here's The Beatles, *Let It Be*. "Let it be, let it beeee" What I said to Nancy *[voice breaking-crying]* that Sunday, Let it be. Aawoohh, shit! "Whisper words of wisdom,"*[voice cracking]* "And though they may be parted, there is still a chance that they will see, There will be an answer, Let it beeeee *[piano] [piano--piano--organ--drums--voices hard to hear--guitars--piano]*-- whisper words of wisdom" *[crying]* "Let it beee. And when the night is cloudy, there is still a light that shines on me," *[voice cracking]* "let it be" *[crying]* "I wake up to the sound of music, Mother Mary comes to me–*[piano]*--speaking words of wisdom, let it beeeee--*[piano]*--ah let it be, let it beeee, There will **TAPE ENDS**

TAPE NUMBER 8A

TUESDAY, JANUARY 22, 1991

Good morning, gentlemen, it's now 8:27 on Tuesday, January the 22nd, 1991. Three months to the day since Nancy's surgery. As a matter of fact, in about eight minutes, it would be just about three months to the day *and* the hour and the minute that the surgery itself actually began. It was on a Monday, October the 22nd, that I was at the cemetery and at 8:35 got this sudden urge I knew I had to go back. I was in the car, I had to go back and see Uncle Morris one more time, and it was later that Joe told me, *[voice soft and slow]* that Joe told me, that the surgery had begun at just that 8:35. And I remember when they got the word, that the surgery was over, and her was beating on her own, and I wished Joe a *mazel tov*. I said to Joe, *Mazel Tov*. They said she was beating on her own. *[angry tone]* They sent down that that good word. They shouldn't have done that at that point! You never know, mehyn. Y' never know y' never know. Almost only counts in horseshoes and hand grenades, mehyn. It does not count in heart surgery. It does not count in life, mehyn. Mehyn! Mehyn! Y' hear dat, mehyn?! Almost doesn't count.

Odysseus was at the shoreline, he could see men lighting the fires. But almost didn't count. He fell asleep, he relaxed his guard, he relaxed his guard, and his men, his men! opened the bag of winds. What a *[signal clicking throughout]* wind-bag his men were! What were the men doing in the wind-bag? Because they thought he was holding out on them. Ha-Ha! It was his men, it was himself who fell asleep, and then his men.

But in life, there is the tragic. Just when you think, you're free as a dove, Old Devil Moon blinds you with love and pain and grief! and death! Old Devil Life blinds you with those things! Just when you think you're free as a dove, Whacko! Whacka-Whacka-Whacko! Here it comes! Right now! Time to close out, over and out for the nonce. With Mr. Phelps, Captain Kirk, Captain Picard, and the away team of Perry Neam, Ian or perhaps Evan Naow, aaannd Peter Burns! Don't get any on your peter 'cause it burns! RIGHT LANE MUST TURN RIGHT! And here we go, 'round again, singin' the song of Molly Bee! Goodbye!

Anybody who hears these tapes or reads my eventual transcript of these tapes might think that I was having a bit of trouble coping with things. But! The fact that I can do these tapes shows that I am finding a way to cope with these things. Right? S said to me once, maybe through literature I could assimilate and cope, take these, these chaoses of life, when life hits you when you're just when you think you're free as a dove, Old Devil Life blinds you with agony and and and *death* and all these terrible things, just when you think. And and to find a way to cope with this chaos, he said, maybe you could do it through lit'ature, as other people find religion. Maybe I There's a sign that's been rubbed off and it says "VIKING

WOMEN DON'T CARE." Somebody grafitied that on a concrete wall, and it h's since been rubbed out. Looks like a very old sign. What's the significance of *that*?!?! *Gentlemen*! Put that in your chaos pipe and smoke it! Whoops! Here comes the traffico mundi, I'd better stop now.

That little conversation about coping and literature. What I was getting to, partly, was also that partly of myself and partly also others, that Ruthie said on the phone last night, incidentally, the last tape ended with the Beatles *Let It Be* from 105.7 WQSR. Ruthie said last night about how Allyson had these resources within her, and all these resources around her, and it made me think although I didn't say it to Ruth at the time what I had said to Darren about his poem about Nancy that if he can write a poem like that, he had more strength inside him than he realized he did. *He* had his resources within him. He used literature to cope and also to express something about, focus the grief of people, of himself and of people, on on that which survives. The sun in her eyes, that which survives. Survives, the sun in her eyevs. Hives!

Hives are an allergic reaction to something. The sun on your hives. Do you have sun on your hives? I don't have sun on my hives. Alllright!

Good morning, again, gentlemen, it is now 9:25, I'm heading down Reisterstown Road in the city! And the song on the radio was just *The Time of Your Life*, we remember the times of your life, on thirteen hundred which is not WFBR anymore, I don't know what the hell it is. But all I wanta do is *[voice breaking]* cryyyy. What contact do I have with anybody?! Jon Krome, my nephew, is in Baltimore. I haven't called himmm in I don't know how long. The last time I saw him was at Nancy's funeral three months ago. 'Course he hasn't called and Sophie always says, it works, it's a two-way street. It works both ways. But I have a greater obligation to call than he does. Greater responsibility. And yet I don't. And I don't and I don't and I don't! And I never talk to Chuck! I know Ronny wanted me to. Sniff. But I'm such a *chicken-shit*! I should've talked to 'im. I remember that wedding! He cried, Ronny cried, *[crying]* and so did I! Sniff. Shit! No one to say *Kaddish*. Oh, how does it work out that way?! How does it work out that way?! How does it work out that way?! I think M and E's daughter or son married a Christian. Sniff. I don't know which one, I think that ended in divorce. Oooohhh, man! Ooooohhh, man! I'm here now at Reisterstown and Northern Parkway. Coming down towards--sniff-- towards the Crest Theatre and the Hilltop Diner. I was never really a Diner hanger, but what was it? Sid Mandell's that was there and near the Crest.

And I used to come up here Friday nights to go to the movies sometimes by myself, often by myself, I would just take the bus and I remember Ruth saying at the time something about how independent I was, I could just go. Do what I wanted. Even if I didn't people who wanted to go, I went. It was all right. And I remember walking to Sid's and seeing ML--sniff. And he was in college then or university, and he s I was wearing a turtle-neck, and he said something about my wearing a hero shirt. A hero shirt, a hero shirt. Ooohh, man, ooohh, man, the Crest Theatre. That time I was having intestinal trouble of some kind. And I had to take mineral oil to help pass out things. And it gave me such awful gas. I remember being in the Crest with A, and I passed some gas. Ah fahted! He fahted! And A got *[laughing]* up and moved, people got up and moved, it was awful. Bennie's. Bennie's Poolroom here at Belvedere. Oh, man, oh, man, oh, man! Garrison Avenue. Reisterstown and Garrison. Oh, man, oh, man! Oh, man, oh, man-oh!

Coming down around the curve now. And there's that white-steepled church. And here I think is where Maar Lesser's house used to be. Taught me my *haftorah* for my *Bar Mitzvah*. Oh-me-oh-my! Y'picked a fine time to leave me, Lucille. Lucille Avenue. It's what just parked [*sic*] at, Woodland, passed that. Woodland. Coming down now towards the old Dominick's. Virginia Avenue. There's where the old Dominick's was, and there is Royce Avenue! 3316 Royce Avenue. Hi, Aunt Freda. Uncle Aaron, Jerry, *[voice breaking]* and Sonny. And Jerry standing out on the street cursing and cursing and cursing, and M saying, That boy is crying for his motherrrr. *[voice very angry here]* And I did *nothinnnggg!* *[quavering but softer, quietly intense]* I did *nothing*! I did *nothiiinnnnggg*! And here we are at Cold Spring Lane. That guy down there from the Penn-Rock Hotel in Penn-Mar, Maryland. A's, family A took care of.

It is 9:31 and coming down now, getting ready to pass Shirley Avenue, and what's now the Shirley Avenue Street Park, Shirley Avenue and there's the IDHS, I Do Hate School, the Isaac Davidson Hebrew School. And now what's used to be PS 59, it's the same building the Louisa May Alcott School, but now it's senior citizen housing. There's where Gleiman's used to be, and that we used to be s P, LP's father, I think it was, attorney at law, and PO's. And Springhill Avenue and up to the right was Jake's Tailor and up farther up to the left was Jake the Tailor, and farther up across Park Heights Avenue the 2600 block, the *famous* and infamous and notorious and wondrous 2600 block of Park Heights of Springhill Avenue. Violet Avenue. Where Kessler's used to be which is now back to being a house and Do you *believe*?! Rockrose, is that where the photographer lived, I remember coming to pick up my pictures there when when class pictures. And Ullman Avenue with Sussman's and Norfolk Avenue. Is that where he lived? And Hilldale with Roland Roland's Barber Shop down there and Lozinsky's Grocery Store. And Park Circle which is now Henry G. Parks Jr. Circle. Sussman's and the time I went into Sussman's. My mother wanted a refill on her Equanil, her Miltown, the S.J. Perlman book, *The Road to Mil Under the Spreading Atrophy, The Road to Miltown*. And asked him for a refill and there was someone in there.

THE NANCY TAPES

I didn't know the difference. And he said that he couldn't refill it without a prescription. Lordy, Lordy, Lordy.

I remember those days, I remember going down to get comics and sundaes on Friday evenings. Chocolate nut sundaes, and mother would get hot fudge. What did Ronny get? I don't remember. And I remember *illo tempo ston gero ekino* those days. *Bahzmahn hazeh.* Oh-me-oh-my. And there's, the reservoir. What's left of the reservoir, what used to be the reservoir. It was cut down years ago, even when we were kids, when we were teen-agers, some time, and turned into ballfields. The reservoir was not even really a reservoir. I used to walk down here. I remember walking in the rain when I was home on Passover leave, was it Passover leave? Or was it leave in May before I went overseas? Oh-me-oh-my. *[voice almost breaking]* Playing pitch at MF's house, in the winter, the snow day. Playing pitch to pitch pitch Roll or bowl a ball a penny a pitch. Playing cards playing cards playing cards. *Asha-i-viatsa. Ashaa-iii-viaatsaaa.*

Mondawmin now to the right, Liberty Heights and Reisterstown and coming past look down and see the Bromo-Seltzer Tower and some of the new buildings. There's the MN Building, I don't know what it is now, it used to be the Mathieson Building, then the Maryland National Building, and I can see the sun glaring, reflecting off the water of the inner harbor. Or the harbor farther down or wherever it is. I guess it must be the inner harbor. Can't be too far down. Although I don't see Fells Point. I'm not sure exactly where Fells not Fells Point, what the heck's it called? Federal Hill.

Good evening, Gentlemen. In the background, *Bridge over Troubled Water*, Simon and Garfunkle. Yes, it's 9:36 p.m.. I'm heading up Liberty Heights from Coppin, after I've been watching Coppin beat Morgan in basketball, 85 to 58. And I heard this song. And it made me think of my *YAAWWWPPP!* Y-A-W-P *YAAWWWPPP!* All these hours of tape, one long YAAWWPP! "Like a bridge" One long yaawwp. "over troubled" Thinking. "water" Thinking, gentlemen. Put this in your "will ease your mind" chaos-mixture, and figure out what comes next. "like a bridge over troubled" I reading last night the review of a book about No Novalis, and the reviewer I can't remember his name talking about how that all of his notes were his kind of an attempt to find order out of chaos, that's not exactly what the guy said but, to find some some meaningful relationship between the world and the world, the subjective world and the objective world the microcosm of human consciousness and the macrocosm of the natural world. *Bridge* ends And thinking about all my notes on this tape thinking about all my notes on this tape. And I realized this is one long fifteen-hour yawp of pain and grief. A child's yawp. Do I find in here anyplace anyplace in which I pose or posit or suggest or think about an order an order an order? Some sense of there's some sense of looking at or for an order, other than just the random emotionalness of it all?

Soph called this evening, or I called Soph, while we were talking and there was a beep th a call waiting. And she said it was Aunt Esther, and Aunt Esther they just got back from Florida, and she wanted to call, say hello. After three weeks in Florida, the first thing that she could say was, she's so depressed, she's so depressed, she's so alone, she's so depressed. She feels rotten. She's so depressed. How many people did I listen to today? How many people did I listen to today? Father confessor. One after another after another. I guess I did I guess I did.

FRIDAY, JANUARY 25, 1991

Good morning, gentlemen. It is 8:01, Friday, January the 25th, nineteen hundred and ninety-one. Mr. Phelps, Captain Kirk, Captain Picard, Jean-Luc. *Jim*!

This morning, on the news, local news there was a report about apparently some kind of a barricade situation. Some guy had was threatening the s I missed the beginning of the report actually. The only thing that I really caught the thing that I really caught was that the place was Spaulding Avenue. And I said, Spaulding Avenue? I said, I haven't heard that name in years. And Soph said, Where's that? And I said, It's in the Pimlico area. Spaulding Avenue, that's where Ronny and D and Eva lived. On Spaulding Avenue. Spaulding Avenue. Up in that duplex, the upstairs, no, the duplex. Upstairs. Was that a duplex? Well, whatever, I don't know, duplex, is that the side by side or the up and down? Anyhow. They lived in the upstairs. Did she have some kind of a kidney problem? Or bladder problem? I don't remember what it was. But I remember being over there several times and being over there once when she was sick and in bed. Spaulding Avenue.

Just passed Royce Avenue, Gentlemen, 3316 Royce Avenue, coming up on Park Lane Shopping Center. Thinking. 1990. October. Nancy's death. And it was actually, 36 wait a second was it 36? Yes. 36 years ago, 1954, in October that Uncle Sol died. Sol Koren. 36 years ago in July in that my father died, and 46 [*sic*] years ago in December that Aunt Freda died.

And I remember them coming back from the Mayo Clinic then, aunts and uncles, Uncle Herschel and my mother and Aunt Esther and Aunt Lily. Was Aunt Menyeh with them? I think so, I don't remember. When Aunt Freda died. What was there about that experience? Thinking about, they lost a sister, and there was a whole bunch of them, and Ruthie this time lost a sister, there's only her, but there was the rest of the family, the cousins who were there. Mainly, Nancy and Ronny and I. Things fall apart, but things can hold together. At least a little bit. Ruthie talking about how Allyson felt that she had all these additional support people. People she hadn't thought of before like m my sister Nancy and Ronny and me and Sophie being there, all of us being there for them at that time.

36 two times eighteen. *Chai* twice. In this situation. In this time. Past Keyworth Avenue PS 59, coming up on Springhill Avenue now. Think about that.

THE NANCY TAPES

Look at that connection. Uncle Herschel coming back, and I remember him saying how strong he was, there goes Springhill Avenue. How strong he was that he didn't cry. And thinking to myself, *Why!* What what's what's wrong with crying when your sister dies? Your youngest sister dies. What would've been wrong for him to cry? Oh, man, oh, man, what would have been wrong? What a connection there is to that. 36 years later. The loss of a sister, the loss of an aunt, the loss of a cousin. No cousins were there then, but sisters and brother were. Sniff. Have to get around to doing the transcription for Ruth. Of the funeral service.

Passing Park Circle, there goes the building, what was that? There was a building on the corner. Was it a restaurant? And it's gone. And they've torn it down. It's like when, that parking lot on Lombard Street in back of the IBM Building. We turned the corner, I turned the corner, I was gonna park in there. Bob and Louise were here and I turned the corner and the parking lot was gone! All of a sudden it was just gone! Things disappear that quickly. *[voice very quiet]* Like people. Sometimes. Things disappear that quickly.

The IBM Building. Turn the corner from Guilford Avenue onto Lombard Street, I wanted to park in that building, parking building, the way we usually did. And I remember, I had heard, that they were gonna d fix the IBM, y'know, construct that IBM Building. And then I didn't put 2 and 2 together I guess, and y' don't think about it, and suddenly construction had not only begun, but they had demolished the parking building, the parking building was gone.

Listen. This is a yawp. But it's also this. It's the raw material, it's the chaos out of which I'm gonna try to find some order. It's the raw material. This is the nothingness, the void, this is the waste. And I want to send my creative spirit over this, into this, through this. To try to come up with something. To see connections. 36 years. To see connections.

Put this in also. That on Monday, January the 14th, that when I went down to Annapolis, for the legislative liaisons meeting. And I went to the the State Department of Records, looking for death certificates, *[voice soft and quiet and slow]* and I put in the slip requesting the death certificates of my father and my grandfather, Charles Krome and Wolf Krome, they couldn't give me copies because they said they were not indexed. They were not indexed. And I don't understand that. So I'm gonna have to go back in and search for them according to the time period of, by myself sometime. But also this. When I found Mushe's death certificate, and I found Rosie's *[very soft and quiet and slow]* death certificate. And I think I found Reubin's death certificate. Or Kathie's Katie's death certificate, Reubin's wife. For father and mother, for a for the women, maiden name was unknown. Maiden name was unknown. And there was only one case, and right now, I can't remember which one, where even the father's name was known. Nothing was down there. Unknown mother's maiden unknown mother's

SIDNEY KROME

name unknown father's name. Unknown maiden name. Unknown! *["Unknown" was whispered]* No information. The line seems to just stop. And, of course, even if I could find their names, because they were they were born in Russia, it said Russia, there would be no way, there would be no records anymore, no way to track them down, to get their birth or death birth certificates at all. *[whispered]* The line ends! The tracing of the line ends. It stops. It begins and that's it. *In medias res.* In the middle of the thing.

SATURDAY, JANUARY 26, 1991

Good morning, Gentlemen, it's 10:04 Saturday, January 26th. When I got up this morning I did go downstairs into the study, and I did work on a note about the photos Zalman's photo the photos of the graves of Wolf and Rosie and Mushe Krome. Okay. Sniff.

Now one of the things I wanted to say *[signal clicking throughout]* is that last night, and I put this in the note, last night when I was looking at the pictures, of the gravestones and I looked at Rosie's, I noticed something, and I noticed for the first time, she died on *Yom Kippur*, it says *Yom Ha-Kipurim*. And I never noticed that before, I just assumed, glancing at it, that it said something that I wouldn't be able to read having to do with the date in Hebrew. Well, it does say something having to do with the date in Hebrew, and what it says is *Yom Ha-Kipurim*. That Rosie Krome that Rosie Krome Rosie Krome died on *Yom Kippur* 1913 at the age of 34, and I also noticed last night as a matter of fact that she was two years older than Grandpa Wolf Krome. She was 34 in 1913. In 1944 when he died, he was 63. So if you subtract 31 years, back from 1944 to 1913, he was 32 when she died in 1913. But she was 34. So she was 32 years, she was two years older than he. Which means that also that he was born in 1881 1881. So he was like he was 29 when Daddy was born. I also so made noted on the note that he died almost exactly 10 years ts before Daddy. He died July 19th, 1944, Daddy died July 15th, 1944. [*sic*]

That is more material for Kirk, Picard, and Phelps. Phelps Pickar Phelps Kirk and Picard, 's in the chronological order. Or Kirk, Phelps, and Picard in alphabetical order. Or Picard, Phelps, and Kirk in reverse alphabetical order. Be that as it may, the order is in there someplace, that's what the purpose of all this is is not simply to yawp, but to put together a packet of material of chaos out of which somehow eventually after I listen to all this, transcribe it, and put it together, there can be some form of orderly orderliness out out of the chaotic chaoticness. Chaotic chaos. Over and out. On my way now to *Tchi-zuk Amu-no*.

This is two Saturdays after the war started, January 10 days 16th was the first attack and, in the last eight days, Israel has been attacked five times by SCUD missiles, most recent yesterday, one person died yesterday, three people died before,

THE NANCY TAPES

I from heart attacks in the I guess it was the second or third uh SCUD missile attack. So I decided I needed to go to services to be with fellow Jews on this, at this time. So I'm going back to *Tchizu Chizuk Amuno* which is where I usually go on the High Holy Holy Days. Although there's a temptation for me to go to Beth Tfiloh. See part of the thing is I have trouble making a commitment to one place or another. But I'm gonna go ahead and go back to *Chizuk Amuno*.

Good morning, again, it's now 12:31, or good afternoon. Saturday, January the 26th. Just leaving *Tchi-zuk Amu-no* to head home. Very briefly and quickly. The *Torah* reading, *Exodus*, Chapter 14, beginning at verse 26, the crossing of the Red Sea, and and manna from Heaven and the the comment by the somebody talking about it was that the rebuke for rejoicing in the in the death of the Egyptians. My creatures God said to the angels, My creatures are dying, and you are rejoicing. But He did not immediately rebuke the He the Hebrews, in recognition of the humanity of human beings, of their fallibility. That this is a part of divinity that human beings find most difficult to accept, and that is the compassion even for one's enemies in their suffering and in their death. And then also *Judges*, Chapter 4, 4 and 5, the story of Deborah Deborah Devorah and Ya-el, the song of Deborah the victory of Deborah and Barak over Sisera. The Canaanites and then also a at the end of that a very brief passage the the a wondering of Sisera's mother, why does it take him so long to come back? She thinking that he's dividing the spoils, not realizing that he is dead. That, speaking of the translation from the Penguin of what? of Biblical Verse? I can't I didn't quite catch that reference. *Exodus* 14 beginning at verse 6 26 verse 26 through 15 and into 16, I think it was, and then *Judges*, Chapters 4 and 5 Devorah and Ya-el and Barak, and Sisera.

Also talking about miracle miracles that the miracle is life itself, the miracles of everyday life, the sense of wonder at life. What I need to talk about again with the at Saint Saint Nectarios and just also for myself the double miracles, the double sense of miracle in Judaism. Number one, the very existence of life, the very existence of the universe as a created thing, created out of nothing, it is therefore miraculous because it depends for its very existence on God. And then within the created universe the miracles are those things which which one would not expect to happen, that require the intervention of God in the universe which He Himself created to alter it at times. Those are other kinds of miracles. Okay, that's it.

Something happened. I must have pushed just the play, and that's why it was not recording, when I thought it was recording about the the death in, wait a second I'm gonna turn this over now.

Actually I'm not turning it over, I'm gonna say this quickly, I was thinking about in in the service today, in the the the the the *Torah* reading and the *Haftorah*, the *Judges* and *Exodus*, that God saved the Hebrews, the Jews, from the Egyptians, drowned them in the sea, that God saved the Jews from the Amalekites, actually, they the Jews were the their own hand against the Amalekites and that God would banish the Amalekites from the Book of Remembrance, and also at the end, that we must fight the Amalekites in every generation, and that's the point! Just as God sometimes saved Jews, but did not for example in the Holocaust, so sometimes you individual human beings live even when they sh seem to be ready to die, and other times they don't. It's **TAPE ENDS**

THE NANCY TAPES

TAPE NUMBER 8B

SATURDAY, JANAURY 26, 1991 (CONT.)

Continuing on the other side. It's as we talked about when Nancy was dying and when Nancy died and Joe talking about some, waiting for a miracle, miracles don't always happen, people do die. It's hard to accept. Sometimes, *nothing* can be done, and God does not intervene. God does not perform the miracle, of intervening, in the universe which He created. He may intervene sometimes, but He does not always intervene even when we call on Him in our pain, in our grief, in our sorrow. He does not always intervene. Nancy *died*. Others *die*.

My father *died*.

MONDAY, JANUARY 28, 1991

Good morning, Gentlemen. It's 9:09 am. I'm just driving through the campus of the University of Maryland. Monday, January 28th. Driving through campus having taken Charlie and his buddy back to school this morning, and just passing Praenkert Field House and to the left previously passed Wicomico Hall and to the right the old SDT House Sigma Delta Tau. Remembering and what was her name? I can picture her. From Baltimore. Kind of a heavy-set Jewish girl. Who introduced me to. Can't remember. Sigma Delta Tau House Sigma Delta Tau. Went there to be the campaign manager for what was his name? from New York, who was running for freshman class president. Hu-ho, what a joke that was!

Okay. I'm eating an apple here, too. That was the crunch of the apple.

Well, now, Gentlemen! Ha-ha! That was actually two apples that I ate rather quickly there. *Habe d'Ehrie. Hunger, hunger,* hunger.

In any case, driving Charlie and his buddy to College Park this morning, at one point, and I I'm not sure what the point was, at what time and it was, I can't recall, but. But I think it was when we pulled off of 95 towards US 1 South, that I saw looked up saw geese or ducks flying. They seemed to be flying north instead of south. And they single file single file, but they also kind of waved their line, I mean, their their line waved as they flew. Which I thought was rather curious. Curiously refreshing.

Yesterday afternoon, Sunday, January the 27th, I went over to Nancy's to take over the pictures. I gave her the picture of Zalman, and a picture of the gravestones of Rosie and Wolf and Mushe. And we talked about Nancy Nancy's grave. And she said Nancy, ah my sister Nancy, Nancy said that she was the one who had told Ruthie that there were stones on Nancy's grave, as though someone had been there, not as though, someone *had* been there. And and nobody could figure out who was there because at that time Joe had not yet been there. And I told Nancy as I had told Ruth that that I had not been there yet. So I don't know who h'd been there. It seems to be a great mystery. Who has been to Nancy's grave?

Visiting Nancy and put stones on it? And Nancy said that she felt very very peaceful there, the only thing that bothered her was that the way Nancy was positioned, that her head, that with the ground sloped, and that her head was on the down part of the slope and her feet were on the up part of the slope. That bothered her. That bothered her. But she said that while she felt no real urge to go see Daddy, to go see our father, she really felt that she had been there twice now to see Nancy. And she felt very very peaceful there. Curiously refreshing. Refreshingly curious. That's even better. Not curiously refreshing, but refreshingly curious. Wonder what all this travel noise is gonna do to this this recording.

That is, all the not the travel noise the noise in the car, the noise of the road and the wind over the car and everything. It's rather loud, today. Course I'm going 72 miles per hour. *[laughing]* In a 55 mile zone.

That's Nat King Cole now on radio station 1-2-6-0, singing *Non Dimenticar*, and I just passed a caaarrr, a Lincoln Continental and thinking about how I said once to Paul, that is, that I can remember a, y'know talking about cars that one wanted now, w for me it was never a Cadillac, it was always a Lincoln Continental. Saying how I used to stand on the corner of Park Heights and Springhill and watch these cars go by and and and it was always the Lincoln. Cars heading through Lower Judea on their way up to Upper Judea. And it was always the occasional Lincoln, that I really admired.

"Don't forget to dream." And now I am on Caton Avenue coming back into Baltimore and guess what? On WITH 1-2-3-R it's *Non Dimenticar*. "*Non dimenticar* my love is like a star my darling," Twicet in one morning. "Shining bright a"

TUESDAY, JANUARY 29, 1991

[signal clicking throughout] Good morning, Gentlemen. It's 8:09 am, Tuesday, January 29th, 1991. Today my brother Ronald is 55 years old. Happy Birthday, Ronald! That's incredible, I can't believe he's 55! And that means that I'm going to be 53 this year. Age grows apace. Apace apace apace. Che-che.

Good morning, everybody. Couple things. *Mey neshumah 'z ah rawzhinkeh.* My soul is a raisin. There's a Plymouth Acclaim with a Purple Heart car with a Purple Heart license plate. *Mey neshumah 'z a rawzhinkeh.* My soul is a raisin. *Mach zuch nischt vischendik.* Pretend you don't know. Make yourself unknowing. *Mach zuch nischt vischendik. Mach oys kayn.* Pretend that it is so. Pretend that it's real. I have to remember where all those, I remember Aunt Lily mainly saying Ma *Mey neshumah 'z a rawzhinkeh.* What's a *mehyr? Mey neshumah 'z a rawzhinkeh?* Or was it also Aunt Menyeh? Maybe it was both of them. And I think in one of them there's a possible title for the book about the Herlich klan.

SIDNEY KROME

Thinking memories memories memories thinking memories of. I think I said this. Ruth was telling me on the phone the other day about how Joe took flowers to Nancy's grave and took roses actually how he had asked her whether they could take flowers. Sniff. And I told Ruthie I'm not sure why but there is kind of a prohibition on by by Jews at least in Orthodox Judaism not a against bringing flowers to graves. At least live cut flowers, and I'm not sure I'm not sure what they're told her I didn't know why, and she said maybe she would look in the book. But it what it made me think of was taking Raizel out in August of 1958 when Ronny and Eva were getting married, when they were here for the wedding. Taking Raizel out to the cemetery to see what she I might later called the *troika*. *[voice quavering-breaking, louder and louder]* The *troika* the *troika* the *troika*! *[voice crying]* My father and Uncle Sol and Aunt Freda. In 1954. Sniff. We passed the 36th anniversary this year of that. And she said, we stopped and she asked me to stop so she could get some flowers, she said she knows y're not supposed to but she had to take some flowers, for Aunt Freda. As for Aunt Freda es for Aunt Freda *[crying now]*, especially for Aunt Freda, *[quavering and singing to Und Sonst Gar Nichts-in German accent]* Falling apart again. Cheh-cheh. *[quiet and soft and slow]* Flowers. 36 years later. Nancy's dead at the age of 48.

I remember when they came back from the Mayo Clinic, was it in Rochester? And we were in Aunt Esther's house. And Uncle Herschel talked about how he hadn't cried and how strong he was that he hadn't cried. And I remember thinking at the time as I've thought since, Why? Why is that a sign of strength? What is wrong with crying when your sister *[quavering]* dies? Sniff. After such a specially in her case after such a horrendous bout with uterine cancer.

And I remember that Aunt Esther showed me a picture of Aunt Freda sitting up, in her bed in the hospital in the Mayo Clinic, I guess it was in the Mayo Clinic. And I remember she looked so scrawny. But her face didn't look so bad. And I didn't wanta make everybody feel bad so I said to Aunt Esther, Well I didn't think she looked too bad. I thought she looked pretty good. She asked me how she looked. And then she said, What's the matter? She looks terrible. How can you say she looks good? She looked like she was dead already.

[very soft and low and quiet and slow] I remember that picture. Sitting up with her arms, her forearms resting on her knees. Sitting up Cheh! in bed. Sniff. I remember that.

Have to write up some of these things. I remember my father taking us, Daddy taking us down on Saturdays. And I remember we went to the New York Dairy Bar, that kosher restaurant, I guess it was on Baltimore Street or on Lombard Street, I can't remember which one. Especially on Passover, so we could eat lunch there, on Passover. And then we'd go to the bar. And Uncle Aaron would brought us home when he was getting off work at four o'clock. And there was a place he

THE NANCY TAPES

took us to The Old The The Europe Old Europe The European something like that on Howard Street. Or on Eutaw. And then there's another place called The Old Vienna which was farther over on Baltimore Street, I think. From which we could even walk down. Che-eh! Che-eh! Pardon me. Walk down to the bar. Sniff. And I remember he took us to I remember that with the icebreaker the Coast Guard US Coast Guard Cutter, the Appalachian. And we used to run around, he used he would sit there and have coffee with the captain or with member of the members of the crew. And Ronny and I would run around on that boat. And then I remember there was there was in one winter there was a freeze. And the freeze and in the freeze there was a freeze and on the front page of *The News American*, I guess it was in *The News American*, there was a picture of the Coast Guard Cutter. Sniff. The icebreaker The Appalachian going through the harbor. Breaking up the ice through the harbor or through the bay, cutting up the ice.

Reminds me, I want to call Martick's because I remember, was it in 1958? When A and I used to go down there, there was that I guess it was charcoal of a man's face in the rain. I wonder where it is and if I could get hold of that. I've thought about that picture several times, and I would like to, and I've thought to myself about calling, I'd like to call, maybe I can call today if I remember, see if it's possible to get hold of it.

Thanks! for the mammaries! Peter Burns! Ian, or Evan, Naow. And Perry Neham, Neam. Sniff. Three heroes. My soul is a raisin. Over and out. Happy Birthday, Ron!

It's now 8:17 and just passing Epstein's which of course has gone out of business. THIS STORE IS CLOSING FOREVER. Do you believe that? A sign in red on Epstein's, here at on Reisterstown Road near RRP. THIS STORE IS CLOSING FOREVER. There's Hechinger's. I wonder if they're open. Wonder if I could get a flag in there. Gonna stop this morning real quick.

But a memory also in December 1954. After Aunt Freda's funeral. In the *shivah* house, our house, and I guess, I guess what happened was that Ronny had probably gone back. Sniff. To College Park at that point, to school. And I was in the house and Uncle Layble and I guess H K came to the door to see about about going to school. Going down to City. And I started crying, and I didn't want to go *[quavers, breaks and starts crying]* because Aunt Freda had died. Sniff. And my mother said to Uncle Layble, You see, *ez nischt geveyzn ah ah tanteh vie ah tanteh me vie men zagt men ah tanteh!* She was something special. *[still crying softly]* Oh, boy! Oh, boy! Oh, boy! Sniff. Aunt Freda. Died. Sniff. Entrance. Hechinger's.

What I did was I pulled off at Hechinger's to try to get a larger flag. 'Cause Paul would like a flag. And I'm going along with it. I doesn't has to, but I'm going along with it. It's now 8:30! Holy Cow! Wee-ga-ii!

SIDNEY KROME

In the background, at 8:33 at the corner of Reisterstown Road and Northern Parkway just switched to WITH and here comes Frankie Lane and *Jealousy*. "No one but me" From the early 50's. "your" Or the mid-50's, the early 50's. "When the muuusic starts" Frankie Lane, one of my all-time favorites. When I went to Atlantic City, thanks to Ronny talking to Mother and letting Mother into letting me go and that was I guess it must have been. What year? I didn't remember what year. Was I 15, or 16? With and somebody else. And saw Frankie Lane! At the Steel Pier. Frankie Lane, the Steel Pier in Atlantic City. "In ecstacy mystery paaaaiiin We dance to a tango of love" And now passing what used to be the Hilltop Diner and on the left Sid Mandell's and "beats with mine" what it used to be the Crest Theatre but is now the Stardom, whatever the Stardom is. "your eyes" Here we go. "give the answer" The answer I'm dreaming of. "The answer I'm dreaming of" Dreaming of. Those soft words "Those soft words" Word your cruel lips "cruel lips will never saaayyy" Will never say.

Reisterstown and Belvedere, the building that that Bennie's Poolroom, I just noticed, it's now somebody's The Tax Corner. And, the storefronts all along the side on Reisterstown Road have been cemented over! I didn't even real then never noticed that before. Obviously it happened before today, but I just noticed it today. Curiously refreshing and refreshingly curious. How things happen and we don't notice them till all of a sudden they hit us in the face. Hit me in the face! They hit me in the face! Death hits me in the face!

I gotta get around to taking those pictures sometime. Make a slide presentation a slide put together some slides of the slides of the slide presentation of the oooolllld oooolldd oolldd oold oold ooooooolllld neighborhood type thingies. Or thinga-type neighbories.

Passing now Rrrrooyccce Avenue Royce Avenue Royce Avenue 3316 Mohawk 4-2448. No! Yes! And our number was Mohawk 4-1014.

Aahh yes, now I remember, just passed Park Circle, Henry G. Parks, Jr. Circle now to you. Sniff. And the building they tore down, they were tearing down, that they are still in process of tearing down, the building itself was down now, they're ripping up the grounds, was was a gas station as I recall, now I recall, I remember now that I recall that it was a gas station though I didn't recall or remember the last time I came by what it was.

The intersection of Reisterstown Road and Liberty Heights Avenue. By Mondawmin. The intersection they've cleaned up and fixed up straightened up polished up to make it easier for f traffic to get through, and they fixed up that corner right here on my right as I'm heading south on Reisterstown Road. And and turned it like into a little stone flattened area with y'know tiled stones or something like that stoned tiles. Pebbled kind of a kind of a peachy color and some trees planted. And look at the trash all over and someone knocked over the trash and

THE NANCY TAPES

there's filth and trash and it's not like it was when M lived around the corner, M and D and B F. M and D. And and B F. And M died was he a fresh? first year? second year? in med school. Testicular cancer. MF, M. Goodbye forever, M.

THIS STORE IS CLOSING FOREVER. Epstein's. THIS STORE IS CLOSING FOREVER. I can't believe it. These people have closed forever. But have they? When I think about Meyer Site. Oh, yes, I f I don't know if I mentioned this. On Sunday, open the paper and the there it was. Oh, you! Meyer Site at dea obituary of Meyer Site. Meyer Site, and it just stunned me. He had died on Wednesday. Which would have been the 23rd. And I saw it on Sunday of Sunday which would have been the 26th, no, 27th. 27th of January. He was 84, he died of Alzheimer's at Levindale. And it just stunned me because even though I thought h I was sure I ha if I thought about it I thought that he was dead. But I didn't realize he was still alive. He had retired in 1966. And I guess I being in D DC area, I just really didn't realize that he had retired. And Sophie h and I had gone on January 15th, Martin Luther King Day, we'd gone down to the Baltimore Museum of Art to see the exhibition of Aaron Sopher's sketches that they had there. Those paintings. And and I told Soph how when I was at Robert E. Lee Junior High School and I had Meyer Site for art, he took the class over to Aaron Sopher's studio. And what a marvelous thing that was. Didn't realize that he was dead, didn't realize, I mean I thought he had died, I didn't realize he was still alive. And so when I read of his death I was stunned. And it said that the services were Saturday, were today were s held on Saturday, yesterda, it said yesterday which would have been Saturday. But actually they were held on Fffriday the 25th. Had I known I m well, I c I don't know if I could've gone, but tsclk I might've tried to go. But I didn't know so I couldn't go.

[voice high and incredulous in this part about Abe Kershman's funeral] How did I ever ever not go to Abe Kershman's funeral!!? What is wrong with me?! I don't believe it! I don't believe it! I don't know what I had to do that I could not go? I had something I know I couldn't take off work, I felt that I couldn't, couldn't take off work, but how could I *not* take off a day to go to Abe Kershman's funeral!!??

Good afternoon, Gentlemen. It's 5:33, I'm on the 695 inner loop of the Beltway, just passing the 795 cut-off, and guess what's on the radio? We will have these moments to remember. *[Me singing along with radio]* "When other nights and other days may find us gone our separate ways, we will have these moments to remember." What year was that? I can't remember. It was in them golden olden daaayyys of the 50's, when knighthood was in flower. I tried to get a few flowers, too, Hah-hah-hah!

"Evening sha" Oh, here she is! It's Connie Whine! *[me singing along]* "dows make me blue" Wawawawa! Connie Francis! "When each day is" Shades of Bad Aibling and HHJ HJ's tape. "all I long to be" 320th USASA Battalion. "my happ" Oh, my goodness gracious sakes alive! "iness" 19-aught-and-uh-60-62! "Everyday I reminisce" *[singing along]* "How I miss my happineeeeessss. [Francis alone]* "A millioooon yeeeaars" *[I sing along]* "it seems" *[Francis alone]* "have gone by since I" Well, WITH is fading out as I come up here past the Woodholme Festival at Woodholme.

[me with Connie] "my haaaappineeeeeeeesss" *[Connie]* "Whether skies are grey or blue"

WEDNESDAY, JANUARY 30, 1991

Good morning, Gentlemen. It's now what time? 8:24 Wednesday, January the 30th, 1991. I'm just pulling out of the SECU lot on my way down to school. Had to get a little cash out so I have enough money for me trip to Montreal this weekend for the Bar-Bat Mitzvah of the Katz kids in Montreal. Going up by train, tomorrow night. I'm taking the sl the coach. Ronny's supposed to get on the train in Washington, be on coach. The rest of them all who are the rest of them all are, of course, whoops! are Nancy and Cheryl, Mother and Lou, Ruthie and Aunt Esther, and Mindy and Joel. Everybody's going up for the big occasion, and I'm gonna be staying at the hotel, the Ruby Foo's, with them. Simply because it's a simply because. And what am I gonna do? I noooo I just as I said to myself before, I feel a need to be with them. Haven't called Raizel, maybe I call Raizel tonight just to tell her I'm coming up just to say hello and whatevers. Sniff. Anyhow, that's where it is.

Last night, tried to reach Ron to call him, it was his 55th birthday, the line was busy, I called Kathie Kathie Bulmash 'cause I wanted to get Sonny's address. As it turns out I *did* have the address, I misunderstood what Jerry said, when I had seen Jerry at Aunt Esther's Chanukah party in December. I thought he said, that if you have, sniff, Olathe, Kansas, you have the wrong address. Well, actually I have the right address. Actually, I think what he really said was if I have anything *before* Olathe, Kansas, that's the wrong address. 'Cause the address is Olathe, Kansas.

Anyhow we started talking she wanted to know how everybody was doing in terms of of of reaction to N y'know follow up reactions whatever to Nancy's death. And and she felt that probably the one she felt sorriest for in a way was Joe because while he had very intense relationship of course as Nancy's husband, it was a *brief* per relatively brief period of time and he does not have roots with her before or in a sense roots after. That as devastateding as it was for Ruthie, to lose her absolute best friend, the woman she had been best friends with, her sister and her best friend all of her life, Ruthie had not only her memories but she has also the support of family, her husband, her kids, cousins, *et cetera*. Whereas Joe is is root-less from the family and that she felt that, she used the term novelistic, that he would just kind of eventually drift away and be cut loose or cut himself loose. And and she felt in a sense that he might, eventually become the grieving workaholic, left with nothing but his his memories and his work to fill his time. That he would not have the kind of support that that Ruth has. And also her concern about Aunt Esther, that Aunt Esther she felt had probably, oh, for maybe even since Nancy was born, have had in her mind the expectation of disaster, an expectation that Nancy would would die and now the worst her worst imagination, her worst, the worst possible case had finally happened had happened. And that she was just absolutely devastated by it and that that she was just and she was concerned about Aunt Esther's well-being and I I said, y'know, I said, she can take care of herself, I said physically it's not a problem, I said, it's emotionally, I said, she, she can get out and, do shopping, it's not *easy* for her but she gets out and does her shopping. And she can cook for herself it's just the emotion of of being alone. And not having anyone to talk to all the time. Or not having anyone to talk to as much as she would like to, as much as she *needs* to have someone to talk to, but she h's is kind of in a state of depression, and I I said how she had come back from three weeks in Florida. The first thing that she said to to Sophie was that she was miserable and grieving and and Nancy was dead and she was sick and awful and, and I said that y'know and Aunt Esther had always been a complainer and and that I I used to say to her that Aunt Esther if you ever stop complaining that's when I'll worry, that's when I'll worry about you. And, Kathie said that y'know she saw the same thing in Aunt Esther, this constant this complaining, and that she understood. And I said, y'know, I said I said I understand, but I said one would've hoped that, that the first thing she would've said would be something like she had a wonderful time, as good a time as she could in Florida, but now that she's back, are all these reminders of Nancy, and it would've been at least some kind of positiveness in the, not positiveness exactly, but some kind of a sense of adjustment. But just absolutely and totally devastated *nothing*, she could say nothing except how miserable she was and.

Anyhow we also talked about Kathie's interest in the Kennedy Assassination and and that she had through Joe gotten access to the 26 volumes and that she wanted to be able to go through it and study it, and see where the inconsistencies were. And she had had lined up all the facts from all of her reading, and she had just done an incredible amount of reading, not only of novels, *not* of novels also but also of of studies of the Kennedy Assassination. And that she subscribes to a thing called *Third Decade*, it's a journal that comes out monthly. Apparently it's a journal about the Kennedy Assassination, and she also said, and this is something that I had felt, that that that that was the day in effect that the music died, that America died, that that things have not **TAPE ENDS**

TAPE NUMBER 9A

WEDNESDAY, JANUARY 30, 1991
Good morning, gentlemen, it's 8:32, I'm on the Beltway heading for 83 South to go to work, 8:32 the morning of Wednesday, January the 30th. To pick up where I left off that this was the that November the 22nd, the day of the assassination was the day that the music died, that America something in America has died and that it has not been the same since and can never be the same again. I told her about my novel *The Far-Off Night*, and she thought the first one I had written was the one that I had written for Freda, the for about Freda, the *Steubenville Is Forever*. And I said, no, I had written this one before. And she would like to see it so I'm I have to make a copy I don't have to, but I'm going to make a copy for her, and I've got to send her a copy in the mail of the poem *The Life of a Star* and also a copy of one of the 8 by 12's of the picture of Kennedy's flag-draped caisson being drawn from from where? From the White House to the Capitol Building on Sunday, November the 24th, that picture that blurred when my shutter slipped, there's somebody drinking coffee, when my shutter slipped. So that's gonna to be going out to her today with a copy of the poem. Okay, over and out now, I think for the temporary time timeoutness, right here, time out! Now!
   Continuation. That conversation, is now, by the way, 8:45. I'm right here by Mondawmin at Warwick Avenue and Gwynns Falls Parkway, at the reyed light, got the reyed light, man, got the reyed light. And that conversation with Kathie last night on the phone, she said that something about how I was indirectly the first person in the family that she met because at College Park, at the University of Maryland, back at, she and Jerry had met in December of 66 and early in 67, I think she he took her past my office in Taliaferro Hall and and told her that that was his cousin's office, and she said he was really proud of that. That his cousin was there teaching at the University of Maryland. And I was so touched by what she had told me, that Jerry was proud of of my being there and I never never knew that, I mean, I never knew that he had taken her around, she met my office before she met me. But she felt that that was a way of meeting me through meeting my office through Jerry taking me to the taking her to my office. Or something like that, anyhow.

THURSDAY, JANUARY 31, 1991
   [train noises and voices throughout] It's 5:02 by my clock, just pulling, we pulled out a few minutes ago from Penn Station on the way to Montreal. *[clickety-clackety]* It's, let's see, Thursday, January 31st. Now past and can see Hopkins Hospital. Three months yesterday since Nancy died. And we're on our way now to Montreal for the *Bar-Bat Mitzvah*. Ron is supposed to be getting on here, I guess in New York.

THE NANCY TAPES

In the distance, right foreground, is City Hospital, Francis Scott Key Burn Center, I think that is on Eastern Avenue. And the sun is above the city skyline, the Hopkins skyline. The sun is going down. Boarding the train in Baltimore, Aunt Esther, my mother and Lou, Nancy and Cheryl, and Mindy. And I'm trying to remember, have been trying to remember. I was walking across campus. And somebody said something, and I changed the wording, something that applied to Nancy, and I can't remember what it was. Damn! I can't remember what, it's on the tip of my mind, the tip of my tongue. There's no clickety-clack. Can you hear the sound of the train? There's no clickety-clack.

Three jets flying off on the right. And the orange golden glow golden orange glow of the sunset. There's a group of eight people going, probably going skiing. Getting off at White River Junction. And I remember we stopped at White River Junction, oh, years and years and years and years ago. And this guy got off, and I saw him walking away toward a house, toward houses in the snow. Passing some military base, Air Force Base, is it Dover, already? It couldn't be Dover already. Ten minutes outside of Baltimore, maybe. I remember that guy got off at White River Junction. I was so young and I had talked with him, and I remember thinking then, how quickly he was into my life, how quickly he was out of my life. How quickly he was *in* my life, how *briefly* he was in my life. Nancy was in it longer, how much did I appreciate of the time that she was in it? How much do I appreciate of the time of anybody who's in my life?

[*train on bridge*] Over some body of water one of the rivers, I'm not sure which one. And the sun has set at the left rear now, dark orange, beautiful color, the water is flowing out east, to the bay, to the sea. It's kind of pale slate grey. Rippled and mottled. The clouds above are tinged with lavender, magenta and grey.

Now we're really rollin', rockin' and rollin' whippin' along, through the countryside, bare trees, barren trees, scraggly-ended trees, and a few clouds on the horizon of the sky, a darker magenta mauve, now darker and grey underneath.

[*train bridge over water*] Another body of water, flowing east, flowing east, pale blue sky, very hazy, very pale not hazy, very pale sky, colored around the fringes with lavender and orange and pink and mauve.

Passing a plowed field, with the light brown of the plowed earth is reflecting some of the pink tinge, the mauve tinge of the sky near the horizon where the clouds are now almost, almost entirely blue-grey pale blue grey.

It's, 7:18, I'm not sure where we're pulling into. I don't see a sign right yet for where we are. Just came from having dinner with everybody and, oh, got all of a sudden overwhelmingly sad. Nancy kept looking and asked if everything was all right, and I just, kind of shook my head, just felt like crying, overwhelming, overwhelming. I showed them the picture that I had done for Nancy, the rainbow with the "earth's the right place for love, I don't know where it's likely to go better," the quotation from from, what's his name Robert Frost *Birches*. And Ruthie obviously wanted to have it, so I'm not gonna give it to the hospital, I'll just give it to her. I think I may also have one made for Nancy; she really liked it also, so I think I will have one made for her as well. Just overwhelming. And Ruth and Ron were, started talking were talking to Aunt Esther about, I gave Ron his pictures of Zalman and the graves, and they were talking to Aunt Esther about Uncle Morris's first son, Edwin, who died the day before his Bar Mitzvah of leukemia and a second son Dean who was severely mentally retarded and was put in Rosewood for a while, and apparently now is still at approximately the age of 65 is in some kind of a halfway house on the Eastern Shore; Ruthie says that he comes to Baltimore to visit Aunt Esther.

I still can't remember what it was that somebody said, at Coppin, that I altered a little bit in my mind and said to myself, and I really wanted to remember, and I just can't remember it. We're still stationary here wherever we are, and I don't know where we are.

We're pulling out now, maybe I can see where we are. Track 1 Location A, I didn't hear any announcement, and I don't see any sign. It was Metro Park, New Jersey, someplace in New Jersey, Metro Park.

[train rushing] I can see New York City across the river, the twin towers of the World Trade Center, the Empire State Building, and the moon rising above the Empire State Building. Incredible lights of the buildings. The World Trade Center's down, I guess, at the south end, it looks like the Chrysler Building down there near them, and the Empire State Building further up here at this end, and that the moon not quite full just a shade off the top, it's kind of a dark yellowish almost orange shade. Incredible lights and down to the right also something in red.

Out to the left now I can see the New York City skyline, the Empire State Building, red light blinking at the top. The tower with blue lights on it and a white-light-topped building, top of the building, and orange-reddish lights below the white lights of the top of the Chrysler Building. Some other tall buildings, I can't, just beautiful beautiful lights. I can't see from here the World Trade Ce, oh, there it is, World Trade Center buildings, if I lean forward, I can look out to the left and see them. *[train rushing]* To the right the lights of the city, there's a church just to the right here, looks li it's a Greek church, I think, seemed to have a Greek flag in front of it. Out past beyond there, the lights on top of a bridge, blue lights, long strings of blue lights, the top of a bridge, to the left the New York City skyline. It's just incredibly beautiful, lights of lights on the top of bridges. There's a church belfry, steeple with a white cross on top and a red light on it, and overhead the lights, flickering lights of planes or helicopters, just a vast sea of lights. Out to the right and to the left to the left, the, it's like a wall of stars, lights, the the New York City skyline, just, just incredibly beautiful. Think of all the millions of people in there.

[slowly slowing train rushing] The throbbing roar of the train, you can probably pick that up in the background here. This, the lights of the bridge more lights on the bridge close, more lights on a bridge close by a bridge far in front, bridge back to the right, bridges and bridges and lights and lights, orange lights mostly but some white lights, lights of neon lights of a bar down to the right, an intersection, neon lights of a bar it looks like, and to the left out across still the New York City skyline looking even larger now from here, I'm not sure exactly how we curve around out from New York. We're going across on a bridge now over some body of water, I can't tell, I don't, obviously I don't know what it is.

And the moon now back to my right still orange higher up in the sky, still edged off at the top, edged off at the top. There's a building with a kind of orange lights on the top, as a matter of fact, it looks a little bit like that building from *Ghostbusters*. I'm gonna stop for a moment now.

Somebody behind me is snoring, to the left rear a little bit. The lights of a plane, the lights inside the train keep flickering on and off. *[train slowing slower slowly]* Just looking out across at the New York skyline, it's like a veritable wall of buildings with lights, and the pattern keeps shifting as you move. Some buildings with a lot of lights in them, some with only a few.

Just, now the Empire State Building and the Chrysler Building are back to our rear. Now are passing what looked like, I don't know whether these are apartments or projects, huge blocks of buildings. They seem to have bars on the windows, maybe it's high-rise projects, hard to tell. We're beginning to leave the main skyline of downtown New York with all the the skyscrapers behind back to our left. Moving up now to the right, factory type lights. And now we've seem to have turned because now the moon is sort of oh roughly at 2 o'clock from here, using the military jargon. *[train chugging louder]* And there's a body of water that we're getting ready to go across, and the lights of another bridge in the distance at approximately 1 o'clock but down at the horizon, not up in the sky the way the moon is, obviously. There goes an emergency vehicle we're passing that left the entrance of a kind of a toll road. I'm not sure what it is though.

Okay. Now green and red I love my heart in New Y Newport my heart in Newport, big white cigarette sign, neon sign. The moon to my right, the moonlight reflecting pale over the wa on from the water. Smoke from a building back to the right and the moon the moon the moon, *tu io la luna el sol*. Some kind of a bus terminal, there's a bus just pulling out from inside the terminal where apparently it's just been washed. Row after row of row after row of buses parked there. And now we're picking up speed again, *[train slowly faster]* and to the left, row after row, in the moderate distance, of apartment houses, block after block after block, just what actually, about 15- or 20-storey apartment houses.

SIDNEY KROME

The lights in the car, y'know, the coach, keep going off and on, right now they're off and pretty soon they'll be back on again, who knows? There goes another plane flying under the moon, just under the moon. And up above in the sky a star, or is that a planet? Planet. Reflected light and directly up above a plane flying through. When I came back to the coach from having dinner with everybody, Nancy had several times in the coach asked me if I was okay, if something was wrong, and I just kind of shook my head. Anyhow, she came back to check on me. To see if I was all right, and she said she thought I was dumping or sick. And I said no, I said, I was just, just so sad. And I was afraid I was going to cry. I just needed to come back and sit by myself. And she said that it was sad, and that she just couldn't keep, couldn't deal with it, couldn't talk about it. And I said well, we all cope with it in our own way. I said that's why I just had to come back here and sit by myself. 'Cause it was so sad. I was so sad. All I wanted to do, I just felt like crying. And I just knew I couldn't do that, just could not do that. So I came back here. And even Ronnie offered to pay for the upgrade for me to sleep there. And I said no, I just wanted to be in the coach. I had thought he was gonna be in the coach. But no, he's, he was in a sleeper also.

[train whistle, clicketing-sound] That was the sound between two coaches in the train. That's the sound of the train coming up from the toilet in the men's room on this train. It's 10:55, 10:56. I'm back in my seat, the coach. I went into the "Le Pub" Car as they call it, and joined them playing the new 1990's Trivial Pursuit. And then I just came back a few minutes ago, to my seat. We passed through, I went in after we came out of New York for a while. They had engine trouble, and we had to stop and wait outside New York, and then we did go through Stamford, Connecticut, and then New Haven, and I'm not sure where we are now. For the first time, I didn't sit by myself in my coach and watch the towns go by. I sat with them, sat with them. Looking up now, the moon is pretty high up above, oh, way up between 12 and 1, and it's whiter now than orange, rather than orange.

As we move, as we shift our direction, the moon's position shifts also. We're passing through a town now, and there's a steeple, a belfry with double-arched, one's above the other, c look like yellow wood, the sun at the moon at times now almost straight in front of us. Other times, more more to the right, almost directly parallel with my right shoulder. Now it is more forward. So that I have to lean towards the window to be able to see it.

When I showed Ruth the picture, the rainbow picture with the Frost *Birches* quotation, she was obviously struck with it. How beautiful that it turned out. And although I had said that I wanted to donate it to the hospital, I could tell that she wanted it and she said, no you made it to give to the hospital. I said, no, Ruth, I said, if you want it you can have it, it's yours. And Aunt Esther saw it, and she wanted one. I said I would give it to Ruth, Nancy, so I showed, took it out and showed it to Nancy, and I think she would like to have one also, I think so, I know so. She would like to have one also. And I said something about making one for her, she said, she said no, it's too expensive. But I think I will make one for her.

[soft voice] Now we are moving, after having been stopped for a while. I look across a body of water. And I see buildings with lights, and cranes, cranes and lights. And I see the ripples in the water of the wind, the ripples of the wind on the water, the ripples of the currents on the current on the water. I don't know where we are, we're on the land spur. There are homes and now buildings to the left. I've missed the sign, the sign would have been on the left, where the station was. But I don't see it. And didn't see it. The moon is slightly in front of my right shoulder. Very high up and very white. The lights reflect across the rippled water. So rippled and mottled. There are slight waves and currents and that now rippled.

There are piers to the right piers p-i-e-r New London, New London City Pier. *[train bell]* So, we must be in New London, Connecticut. Fishing, cruise and sightseeing. Sign. New London City Pier. The whole bottom with blue writing: Fishing, Cruise, Sightseeing Eveh and then on the right side Events. Like two columns but in the right column only the word "events" above that blue with yellow writing New London and then under New London City Pier in much larger letters.

Passed, just passed a sign on the wall, incidentally it's 11:35, sign on the wall, white metal, black writing, with a red arrow pointing, a red arrow pointing to the right at the bottom, Long Island Block Island Long Island next line Block Island next line Ferries. Curious.

The direction has shifted again, in such a way that the moon is now, though high in the sky, behind me a little bit, and I have to look out and up and back to the right to the right and back to see the moon high above me. Things change positions, or appear to change position, but it's really our direction that changes. The direction the train is moving. The direction I'm going. That changes the relative position of others vis-a-vis me. And vis-a-vis others, other things and other people.

We just went under a bridge that is perpendicular to us. I turned around, I looked back, and out there are the lights of the bridge going over. Over on a point of land. We seem to be getting ready, to the right is some water and lights, spaced out lights, spaced between spaces like lights on a road, lights on a road up above the water's edge. At water's edge and above the water's edge. We seem to be getting ready. No, no, on a shifting tracks.

[voice still soft] Passing, we have passed piers and wharfs sticking up out of the water on wooden legs sticking up out of the water lighted here and there the black silhouettes the black bulk of them suddenly and here in places here and there becoming lighted, brown grey wood. And now we're picking up speed again. *[train slowly speeding faster] [clank]* Might be the clack, but there's no clickety-clack anymore. There is no clickety-clack. But there's sort of a clickety-clack.

[whistle-whooo] Chunk-a-chunk-a-chunk-a-chunk-a-chunk-a-chunk-at, like.
   [train sound, as if on bridge--chunk-a-chunk-a-chunk]
Bright orange lights high up on poles, along the water's edge, over buildings to my right, and the lights seem to speed across the rippled water, across the wind breeze-speckled water the dimpled water, smooth and rough in places. Sand-paper edged, sand-papered in places. *[train sound slowing]* Sliding along with me, they seem to move. Now there are more 8 10 of them in a row, lower down on building walls, I think, stretching their reflections stretching s stretching across the water toward me, moving in my direction as the train moves, their reflections moving. Reflections of dozens of lights high on a hill, too, a vague, a vague conglomeration of reflection, not like the individual rays of light, reflection reflect wave reflections of light on the water. Like the moon they seem to change their position, but they don't, it is I who do. And as I move, the po the position the apparent position of the others seems to change.

Here on the train, I am moving through space. *[train-chunk-a-chunk-a-chunk]* But also time is passing, in my life, I'm moving through time. But also space is passing. And as I move through time, just as when I move through space, the relative position of other things changes vis-a-vis me, the relative position vis-a-vis me appears to change but those things are always still in the same place. Now I hear the train whistle, like the train whistle, the horn of the train, that I mentioned in *THE FAR-OFF NIGHT*, blasts out from forward from the head of the train, the engine of the train goes overhead and blasts back, even as I move past it trying to catch up to it, but I can't catch up to it even though f as it goes past me overhead. *[train--chunk-a-chunk-a-chunk-a]*

More lights on more water, position shifting, more lights in front of other lights and buildings in front of other buildings and smoke in front of buildings and steam, all changing positions. Now a big building with spotlights pointing down on this small body of water next to the parking lot, everything moves over. There go the lights on the building moving. *[wheels going around a curve]* Steel towers of electric wires, gray steel, moving moving back, the lights moving shifting their position, *[train whistle]* going back, some going forward, some in the distance seeming to go forward, and the middle ground staying still compared with what's in the back and what's in the front.

Do you hear that, gentlemen? Mr. Phelps, Captain Kirk, Captain Picard. Those are the, some of the meanings, some of the chaos out of which can come meaning. *[wheel on track]* That's your Mission Impossible, your task should you choose to accept it. But you have no ch **TAPE ENDS**

THE NANCY TAPES

TAPE NUMBER 9B

FRIDAY, FEBRUARY 1, 1991
[train whistle] It's just 12:01, we're coming into or going through some town, the train whistle is blowing. And I was reading this line from Octavio Paz's Nobel Lecture: "The tree of pleasure does not grow on the pasture in the future but at this very moment. Yet death is also a fruit of the present, it cannot be denied, for it, too, is a part of life."

That reminds me of what it was that I heard today and thought of at Coppin that I haven't been able to remember. Somebody said something and then I changed the wording and it had something to do with death being a part of life. But I can't remember what it was. *[train-chunk-a-chunk on a bridge]* Some town with Christmas lights still out. On the trees in front of the town hall red lights and green lights also here and there, but the lights on the trees were all white.

I started this side of the tape at just about 12:01, it's now about 12:5 or 6. You hear the sound of the train going over a culvert or some water. And we passed a town, and we pass apartment houses, we pass individual houses. And there are lights, lights in windows and lights covered by shades, and lights covered by blinds and lights of the inside of the rooms, and I try to look in and see things, and occasionally I see a piece of furniture, but mostly I see nothing but light, don't see people, don't see anything that is happening, don't see anything of the life that is in there. Strange flashing orange lights, two up and two down, two up and two down, *[wheel on track]* two up and two down.

Now there seems to be some snow on the ground here. It's hard to tell though if it's snow. No, I don't, no I, no, it's just, no, I don't think it's snow. But the position of the moon now has changed so radically that I can't even see it. Just passed, across the road there was a bridge coming toward us, road overpass. There was some water, a red light flashing. Now there seems to be some snow, clumps of snow. It's old snow.

And an occasional car passing. Not too many. And there's a big red sign that says HOTEL or MOTEL. I meant to call Raizel last night, no, Wednesday night, and never got to, or Thursday during the day, so busy trying to get that report done.

Curled up now with the light out. Ready to try and sleep. Thinking about how Ronny earlier offered to pay for the upgrade if I wanted upgrade to a sleeper and Nancy saying there were none left, and my saying, No, I just wanted to go via coach. And how it is partly the money, of course, I don't want, but it's partly just that I wanted to go by coach. As I did so many times before. So many times before. Thinking how in 1975, I guess, when Barbara, Sam's wife, oh, I guess they were ex-wife, I don't know if they were divorced, whatever, but when she died, went up for the funeral and just stayed for the day for the funeral and was catching a train back that night. Faygie, I guess, said something to Ronny about how I maybe I should take a plane, and and that maybe I was taking the train because I didn't have money, but he understood I was taking the train because I wanted to take the train, I didn't want to fly. And he called me over and he said, Sid, tell Faygie why you're taking the train. And I told her because I don't like to fly. And I'm not in the sleeper here because this is the trip to Montreal, it's not like going down to Atlanta. This Montreal, oh, pardon me, and I go to Montreal in a coach, not in a sleeper. I might consider if they had a Pullman, but they don't have a Pullman anymore. So, I go on a coach. As I've done all the time, on a coach. *[whistle--whooooo]*

As I told Cookie, I guess, it was, it must have been in '78 when I came up for, was it Joy's or Gail's wedding? That I can ride the train to Montreal, and while I'm riding it, I can make a trip back into my childhood. *[chunk-a-chunk]* And it's OK. Because I can do it while I'm riding the train, when I'm going to Montreal. And when I come back, when I get off the train, I'm an adult again. Well, about as much as I can be an adult, I suppose, right now, the condition I'm in. Hey, Mister Tambourine Man.

It's 20 to 3, the middle of the night, and there's snow all over the place out there. I can't tell if it's snowing, but there's snow all over the ground.

It's 3:05 am, just passed a white wooden church, typical New England style architecture in the snow, right by the side of the road. There's a white lamppost, bright white light next to it. Oh, my, 3:05 am.

Seeing this, passing houses in the snow, most of them new, this, since my regular, winter trips to Montreal when I was a teenager and younger, not late, not that I made that many. Oooh sometime since most houses that I'm seeing now built sometime since that time I went when I was 18, it's it's it's a river. '56, January 'fifty-sev, Ruthie and I came up, it's houses by the roadside, the houses occasional houses scattered houses, very scattered. The lights in the darkness, lights in the background, I can see in the hills where the trees, the tree-lined hills, though I can't see the trees right now, all this in front of, close to the train there's snow.

I think of the speech I gave in speech class. That one that L to tell to tell somebody later and said I I had a fine mind. I remember that speech, it was a speech about lights in the darkness, the presence of human beings in the darkness, that life is or can be oases of light, oases of humanity, oases of the potential of humanity to be potential human humanity's human beings beings human human beings being human in the darkness. And those lights that are less the lights in from trains, as I recall, I recall I recall. Then I recall that then there was the lights of trains that gave me the metaphor that gave me the thing to talk about in the speech class. I recall now that it was the speech class, of which I'm reminded by the sight of the lights in the darkness of the night. *[faint and soft and quiet]*

And the snow-covered fields in the front and the snow limbs of trees in between. The fields and the homes and beyond the hills in the dark, hills, tree-covered hills, I can't see the snow between the trees *[slowly and very softly]* on the ground under the trees between the trees. Right now, there're very few lights to be seen, I don't know how many, if there are many, I take it back, and up on the hill, toward the hill, lines of trees, lines of trees along the track, not quite beside the track, though sometimes beside the track, and lines of trees and clumps of groups of trees and roots of trees. And the snow and the snow between the trees and the fields it's in the snow. And there are box cars. *[very loud sound as of train passing on next track]* And they change their position, relative to each other. As they do change their position relative to me as we move, as the train moves the train flows into the night deep in the night.

As I look out the window at the light, very suddenly there are closer hills. In the night. And there's that light, now I see just one light. It's incredible to see just one light. Looks like a street light, that light a light over a house. I wonder how much of this will be audible.

The sound of the train whistle whooo whooo who-whooo. Crossing the road the barrier down. The red lights. Now some kind of a some kind of a factory building or a warehouse, maybe. Trailers of tractor-trailers, dozens of them outside. GP, Georgia Pacific. Big building, big yellow brick building. Whoa! Comes right on up to the roads to the to the train side, track side. Still going! Incredibly sized build, and there's the end of it. *Quelque chose d'énorme de grand.*

Stopped someplace, snow-covered cars. There's a sign "Bob's Service Center." And lots of vehicles parked along the side. Looks cold out there. But I don't know where "there" is right now. Actually, it's cold in here. I just looked out the left window, it's Brattleboro, Vermont. Brattleboro. And here as we cross this little, there's a car pulling up, stopping at the barricade.

Sto 10 of 4. Stopped in some town, I can't see the name at all, yeah, but lots of footprints in the snow. Right here alongside the train.

Moving again. Very soon after we stopped. Crossing a road. Whoops. White lights are flashing. Seems to be a station here to the right. What's that say? Green Mountain Something. Green Mountain Railroad. It was Green Mountain, Vermont? Bellows Falls, Vermont. Bellows Falls. There's a guy, I don't know if he just got off the train or what. Bellows Falls, Vermont. In the night. 10 of 4, 8 of 4 in the morning. Lots of snow. Oh.

Crossed another road. Seems that the snow on the road has melted. The road looks just wet. Not ice-covered. Just wet. White wooden houses. And that looks like a, no, I thought it was a church, but it just, apparently it's just a big house.

THE NANCY TAPES

Houses coming right down to the tracks here in Bellows Falls, on both sides of the tracks. Brick houses, wooden houses, with those sloped rooves, whatever they're called.

There's cold air coming into this car, somehow. When I got up and went to the bathroom, I could really feel it. Very very cold air coming in. I can feel it sitting here by the window. But I can't quite figure out where it's coming from.

There's a road alongside the hous alongside the tracks houses and a road and houses and houses and a road. Sniff. There's a fair amount of space between the houses too. Now, we're picking up speed now, picking up speed. Leaving Bellows Falls, Vermont. But there's still numbers of buildings around here.

Warehouse and warehouse types buildings with big kinda floodlights spotlights on the corners, on the corners, on the roof.

It's about 20 to 5 and just came in and woke these people up, these 4 couples, they're gonna, getting off at White River Junction. Driving past some town over there. There's some lights on top of the hill, there's one that's turning around relatively almost like it's like a lighthouse. Here a quaint little town over here now.

This scene here at White River Junction, lots of snow but, it's not like. I have this memory in my mind of, as I've mentioned this before, of talking with some kid, he was older than I. He wasn't a kid, not a kid kid, I was a little kid, he was around a teenager, he was around 20, something like that. *[voice very soft]* And the train stopped, it was early, early in the morning, and he got off, and he walked down this road towards this house, this farmhouse, it was, it looked like a farmhouse, towards this house. In my life that briefly, out of my life as quickly.

Okay, and we sat White River Junction, it's just 5 o'clock, just sat there, and then all of a sudden there were two quick toot-toots, and then here we go, White River Junction, Vermont, the dark red brick train station, and there's a police car sittin' out there. Look at that new building District Court of Vermont. Brand new building.

Course by the time we moved, couldn't see where those four couples were. Where'd they? Probably gotten into a bus or something or a cab and gone on up to their ski lodge.

Course now I think it could have been Essex Junction where that kid got off the train. Essex Junction. Or someplace between White River Junction and Essex Junction. Must have been the summer then, not the winter, because it was lighter out. Or't was getting light out. It was grayish light out. In my memory it was grayish light out.

There is lots of snow here at White River Junction and when the people when those couples got off, they just got all excited about, Oh, snow, oh, look at the snow. Lots of snow. And hills, lights going up the hills, lights climbing up the hills. Lights climbing up the hills.

Road alongside the tracks. First one 18-wheeler pulled off on the side like just a little slip dug out of the snow plowed out of the snow and then another and then another. And now the road has turned off. I'm not sure where it's gone, but there seemed to be like a warehouse parking lot area, and then the road was gone. Roads come, roads go. Roads come, roads go.

I don't remember if I mentioned that after dinner when I came back to sit here, after a little bit Nancy came back to see if I was all right and make sure I was okay, I think I talked about this, I'm not sure. And I told her I was just sad, and she said, yes, it is sad, and she just, it was just too painful, and she just couldn't wouldn't talk about it, and I said, okay, and I said we all have our own way of coping, and I said, But that's why I felt I had to come back 'cause I felt like I was gonna cry any minute. I'm thinking, yeah, thinking afterwards, sometime later in the middle of the night, about how for her and for Ruth, this must be really the saddest of all because this is, what? five years ago that they took the train up to Montreal together, the first reunion in Montreal, in the winter, in January. *[voice like crying]* All of a sudden, it's really a rocky road, we're moving along here.

It's 5 of 6, think I'm gonna go shave and washup, go and get a cup of java. Java java jing jing.

It's now 6-29. We're in Waterbury Connec Waterbury Vermont, I guess, Waterbury. One of the trainmen just talking about the snowplowing, he said that we'll be on time as long as they plow the tracks out ahead of us. Said the drifts in Essex were higher than the trains where they plowed the snow off the lot, piled it up higher than the trains.

There are houses backing down to the road here in Waterbury. And the sky is lightening in color. Graying greying up a little bit, lighten lightening grey a little bit. Lots of snow, lots of snow.

It really is a much lighter sky now. Much much clearer and lighter, brighter. Leaves and bushes sticking up through the snow, there's a road nearby, couple hundred yards away with traffic on it, little bit, cars, pickup trucks going by. Every once in a while, a house. *[wheel on track]* Set with dark soil with trees around it and light on it, solitary light and a solitary house. And the dark of the trees and the white of the snow and the grey of the sky. Hills, the Vermont hills, the Vermont mountains, treed. There's another house with a light on the outside, on the door. Hills, dark, treed hills, snow-covered, between the trees, among the trees. One sticking up at the top beyond the first row arc around us.

Reminds me of that drive to Montreal up Route 9 when I was 16 with the other guys, T, HR, was there someone else? I think T and HR, Ronnie and I, we drove up in 1954, that summer, hills rolling high, hills rolling high, yeah, and we came around a bend in New York, in New York State, and suddenly this hill, just sheer almost sheer rock face. Later I guess I would say it was looked something like

THE NANCY TAPES

Delphi. Out of the mist of rain and fog. Suddenly now there are ma more lights like there's a small town a village, lights on the roads not just lights by the houses. Hillocks within the hills sticking out from the trees, bulbous whitenesses, bulbous whitenesses of snow sticking out. Cars and vans, a white van not quite keeping pace with the train as they drive along beside us. And there's another road off to the side there.

Some of the hills are big and tall, and some are smaller smaller peaked hills, there's a smaller peaked one, trees and snow on it and a barn in front of it with silos and a light in the house. And low peaked and rounded hills, another red dark red barn it looks to be, peaked and rounded hills with snow, and dark dark remnants of trees, trunks and branches, sticking up and clumping, and now here between us and the road nearby, a few trees sticking up and some bushes and shrubs getting in the way, cars moving along the road.

7:05, just leaving Essex Junction, beautiful snow, beautiful.

7:20, sky is clear and the moon is out to the left side of the train. *[clicketying]* That hazed-off part is now down to the right instead of the top.

Okay, it's 8:09, we're crossing some body of water, the Customs just made their announcement. The river is frozen solid in most places, frozen solid, and the ice is snow-covered. Oh, no, here's a place where there's some water showing through. Seems to be bubbling up a little bit. The sun is now, we've altered our direction a little bit, and now the sun, it should've, which rose on the right is now shining int shining in from the left. Which means our direction, we must be heading sort of, what? southerly. Westerly? It's hard to tell. The snow on the ice has swirls and swirls almost like it was like the waves underneath, except that they're running the wrong way, sideways to the current, the way the current would be. A little while ago the sky was clear, almost perfectly clear, but off to the left on the horizon over some mountains, there're some clouds, just a few on the horizon. At one point we passed a white house, white wooden house with a dark red barn and a tree to the left of the house, the barn to the right of the house.

Moving very very slowly over this *[whistle-whoo]* ice-covered body of water, very very slowly. The position of the sun has changed, now I see the train is gonna curve around to the right, which means that the position of the sun is going to change again. Some boxes set out on the ice, have no idea what they were for but see so also see some tire tracks on the snow, on the ice. Now we're on land, and the train is curving around to the right *[whistle whooos-whoooos]*. Curving around to the right. Crossing the snow-covered road, and now the sun is coming in from the right rear, and we're curving more around to the right. The position of the sun changing vis-a-vis the train because the chan the chan the train changed its position.

Now the sun is almost directly perpendicular to me on the right. And there are hills off to the right under the sun. Hills and low mountains with the clouds over them, directly under the sun. The sun is just oh, roughly at 3 or 4 o'clock if you use the sun dial, to my right, almost directly to my right. Oh, no, closer to 4 o'clock I guess, right, slightly rear.

The ground here is mostly flat with very low rolling, very very low rolling very low rolling.

The train is kicking up blowing snow along the side of the like the wake of a boat speeding through the water. The snow is spraying up and blowing past the side of the train. Moving backwards toward the back of the train as the train moves forward through the through the spray of the snow being kicked up by the train moving forward through the spray of the snow moving back towards the train moving forward through the spray of the snow. And in endless variations thereof.

Suddenly we're crossing a flat with clumps of trees to the right, single trees to the right. To the left, clumps of farmhouses and silos and barns and trees.

And the sun is now pretty much to our rear. Right rear but rear.

Just went over another icy frozen river with channels of water in one of which was a duck swimming along, of all things.

Over another river now. It is mostly unfrozen flowing water. Only here and there mainly by the banks along the banks is there still ice.

Alongside that last river, wooden houses, apparently vacation or fishing houses for people. And flat fields, plowed fields apparently, although they're covered with the same snow figuration as on top of the rivers, where they were frozen. Wave waving white lines and blotched ripples in between.

To the left, wooden barns wea with boards weathered and grey and greyed and black from the weather. We're veering around now to the right, the train I can see it up ahead, veering around to the right. Sniff. And the sun which was kind of behind us to the left is gonna be moving around now, it is moving around now to behind us *[train whistle whooos]* to the right. **TAPE ENDS**

THE NANCY TAPES

TAPE NUMBER 10A

FRIDAY, FEBRUARY 1, 1991 (CONT.):

Okay, it's 8:28 now. The last tape lasted, the second part, half of the last tape, lasted from approximately midnight till 8:25 a.m., Friday, February the 1st.

And what I was about to say was, alongside the alongside the track in a little ditch like are I guess cattails and bullrushers, using Huck Finn's terminology for the kind of growth here.

[train whistle] And 9:07, we're finally taking off after Customs has checked through, Canadian Customs, they're very, a quick job, just want to know, didn't even really look at our identification. Very superficial.

Cross more flat plowed land, with clumps of trees and lines of trees crisscrossing and houses in clumps and rows of denuded bushes and trees, bushes mainly, alongside the train tracks. And the wind blowing the wake of the train, blowing, snow blowing out to the side of the train, blowing back towards the end of the train, as we plow through it, moving forward as the snow moves back. But it all seems to be on the right side, on this side, as I look out to the left. But the land is all so flat, with lines of trees and houses in the distance. I see no blowing snow to the side of the train. See the wake is all on the right side, there is none on the left.

The question now is do I want to continue to sit here by myself. Or go join them maybe in the cafe car. And see what's going on for the last hour or so, hour and a half of the trip. And suddenly I think about last night and how I sat, thought I was going to cry, and I had to come back and sit by myself in the coach, and Nancy came back and I told her about how sad I felt and how I felt like crying. And she said about how she felt and she just couldn't stand it, and had to deal with it. I think about talking to Ruth on the phone the other night, when she said that, something like, I miss her so much. I think about Soph talking about her mother, the year just past, January the 8th a year since the death. Sophie saying, "I miss her so much." Because they were such good friends.

And there is a wall about a hundred yards long, maybe 75 yards long, a bin for corn, not a silo, but perhaps a hundred yards long, 75 yards long, maybe 20 feet high and maybe 5 or 6 feet wide. A bin of wire mesh, and inside corn after corn after corn. This flat land. And off to the right now, I see the mountains on the horizon. To the right rear at approximately 4 to 5 o'clock, the sun bright and warm, shining through the window of the train on me, warm. It's the cold outside, clear, cold, windy, snow-blowing.

This is the sound between the two coaches, standing between the two coaches now. *[loud click-clack]* It's 10:17, we're approaching Montreal, real close, just about ready to go into the city. We crossed the St. Lawrence Seaway. Saw the

Expo si 67 site. Curving around now to the right, the skyline's gonna switch from our right side to the left side now. Switching sides, everything switch sides depending on which way you're looking at it. And there's the Farine 5 Roses. Able to see the skyline for about last 10 or 15 minutes. Marvelous sense of excitement coming into Montreal. Cross the river flowing well, but some ice pieces of ice flowing through it also. More flowing through it. Channels of water, clear water, mostly clear water flowing with some ice in it, passing over something now that's frozen solid.

A graveyard of buses, *Connaiseur*, some with the top burned out, oh, my God, and just like the rusted girders, like a st gravesti grave of of buses. Swinging around now to the left to come into, go through, into the station the main station. I always loved the feeling of coming to Montreal on the train, the excitement, just the real vibrancy, to the city. I still feel it, that excitement inside. It's a bright and sunny, beautiful, crisp winter day. Lots of snow, the sidewalks are, seem to be pretty clear, the roads are clear. Pulling in now pulling in now pulling in now into the tunnel of the station now, everything dark around us, into the tunnel just some lights and the grey cement and the platforms, and here we are, in the station. Love it! Pardon that last remark, we got a little carried away, I do love coming into the city but that's a cliche way to put it.

It's 8:50 p.m., Friday, December, February the 1st, we're at the Restaurant *Le Mas des Olivier*, I wanted to offer a toast, told Nancy it would be "To those who are here, to those who are not here, but who always will be with us." She asked me, personally, not to make the toast, I didn't. Ruthie made a toast, she said, "I'm glad that we're all here, I wish that Nancy could be with us, but I'm glad that we're all here together." She almost cried, she almost cried, and I almost cried. *[almost crying voice]* I'm in the bathroom right now, I'm going back out now to the table.

The soup I had, call they call it a *pescado*, it was a *bouillabaisse*-based soup but instead of the soup with the pieces of fish and everything, it was pureed and they had pieces of French bread which had been toasted to a kind of *paximadi* and what they called a garlic mayonnaise, which was garlic and saffron and mayonnaise which gave it that russet color and grated *Gruyiere* cheese and you put some of the garlic paste on the toasted French bread, sprinkled some of the cheese on top of that, then lowered it into the soup and spooned some of the soup on top of it so it melted the cheese and softened the toast, and then you ate it and it was wonderful. Wonderful.

SATURDAY, FEBRUARY 2, 1991

Last night, Good Morning, Mr. Phelps, Captain Kirk, it's Saturday morning, February the 2nd, 1991, the clock time is 7:08. And I know that's, the clock is too fast. And the actual time is 6:49. Yesterday evening I did manage to call Raizel, get through to Raizel, and she invited us all to come over after dinner and I told her I didn't know, but I'd let her know if we did, and I told her that we all had had really wanted to just be together and that it was very important for us to be together. And that I wanted to talk to Ruth and that, *[yawn]* pardon me, and time out.

Oh yes, and Ruth got out for me my copy of the Craig's girlfriend, Amy, made a looked like a pastel sketch of the hou 2614 2616 houses Springhill Avenue, based on the photographs I had given I had given Ruth. She asked for them so that Amy could do that. And I have to say frankly that that it's that I like the photographs better even though even though I know that she tried to restore in her sketch her painting drawing whatever it is, she tried to restore the original quality of the houses. I think the picture shows something about them that the sketch does not. It, the sketch is ethereal, idealized, abstracted. And the houses were never that. They were always concrete and specific and alive and rich. That's what it is: they're too ethe, the sketch is t they're the houses are too etherealized and abstracted, too much like a hazy dream, too much like an idyllic dream without without the the vibrant reality of those houses, of the life that went on in those houses.

Anyhow, Ruth, she also showed me a picture that she had had made for Nancy, for my sister, it showed Ruth and Mindy and Nancy and Allison *[yawn]* pardon me, and in the picture Nancy just looked so bright and lively and alive and alert, and her face was so full of life and her eyes and the smile just just positively really kind of radiant, and Ruthie said that the picture was taken in October of '89 was which was just about the time that they learned really how how devastating Nancy's condition was, how how it had much it had deteriorated and that how badly she was going to need new surgery because her her heart condition was just deteriorating so badly, and there's such a contrast between what the news meant and the way she looked. There was nothing by etherealized about it it it it was the the absolute full hard harsh intense concreteness of life, that contrast in there between what she looked like and what the news was.

And we went out because she was going to give my sister her copies and nobody answered but anyhow we start and Ronnie was *[yawn]* not quite decently dressed, pardon me, but boy it's early in the morning. So I said something about how this was all making me flash back to 1954, and she said, "You mean your father?" And I said, "That," I said, "But mainly," I said, "Aunt Freda." I said, Sniff, "I remember when they all came back from Rochester." And she said, "It there wasn't Rochester," she said, "it was Sloan-Kettering in New York." And I said, "Aw," I said, "I thought it was the Mayo Clinic in Rochester." Anyhow, so I guess maybe it was Sloan-Kettering, the specific place was not important to to all that happened and to my memory of it and to the meaning of it.

THE NANCY TAPES

And I talked about how her mother, how Aunt Esther had showed me this picture of Aunt Freda sitting up in her hospital bed *[yawn]*, and she looked, how she looked thin and scrawny, but her face, her face had this vibrant smile this richness of life coming out of it. Even though it was gaunt. And and now that I think of it, I think that at the time Aunt Esther said that she looked like a chicken or like a rooster. And I told Ruth that Aunt Esther had asked me how how I thought Aunt Freda had looked, and I said that while I thought she didn't look that great, I didn't say that, and I said that I thought she looked okay. And that Aunt Esther replied something like, "Oh right, how can you say that? She looks terrible she looks awful she looks like she's dead already." And she, Ruthie said she didn't remember that she didn't remember the picture and I said, "Yeah, yes, I remember that picture."

And she said, "Do you wanta kind of talk?" And I said, "Well, no." And I I said, "I don't want to get into that right now. And 'cause I had been planning to go down to have a beer." And so I did, I went down to have a beer. *[noise-tape slip]* went out. I don't know what happened then, but it glitched on the "over and out." And if my voice sounds really tired out that's because I'm all, y'know, it's it's not even 7 o'clock in the morning yet. I just woke up, and I just feel I could probably talk about this stuff a little bit.

Good morning again, gentlemen. It's now 7:45 by my watch. Just wanted to make another comment about the sheer excitement of coming into Montreal on the train. It was a bright sunny day, the sunlight glistening over the snow, the the water the icy water of the Saint Lawrence underneath, flowing, the buildings, the construction, it was just that that excitement of coming to Montreal. And now I'm standing at the window of my room in Ruby Foo's, room 467, and now I can see--I didn't notice this before when I looked out--but looking out to the to the left which is towards the city and the mountain, I can see St. Joseph's Shrine, there on the hill just, and it's beautiful the cupola the dome sticking up on the horizon of the hill. It's not that far away, it's pretty close. And then to the left there's a big positron building, green green glass and kind of grey concrete slabs, and above it to the left I can see the top part of the tower of the University of Montreal. Which I wonder was that was built to look like the University of Pittsburgh. The tower of learning. Over and out.

Good morning again, gentlemen. It's now 8:47. Just a comment about our very being here and the importance of our being together last night. Ruth and I, on the way home, back to the hotel, I said that I was really glad that we were all together, that it was a good dinner, and was it was more than worth the money, and and the cost in our our in our being able to be there to be together. I have to watch because if I if I stop talking, it's it's set on AVF. Let me turn the AVF off. It will go off, it will stop recording. Talked about how good it was for all of us to be there, to be together. It was the first family *simcha*, the first joyful occasion since before Nancy's death. We were all conscious of the fact that she should have been here with us, that she would have been here with us, had she still been alive. Ruthie said it last night, "I'm glad we're all here together, and I'm sorry that Nancy can't be with us. But I'm glad that we're together." We needed this, to be together. We need to be in, I needed to be with the group here in the hotel, and I told Ruthie that, not for me to call Raizel or somebody and get some place to stay but to be here with them. We needed to be together.

Who was there? Twelve people. Mother and Lou, Aunt Esther, Ruthie, Mindy and Joel, Ronny, D, Amy, Nancy and Cheryl, and me. We were the twelve. And Nancy was the missing one. Our coming together, coming up together, our being together, it's not life as usual, it's a reassertion of our living, a reassertion of our being alive, a reassertion for Nancy, and for ourselves. It's a reassertion of life. It has great, there's a great emotional great emotion there's great feeling to our being here. We all needed this. To be together. I don't want to over-exaggerate that, but it is important for us. I don't want it to be somber either *[peculiar intensity of voice]*. But it is important for us. We were all conscious of the fact that Nancy wasn't here, my sister didn't want me even to mention a toast, but Ruthie did, and I'm glad she did. Nancy had asked me personally as a personal favor to her not to say anything and so I didn't, but Ruthie wound up doing it.

Good afternoon, gentlemen, it's 2:54 Saturday, February the 2nd, 1991, I'm back up in hotel room 4 room 467. I've gotten back from the *Bar-Bat Mitzvah* and the luncheon following the *Bar-Bat Mitzvah*. And I'm getting ready to go downtown to do a little souvenir-type shopping, I think Mindy and Joel are gonna come with and maybe also Cheryl, I don't know. In any case, during services towards the end, they asked people to get up who had to say *Kaddish*, and Ruthie was sitting behind me and she got up to say *Kaddish*, and I could tell that she was having trouble finishing it, and I started to cry, and I could tell Nancy sitting behind me next to Ruthie was crying and so was D a little bit oh there's the phone ringing time out. Yes, and, so Ruth and and there was and afterwards I said something to Ruth and she said something to me and she said she didn't know why she just could hardly get through it, she could barely say it. It just overwhelmed her, and she said she guessed it always would overwhelm her and she would never get used to saying *Kaddish* for Nancy, and I said, "I heard your voice and I just I couldn't believe that I was hearing you say *Kaddish* for Nancy. It's just it really kind of overwhelming." Overwhelming.

Elliott looks just incredibly Elliott. Sat with him and Lison, and talking about his older son *David*, David, who plays the guitar and has a band, he's off skiing today, Elliott was saying he's tough to get him to do things and I mean the kid's 12 years old but anyhow. I'm gonna be off and going in a few minutes.

THE NANCY TAPES

I had thought our group would not really be sitting together at the luncheon, but so I went to sit with Raizel. Anyhow, and then I looked up and they were pretty much all sitting around the table, and I felt that somehow that I had been left out or that I had abandoned them, but that's I don't know and now and I said I wanted to go downtown and walk around and do some souvenir shopping, and Ruth asked me to pick up a T-shirt, and I think Mindy and Joel might be coming down, but basically now here everybody else is going with Ron too and probably D and Amy, and Ruth and Nancy and Cheryl are going to this other mall, a closed-in mall where of course it'll be easier for Amy. And I'll be downtown. Probably by myself again. Looking for T-shirts for the guys. And maybe some Cuban cigars for Paul. Over and out. Or maybe I should say under and in. The first call was Ruth, the second call was Cheryl. Cheryl's going with Nancy and Ruth and them, so it'll be Cheryl, Nancy, Ruth, Ronny, D, and Amy. The six of them, that'll take care of that car.

Good evening, gentlemen. It's 9:47 Saturday, February the 2nd, 1991. I'm sitting outside the *shule* where the *Bar* and *Bat Mitzvah* of Avi and Adina Katz or Adina and Aviron Katz, sons of Chaim and son and daughter of Chaim and Lorna Katz. We're at the reception, the dinner reception. In her in her statement in her presentation, her speech her talk, Lorna talked about people who could not be here, who were here for Ilan's *Bar Mitzvah* but could not be here for Avi's *Bar* and Adina's *Bat Mitzvah*, and she mentioned Nancy Kanow Simpson. And in the video in the video in the video the Chaim kind of narrated or talked about presented, he included a picture of Nancy, I think it was Nancy with Mindy, a picture of Nancy, and afterwards I went up to him and I said, "I don't know about I can't speak for everybody I wanted but I wanted to personally thank him." I'm standing outside, what you hear also is the wind blowing over the mike *[loud wind sound]*. It's not that cold but it's cold but anyhow. I said, "I wanted to personally thank you personally for including Nancy." And he said, "Was there ever any doubt?" And I said, Well, I still wanted to thank him. And he said that tomorrow when we come to the house for the *[wind noises]* for the brunch he would show me a note that he had gotten from Joe that was very sad but also very beautiful.

Anyhow, Mindy started crying, Mindy and Ruth, and they went out, and Nancy went out, and Cheryl went out, so I went out, and Ronny went out, we went upstairs, and they were sitting up on some benches by the cloakroom, some chairs. And it turns out that one of the things that Mindy was so upset about that I didn't know. The cousins came down for Nancy's funeral, but the day of the funeral after the funeral they went out shopping! I couldn't believe it! And Ronny talked about how you could not change them, they were what they were; anymore than they could change you to live their way you could not change them to live your way. And I said to Mindy, "I'm on your side." And and somebody said something about choosing sides, and I said, "No, it's not a question of choosing sides," I said, "But it it's just I'm so offended by it, I'm just so offended by it, that they would do that. I can't believe it! That after the funeral they would go out shopping! It's just incredible." And Nancy said that the summer, it must have been the summer of '62, the year after Eva had died, that she was up in Montreal, up here visiting, and she was with some of the cousins *[wind]*, and they were talking about, and she said they were talking about how sad it was and they just couldn't get over Eva dying, and she said she just got really really really upset and argued and yelled at them, how dared they say that, they didn't know anything about Eva, they hadn't come to the funeral, they didn't know anything, and how could they even bother to talk about it. And she said that even today, even now, almost 30 years later, they still talk about how she gave them hell for that.

SUNDAY, FEBRUARY 3, 1991

Good morning, gentlemen, it's now 1:39 am, Saturday night to Sunday morning Sunday morning February the 3rd, 1991, and I'm back in the room after the *Bar-Bat Mitzvah* reception and dinner and all that stuff, and just a couple things.

First, let's see. Avi Adina Adina who had *davened* so well this morning was called upon to do more. She obviously she wanted to sing, she's quite a show girl, and she she started singing. She sang, "Did you I was you hero?" And she got a real round of applause and suddenly I realized, that she had everything going for her, and I thought about Amy. And the next song that Adina sang was *Yesterday*, the Beatles' song *Yesterday*. And so I went over and I asked Ronny and D if there would be any problem if I picked up Amy picked Amy up and danced with her. And they said there'd be no problem, the only problem might be could I hold her up. So I went over and I asked her to dance, and she said, of course. Picked her up and it was really kind of tough. But I did it, I held her up, for the whole thing, and we danced *Yesterday*. And then I brought her back and put her down, and then later when they started playing some boogie music, she yelled for Joel, now right after that actually that was before that right after that they played some boogie music and she got up and danced I guess with Cheryl and Joel and Mindy, they all kind of danced with her, but she was she was in her wheelchair, and they held hands with her, and danced that way. And then later then when I went and sat, when I went and sat down, Cookie and Raizel were at the table. And Cookie said something about crying, and Raizel held her hand out and I said, "I can't talk, because if I talk I'm gonna start crying." So I didn't. Sniff. And anyhow and then later, I asked her again if she wanted to dance some more and she said, "Yes." And so we danced to that Louie Armstrong song, *What a Wonderful World*. I had a little trouble then holding her up 'cause she was she was a big girl, she was 21, she's big she's heavy, and it was hard to hold her up. I almost, she kind of slid down a little bit, but I managed to pull her back up and hold her up. And then she, we got done and I put her back in her chair, and then they played some of that boogie music and she yelled for Joel, and took off and Joel danced with her, in her chair. He's a real nice guy, I just, incredible that he would do some of the things that he does with this family.

And then later, actually it was before before the second dancing while I was sitting there with Raizel and Cookie, Myron came over and started talking. We were talking about Montreal, and he was talking about maybe moving out to Toronto, and he was talking about writing and how he was had written this piece on the view from his apartment and how they've put all these put all these whats? Put all these neon signs on tops of the buildings and hurt the skyline view from down below but also his view from up above. And he had written a piece about Zack, when Zack was born, their son. And he said he just hasn't shown it to too many people, and I said, "They print things like that." And he said that he had to think about that one. And I started telling him about some of my pieces, two actually, just two and what happens sometimes as a result of them. I talked about the piece on giving blood and the letter from SK, I said, who turned out to be, his father and my grandfather turned out to be brothers; he was my father's cousin. And he just kind of flipped out on that, well, he didn't flip out, I still don't use that terminology. He thought that was, really kind of gave him the chills. He says about how he cries even at his piece about Zachary, and then I told him about the piece about *Porgy and Bess*, and it was funny how I couldn't think of the opening number from *Porgy and Bess*, it was *Summertime*, I just couldn't think of it. And I asked Raizel, and she said, Well, she says, it's not *Summertime*. I said, "Yes, it is," I said. And I told him about writing that piece and about the personal feelings, *Summertime* that Aunt Freda used to sing and he said, "She was the youngest sister." And I said, Yes. My aunt. Jerry and Sonny's mother. And I told him how I saw Sonny sometime after that with at at my mother's house for *Rosh Hashana*, I think it was *Rosh Hashana*. And how he said that I had sent him and Jerry a copy 'cause I mentioned Aunt Freda *[yawn]* and how--oh, pardon me--he said that he had been, that *Porgy and Bess* was not one of his pieces was not one of his things but he'd been singing *Summertime* as long as he could remember but he never knew why. I said the reason he was singing, I said he was 3 years old when his mother died, and she used to sing it when he was a baby. That's, and he just he said, that really gave him the chills. And I said, "It gives me the chills every time I" **TAPE ENDS**

TAPE NUMBER 10B

SUNDAY, FEBRUARY 3, 1991

It's now 1:46, the tape ran out. And he said that it gave him the chills. And I told him that it gives me the chills every time that I think about it. And I told him that I had given Raizel, I had given his mother some copies of a bunch of my pieces, and he said he would get them from her. And I asked him to please send me a copy of his piece is coming out on Wednesday, in *Montreal Today* or *Montreal Tonight* or *Downtown Montreal* -- something like that. He said he would. I told I wanted him to send me a copy, and then he said that it was such a coincidence that we had talked together like this, we hugged and he said he loved me and I told him I missed him and how good it was to talk with him and that if he and Marilyn were leaving. Then I sat down, and then I went up to him, caught him before he left and I said, Myron, I said, you know, I said, there's no such thing as a coincidence. It was not just a coincidence that we got together, that we talked about that.

There was actually something else. I don't know if I mentioned this on the other tape, on the other side, but earlier in the evening, Lorna had talked about people who were not there, and she mentioned Nancy Simpson, and when Chaim showed his videotape, there was a picture of Nancy with Mindy and I thanked him for, later when I got the, I went over I think I said this but I want to repeat it quickly, thanked him personally for putting her in and he said, Was there any doubt? And I said, well, I thanked him anyhow and he told me that Joe had sent him a note, and it was really sad but it was beautiful, and he would show it to me tomorrow when we came for the brunch.

But also I noticed that Mindy was very red and broken up, and Ruthie and Dave went out, and then Nancy went out and Ronny went out and Cheryl went out, and so I went out and went up, and they were sitting *[yawn]* up in the lounge and by the coatroom. And that's when Ruthie and Mindy said that the day of the funeral, after the funeral when they got back to the house, that they had gone out and gone shopping. I said, who went? The cousins. They had gone shopping! I it was just And and y'know Mindy was talking about how angry she was and still was, she was so angry about it, and Ronny said something about how you have to take them as they are and and you can't make them live your way anymore than they can make you live their way. *[yawn]* And he Mindy took that to mean that that she shouldn't be angry, but I understood, and and Ronny didn't really mean that she shouldn't be angry, and and so I said at one poi, well, Mindy, I said, I'm on your side. And Ruthie said something about choosing sides. And I said, No, it's, we're not choosing sides, I said, but, I said, I'm just appalled, I said, I'm just I'm so offended by it, that they would do that that they would go shopping! I said that's just incredible, on the day of Nancy's funeral that they would go shopping.

THE NANCY TAPES

And anyhow then Nancy talked about how, I think I put this in, I don't know, in 1961, when Eva died *[yawn]*, none of them came down for the funeral, and the following year, I ca, in 1962, she was up in Montreal, there for the summer, up here for the summer, and they, I guess it was with the girls, and they were talking about how how sad it was about Eva and how what a terrible thing it was. And she said that she got so upset with them that she kind of, she even yelled at them got real angry with them, what did they know about, they didn't know anything about it and and they should just stop talking about it, because they hadn't even come to the funeral. And she said that every once in a while they still talk about how she yelled at them, for what they said, about Eva and not having gone to the funeral.

It's, hello, yes, it's 12:4s, 12:49, Sunday, February the 3rd, 1991, I'm walking up Crestwood just getting a little air outside of Chaim's house after the brunch. We were looking at pictures of Chaim's *Bar Mitzvah*, and there were pictures of Nancy and Nancy and me and Ruth, sniff, and Aunt Esther, about three pictures of Nancy, as in Nancy Kanow Simpson, one with Nancy and Sonky, and Miriam Lehman, one at the table, and one now who was at the table, my sister and Sonky and a couple other kids whose names I don't know. Sniff. And then there w's one with her in the whole family group picture, and in that one Ruth and I were right next to each other and Cheryl said it looked as though we were dating or seeing each other. Then Nancy said that we were good friends, and I said we were best of friends for for that time, and I remembered that and, thinking of Nancy's picture, I felt like crying, it's been so hard not to cry now. Tough weekend.

And thinking about how close I was with Ruth at the time, that was in February of 1959, sniff, and I had thought I had not come up here but actually I had, what happened was I finished, as I mentioned to Ruth just a few moments ago, I had just finished University of Maryland and I came up and I think I spent three or four weeks here with Raizel and Ken, that's where I have that picture of me with Raizel, in the house on Braille 4-1-5-7 Braille. And then I went back, and I went in the Army, and I remember now sitting and talking about going in the Army and saying something to Sam Herlich about how I would be, sniff, I was 21, hell, I was almost 21, no no responsibilities and that I would probably have gotten drafted, so I decided to go in, go into the Army. Sniff. That was in '59.

What else was I gonna say? Something else about that. Yes oh at that time I think it was at that time that I was out for a ride with Beryl, and Beryl said that he said, You probably tell me want to tell me that I'm a schmuck and tell me to fuck off, he said, but I I just want to tell ya that, he wanted to tell me about, he wanted to tell me to find a rich girl to get married to, and he was saying that he was making at the time 20,000, that seemed like a lot of money to him but it wasn't really. And that that he needed money, he needed a lot of money to get to be able to get by. *[wind over mike]* Sniff.

SIDNEY KROME

I remember that in '59. DD, University of Maryland, the night before my last exam. Did we get a six-pack of beer someplace? And some pizza? Listening to Frank Sinatra. The night before my last exam. Oh, God, I remember that. That's another reason I feel like crying. Every time that has passed so fast, that was 32 years ago, sniff, 32 years ago, 32 years ago, 19-ought-and-59. 19-ought-and-59. 19-ought-and-59. Eva. Eva. Ronny said something last night or the night the night before it must have been, how Mother at one point at one time asked her, this was not that many years ago, just fairly recently sometime, Mother asked him if he knew when he married Eva that she was so sick and he just got pissed off. 'Cause first of all she wasn't so sick, she had a minor, it was kidney or bladdy, blad it was a minor nephritis of some kind and he said, it was not big deal. And he knew because they had done an autopsy, I thought they had not done an autopsy, they had done an autopsy. She keeps bringing things up over and over and over and over and over and over again. *[wind]* We talked, it must have been on the train, how, sniff, she always said that she just wanted us to be happy, but she always wanted to be the person to define for us our happiness. Such happiness, such happiness. 19-ought-and-59.

Flashing back. I told Ruthie the other night, flashing back to 19-ought-and-54, when they took Aunt Freda away, *[crying]* they brought her back and she was dead. And then 1990, Nancy, Nancy, came to Baltimore, to Hopkins, and when they brought her back she was dead. Sniff. And I remember, I'm beginning to remember having been here, February of '59, Oh, Gawd, Sic transit, Gloria, Mundi.

Now in the pictures of Nancy at Chaim's *Bar Mitzvah*, she was so much thinner, her hair was black and kind of page-boyish type length and much thinner, and Cheryl said it didn't even look like Nancy. And I said, Oh, yes, oh, yes, that was Nancy. *[crying]* Dammit! February of '59 also, that's right, the blonde Italiano. I remember that, too, now, 19-ought-and-59. Sniff. What would have happened had I decided to stay in Montreal? I didn't stay in Montreal, I didn't stay in Baltimore, I didn't stay in Israel in '62. I didn't I didn't I didn't stay, I didn't make any commitments. Until I got married in '68. Oh, dear. Oh, dear.

Oh, yes, now I remember what else I wanted to talk about Nancy. We were talking about phone numbers, and Nancy asked, asked Nancy if she remembered our number, and she did it was MOhawk 4-1014, if she remembered Aunt Freda's, Aunt Freda's *[voice cracking]*, and she said 331, and I said, No, she said, well Forest, I said, No, I says, MOhawk 4-2448. And she said, that's right. And I said, the address, and that's when she realized that the address, the address was 3316 Royce Avenue. And then she asked me what Aunt Esther's phone number was, and I said, I didn't remember. I didn't remember because I hardly ever had to use it, because it was always just next door. And it was FOrest 7-3756. That's what she said, FOrest 7-3756. Then she asked Ruthie, and Ruthie remembered, of course, FOrest

THE NANCY TAPES

7-3756. Sniff. FOrest 7-3756. And Nancy talking about a party, and Ruthie and I used to have parties and never invited them. Of course not, they were too young, I was 16 or 17, Nancy was 10 or 11. My Nancy, sister Nancy was 10 or 11. So she said one time that she hid, she said there were so many people that they were spilling out over on the street, on Stringhill Avenue, Springhill Av Avenue on the street. Sniff. So she and Nancy hid downstairs in the front room of the basement of Aunt Esther's house, waiting for people to come in, but nobody came in because it was so crowded everybody just stayed upstairs and spilled out on the street out on the street on Springhill Avenue.

Ruthie and I were such good friends. And then I went in the Army. And then I went in the Army. And then I went in the Army.

5:11 p.m. Sunday, February the 3rd, we're now moving, pulling out of the main train station, in Montreal. Here we go. Now I was thinking about 1978 when I was up here for Gail's wedding, Gail and Simmy Simon, up to Montreal for that. That's when I gave that kind of tribute to Beryl. Thinking about how I went to Beryl's house, we saw the pictures of his wedding, his and Ann's from 1953, June of 1953, and Aunt Freda in there and Jerry and Sonny. Oohh, and I was there, was I there? No, I don't remem, I don't think I was there. No, I don't think, I don't think Ruthie was there. Here we are pulling the end of the city, dial back to the right, aahh, would be where the building was with the Henry Moore sculpture.

Sky to the right rear hazy clouds light clouds kind of a red pale orange very pastel orange clouds, and the sky is a pastel grey blue. The skyline is directly behind us, can't really see it too well now. We'll curve around to the right, I think, before we curve around to the left.

Pictures of Aunt Freda, Jerry, and Sonny at Beryl and Ann's wedding. And Beryl gave us a copy of the picture of of Raizel and Jack and him when they were little kids. Oh there's the skyline now, there it is, God, it's beautiful! So exciting. But eventually it will probably become a separate country. They're gonna go for their independence someday soon probably within two years. I think that looks like the, let's see, where is that building with the with the Henry Moore sculpture? It looks like the building that they're putting additional additional stories on. We're crossing part of the river, that looks like the Sheraton symbol on something. There's Mont Royale, can't see the cross from here 'cause it must be around the other side, yes, it's around to the right back there. Goodbye, Montreal. This store is closing forever. The sign on Epstein's on Reisterstown Road. The buildings are shifting their positions cough as we shift ours. Now we're curving around to the left. Cheeh-cheh. The skyline has shifted around to the left. Passing freight cars, Union Pacific, CNN, and flat cars. All righty, here they come. The skyline is to the left now. Farine-Five Roses.

The skyline's to the left rear. Farine Five Roses in red. On the bridge now we're get, moving out *[train on bridge]* nicely over St. Lawrence, and here I go, now I'm over the St. Lawrence, just got to get over it. It's clear. Habitat. There's the EXPO '67. Noisy noisy car tonight. Noisy noisy car, and the AMTRAK woman is officious, this guy back there's officious.

The big red CN sign on the station building. There's the biosphere. Here comes the conductor. There's the there's the skyline.

Sound of the going over the bridge, the bridge over the St. Lawrence now. The lights are really on in Montreal, and the sky is turning, over the city there's a cloud streaked with bright mauve, bright lavender mauve.

On my way to the sleeping car where everybody is, it's a few minutes later, I don't have my watch on, but we're on dry land now, on the other side of the St. Lawrence, heading south, and I can look back and on the left side *[wheel on track]* of the train and see the city skyline and over. The clouds have deepened and darkened and richer oranges and lavenders and mauves, and there are streaks where there were some contrails of some planes that went overhead. Aahh, and the lights of the city, there's that red CN still there. And now most of it is going back behind the building as we move over to the left where the sun is setting, the sun actually probably has set, there's a glow to the left, far to the left where the skyline is there's a top floor of the building lighted in white. *[wheel on track]*

Okay it's 5:3 Cheh pardon me 5:36 in the evening. We've been stopped for about maybe 15 minutes here outside of Montreal, I'm not sure why. But I can look back to the left and Montreal's skyline has disappeared, it's blocked by freight cars. PROCOA CN PROCOA CN PROCOA on the top Was it PROCOR? PROCOR. Grey on the top and CN, no, or is that two different cars? It's hard to tell in the dark. Now that obnoxious AMTRAK woman who gave us our instructions orders wanted to know what my taperecorder was for, and I I said told her it was just for me. She said, Well I thought you had to have somebody's permission before you taped them. I said, Well, I was just taping myself. People can be a real pain in the ass, and it looks like she's gonna be one.

A guy sitting just one seat behind me and to the left talking talking talking. I'm in the club car right now. And this guy, just obnoxious, really pompous, loud, sees all and knows all, talking about how he caught scorpions by the tail, making a a lasso, a loop of thread, and then the guy sitting on the side talking about how he used to find tarantulas in New York or something like that to take it to New York, and the couple behind me, the guy was saying something about how it's can you top this? Just knocked out the older guy how that too was non-stop, grey hair, tall, slim, grey hair, slightly bald, and wearing a sweater and just non-stop talk-talk-talk, it was just incredible. Aahh, couldn't believe it. And when I went back, took the suitcases back to the car, he was still talking, just talk-talk-talk, just incredible how much people can talk-talk-tal blah-blah-blah-blah-blah.

Okay, I had to cut the volume down a little bit, it was obviously too loud. That woman giving her obnoxious her orders in an obnoxious manner. Just people are just absolutely incredible. Anyhow, in the station again, we were talking about, they were talking about how, how what how how they'd gone shopping that day after the funeral. And Ruthie said she thought that was probably the instigator, and I said, I know what Ronny said about how people are different and you can't make them live your way anymore than they can make you live their way. But I said it was really just, I found it just so offensive, that they would do that, that they would go out shopping after Nancy's funeral. I don't understand that.

Well, I just wanted to mention, if I have not already, that Myron said yesterday last night about the the hotel Ruby Foo's, that he used to say that everytime he heard that people from from the family were being put there put up there to live he that he wondered where where the hookers went, or would go. And I told him about having been in the bar and that I thought it was a real swingle singles place. And he said, They're not exactly singles. It's a real working place. For the hookers of that area of Montreal, it has quite a reputation, it's quite well known, according to Myron. I find that just intriguing. He also today at Beryl's was talking about having gone to Woodstock, August 15 and 16 and 17, 1969, and August the 17th was his birthday and he turned 19, and that it was just incredible that so many people could be in one place. Oh, we're starting to move again, moving. At 5:43 we started moving again. People had, 500,000 people, and the worst there was was that it was the biggest traffic jam and that they were stoned on the way there stoned there and just stoned out.

Actually we seem to have stopped moving again now. Saturday morning, at the *shule* for the *Bar Mitzvah* itself, *Bar-Bat Mitzvah* itself, and for the luncheon, I wore the *yahmukuh* that I carried in my pocket, that I've been carrying for the last three months, the *yahmukuh* I got at the funeral home for Nancy's funeral. I hadn't seen any *yahmukuhs* for the *Bar-Bat Mitzvah* so I wore this one that I had in my pocket. Yesterday evening, however, when we went back for the dinner, there were *yahmukuhs* around and I did get one, it's grey corduroy.

At the dinner Friday night when we went out to *Les Mets d' des Oliviers*, Ron and I had the *biscadoux* of that soup, a pureed *bouillabaisse* with French bread toasted that on which you put garlic mayonnaise, a shredded *Gruyere* and dipped it in, floated it, put it in the soup and let the hot, spoon some of the hot soup over it to melt the cheese and soften the bread and then ate it. Joel and I had the lamb, and they called kind of a fillet of the lamb, sauteed marinated in herbs and wine, and it's in Nancy and Amy and a couple of others had the veal scallopini, it was extraordinarily light, thin sliced, marvelous. Most of them had the salmon, poached or broiled, grilled, grilled with lemon on it. Cheryl had some other kind of fish. For dessert Nancy and I split a strawberries melba which was ice cream, whipped cream, and strawberries and almond slices. I had the espresso, and the guy brought me a double espresso. It was marvelously good coffee. Ronny and I guess it was Joel had the profiterol profiterol which was like a cream puff filled with ice cream with some chocolate sauce on top. Amy had a chocolate mousse. We had wine, we had a couple bottles of wine. There was a white one, it was just marvelously slightly fruity but not overwhelming. The total tab came to $480 dollars plus $64 dollars tip which made it 5-4-4 and divided by 12 was $45 each which was really not bad considering the quality of the food and the service and the kind of food and the kind of restaurant it was. I thought it was marvelous.

When I listen to the sound of my voice played back, at times like this when I'm talking quietly I do sound a lot like Ron. It's now 11 minutes to 6, and we've started moving again. It's 11 minutes to 6, and we're moving again. In addition to the picture of Aunt several pictures of Aunt Freda, a couple of which had Jerry and Sonny in them, there was a picture of Elliott, Raizel's Raizel's Elliott and Chaim and *[whistle whoooo]* Nancy said to Cheryl something about, Doesn't that kid look like a real *mumzer*? Which was what he was when he was a little kid. Nancy said that in '53, *[whistle whooo continues]* when she was 9 years old, Mother--hear that lonesome whistle blow, can you hear that whistle? I don't know. Delay due to switching problems. In 1953. It's long line of cars stopped here at the road, the flashing, blinking red light, long line in both directions, moderately long line in both directions. Sign, a white sign with red writing on it, all lower case, "desordy" d-e-s-o-r-d-y the first d large but not capital. That Nancy said she remembered she stayed home with Aunt Esther and Ruth and Nance. I don't know where I was that summer of '53 when I was 15. Did I not go to Beryl's wedding? I don't remember, I have to backtrack and think about that. But she said that she stayed home, right after they left, Ruthie and Nancy took Nancy to the hairdresser's to a hairdresser's, and they got her hair cut. Nancy had had real long hair that Mother used to curl, and she and wear in a ponytail, that's right, in a ponytail. And that they cut it off right at the end of the ponytail, right at the top of the ponytail, and that when Mother came back she almost killed them.

Thinking now of the picture of the family all together at Chaim's *Bar Mitzvah* and what Cheryl said about about Ruthie and me looking as though we were seeing each other or dating or something like that, we were so close then. And then later today at Beryl's house, when Beryl brought out the pictures of the time in '68 or '69 when they came down to visit just for no special reason, but just to visit. And I remember that morning that Beryl called and I was really kind of angry on the phone because not at him, I didn't know who was on the phone, but it was a Saturday morning, I didn't want to answer the phone, and it was ringing and ringing and ringing and so I got up and I answered it. And I was really kind of pissed, and I guess I kind of yelled Hello into the phone, and there was a moment of silence. And it was Beryl, and anyhow, I get, I didn't remember that Sophie and I had gone up to see him at the hotel where they were staying, but we did 'cause there's a picture of Soph and me with them and their kids at the at that whatever the hotel was a Holiday Inn or Sheraton.

[whistle whoooo loud] Can you hear that? I don't know if you can hear that in the background. We're just passing pharmacies and *chaussures* little shopping centers. Whipping along like crazy now, we're passing through a residential district. **TAPE ENDS**

TAPE NUMBER 11A

SUNDAY, FEBRUARY 3, 1991
Continuing now on the train 5:55, houses on both sides, just kind of whipping along. And I was gonna talk about something. Oh, yes, when when Beryl and Anne and the kids came down to came down to Silver Spring, and they called and we had gone we went over to see them. I didn't remember that we had until I saw the picture of Sophie and me with them.

Lights in the distance lights in the distance lights in the distance lights on the right close by lights in the houses people sitting in their dining rooms a woman carrying a plate to the table.

And then another time I remember, I went over by myself to see them. It must have been one evening that evening I don't know what evening. Ruthie said something today when we were talking about the pictures, that--there's paneling in a house we just went by and there's tv on in the house and people around the table, lamps inside the house. And she said that she didn't know why but there was tension between us at the time, and she couldn't remember what didn't know what it was about or why but that there was. I said I didn't remember it. However, now at this point, now that I think about it, I think about the fact that there was because I remember I went over and I was talking with Beryl. And Beryl said something to me about me and me and Ruthie, and I didn't understand why, and and he I I said something I remember now the conversation with him, saying something like that I something like well, y'know, one never knows what problems one has, they don't know what they have and I don't know what I have, *[whistle blooooows]* they don't know what I have, I don't know what they have. But, here it was it was 1969, because I said, Here it was, I said, Beryl, I said, we got married, I said, Before we went, *[whistle blooooows loud]* before we went on our honeymoon, we left Mother's apartment, and we went down to the Sinai Hospital and we stopped in to see Sol. And I said, When we came back, and I said, and I said, Now, I said, We were waiting for our first anniversary. We couldn't celebrate our anniversary because we knew Sol was dying. And I said, And as a matter of fact, four days after our first anniversary, he did die.

I said, I don't know what kind of stress they're under, I said, but but that was mine, and and they've got theirs. I've got my stress, and and maybe that's was the stress that I was under at the time.

In the car this afternoon with Beryl, coming back from the airport to his house before we all left to come down to the train station, talking about the Gulf War, he was saying that he felt the United States did not have much choice, but to do what it did. That, and then he said something like, The world would not exist, there would be no world without the United States. He said Hitler would have destroyed the world, Hitler would have taken over England, there'd be no Israel, there'd be no world. There would be nothing were it not for the United States to provide the opportunity *[train chugging]* for at least some significant parts of the world to live in relative freedom, relative peace. Without the United States that could not happen. *[whistle blooooooows from time to time]* The same thing was going on here in the Middle East under Saddam Hussein. We need only imagine what would happen if the United States were not there to protect Israel, for example. It just just. We talked about how, I said, with hell with all the criticism, countries that, from countries, people abroad about the United States about pseudo-imperialism and stuff like that and. Told him about teaching, guest-lecturing in some classes that that, for all of that, if you gave most of those people in those other countries a chance if they had to leave their country where'd they go? I said, They would go to the United States. He said, All of them would, not just some of them.

Out to the left, out towards the front, across, a large area of darkness, triangular, widening out to the rear, narrowing to the front. Long line of lights, some bluish, there's bluish lights, some orange, smaller orange ones, some white, tall white ones, there's a red light, looks like a tower, not blinking, but it's back there. And the positions of the lights themselves are changing. The blue lights in the rear seeming to move to the right with the train. A long line of orange lights right here in the front seeming to move to the left. And some move in front of others. There's a double row actually, the ones in the front seem to move to the left of the other ones as we move forward, they're moving to the rear and left. Long lines of lines of lights white lights on tall poles, tall lights. There are orange ones. Car lights moving headlights moving, headlights moving and cars silhouettes of cars moving. *[whistle whoooooooos loud]* Can you hear the whistle of the train? Just went off.

Suddenly we just crossed the double row, the road with its double row of white lights, one row on either side of the road angling in from the left. Red lights blinking to keep the traffic away. Buildings with white lights that come up from below. Lights like but shorter.

Couples around me, in front of me, on the car, in front of me in the car a white kid with sandy colored hair, but kind of Oriental with a girl with him. Lights, outside, now going off. She's wearing a red sweater, he's got kind of a grey one on, drinking 7-Up.

Look at my. It's now 7:40. We're still stopped for Customs, Customs has been through our car. And this guy in the seat behind me to the left, seat to the left and then behind, back one. They the balding talker talker talker talker talker talker talker talker. The couple sitting behind me, at one point I heard the woman say to the husband if, this is worse than having a crying child in the car with us. Guy is unbearable, never shuts up.

SIDNEY KROME

Going to Chile next year, may go to Argentina, he knows about this, he knows about that. He knows about money, he knows about social customs. Is there anything the guy does not know? Southern Argentina, now he's talking about specific places. Can you hear this?

I asked the Customs man when they went through, they had pistols in holsters on their belts. I don't recall ever having seen them armed before. And at one point when the second one, the younger guy, not the one who questioned me but the younger guy, went out, he looked on the shelves and checked, there were some bags and boxes there and he looked in the, actually looked in the trash bag, almost as if he were looking to see a or a a bomb or something there.

Before the guy was talking about something about Chichenitsa being halfway between one place and another.

Good evening, Gentlemen. It's 11:16, Sunday, February 3rd, back in, my coach, after playing Trivials Pursuit, sitting *[clickety-clackety]* in the club car from about eight o'clock, 8:01. When the train started up at eight o'clock from Saint Albans, I went on down to the club car and got a table and we all had dinner. And we played Trivial Pursuit, but at one point, let's see, Ruth was *[whistle whooooooing]* telling us was what she said this afternoon in the station that she would tell the story about how, the conversation she had with the wife of one of the cousins last night, about, the question of where to bury her mother, who had a severe stroke, and she didn't know where to bury her 'cause her family was buried in in her home city. Her father is buried in there, she's an only child, her mother is now in the hospital in Montreal. Ruthie said that she spoke with her cousin in Florida who said that she should just, since her mother would go along with her, usually did go along with her. she should bur just bury her *[wheels on track]* wherever she wanted. And her husband said essentially the same thing, that she should bury her wherever he she wanted. But she came to Ruth, and Ruth asked if she had discussed it with her mother and she said, No. And she said, Well, does she ever have lucid moments? And she said, Yes. And Ruthie suggested that she talk to her and find out what her mother would really like. And then, if when she finds out, then she could do, that means, of course, she would have to decide what she wants to do. Because if, if her mother says she would rather be buried with her husband, then that leaves her with a decision to make. And if she says she wants to be buried in Montreal, then it's okay to go ahead and do it. She said that she found it strange that, with the congestive heart failure that her mother had, you know, months ago, and then into something potentially could happen, that she didn't even discuss it with her, with her own mother in that time, intervening time.

Then Nancy, later later on Nancy was talking about, we were talking about that conversation where people would be buried *[clickety-door open thruout]* led to the question, does it really matter? And life after death and the soul, and Nancy talked about a friend of hers, another nurse, who had gone to a kind of a spiritualist, and the other nurse said told Nancy that she went there, and the spiritualist said, You know, I sense in you the spirits of some people, and and she mentioned the names of some people who were in this nurse's family before she was even born, which was kind of incredible. But, and then she said that the night Nancy died, we were all sitting in the in the waiting room in that lounge. The doctor came in and *[clickety chugging]* said that Nancy had, Nancy said that, she felt that, she heard Nancy calling her. But, she couldn't imagine that it was really Nancy calling her so she just kind of pushed it out of her mind. And then she had a dream, 'cause I asked Nancy if what she thought about. Oh oh It started when she said that Ruthie had said that she thought that if anybody, this was in in what Ruthie had to say at Nancy's funeral, that Ruthie had said that if anybody could if anybody could be a good pleader, a good intermediary, for us on the other side, it would be Nancy. And Nancy, my sister Nancy, said that that she thought that if anybody could come back and and let her know let that that there was another side on the other side, that it would be Nancy.

And then she started talking about, first of all the fact that she heard Nancy's voice that evening, *[wheels on track]* but she couldn't imagine that it would really be Nancy, and so she she just kind of pushed it out of her mind. And then she had a dream in which Nancy came to her in the dream, and my sister Nancy called this a goodbye dream. She said she felt that there were two kinds of dreams that you could have. One would be the goodbye bye dream, where your own psychological and emotional state says goodbye to the person. Because she felt that that while people had told Nancy that they loved her, she was not sure that anyone actually said goodbye, that anyone said that if you don't make it, y'know, we love you and and we just have to say goodbye to you. I know I didn't. *[loud clickety chugging]* I didn't. That sound you hear in the background is the clickety-clacking of the train on the tracks as we apparently were switched from one track to another. And in the dream, Nancy came to her, and and my sister asked her if she knew that we were all there, during that eight nine days. *[clickety softer]* And my sister Nancy talked about how Ruthie said she had had an out-of-body experience when when Mindy was born, and and that people have out-of-body experiences, and she said that Nancy answered by talking about how you didn't have to have an out-of-body experience, and she went onto this long dissertation. *[whistle whooooooooo]* And finally my sister Nancy said j, But but were you aware, did you know that we were all there, that we were with you? And that Nancy said, Yes, I did, I knew. But, it never, she never, even in that dream she didn't let Nancy say she never g she didn't give Nancy a chance to say to say what? Whether she had been calling my sister, and if she were calling my sister, what she *[whoooooo]* was calling her for, what she wanted to say. And so that just that dream ended without, and she never did find out whether Nancy was calling her, and if she was, why she was calling her, what she had to say to her. Which I thought was very interesting. *[whooooooo]*

And we talked also about where, you know, about being buried. I said that it was, that Sophie and I had a discussion about that, and I said that, you know, when when my mother-in-law died, that they family bought a big plot in Steubenville and that, y'know, Sophie wanted to be buried there, and and I wasn't sure that I wanted to be buried there. And Ruth said that she thought it was very interesting that that after even after all these years Sophie would want to be there. But then she said like like for her and Dave, but I said, Well, well, but you have, you know, they have a plot, *Sharei Zion*, near where Nancy is buried. So that it's it's not a question of being from one city or another, although I thought that was different.

She said that Mindy was a little bit upset about the fact that they bought plots in Baltimore not in Washington, where they lived, and she said that she told Mindy that she had no idea where Mindy was gonna be living anyhow. And I mentioned, of course, I mentioned Thea, and I said I think she stayed where she has been for all these years because her husband is buried in Arlington National Cemetery, and she didn't want to leave him. That's really what I think, that she just doesn't want to leave her husband her husband.

And, Nancy was saying that that I guess it started off because Nancy was saying that that she didn't think that where your body was mattered and 'cause it in heaven it would all be one and the same thing. I didn't comment on that 'cause, frankly, I'm not so sure that I believe in heaven, in that sense.

[voice softer] Roads suddenly appear out of the darkness. Lighted at the intersection with the train. With the track. A bright white or orange light and by blinking red lights.

MONDAY, FEBRUARY 4, 1991

Good morning, it's 12:05 AM, the night of Sunday, February 3rd, to Monday, February 4th. So it's actually Monday, February 4th. *[soft clickety]* In the train, just finished reading, getting ready to go to sleep. And I try looking out the window, and it's so dark. I can't see anything unless I lean against the window, and look down below at the light. It's the light from the light over the seat in front of me. The light cast outside the window by that light over the seat in front of me. That is casting a light spot that runs along the train, that moves along with the train, on the ground as the train moves through the night, but otherwise there is darkness. And all I see looking out the window is the reflection of a blonde woman and her white pillow and a white jacket *[louder and faster clickety]* and and the ceiling, the very faintly lit orange lights one two three four right here. Every other light, and then overhead, and to the left front in front of me, a light that is green under the under the seat tags of the people, which say NYP New York Penns Penn Station

THE NANCY TAPES

New York Penn Station, New York Penn Station. Lot of New York Penn Station people getting off getting off at New York Penn Station. This is the way it is at night, on the train. There is a clickety-clack sound. *[loud as mike is held up-goes on longish time-then quiets back down]* But the train is moving in darkness, in the darkness of the night. *[clickety louder and very clear]* Moving so swiftly, the light from the light, the light cast on the ground outside moving so swiftly with the train, that all it is is not even a rectangle but a glowing light-colored beigeness, light that moves along, and there's nothing I could see, and I can't tell what's in the light, and I can't tell what's in the darkness outside, whether there are trees, or houses, but there are no lights for me to see out there.

    Now all of a sudden there are lights, tall lights, and lights in a building. And then suddenly there are more lights. And there are street lights that are orange, lights on poles that are orange. And there's factory of some kind and tractor-trailer trailers of tractor-trailer trucks. And railroad tracks alongside this, *[whistle whooooooo]* I think they go over to other tracks. And there's a line of lights, orange lights moving down to the distance. And there are two big white lights spotlights in the backs and more lights in the backs of more buildings. Warehouses and that big red sign white letters that says SUBURBAN PROTANE off in the PROPANE off in the distance. Red motel sign and then here a building a factory or plant of some kind. With light coming through the translucent windows and tall street lights, lampposts, but tall ones and a far off in the distance a store with a red sign over it, I can't read it. And there where before there were f furniture stores. And grocery stores. And gas stations. And. Now the lights are coming and going, and now the lights have disappeared again. And there are some lights glowing up from the glass sskylight of a building. *[loud clickety]* We're rocking now, *[thruout this part voice has been quavering as train rocks]* rocking and rocking. And a house and now a barn, is it a barn? With lights on the corners of the barn, and an occasional street light. Orange and tall.

    [voice very quiet] Back again. It's approximately 2:01 or 2 2:01 AM. On Sunday night to Monday morning, still on the train. *[muffled clickety]* Just passed a town, and there was just up to the right a blue, blue white church with very tall and narrow belfry, steeple. Very tall and very narrow. Some time, it must have been about one o'clock, I guess, the sky seemed to have cleared, 'cause I know at one point I was talking about how dark it was, all I could see outside the window were reflections. Now I can look up and I can see stars. Curiously refreshing thing about them. The refreshingly curious thing about them is that they change their positions as do every does everything else. *[wheels squeak]* The position of the train changes, and the direction of the train chain *[slow and quiet clickety]* the direction of the train changes. And I'm so sleepy I can hardly thlink, can hardly speak.

Coming into or through someplace now at 2:20 AM. *[slow chugging]* Suddenly I looked up and there was a moon overhead. Roughly three-quarters, little bit less. And then our position changed, changed in our direction, curved around to the left, *[wheels squeaking]* curved around to the right a little bit, and then the moon was gone. Gone behind the top of the train, or our passenger car. And there was also the sound of the grinndiinng, of the wheeeels on the tracks.

Good morning, Gentlemen. It's about 6:50 AM. Just pulled into New York Penn Station. I'm in the dining car, club car, getting ready to get some breakfast. Actually woke up about 6:30, woke up before but it was really 6 it was 6:30 when I woke up. Passing through New Rochelle. And went farther down out to the right past, like looked like artificial lakes, couple small ones. Just block after block after block of huge apartment houses, they were new, they look nice from outside, from a slight distance. But they were enormous. Numbers and numbers and numbers, there were probably about fifteen to twenty stories high. In a cruciform sort of, and then a kind of a it's hard to tell how many there were. Probably at least twenty-five to thirty. And they were just so big. I thought of thousands and thousands of people who live in them. What do they do? Where do they go? What if there's a power failure with all those thousands of people? What if there are all those thousands of people right there? Just an incredible number of people. Incredible number of apartments. I didn't get to see the New York City skyline as we were coming 'cause I had to, go to the bathroom to wash up. I had to stand and wait in line for that. It was really kind of messy there, I didn't, I didn't even shave at all, I have to wait and see if I can get into the Nancy's or Ruthie's compartment so I can go in and shave and change in there.

S I'm still in the club car, reading Stanley Kaufman's review of Mel Gibson's *Hamlet* in the January 28th, 1991, issue of *New Republic*, page 25. Oh, in line, lines, "When he can speak quietly in prose, like the bitter prose of the address to Yorick's skull, Gibson is affecting. In the larger moments, particularly where there is verse to be carried, to be used as the medium of heightened being he flails about somewhat." That phrase: "verse to be carried, to be used as the medium of heightened being, the medium of heightened being, the medium of heightened being." Poem about Nancy?

Sitting here still having breakfast. The breakfast basket. And now I'm on the second half bagel and cream cheese, marmalade and my coffee. I've had some Rice Krispies and orange juice and a small coupla small slices of of apricot and with my Rice Krispies.

Thinking about some of the conversation last night and how at one point, I was gonna say we were talking about, I guess talking about *Malka Bubbeh Malka* died in in '61. Ruthie said she died in April shortly before Ruthie's wedding. And

I said she and Dave got married it was the 17th, wasn't it? And she said, No, it was the 19th, and now that I think of it, the 17th was K's birthday, birthday.

But I was thinking also about how that was the year Eva died. I think I said that. But what I was thinking about but what I didn't say was it was Ruth who called me when I was in the Army in Germany to tell me that Eva had died. We were on bivouac, and the Wall had just gone up, and we were kind of wild in the woods. And the call came, and they found me in my tent, with Shor, and and I remember Ruthie said something, I said, How are you? Well, I guess I just have to tell you: Eva's dead. Right now I can't remember how how to say it? Let's see, I told her to call the Red Cross to confirm, and I went, I went back to the they gave me a ride back to the base. And I talked with that Captain C, and told him I wanted to take leave, but of course they could not count it as emergency leave because Eva was not considered immediate family, not my blood relative.

Thinking now how things were shattered apart. The Wall going up, the possibility of Eva not, possibility of war and Eva all at the same time. I remember when I came back, and I was at the *shivah* house, AB asked me if I thought there would be war. What did I know? What did I know? I was a lousy PFC. Buried in some, quasi-intelligence unit. And I remember when the, who picked me up? Was it K and Ruth and Dave? At Washington National Airport. I had my tie off. And some guy came up to me, some other GI, and he said I should put the tie on because the MPs patrolled around the the airport, and they would get me for being out of uniform.

And when we pulled up in front of the house, Ronny was on the porch. *[voice breaking]* Mother came down to meet me. And I remember hearing somebody say *[voice breaking]*, Sniff. This was the brother they were worried about. Sniff. *[now a whisper]* Can't stand it. Can't stand it. *[voice almost broken crying]* Aaww, yes I can. And we'll muddle through. Muddle. And muddle. But actually, I think my whole life has been a muddling away, a barely muddling through. Never quite going g'zonkers. The way I sometimes want to. Oh, Eva. I haven't been out yet even to check on your stone to see if the guy fixed it or not.

Still in the club car. It's after eight, I'm not sure what time right now. But reading review by David Bromwich of, the review is called "The Unamerican Mind," review of Allen Bloom's book *Giants and Dwarfs: Essays 1960-1990*. On page 29, he talks about Bloom's, of a book by John Rawls R-A-W-L-S, *A Theory of Justice*. And and in here, he says that "Bloom challenges Rawls' assertion that quote 'the self is prior to the ends which are affirmed by it.' unquote Rawls asserted that quote 'the self is prior to the ends which are affirmed by it.' unquote Just prior to that, 'It is also prior to the ends which are asserted *for* it. By others. By themselves."

SIDNEY KROME

Actually when I made those last comments about that book review and the the self, it was, "The self is prior to the ends which are affirmed by it." It was actually a couple minutes before eight as it is now 8:02. The conductor said we'd be leaving New York just about 20 minutes, at about 8:20.

The review is in the January 28th, 1991, issue of *New Republic*. *[staticky kind of noise, then silence]* **TAPE ENDS**

THE NANCY TAPES

TAPE NUMBER 11B

MONDAY, FEBRUARY 4, 1991

All right, this is the next side. I have to start paying attention to how much tape is left because I missed a lot of this that I was saying into it and have to get back to it. What I have to do, as I was saying, what I have to do, what I want to do in this poem about Nancy is to bring together, these two quotations have crystallized, what I need to bring together. Quotation from Stanley Kaufman's review of *Hamlet*, page 25, the quotation is: "In the larger moments, particularly where there is verse to be carried, to be used as the medium of heightened belief heightened being, he flails about somewhat," speaking of Mel Gibson. Quotation: to be used with/as the medium of heightened being, the medium of heightened being.

Then the quotation in this review *[page turning]* about Bloom's book. It's the both of them the January 28th, 1991, issue of *New Republic*. From John Rawls' book *A Theory of Justice*. That quote, "The self is prior to the ends which are affirmed by it." unquote Or? also assertion that quote, "The self is prior to the ends which are affirmed by it." unquote.

Link together, those two quotations, those two ideas, the medium of heightened being and the self as prior to the ends which are affirmed by it, we might say also with the ends which are affirmed *for* it. Bring the two of them together: the medium of heightened being.

It meant reminded me also thinking now also of the article quoted at length in *Harper's Magazine* about cooking, the article I clipped out and already put into the folder, about about cooking, taking the time to prepare and cook and to chop vegetables to chop mushrooms, to chop to chop all these things rather than putting them in a in a blender or a salad throw thrower whatever they're called. And then and instead of cooking by microwave to take one's time with the cooking gives one the heightened sense of being alive to cooking and to eating. And I remember how when I read that that made me think of the process of dying, of Nancy's dying, of all of us that week, *[wheels on tracks]* those nine days in that lounge at at Hopkins.

And what I've been thinking about also as I said to Ruthie is about flashing back, and she said, To your father's death? And I said, No, I said, To Aunt Freda's. And while we didn't get, did not get the chance to finish the discussion, this was Friday at the hotel, while we didn't get a chance to finish the discussion then, I want, I was thinking about the way they, I mentioned this before I think, on the way our aunts and uncles our aunts and uncle Herschel, the way they took Aunt Freda away, I had thought to the Mayo Clinic in Rochester, and Ruthie said, No, it was Sloan-Kettering in New York. Can't remember which one it was, but family was in dis disagreement on our part which one it was or or or difference in memory. But the point is that the same, essentially the same kind of thing with Aunt Freda as with Nancy. In in both senses, for us now there is more the medium of heightened being as in in terms of becoming aware of the self that is prior to anything that we might affirm, that might have been affirmed by her, that we might affirm for it. The medium of heightened being. Not verse but life, but the right kind of verse can help it.

Review by Jasper Griffin entitled "The Real Founding Fathers." *[clank-as door open]* Talks about ancient Greece and Rome. "On the far side of the abyss of barbarian invasions et cetera we can distantly see another high culture like yet unlike our own in which the ideas of democracy, liberty, and the rule of law were memorably debated. Such a society existed and then ceased to exist: colon those are both momentous facts." It's on page 33. One might say that about those who lived, the souls that are prior to what is affirmed by them, what is affirmed for them. The medium of heightened being. Such person existed and such a person ceased to exist. Both momentous facts.

Same page, the very the next paragraph in the review. The book by a German Frenchman and American Christian Meyer and Paul Vain. Part II. "The most powerful historians now writing on the world of ancient Greece and Rome. Philosophical rather than ha com Greece and Rome, comma philosophical rather than antiquarian writers, comma who generalize and impose patterns of meaning on the evidence." unquote Philosophical rather than antiquarian writers who generalize and impose patterns of meaning on the evidence. Isn't that what your mission is? Kirk, not, what's his name? Phelps, Kirk, and Phelps, Kirk, and Picard.

Family of five, kids and the father came in taking pictures. And now it's a it's a bright full sunshiny sunny, day. It's 8:24 and we're on our way. Kid in a vest. Can see the blue sky and now we're going into the tunnel.

Here come Ruth. Or here comes Ruth. And Aunt Esther. And some of the rest of them.

It's 1:00 P.m., Monday afternoon. I'm in my office. I've been back here on campus since about ten of 12. But very quickly I just needed to say that this morning when we, after we passed through Chester, Pennsylvania, parts of the tracks where there are switched tracks over to the east of us, there were there was tall dried yellow grass and dried, small trees, very very small saplings, I guess, or or bushes in between and the middle of, the tracks. So that it had been obviously been looong time, years since the tracks have been used. Years since they've been used.

TUESDAY, FEBRUARY 5, 1991

Good morning, Gentlemen. Couple surprises for you today. First of all, it's 7:21 AM. And I'm just back at Owings Mills, Owings Mills at Wimbledon Lane, pulling away on my way down to work again. You know where I have been the last three days. And who knows where I'm going for the next three days other than right here. I have to stop this for a moment while I go over the, while I go over this beump.

On Village Queen Drive right now heading I guess this would be west. Straight up and now bout roughly of the 11:30 according to the clock time arrangement of the sky is a half-moon, very pale, but still white. The shadows are faded blue almost the color of the sky so that it looks as though it has holes in it almost, as though it has holes in the moon. The light changed. Raiiight. On my way, troublemaker.

I have to rearrange the date and time on SIDE A. I have it as, ei 2/3 at 8:02, I remember it must have been 2/4 yesterday morning, at 8:02 in the, in the club car. Now anyhow I'm down I'm at the intersection of of Hooks Lane, and the sun to approximately the ten o'clock hour is a bright, bright, golden orange, and it's the orange it's it's past paling now, it was bright orange about thirty seconds ago. And it's it spreads up into the cl few clouds that are right around it. Like the color like the like the glow in the sky when we went up to to Steubenville. When was that? Was that when I was with the boys? Going up for Mother's funeral.

And that was on that back route, 88 548 whatever it was, heading up the back way to Steubenville from little Washington.

I just switched the radio to 1-2-3-0 WITH, the *Memory* song was on. From *Cats*. And the last phrasing of it, "Let the memory live again." Or, "Let the memories live again." Yes, "let the memories live again."

How ironic that yesterday in the mail when I got home was the newsletter from Amy with my piece on Nancy. That I, who was I talking about how much I had rushed? Was that Ruthie? That I had rushed so much to get it in and to mail it off and Federal Express it and all that stuff. And it was, it was probably a good five weeks after that before she mailed it out. For whatever reason it took took a month and a half almost to get it mailed out.

Anyhow, Gentlemen, I'm I am on my way back down Reisterstown Road again. Good old Reisterstown Road. Comin' down now towards Slade Avenue.

Elton John and *The Crocodile Rock* in the background. And here I am at Fordleigh and Reisterstown or Reisterstown at Fordleigh and the Fordling Shopping Center Fordleigh Shopping Center. And looking straight ahead I see that there's the it looks like the radio tower for the police station down there. Radio tower for something. And it's sticking up through the clouds. And the one also to the left down there I can see the old triple triangular top triple station tower, over over in our old area Springhill area Springhill and Violet area. And that too is sticking up through the clouds, where the sun is, more to the left over there. But I don't know what this other tower, I don't know what this shit! Pardon me. I don't know what this other tower is that's more straight ahead. 'Cause I didn't think it was that far down. But it must be far down. It mi Look at But the cloud level, must be really low for that one to be going up through it. Oh, and look at the the golden glow of the reddish-burnt glow of the sun. It's now just about wish I had my camera, is now right on the triple, points of the triple antenna. And there is the the W-B-F-F tower over there also into the clouds, and this one straight ahead. This must be oh, that's what it is, it's that smoke, from that fire over in Woodlawn that that stump, that smoldering stump thing. That's what that must be. Yes, 'cause that is kind of acrid. Okay.

Now right about now, yes, that tower was for the police station, northwestern district, here, and I'm now down just almost right parallel to it and I can see the smoke that was drifting overhead and and right in my position now it seems to have faded out. 'Cause I'm right under, what's it? Hayward. Right, just crossing Hayward. Whoops! I better watch out, and now here's the police station. Okay.

And this was where the pall of smoke was, and I can still see there's still a bit of haze ahead. I'm not sure what this has to do with anything, but I think that haze is important. Isn't it? Isn't haze important, when you're looking for the significance and meaning of things? And there goes the the Baltimore Metro overhead down straight ahead just crossing Belvedere and Benny's. With the okay, a cement blocked up windows and stuff. Store fronts. I better put, something down 'cause I'm havin' trouble driving this carrr with this traffic here and the coffee in the left and the the casse microcassette in the right. And the the the burnt glow to the sky is gone from in front of the sun now. It's all around me actually *[laughing]* is what it is. I can see the smoke in the air right around here where I am now. I passed Garrison and heading down. Sniff. Boy and I can smell it! Holy cow! And I'm gonna be spilling coffee all over myself in a second. I can smell it, in the air and passing the church near Maar Lesser's house. There is smoke in the air, there certainly is smoke and haze and haze and smoke and hoke and smaze in the air. And I'm coming down there just passing Beeler Avenue. Was that after we used to live on Beeler? I don't know. Anyhow I I better get over here I'm coming Woodland Avenue. And coming down here now. Sniff-sniff. Boy, is the smell of this stuff strong in the air now! I'm telling you, you put the window, Virginia Avenue. Virginia. Even with the window closed, windows all closed, coming now there it is! St. Ambrose, and here we come to Royce Avenue. Good morning, Royce Avenue, 3316, Mohawk 4 2448. How you doin', Aunt Freda?

Yes, we talked about phone numbers. Course I've got that recorded already. Forest 7-3756, Aunt Esther's old number that I didn't remember when we were in Montreal. Because I didn't have to call it that much.

Che-che. Pardon me. Passing now Keyworth Avenue and the Francis Scott cav Louisa May Alcott School and what used to be P's office there and the

Gleimans' drugstore. And here coming up now uh PS 5- past PS 59 Springhill Avenue. Crossing Springhill Avenue now, Jake's up there and the block, farther up, the 26-hundred block, the famous block. *The* block, of the Kromes and Kanows. And now passing, Violet Avenue! And up there what used to be Kessler's, but now is back to a house. I remember, was it in '77? When they were reconstructing that back into a house. No longer Kessler's Delicatessen. Even though Paul is now friendly with Barney's grandson. Over and out! Under and in!

That burnt smell from that stump fire, smoldering stump fire, is still strong in the air even down here at Henry G. Parks, Jr. Circle.

And thinking now that about all the times I go along with people. And it reminds me of how when I was talking to Ruthie about something having to do with Jewish practices, and there was something that that she didn't understand, and I remember thinking to myself, Isn't that surprising, that she didn't understand that? Why is that surprising? Why should I think that? And why, y'know, it's like even with the the the girls the group from Montreal going to going to shopping. Why should I be surprised that people that I love and respect for other things would do stupid and inconsiderate things at other times? They're human beings! And it still surprises me. Heh!

And I think, remember thinking yesterday at one point that I have not been able to get away from 1954. And thinking about all this stuff, and how this with Nancy last fall reminded me of Aunt Freda in December of '54. I can't get away from '54. Sometime I said something about how I was just muddling through. Part of that I know is my negativeness towards myself. That I'm just muddling through, that I'm not, there's no breakthrough into either a a kind of a breakthrough into a momentary madness from which I would come back. Or a real integration into myself of what happened. It's the muddling through middle. Maybe it's more positive than I think, maybe that muddling through is more positive than I think it is. And, or again then again, as I thought to myself at one point, maybe my madness is in what I have done by distancing and separating myself! Isn't that incredibly strange? No, it's not incredibly strange, but oh okay I better stop this, I I have to remember to say something about burial sites. Burial sites for me and Sophie. Or did I already say this? I gotta stop.

The smell of the burning is just incredible. I'm back down here at Coppin, and this is very very strong. Sniff. Very strong scent of that burning, that stump, smoldering stump burn. Talking about being buried someplace. Oh, Nancy was talking to Ruth about how she wanted to call the *Shaarei Zion*, cemetery thing so that she could order a plot for herself near where Ruth and Dave and where Nancy are. And somehow I said something about che-che y'know that that Soph wants to be buried in Steubenville, and they have this plot, the family plot where my mother-in-law died, and I just really haven't decided what I want to do. And Ruth said that she was surprised that after so long, not surprised, that's not the right word, there was something that that, after so many years, Soph still thinks in terms of Steubenville and the family, and, it's not really that surprising, it's not really that unusual. Although I suppose it would be like, twenty years after marriage in 1953, had my or '54, let's say, had my mother died first, would she have wanted to be buried in Montreal? Course, the difference is, or like Aunt Freda, even. The difference is that at least, with them, Aunt Freda still had my mother, and her sister, so she had two sist, her mother and Aunt Esther, my mother and Aunt Esther, so there were at least, there was a clump of family here, not just, Aunt Freda and Uncle Aaron. Whereas in the case of Sophie, it's just it's just the just us down here, and the rest of her entire family is there in Steubenville.

And Nancy saying something about how she didn't think it mattered where your your body was, it was where your soul would go, and and the whole idea of of heaven and where people would be together in heaven.

And ironically also yesterday there was that article in the *Accent* magazine of about people's views towards death towards the afterlife. And that one woman, really rather fundamentalist, very rigid that, you know, you don't get into heaven unless you're the only way you can get there is to be saved by Jesus Christ, to accept Jesus as your savior, and that's the only way you can get in. And she knows that she's in. What arrogance! What arrogance! Not necessarily that to believe that you have the best way, but to believe that you have the only way. It needs to be the right way for you. That makes me think now also that column about that guy, in Athens, from Cyprus or from Crete, that you say you love your island, and he said his island was the most beautiful. He did it for two reasons, first because he felt that everybody should feel that way about his home place, and second because it's right! It's the truth!

Everybody who believes in a religion should believe that his religion is the is the right one. But is it the truth that his and only his is the right one? Is it objectively the truth that one island is more beautiful than another? Is it objectively the truth that one religion is not simply the best but the only way? Things are better for people. But it cannot, you see, there's a difference. There's a difference. It cannot be obj, I don't, I To me it's absolutely impossible for it to be objectively true that one *must* believe in Jesus in order to be saved. It's objectively impossible! I can't believe that this would be the universe that God would create, this would be the *world* that God would create. This would be the nature of spiritual reality, that the *only way* to attain salvation of one's soul is to be a Christian in that sense. I just, that's spiritual arrogance. That's spiritual arrogance.

On the other hand, what about our claim, the Jewish claim to be the Chosen People? To be chosen, not in the sense that that we're the only ones to be saved, but in the sense that we are to be the ones to reveal the way to salvation, to reveal spiritual reality to the rest of the world? And what is, but then there's the question of what is the spiritual reality? Is the spiritual reality the Thirteen Articles of the Faith of Judaism? Is the spiritual reality the particular Jewish way of worship? Or is the spiritual reality or is the spiritual reality the existence of *God*? And the consequent demand, spiritual demand on humanity, spiritual and moral demand on humanity, in the *Old Testament*? Does one have to keep kosher in order to be saved? One has to keep kosher in order to be Jewish. But does one have to keep kosher in order to be saved? So maybe from that point of view, Paul was right, not Peter. That is, the spiritual reality is not in *kashruth*, the spiritual reality is in Judaism, not in Jewishness. Does that make sense? Makes sense to me. Because if that's what the spiritual reality is, then it can be, then it can be accommodated by almost any religion, which recognizes that spiritual reality and that spiritual truth. Anyhow, it's 7:53, I better get in and get ready for this meeting. Over and out. Under and in.

It is 4:57 on the *apres-midi d'une faun*, on the afternoon of February the 5th, 1991, Wednesday *[sic--actually, Tuesday]*. I'm on my way home, and here it is on W-I-T-H, 123 1-2-3-0 on your radio, it's *On Top of Old Smokey*! "On a green willow tree, For the leaves they will wither, The roots they will die, You'll all be forsaken" You will be forsaken. And and *never* know why. "And never know why" The leaves they will wither and the roots they will die. Aaaaaaaaahhhhhhhhh. The crunch of an apple. *[apple crunch]*

WEDNESDAY, FEBRUARY 6, 1991

Good morning, Gentlemen. It's 8:25 AM, Wednesday, February the 6th, 19-hundred-and-91. I'm here at the intersection of Greenspring Avenue and Cold Spring Lane waiting for a traffic light. Pipe that in your put and moke it smoke it. Or whatever you do with it, when you get, news. Heading down a back way. Why? Can you figure this out? No, I'll have to tell you why. Just took my mother to drop her off at. What's the name of that the Hoffberger Building at Sinai for her colonoscopy. And I had actually I had forgotten she had asked me to do it, to take her down, and I had forgotten about it. But fortunately she called about 7:20 this morning to remind me. And that's interesting also, I had completely forgotten. *[clunking thump]* And that sound you hear in the background is the windshield wipers, moving slowly, intermittently, intermittently. And I'm getting ready to go down Greenspring towards Druid Park Drive and then into Druid Hill Park.

Paul is now significantly taller than Soph. This morning his his shoulders were a good three inches two to three inches higher than hers and Monday, when I got back from Montreal and I saw him Monday evening, after he got back from school, he's just I thought he was, as tall as I am, he's not quite, I mean, not that I'm that tall, but he's, he's almost to my height. You asshole! Pardon me. He's almost to my height. And I'll tell you one thing, he has, in fact, he grew, he got taller! In the time from when I saw him Thursday morning going to work before I left for Montreal Thursday evening and the time that I saw him Monday evening, so it's Friday, Saturday, Sunday, three full days, till Monday four full days, four days and some hours, and and I know he got taller, and of course a little bit thinner. Here we are coming back coming down Greenspring, and I've passed Keyworth, we went just went past the Martin Luther King, Jr. Elementary School. Coming down now the hill towards Druid Park Drive. Out and over. Over an under and in.

Ah, yes, yesterday I heard that Dean Jagger had died, he's the one who played the general Wainwright in *White Christmas* and then this morning on the news on at A-B-C Good Morning, America, they talked about the entertainment world's saddened, Danny Thomas died of a heart attack, 79, Jagger was 87. Dean Danny Thomas was 79. And I remember him doing that Wailing Lebanese bit on his old original "Danny Thomas Show" on television what? not forty years probably thirty, thirty-five.

And here we go passing on the right, Hogback Hill, the notorious and infamous Hogback Hill in Druid Hill Park. It's now barricaded off. You can't drive on there, they've got a barricade on it. And coming up on the left will be, here just as we go round this curve is Three Sisters. What's it? The three ponds, I think that's by, there's the other barrier, the top part of Hogback Hill, and the sign says "Test Area/Do Not Mow." The left is Three Sisters. To the right is that flat little area alongside the reservoir. God, it looks so small now! Where we used to play football. To the left is the old cemetery. To the right now, here's this, tree, the one that's half on its side. I have to come by and take pictures of that sometime, half on its side by the Reptile House. What used to be, I remember this the Aquarium years and years and years ago and the the reservoir which is gone, has been gone for years, I mean, even when we were teenagers it was gone. When we used to play play softball there, and I was so, played way too far back with my eyes I couldn't see, man, I couldn't judge distances anymore. The old Cavalier Club and there's the the *shule*, gee, I don't even know what it's called other than the Auchentoroly Terrace *shule*. Okay. And here we are, and there's the old, the pagoda down there. By the entrance to the zoo.

THURSDAY, FEBRUARY 7, 1991

Good morning, Gentlemen. 8:00 AM, Thursday, February 7th, 1991. I just crossed the I'm on Reisterstown Road, just crossed the overpass over 695, the Beltway. It's a rainy misty foggy day, and this schmuck is coming out. If I didn't have the coffee, well, whatever. **TAPE ENDS**

TAPE NUMBER 12A

THURSDAY, FEBRUARY 7, 1991
Good morning, Gentlemen. It's 8:03 at, the last tape. Good morning, Gentlemen, it's Good morning, Gentlemen, it's 8:03, February the 7th. Song that was just on what used to be W-F-B-R was *Solitary Man*, and now it's The Mamas and The Papas. *Dedicated to the One I Love*. Anyho "Each night before you go to bed, my baby" Say a little whisper a little pray for me, my baby.

What I was saying before the last tape ran out was that I tend to ignore the world around me a little bit. "and tell" There's been a war on in in Iraq. Our coalition forces as they're called January 16th started "this is dedicated to the one I love" started the air assault "something I want you to do" on Iraq, missiles *et cetera*. "I want it to be" Airplane bombing. "I won't be satisfied" And Israel was hit a few several times by SCUD missiles fired from Iraq. Fortunately, they were not chemical warfare. They were trying to provoke Israel into an attack that would lead to an Arab-Israeli war. But it didn't work, fortunately. But that'ss the kind of thing that's been going on.

Paul has grown incredibly tall. Last weekend when I went to Montreal, and I came back on Monday, and when I saw him Monday evening, after he came home from school, and I came home from work, he h'd I think he had grown probably a half an inch or an inch, over the weekend while I was away since I had seen him Thursday morning. "Is just before dawn" Dawn.

I really screwed up yesterday at that budget hearing. At, that student, that girl got me all screwed up in time, she was supposed to be here at 9:30, she didn't get there 'till 10:30. My impulse to take out a copy of that project report I had done just got lost. She just. Damn! I should never have done that! Should never have allowed that to happen! It's my own fault! As they say. Although he was nice about it afterwards, called me in and apologized *et cetera*, and I apologized and, anyhow, he said 95%, as of July 1st I'll be Acting Vice President for Academic Affairs. I'm not so sure, I do wanta do it, but I don't wanta do it. P asked me in the car coming back from Annapolis how I found time to do the writing, and I told him, well, summers and early mornings, you know, five o'clock and working for an hour and a half in the morning. I really really really would like to teach and write, but there's something really attractive about being a Vice President for Academic Affairs. I hope I don't screw it all up, that and myself. Oh, well. Oh, well, oh, well!

I woke up screaming, horrible, from a nightmare last night in the middle of the night. It's hard to remember what it was. I was in a rheum in a zimmer in a room, and there were something underneath and then the floor started to burn out, it flash burned. And there was something underneath. And I got out and closed the door, and there was something before that, I don't think I think that was where it ended. That was where I started screaming. But I don't remember all the details, I don't remember all, something about that room. I still have not remembered what it was I was thinking of that Thursday that was a week ago tomorrow, a week ago today! At school. And somebody said something, and I said the something of the something. And I can't remember it all.

The mere fact of my having forgotten what it was becomes significant. As my having forgotten to take along that project report. Oh, how I'd love to go back to yesterday morning and put that project report out. I'd love to be able to go back to last Thursday and pick up this thing, pick up my cassette recorder, to record just what it was that I thinking then. But I can't go back to then, and I can't go back to then. I can't go back to yesterday, I can't go back to last Thursday. It's forgotten. If you don't do it right away, it disappears.

Something else I forgot. I meant to bring the camera with me today, I have about three pictures left, black and whites, taking back pictures of the basketball game last night, and I forgot to bring it along so I could finish off the pictures, and take them in to to get developed. But, of course, I forgot.

How much have I forgotten of everything? You see, part of the clue is not only what you remem not only what you can put together, or how you put together what you remember, but part of the clue is, what do you remember? And some of what you remember, you remember because partly it's important to you, and so you remember it. And other y and and apparent apparently that would mean that what you forget is something that you find is not important to you. But sometimes you forget things because you forget things. And so I've forgotten things. You can't remember everything. So what I should be doing, in one sense, is is speaking into this thing and telling it everything that I can remember, everything that I can think of, like that memory tape I started a number of years ago. I need to do one of those again. Or or at least include mem memories in here. Sniff.

I need to respond to that thing of Nancy's, the request about information about the the the reunion. I need to put in my if I'm gonna do it, need to hurry up and do my Rumkowski paper, redo that so I can send that off. I need to do the CHOICE report, I need to do the other report, the MCTS report. Work on it this weekend.

SUNDAY, FEBRUARY 10, 1991

Sunday, February 10th, Godparents' Luncheon at the church, it's 12:09 and one of the one of the doves that they've kids've put up on this tree down here. "Please, God, give us peace. We hope for p we wish for peace and we hope for peace. But we proble p-r-o-b-l-e proble we'll never have peace, but we still pray for peace pray for peace. Never have but we will probably never peace, but we still pray for peace."

SIDNEY KROME

THURSDAY, FEBRUARY 14, 1991

"Summertime and the livin' is" Good morning, Gentlemen. Cheh-cheh. "easy" Good morning, Gentlemen. It's 7:53 AM "fish are jumpin'" Thursday, February the 14th, Valentine's Day, and I'm heading south on Reisterstown Road towards going to work. In the background you can hear the music of *Porgy and Bess* playing. "your ma is good lookin'" Or maybe in the foreground, I'll put. "so hush, little baby, don't you cry" "Old man Seven, come down from" It is a very gray, very overcast, foggy day, miserable, miserable! Warmish, though. "What?" That child ain't asleep yet. "That child ain't asleep yet?" Give him to me! "Give him to me." There seems to be a traffic tie-up here. And listening to *Porgy and Bess* and *Summertime*, and thinking about what I told Myron, about how "your daddy warn you" when I had sent a copy of the Gershwin the *Porgy and Bess* article to Sonny and Jerry 'cause I mentioned Aunt Freda, and then I saw Sonny and Ellie at "love and mourn you" it was either Rosh Hashanah or whatever, one of the things at dinners at my mother's house "buuuuut" that's "a woman" when he told me that he had been singing and humming *Summertime* and he never knew why. And I told Myron he was *[voice breaking]* under three he was three years old when his mother died. "claim you" How could he know why he was singing *Summertime*? That his mother used to sing it, *[crying]* Aunt Freda used to sing it when he was a baby. "woman comes to claim you" Sniff! "'Cause" Oooouuuhhh! Man! "A woman is a sometime thing" Oh, man! "yes, a woman is a sometime thing" Oh, man! Let me hear from you, Myron! About a copy of your article. Sniff! "Don't you never let a woman" Uh-huh-huh Fit that in.

The other day, cheh-cheh! I guess it was at the Sunday School Godparents' Luncheon, "'cause" the church, "a woman is a" it must have been when Sophie was talking about, I'm not sure what it started as, it started about talking about the chaos, and Father Constantine said that that anybody who could make order of out of chaos is to be blessed. Did you hear that, Gentlemen? Anyone who can make order out of chaos is to be blessed. Mr. Phelps, Captain Kirk, Captain Picard, earn your blessing!

[voice breaking] It's so dark and gray today. It's so dark and gray! How did I leave Eva's name off that list of our young dead? That went with the pictures I gave to Ronnie and to Nancy? *[crying]* How did I do thaaat?! I don't understa-and how I did thaaaat!

Rogers Avenue, Rogers Avenue, the Crest to the left. "ain't that I mind" The Diner "workin'" to the right.

[voice breaking and crying] I can't stand it todaay! My man's gone now, since my man is gone just plaaaayyed and I'm falling apart again! Coming down Reisterstown towards Royce Avenue nooow.

THE NANCY TAPES

"and I'm leavin' at" Okay, now, getting ready, and here we go, passing, Rroyce Avenue! 3316 the home of the first place and time I heard *[crying] Summertiiimme* from Aunt Fredaaaa "it take a long" who is gooonnne long since. "pull" It take a loonng pull to get there. "loong"

Just passed Keyworth Avenue and PS 59, now known as Alcott Place. "what for?" And now here's Sspringhill Avenue Springhill Avenue! Springhill Avenue! Springhill Avenue! 2614 and 2616. Numbers and numbers and numbers. Symbiosis. Symbiosis. Symbiosis of 2614 and 2616.

Two numbers, one double-digit apart, one one even number apart. One wall apart, one porch apart. Separated. Or joined. By a wall, by a porch wall. Sniff. Separated by a number. There is no gap, actually, between 12 and 14 if you're counting by evens and odds. If you're counting by evens 'cause it ain't odd!

[very loud] Look out at da buzzard! Da buzzard haangin' round my door all de time! Even when I don't see 'im, even when I don't look for 'im, de buzzard is always there. "burning trouble" *[very quiet]* The buzzard. "watch" The buzzard. "right over your house" The buzzard. "all your happiness done dead" All all your happiness done dead, nooo, your happiness is still there, but the buzzard always lurks behind and beneath it. "buzzard"

The buzzard don't never keep on flyin' ovuh! "shadow" Don't take along his shadow he g always casts a shadow, his shadow is cast when you try to see through the shadow, what you can see through the shadow.

Ain't you heard the news this mawnin'? Po'gie's young again. "Step" Step up, "up" brother "brother" hit the gaveled. "hit the" The problem is "gravel," the news no matter how good the news is, the shadow of the buzzard "Po'gie who you used" is always, lingering, "beat on" always lingering, sometimes you can't see it, but it's aaallways there someplace, the shadow of the buzzard.

Okay, it's now 11:11! "sister" The morning of what's this? Thursday, February four-teenth, 1991. I'm here back, just leaving home, just dropped off Valentine's flowers for Soph, and in the background is more "take it, take it" *Porgy and Bess*. There's lots more where that come from! "that's the t'ing" That's the thing, ain't it? "remember there's plenty more where that comes from" There's a boat dat's leavin' soon fo' New Yo'k.

Anyhow, one of the things I wanted to do today, I picked up the flowers for Soph, went down and ordered them yesterday, and for Mother, but Mother's being delivered. And, what I wanted to do today "Come wid me" was to "dat's where we belong" also to pick up a cake from Muhly's, 'cause this is 20 years ago, this Valentine's Day, Soph was in Steubenville, "can live that high" and I went when I went up for the weekend, I made the ca took a cab down from from Beethoven down to "won't go wrong" the bus station, and we stopped at Muhly's at L at Lexington Market, and I got a Muhly's Valentine's cake to take up and sat with it on my lap all the way up to Steubenville. And I wanted to get another one this time, and I parked the car and walked down Charles Street, and suddenly realized that even though it said BAKERY and COFFEE, the Muhly's sign was not there, and I thought, Well, that's whatever, it just faded out. But then I realized that it's a Chinese restaurant, breakfast, lunch and Chinese food! "and all your blues you'll be forgettin'" And I walked inside to pick up the flowers at what's-a-names? Mary Johnson's, "come along wid me" and I said something about Muhly's being gone, and she said it just happened suddenly. And then suddenly, *[voice higher and higher pitched]* I realized something that I didn't even realize "come along" yesterday: "come along" something else is gone, not only is Muhly's gone, now a Chinese restaurant, but Mary Johnston the Florist, *[high pitched throughout]* the little old ladies who used to run it, and the gays who used to answer the phone and do the flowers, the florists and all this stuff, they ain't there no more! And it's I think it's a Korean family or Vietnamese family, an Asian family anyhow, that's running the place. "That's where" And "we belong" How 'bout them apples?! "loooonnnggg" There is "looonnnggg" no more little old ladies at Mary Johnston, it's Mary Johnston the Florist still, they've got the same name, but it's not Mary Johnston the little old ladies anymore. Well, how 'bout that? So that's two things, it's like the IBM, the parking lot, down by Harborplace when I went down when we when Sophie and I went down with Louise and Bob and turned the corner, the parking lot was gone! "Bess oh where's my Bess?" Turn the corner, "oh where's" Muhly's is gone! It's a Chinese restaurant. Turn the corner, the little old ladies are gone! It's it's a Korean-owned store. Which is fine for them, but, *[higher pitched]* what happened to the little old ladies? What happened to the guy gay guys down there? I miss *[back to normal pitch]* my friendly people down there.

It's like that article, nations live and nations die, they come and they go, and that's a fact of life. Muhly's Bakery at on on Preston and Charles Street "oh where's" is gone! Little old ladies, they're gone! What's it? "Bess" Life goes on, ma-yn! Mehyn! Mehyn!

More more grist for the chaos mill, Gentlemen. Keep that in mind.

TUESDAY, FEBRUARY 19, 1991

Good morning, Gentlemen. It's What'sah? What'sah?! It's 8:03 AM, on Tuesday, February 19th, 1991. It's a very, pardon me, gray, rainy, misty, foggy, but mild, February day. Temperature's 45 or so. That sound you hear in the background is the sound of the sound of the windshield wipers. *[singing]* Window wi-pers, win-dow wi-pers, wipe those windows, wipe those windows.

Anyhow, Friday night and Saturday we went to the Hyatt Regency for just a getaway weekend. And, Saturday morning, while Soph was in the bathroom, I put the tv on, and I think it was it was either the Discovery channel or or public broadcasting, and they had a program called *The Rattlesnake and the Squirrel*, or it it was called *The Squirrel and the Rattlesnake,* I think it was *The Rattlesnake and the Squirrel*. And it talked about how the the squirrel, the rattlesnake, would go after squirrels, and spotted one, and the squirrel, kind of backed into its burrow a little bit and was throwing dirt at the rattlesnake, and the rattlesnake hit the squirrel. But later it said that the hit bit the squirrel, said that the squirrels had developed over evolutionary periods kind of an immunity against the fatality, oh of the of the of the of the rattlesnake bite. And the face got very very puffy, but it didn't die. And as it backed in, it blocked off the the passageway, eventually it blocked off the passageway as much as it could to the burrow, while it then moved its baby squirrels to a safer location, and and and I was thinking about how here the cameramen were recording this, and of course nobody would think of intervening to to protect the squirrel. And whereas if a and would people intervene if if a human being were being attacked like this? That is, would journalists intervene? And and the answer is that they probably would, at least in some cases, they would, if they thought they could and get away with it. But they don't for the squirrel because because that's part of nature, that's nature's way. That is, that there's a c a qualitative difference between a rattlesnake killing or going after and attempting to kill a squirrel, which he would kill for the sake of its own food. There's a qualitative difference between that act of killing and and murder of one human being by another human being. But some of the news photos indicate that that, of course, people would not intervene, at least journalists would not intervene, and the question is, of course, should they? And the answer is probably not. Depending on the nature of the act about to be perpetrated, by the alleged perpetrator. On the perpetration of the perpetrated.

That was one point about the and then Was it Soph? or somebody said something about how oh and then anyhow what happened was that the squirrel did manage to get away, the squirrel managed to get its babies away, and so this time, particular time, the squirrel and its and its babies escaped death at the fangs of the of the of the rattlesnake.

And and somebody I I think it was the announcer said something about how the the squirrel escaped, and it was good for the squirrel. Well, it's good for the squirrel, but is it good for the rattlesnake? I mean in in a in a natural situation like that who's, do we take anybody's side? I'm take a side of the squirrel over the rattlesnake? I mean, the squirrel is, obviously, cuddlier, cuter, it is a mammal like a as we are, and and the rattlesnake is, looks cold, and it's got that cold skin, and it's a reptile. And it's it frightens us. And we dislike it because it's a reptile. And interestingly enough, last night, Sunday night, while Soph and Paul were at church, and I was folding laundry, I put on *Alien* was on on channel 25 channel 5. And I saw two parts of it, basically, one part where the the the s s baby reptile alien comes out of the guy's chest. And then later when it sort of an adult, I guess an adult, and the rows of teeth come out and it gets one of the guys, and I couldn't see where it zonked him, but it it really zonked a guy, the teeth came out chomping.

But interest interestingly, this was a a reptile type alien. That is, it was not a a mammal type alien, it was clearly reptile. In other words, the alien was associated with, at least in my mind, and I think also in the director's and producer's minds, associated with rattlesnake, with with a reptile as opposed to a mammal, that is, it was not like a lion or a tiger or a bear, but instead, was r a reptile.

And that also reminds me of the the *Star Trek* program "Arena" where Kirk has to battle the Gorn, who of course is also a big a big lizard, a big reptile, and not not a mammal. Okay. Put that in your smoke and pipe it. Out and over.

I really almost went bonkers at home today. It took me approximately 35 or 40 minutes just to get 35 minutes just to get my lunch together and get myself ready to get outa the house after I'd had breakfast. That's just incredible! I just can't move! I just I just can't move. The sound you hear is the sound of the window wipers wiping windows!

Also bought two hats this weekend down at Harborplace, one a kind of a grey plaid called a Plaid Walker, and the other one a call a black called Light Felt Safari. I'm starting off with the Walker today even even though it's it's a rainy day, I'm wearing the Walker. Walk walk walk walk walk walk walk! Whittaker Walk!

How many people would understand the allusion of that "Whittaker Walk"? Whittaker Wault! *The Russians Are Coming, The Russians Are Coming!* Alan Arkin referred to Carl Reiner as Whittaker Wault. And wok wok wok the wok w-o-k, the Chinese Whittaker Wok, Whikkaker Wok.

Coming down now, approachiiinng Royce Avenue, and there's a, billboard says You've just Did you just say, Thanks Canada House? And here we go, crossing Royce Avenue. Whattaya say, Aunt Freda? Uncle Aaron?

THURSDAY, FEBRUARY 21, 1991

Good morning, Gentlemen. Now there's bus going past me. 8:14. Good morning, Gentlemen. It's 8:14 AM, on Thursday, February the 21st, 1991. I've just emerged from the escalator from the Mondawmin Subway stop. It's a light haze, the city skyline is silhouetted in a grey haze. This should surprise you.

I'm now walking across heading towards Mondawmin towards Coppin. In the morning heading towards work. Put this in your chaos factor and smoke it. This morning on the subway just about 8:08 as we came up to I could see, what an aviator says, see, Saint Ambrose Church. And then I could see the *Agudas Achim* in the distance on Park Heights Avenue. That was where one Saturday AA and, was it JS? I can't remember whether it was JS or A A, one of them said something about about something about why wasn't I in *shule* and something about it was for

Jews. And then the other one said something about how I was doing so much to help the kids of Isaac Davidson on Saturday, going to Saturday services there. Anyhow, I saw it from the subway.

Thinking again about how one thing I really want to do sometime is ride the subway down and take pictures of the old landmarks in our historic youth or our youthful history. Saint Ambrose, *Agudas Achim,* Avalon street the street that the Aval the section where the Avalon is. 59, Louisa May Alcott School. As I went past. Also the School 59, I saw the, School 59, came down to the east side of it south side and could see that the southeast side along Keyworth Avenue was in sunlight, because of what direction of the sunrise. And I could also see it through the through the branches of the denuded trees. How's that for a word? Trees without leaves. Since the trees have not yet gotten their leaves back.

Thinking about how that's how I see 59, that's how I see, actually that's, panting and puffing as I speak and walk, including my childhood and my youth. Through the haze, not the haze but through the dry the dry barriers, no, I wouldn't call them barriers, but through the branches, the haze of my memory, the trees, the leafless trees of my memory. But maybe actually my, now that I think about it, maybe the trees of my memory are full-flowered because they're basically so good. Anyhow, through the leafless trees of my memory.

And then a moment later, as the subway kind of went past, I remember thinking also of taking pictures went past Towanda where that kid burned himself, oh, my God! And then, there was that write-up in the paper, was it yesterday? or Tuesday? About the guy in, was it Boston Com? in Boston Common, doused himself with some kind of flammable liquid, set himself afire to protest the war. Does it help? And even if it did help, does the end justify the means? The means that he took, burning himself alive?

But also a moment after passing Towanda, and then seeing 59, through the haze of the leafless trees, the branches, the trunks, grey and sere and dry and sere and sere and what else does sere mean? And then while going down, as the subway dipped down, suddenly it turned at the angle so that the sunlight came through the window opposite. I was facing sideways in the a seat that was to be reserved for handicapped, disabled, and se Senior Citizens. And suddenly, I was facing that way, and the sun came, full in my face, and it was full in my face for a moment, and my eyes my my pupils constricted. And I blinked my eyes, and then suddenly we dipped down below the level of the wall of the tunnel, of the coming tunnel into Mondawmin. We dipped below the level of the wall and suddenly, the sun was blocked from my face, the sun was blocked from my eyes, and we went down into the darkness of the tunnel into Mondawmin. And then when I came out, came up the escalator, that looonng, long escalator ride up from the passenger floor. After the elevator ride up from the subway floor, and I came out and looked into that city skyline. It was in a haze, it was a hazy grey silhouette, hazy grey silhouette. A hazy grey silhouette down below and I'm comin' below the hills after going down into. That's the sound of an 18-wheeler going past me down Gwynns Falls Parkway ready to go down on Warwick Avenue, and I think I'm gonna cut this off. After going down that sloping wall that sloping tunnel that sloping wall of what was to become the tunnel very briefly, very instantaneously almost, into Mondawmin, into Mondawmin Metro stop. Coming out up the long up the elevator ride the sloooow sloow elevator ride, and the slow and very long and very steep escalator ride, coming out to see the skyline of the city in the grey hazy silhouette that it became, had become.

I remember now, speaking of all this, thinking of what I could write from all this, lying on my bed, on Springhill Avenue, *[walking and panting]* my head down. There's that grey three-toned grey sweater, light grey to medium grey to almost to a black, lying in the street here on Warwick Avenue. But suddenly remembering as I think about what I could write from these tapes, remembering. I must have been 16, 17, it must have been after my father died, yes, it must have been after my father died, it was after my father died, 17, maybe 18, lying in my bed on Springhill Avenue, looking out at the W-B-A-L tv antenna that just, tall huge towered antenna. Thinking about it. And in my mind then I was writing about it, about the white and red metal, reaching up to the sky, focusing in even narrowly as it moved up, and the red lights blinking. And thinking about writing about that. Moving, all that there was that I had thought and seen but which was not much at that age. But thinking now also how at one time talked to talked about Raizel about it and something about how I could have written something or wanted to write something. That was just a professional cleaning pick-up van passed us, it was making a squeaking noise, it was white with red and blue lettering. Thinking about saying to Raizel that what I, could've been like another *Leaves of Grass*, and she went, Oh? And it was sheer arrogance that might pretend what I might write to Whitman's *Leaves of Grass*. And while it might no have been this good, it would, you know, whether it was. Taxi, red top, white bottom, white middle, blue bottom. Might not've been as good or as great as Whitman's poem, it would've been my own *Leaves of Grass*. Maybe I wasn't quite ready to write it then, maybe I'm ready to write it now. I need to write it now. I need to write it now.

How could I have left Eva off our youthful dead our young dead our dead young? That I wrote about the for Ronny and Nancy. I wrote about Rosie and Daddy and Aunt Freda. And then Nancy. But I left out Eva. How could I have done that? I have to go by there, check out her stone, and make sure the guy fixed it.

Just passed walking in the street heading in the opposite direction up Warwick Avenue. And had Muslim woman, impossible even barely to see her eyes, in white pants and shoes, a white chadoor and a grey whatever it's called under the chadoor. Absolutely stunning, like an apparition. Like an apparition walking the streets.

Two little kids walking past. She in a pink jacket, he in a blue, with the blue, mid calf. Both looking at me carrying this thing and talking into it. And noticing how many people have looked. How strange it looks. Noticing now, after a couple blocks even, a pale blue-green *[panting]* paint dripping on the sidewalk, long trail. I wonder where it started, what it's it's, it's way back there up, and here's here's where it starts. Right here by the entrance to the parking lot of the Baer School. And it goes all the way farther up. Whoa! Look out for this! And there is a contrail, there are two of the contrails criss-crossing in the sky, old ones. But there's a new one just getting made. Heading south.

SUNDAY, FEBRUARY 24, 1991

Sunday, February 24th, 1991, 12:17 AM P.m.. Reading, *Chronicles*. And sitting the *First Book of the Chronicles*, sitting in the Sunday School office. And here is Chapter 1. No, it's Chapter 2, Verse 7. The sons of Chambi *[?]* Achar, the trumpet*[?]* of Israel who transgressed in the matter of the devoted thing. With no explanation.

MONDAY, FEBRUARY 25, 1991

Good morning, Gentlemen. Morning, Gentlemen. It's 8:04 AM. Monday, February the 25th, 19-hundred-and-91. On my way down Reistrestow Reistrestown Road. Couple things couple things. Listen. Have I told you lately that there's a war on? In the Persian Gulf. I don't know if I've even mentioned that at all, but anyhow, on January the 16th at night, US forces and our coalition forces began bombing and missiling Iraq and Iraqi positions in Kuwait. And on Saturday evening, w launched the ground war to liberate Kuwait. Some devastating things going on over there, but anyhow whennn last night we saw on the news, so I guess it was on CNN. Incidentally, an idea f my idea for my idea for my terrorism novel would be to title it CNN: The Gulf War: DAY 300-'n' or maybe 4-hundred-'n'-twenty-five in the summer of '92 when the terrorism attack would take place, after the war itself was over. Then, of course, I realized that it's not CNN! that uses the GULF WAR: DAY Number, it was ABC. ABC: THE GULF WAR. CNN uses THE WAR IN THE GULF, which is a little bit different from THE GULF WAR. What the hell is this guy doin'?! Anyhow, last night on the news, what what we saw was a report on the the prayers in Baghdad, and and they showed the Ir Iraqi Christians, saying that they and and the the bishop in his robes very ornate robes that they pray in. Look at the way that woman is driving! in that truck! Holy Cow! That they pray in the lang in the ancient Aramaic, the language probably spoken by Jesus. But anyhow they showed on the outside, a couple of Muslim women, one a Muslim woman with her daughter. Right through the reyed light! One of the Muslim women with her daughter using the holy water out what was supposed said to be holy water outside in a little basin in front of a a statue of the Virgin Mary and washing her face and and performing as as the announcer said the Muslim cleansing ritual, and then doing the Muslim cleansing ritual for her daughter's face and and praying that the Virgin Mary would would help to make the wor the war short. Now thisss was a Muslim woman. Then another Muslim woman shown and and te encouraging her daughter to kiss Mary or give Mary a kiss. Then another Muslim woman with tears coming down her chee **TAPE ENDS**

THE NANCY TAPES

TAPE NUMBER 12B

MONDAY, FEBRUARY 25, 1991 (CONT.)
Okay, that was just a quick tape change. It's 8:07 AM.

And then they showed another Muslim woman with tears running down her cheeks, also standing in front the of the the water basin and the the statue of the Virgin Mary and and holding asking for for special care I think for her son and for the others so that that not too many people would be killed and that the war should end soon and and holding her hands out open and palms up looking like looking like a almost the way that priests in the Orthodox Church hold their hands out while they're they're praying, hands out and open, palms up. And the two images of the two women were among the the most devastating in one sense, although they weren't dying, they weren't hurt, they weren't in pain. Their anguish over the war and that they would, Muslim women would pray to the to the Christian Virgin, almost almost as though they were looking for help from from quote unquote the god of their enemies, to make things easier on them. It was a very very moving moving thing and and, you know, Sophie started crying and I talked about it. And then we a we talked about how devastating it was, but then also talked about how devastating it must have been all this time for the Kuwaiti women. For all that that the the Iraqi soldiers had done, raping and and killing and torturing in Kuwait. And and Ruthie when we were out there Saturday night, talking about again about how how he was like a Hitler and how could anyone say he was not like a Hitler, given the way he was behaving, the way his troops were behaving.

And incidentally, we were out, Soph and I went out Saturday so Ruth and I could talk about our work on the book and also just to have dinner and and I took out the the rainbow picture with the inscription for Nancy that originally I was gonna put in the in the hospital, but when I showed it to Ruth on the train trip up to to Montreal, Ruthie obviously liked it so much that it was obvious that she wanted to have it, so I told her that she could have it. And and she said, I know you maded it for the hospital, and I said, Well, no, it, that's what it was originally intended for, but if you want it, I said, I think you're the one who has to have it. And and Joe l and Dave when he soon as he looked at it, he said it was he remembered 'cause he was he and Ruth had decided which picture they wanted of the rainbows. And he even asked if I used his picture. I said, Yes, that was the one that he had picked out, and and he said that it was that it was so beautiful that that he wanted to cry, just just looking at it, it made you wanta cry, and that's precisely the feeling.

And when Joe looked at it, Joe asked about the quotation from the poem, and I said that I had been listening, I said, that whole week that Nancy was in the hospital, I had I had made a tape of of albums of the poems of Robert Frost and of Dylan Thomas, and that the, originally most of the time I was listening to the one by Dylan Thomas, *A Poem in October*. And I found myself suddenly sitting there in in in Ruthie's family room hearing the poem on the tape and and feeling myself back in the situation of driving back and forth to Hopkins with that poem playing, "The Poem in October," and hearing "Oh, may my heart's truth still be sung from this high hill in a year's turning." In a year's turning. And thinking about the line the "that the weather turned 'round." "The weather turned 'round" and her condition turned round. And thinking about and it was like I was back in the car, and like I just I had to stop talking for a moment because I was afraid that if I kept talking, I was gonna break down and start crying. *[very subdued]* And so I had to stop. And so I had to stop. And so I had to stop.

One of the very very popular songs is *"God Is Watching Us," From a Distance*. "God is watching us from a distance." And how Bette Midler had a big hit on it. And how from a distance, there's harmony, from a distance, I don't know why we're not friends, from a distance, there is no poverty, there is no disease. There is no war. From a distance I don't know what all this fighting is for. Part of the problem iizz, number one, that we don't live at a distance, we live in proxsimity. That makes it very very difficult sometimes to see things from a distance. Aaannd from a distanccce, does that mean that all those things are so petty and small, that we need not worry about them? That we ought to overcome them. Very very glibly and easily? No, what has to happen is that if I'm close up from the proxsimity, we have to work through those differences. We are not Gooood. We are human, so we need to work through them.

"oriental music and you in my arms, perfumed flowers in your tresses, lotus scented breezes and swaying palms" 7:18 Monday, February 25th, 7:18 P.m.. "Rose I love you, with your almond eyes, fragrant and slender, 'neath tropical skies, I must cross the seas again" Fffrankie Laine! Come back to the good old days! Time to go! "back to my home on a dis"

DAY UNSPECIFIED, FEBRUARY OR MARCH DATE UNSPECIFIED, 1991 [DAY/DATE IS SOMETIME BETWEEN TUESDAY FEB. 26 AND FRIDAY MARCH 1, SINCE PREVIOUS ENTRY WAS MONDAY, FEBRUARY 25, AND NEXT ENTRY IS SATURDAY, MARCH 2]

Good morning, Gentlemen. Whoaew! You're now listening, in the background you're now listening to the piano solo on towards the end of Benny Goodman's *Sing Sing Sing* in the *1938 Carnegie Hall Jazz Concert*. It's now 8:30 AM, heading south on I-83, the Jones Falls Expressway. And I've been listening to this. Listen to this. *[drums]* Listen to this, man, listen to this! *[Krupa-drums-finale]* Listening to this on the way down to work. And thinking about the crisp clarity, the incredible beauty of the piano solo in this in this *Sing Sing Sing*, and thinking about how beautiful it is, and talking to my students about the the the detail, the im the critical critical importance of detail in writing. And thinking about how beautiful this was and how it it brings just about brought a tear to my eye it's so beautiful.

And it made me think of couple things. Number one, F. Millard Foard back in 1954-ish or so, when P or D D played *Stormy Weather* on the trumpet, and and Foard talking to the class about how he ordinarily does not like jazz or or popular music of that type, but that this was so beautiful, that the the playing was incredibly, that the, I remember him speaking of the crisp clarity of each note sliding from one to another, but each one distinct at the same time. That there was no sloppiness or slurring in the playing or in the music, and it was just incredibly beautiful. And it made me think also of of of last Saturday, the 23rd of February, when Sophie and I went to have dinner with Ruth and Dave and Joe, and Craig was there and we and and I brought in the the rainbow, framed rainbow picture with the quotation from R Frost's *Birches*, "Earth's the right place for love/I don't know where it's likely to go better." And Dave looked at it standing in the foyer, and he said, It's so beautiful it makes you want to cry. It's so beautiful, *[breaks into crying]* it makes you wanta cryyyy. You haven't liiivved either until you've hearrrd Lionel Hampton's vibe solo on *Stompin' at the Savoy.*

Okay now, Gentlemen, good morning. That's today's this morning's message for you, Mr. Phelps, Captain Kirk, and Captain Picard. Add that to the complex complexities.

We got *Big John's Special* in the background right now. I just played back what I heard what I said and "complex complexities." And thinking about last night, I think it was on channel 20, I put on channel 20, switching around at oh roughly 9:30-ish. There was a program on astronomy, and it came on with a quotation from Goethe, who said something like, The task of of man as a thinking being is to learrrnn that which is knowable and to quietly revere that which is unknowable. To quietly revere that which is unknowable. Quotation from Goethe. But it didn't say where from in Goethe.

Big John's Special at 8:35 in the AM. Comin' around Druid Hill Park, just passed the reservoir, the real reservoir, not the old reservoir. That was cut down. Badada duh dum duh. All right, you s

SATURDAY, MARCH 2, 1991

With Lionel Hampton's vibes in the background on *Sing Sing S* not *Sing Sing Sing, Stompin' at the Savoy.* Catch that, Gentlemen? It's now 4:17 P.m. on Saturday, March the 2nd, I'm returning from Towson State University conference on thinking for writing for thinking for writing for thinking for writing. When what to my wondering eyes should appear while I was walking up with, what's her name?

THE NANCY TAPES

EA from lunch to the afternoon sessions. When suddenly someone stopped me and said, Do you remember me? And it was G. Fifteen years ago at Coppin State College, sixteen years ago. The last time I saw her was at Charles Pryor's funeral. In August of 1975. Fifteen and a half years ago. And we chatted for a few moments, and then walked in and she went to her session, and I went to my session. And afterwards, there was gonna be this, like, plenary session, as they call it. And I stood there waiting for her to walk in, and she walked in, and I told her about how I'd carrying around this picture of her standing alone at Charles's funeral. And I said, I'm sorry, I said, I hope I don't. And she said, No, that's all right. And I said, Well, and finally I said to her, Look, do you wanta stay for this? Or would you like to chat? I said, We can either stay for this or we can chat. She said, Well, what would you like to do? I said, I would like to talk.

So we went out and we walked the campus a little bit, then we sat on a bench, and we talked. And what I I told her at one point that it was like, we talked about Charles's funeral, his death and his funeral, and Sam's death and his funeral. *[Hampton]* And their homosexuality and about FD, what she said to me about how she never thought she'd be able to say that Charles was entitled to have his own life without someone killing him and and she said that she thought it was very difficult for her to say that. And I said, it was funny, because at lunch, we were talking about how that teacher had seen the our Eagles, our basketball, Coppin's basketball team on Spanish tv last summer, summer of 1990, in Spanish and they were talking at the table, and I said, it was one of those totally disorienting *[Hampton]* experiences, where you just don't know what's going on. And so I said to G that it was just like that, seeing her was just like that, and I said, I'm sorry, I'm just, I'm really still disoriented. Suddenly, after 15 years, there you are, and we talked about about the death of Charles Pryor. And about the death of Sam Jones. And my going to the funerals, and then going to the tri-als the tri-als the tri-als of both, and my comment about Sam Spade, that you don't let them kill your partner, and how H said, No, it's that, but it's also Antigone, you don't let them bury your, they don't let, you don't let them leave your brother's body unburied. *[Hampton and Krupa]* Well, we talked about that. And we talked about our kids, her kids and our kids, and stuff like that. And there were hugs at the end. And then hugs again at the end. We hugged outside Hawkins Hall, then we hugged again inside. Take care of yourself. Drive safely, G. And I have to send her, she wants a copy of the poem for L C. We talked about L C, E T, M C. And have to send her a copy of the poem on L C and a copy of the new Kennedy poem *LIFE of a STAR*, the new version. With Part IV that was not in the one that she has. It was a really disorienting, disorienting experience. *[Hampton]*

MONDAY, MARCH 4, 1991

"a little love" 7:46 AM, "love that" Monday, March the 4th, 1991. And here's this song, *"That's All I Want."* "that's all I want" From you. "from you" What year was this song? It sounds familiar, I know I know it, I just can't remember what year! W-I-T-H. Actually, I don't know sure if it's called W-I-T-H anymore, it's 1-2-3-0 on your dial.

"Tomorrow might not come when dreamers dream too late." "a little love that slowly gr"

It is still called W-I-T-H, they just gave the call letters, and here's more music from my wonderful past! trumpet-da-da-da-da-daaaah

Good morning again, Gentlemen. Twicet in one day. It's now 7:56 AM, Monday, March the 4th, 1991. I'm heading across Hooks Lane towards Park Heights, I'm tak taking a different rowt or root this morning. Or going in a on a different road or whatever. And look at that poor kid with all his stuff! Oh, it's lacrosse stuff, running to the school bus.

Anyhow. Some stuff I wanted to add put on the tape today. Got home from taking Charlie to College Park and visiting with Thea yesterday and got home about, what was it? about 8:30-ish. And there was a message on the recorder from Nancy, RK had died, B's sister, and I called her, and we talked about it, and I I said, There were three sisters, and I said, There was R, I said, there was F. I guess F had died years ago, I didn't realize that. And a third one who I thought was in some kind of hospital or something for the incurably ill, and Nancy said, No, she thought maybe that was the mother. That door is open! Son of a gun! One second. Time out, Gentlemen.

Turning right from Hooks Lane onto Park Heights Avenue. Anyhow, she said she thought that the other sister was at had died in childbirth or shortly after childbirth. And I said, No, I didn't think so. So we talked about who was gonna call Ronny and so I called Ronny. I said I would call Ron, and she would call Ruth. Aaannnd I spoke with with D.

I spoke with D and then with Ron, and he seemed pretty kind of devastated, asked me to get B's address for him so he could write him a letter. What else, man? What else, man? And he said that that he thought it was B's mother who was in the home for the incurably sick. But I don't remember that. And anyway, I talked with Nancy last night, I said it was his, y'know, it was his his father had, I remember, B's father, SK, he had diabetes. I remember they had to amputate his leg. And he, when did he die? He died years ago. I don't know about the mother. I I thought it was, I thought it was. And anyhow they they there were three si sis two sisters in addition to R in the newspaper, the *late* FS which obviously was FK, I didn't know that she had died, and and DK. I think she was in in that home. Anyhow, when I talked with Mother, she said she thought that the sister was in was in a mental institution, a mental hospital, but I don't remember that. But anyhow I'm going to the funeral today at 12. Nancy said she was gonna try, but she wasn't sure.

Aaand what I also wanted to add this, we were at Thea's yesterday af evening, and *60 Minutes* was having interviews with the Bob Simon and the the other CBS newspeople who were taken prisoner by the had been taken prisoner by the Iraqis, and they were freed yesterday. And in the course of their discussion, their interview, the last this was the last part that they showed, and they ended with this. Bob Simon was talking about how, while he was while he was in there, while he was he was being held, and he thought he might be dying might be going to die the the bombs the the building they were in was hit by allied bombing. And he said that what came to his were not the big news events, the major stories he had covered in the world contemporary world. What came to his mind were the thing he one thing he thought about was the first time he carried his his daughter his little daughter into the Mediterranean into the water of the Mediterranean Sea, and the time he had gotten a bike and took a ride in the French countryside to go flirt with this young with this beautiful French girl who eventually became his wife. That these were the things that he thought about, not the major stories he had covered, the major events in the world, but instead what what gave him the sense of the joy of life were these these small things. And he felt that that if he were to die, that it would be okay because he had experienced this joy of life. And his life did have beauty and joy in it, but but, of course, he wanted to live, he wanted to have more, he didn't want to give it up. And that's that's kind of where it ended with him saying that with his saying that. With him saying that. That it was it was the joy of life, of of carrying his daughter into the Mediterranean for the first time, and of getting on this bike to ride in the French countryside to flirt with this beautiful French girl who became his wife. And not the major news stories and the major events that he had covered. And it it's interesting, though, that this experience of the the joy of life and the small home family things, his daughter in the seeaa, his his wife before he married her. That this this came to him in a situation in which he was in danger and while he was on a quest, a major quest for a major news story and put himself in extreme danger by by *not* following the the press rules of the US military. In other words, he went he exceeded the bonds or bounds set by the by the military. And he went out on his own, this whole crew of four went out on their own. And thus put themselves into into dangerous situations, got caught, got captured. And it was as a result of that k that kind of daring, that kind of quest, that he was in a situation where he was, in fact, seriously endangered, his life *was* threatened especially *his* life, because the guy realized that he was a Jew. It was interesting that he said that when the guide spat in his face, called him, *Yehudi Yehudi* and and beat him and slapped his face and spat in his face. He said it was like this sixth sense that anti-Semites have because, of course, there was nothing specific to identify him as a

Jew, he'd have no identity cards that he carried or anything that said he was Jewish. But but the guy knew or could tell that he was Jewish.

And anyhow it made me think of of *The Ulysses Factor* that book that I saw in Steubenville at the bookstore and and read about someplace else. And that thing that I had thought about, the *[louder]* the the the what?! *[back to normal]* Oh, the image of dust of the image of God and the dust of the earth. And and also back to Gilgamesh, what the is it the harlot? No, it's Siduri. What Siduri tells tells Gilgamesh. That that. Enjoy your the the pleasure of your wife and your child 'cause this too is what life is, and and this conflict betweennn the simple pleasures, the simple joys of life, and the quest for for some kind of achievement. Bob Simon, the journalist for 25 years, when they accused him of being a spy, he got very very upset and angry, and he spitted out, I'm not a spy, I'm a journalist! And they said, Well, maybe that's a cover. And he said he got angry, and said I've been a journalist for 25 years.

[voice subdued] That quest, that search. Now, Nancy did that, but she did it in terms she did it in terms of the family life. Isn't that interesting?! That is, her struggle to live, her quest for life, her willingness to face the challenges of of heart surgery. Her willing willingness to s to face the challenges of heart surgery for the sake of living, and living with her family, not for the sake of any kind of of of professional or or major achievement on her job or her profession or or any achievement, recognition of honor, quest for glory *et cetera*. Whether it would be personal glory or or public glory, but whatever it might be. Not for that. But for the sake of life and her family. Her family in life. How bout that?! Something you didn't think about. That conflict between the simple joys of life and the quest for achievement. And in Nancy's case, it w the two came together, the quest for achievement, the willingness to face the risks and the challenges. Isn't that something!? The willingness to face the risks and the challenges of heart surgery was for the sake of her family. The sake of love of of and for and by and with her family. Bob Simon was facing the risks and the challenges for the sake of achieving his story, of getting his story as a journalist. Like an epic hero. But what he thought of afterwards, in the moment of danger, the times of danger, was not his achievement. And not the potential for achievement. But rather the family. And and you could tell, I could tell from his voice that he was practically crying. And Nancy faced that for the sake of the family.

Back again. Very shortly thereafter. 8:07. Late yesterday afternoon, I took, well, I when I stopped working on the report, I took time to gather together some material on Sam and on Charles Pryor to send to G. And oh I just it was like I could cry again. And very emotional. I almost cried when I spoke with her on Saturday, talking about it. I told her I was having flashbacks, I was flashing back. To Charles and to Sam. And I pulled out the yellow piece of paper on which I had my notesss for my, what I said about Charles at the at the ceremony we had for him on campus. And thisss be the first time in what? it'd be almost 16 years, 15-and-a-half years, that I've really looked at it, and I'm gonna type it up so I can send it off to G.

It was something I should've typed up a long time ago. I remember what what M said after I, after that program was over. She came up me as I was walking down the hall, and she said something about, One day we're gonna see that you're gonna be a rabbi. Oooh, looks like another accident.

She said, You're gonna be a rabbi. You should be a rabbi. Becau I guess because of the nature and quality of what I said. And and Sam I could see Sam Jones sitting in the back. And he said afterwards that it it really had, what I said had a tremendous impact on him because I was the first person, I was the only person actually who who talked at all about how Charles had died, that he had been brutally murdered. Not that he had simply died. And interesting, here I am saying those words coming to the red light here and stopping at the red light Sumter Avenue and Park Heights 31-hundred block Sumter Avenue 46-hundred block Park Heights. Right out in front of Saint Ambrose Catholic Church here on Park Heights Avenue. Saint Ambrose.

Crossing Wylie Avenue and here's Park Lane. Park Lane Shopping Center. *[voice quiet for this part]* I remember that years ago when I was a kid, I used to walk up and go to that hobby shop on Cold Spring Lane around the side. The side part of Park Lane and and what used to be READ's drugstore there on the corner but which is now REVCO. Park Lane was such a wonderful place then. That must've been in the early '50s, probably '51, maybe even earlier. Maybe even fift Was I in I don't remember whether I was in 59 or 49 at the time. But around 1950, so we're talking 41 years ago.

Coming up now the fish market which used to be CARMEL's. I remember seeing the article about S, the kid from from Carlin's Park. And there's what looks like a burned-out marquee and of of Avalon and the boarded-up burned-out beaten-up shops. And near where the there's the *Agudas Achim shule*. And there right by the corner by it was where that little haberdashery was, that guy where I went in and bought that cardigan sweater, cardigan jacket, for 15 bucks, and he was gonna let me pay it off a buck a week, and my mother made me give it back, take it back. Had to take it back. Took it back.

That article in *The Washington Post* yesterday at Thea's about terrorism and how the terrorism net terrorist network was broken up. And I went by the 7-11. Passing Keyworth Avenue, there's there's Louisa May Alcott School, and here we are coming up on on Springhill Avenue. Something musta happend, there's a police car at the corner. Was it another accident in the rain? Miserable. At Springhill Avenue and on that corner, the far corner, the south corner, southeast corner I guess southwest corner I guess it would be. Yeah southwest corner of Park Heights and

Springhill. That's where the Fs lived and here on the on the the northeast side northwest side of Park Heights Avenue where, was it MW or BW lived? Oh, ye cops got somebody up on that porch for something. Okay. I'm coming now down towards Violet Avenue. Where Kessler's used to be, but in 1977, it was reconverted back into a house, and how many times have I mentioned Paul's buddy, the grandson of Barney Kessler. Is that coincidence? Or is that coincidence? Or *are there* coincidences in life? Who did I say that to one day? To somebody, that there's no such thing as coincidence. Somebody at school, Coppin, was saying that. And then there's the which *shule* was this one? The *Shaarei Zion*? Down here at Hilldale right opposite the corner where Roland's Barber Shop used to be, Roland. Oh, good old Roland's! And I used to go in there sometimes in the summer to get my long hair cut short. And I remember the women in there with their their their kids getting haircuts, and they would just say, Oh, look at his curls! and How could he cut them off? And stuff like that, and that they wished they had curls like mine.

Good morning yet again, Gentlemen. Same day, March the 4th, 1991, Monday. It's 11:25. It's 11:26. I've just left Coppin, I'm on my way up to Levinson. *[subdued]* For RK's funeral. It's been so many years since I've seen her. But I can picture her in my m **TAPE ENDS**

THE NANCY TAPES

TAPE NUMBER 13A

NOTE: THIS TAPE ORIGINALLY BEGAN ON 03/04/91; HOWEVER, I ACCIDENTALLY BEGAN TAPING OVER SIDE A ON 03/07/91, AFTER I HAD FINISHED TAPING ON SIDE B. THUS, THE TAPE BEGINS ON 03/07/91, THEN SHIFTS BACK TO 03/04/91, THE DATE ON WHICH TAPING ON SIDE A ORIGINALLY BEGAN.

*THE FOLLOWING NOTE WAS HANDWRITTEN ON P. 1 OF 910304A.001:
NOTE: BECAUSE OF OVER-RECORDING, PAGES 1 - TOP OF P. 4 BELONGS AT **END** OF 910304B.001.*

*THUS, ALSO 3 PAGES OF WHAT WAS ORIGINALLY RECORDED ON 3/4/91 ARE IRREVOCABLY & IRRETRIEVABLY **LOST**!*

*12/4/96
9:35 AM*

THE FOLLOWING NOTE IS FROM MON 7/14/97 4:00 P.m.

ACCORDINGLY, I SHIFTED THOSE PAGES FROM HERE TO THE END OF TAPE013B.ED1; WHAT BEGINS HERE BEGINS ON P. 4 OF 910304A.001.

THE FOLLOWING NOTE IS FROM P. 4 OF 910304A.001:

[NOTE: AT THIS POINT THE MARCH 4 RECORDING CONTINUES, WHICH I HAD RECORDED OVER AND IS GIVEN ON THE FIRST 3 PAGES OF THIS TRANSCRIPTION.]

MONDAY, MARCH 4, 1991
    [very quiet] That's when I said to him that he was dead already. By the time we got there, my father was dead. And I didn't stay. I didn't stay. I let myself be talked out of it. I didn't stay. Talked out of it by Aunt Esther. Talked out of it by Aunt Esther. *Sic transit gloria mundi.* That's the way I've always been, let myself get talked out of everything. No matter what I want to do, I let myself get, not everything, that's not quite true. I stuck with being an English teacher. But now, of course, I'm an administrator. When what I *really* want to do is teach and write. So many things to write, so many things to do. There's an empty open area where

THE NANCY TAPES

there was something before, and now it's just a field of dirt. In the midst of these rowhouses here on Park Heights Avenue, there are some with yellow ribbons on them.

Now at Park Heights and Garrison, up to the left. What used to what used to be the Uptown Movie Theatre. How many years ago did that close? Decades. Probably decades. Now it's the, what's it? the Kingdom Hall of Jehovah's Witnesses. Which it has been for quite some time. Just passed Spaulding Avenue to the left, where Ronny and Eva used to live. And what I guess Goldenberg's is what used to be the Pimlico Theatre. Crossing Belvedere. And moving on up now, Park Heights Avenue.

[still quiet] Think I'll turn down Rogers Avenue to Reisterstown. To go up to Levinson.

The Rogers Avenue *Shule*. Then back there to the left would have been where A B, A and C lived. I can't remember the number. But just passed that. That's where I first saw my mother eatin' crabs. I remember how disturbed I was about her eating crabs. The fact that she had told us all about being kosher, and I was trying to be kosher, and she was eatin' crabs. What a letdown that was.

[quiet] 12:21. The funeral service in the funeral home is over. We're getting ready to head out to the cemetery. R C R Bas Reb S S told me that it was ovarian cancer, got diagnosed in August, and it was a terrible death. Very painful. Just very very, lot of agony. She also told me that that we the Kromes probably never realized it but that we by making life kind of normal for B and taking him into our house had gotten him over a very very difficult period in his life, that he might not've gotten through without our being there. Without our being with him, the way we were. And I said, No, I never knew that. Now. And B said so he couldn't believe that I was there, and when my mother came in, he hugged her. Course called her Mrs. Krome. C R Bas Reb S. The, born on, what was it? the 7th day of Adar, the same day as Moses, as the rabbi said. The same day as Moses. C R Bas Reb S. Struck by how much. There was something about B's appearance, B's appearance, that startled me. And what I reallylized it is realized it was during the service was how much he look, he looks like his father. And looks like R. And the rabbi talked about how blessed was your coming into the earth. Because you lived your life to its fullest. And enriched it for y family and friends as well as for yourself. And he referred to the cemetery as as being known as a *Bet Chaim*, a house of life. Because some of those who die even in their deaths remain an inspiration to the living, their spirits continue to live. And through their memories they help the others, the the living, to go on living. Through the memory and their inspiration, they provide a living, a spirit inspiration for the living. There's the hearse and the limousine and then a car and then a car and then me and then another car. And the rabbi said that one way to to show your memory is to to be there for

one of the services. There's not gonna be any *shacharis* service tomorrow, but there's a evening service tonight at seven. Another one tomorrow night at seven. Stevenswood Road, just past Old Court off Liberty Road, go left on Fortliegh? or Fordleigh? or F, something like that. I'll have to try to get there tomorrow night, I don't know if I can get there tonight. Maybe I'll go tomorrow night. Over and out now.

Curious that you should pass the 22,000 mile mark on the car now.

Waiting for the light here at we're on Northern Parkway, facing Park Heights, and a funeral just passed through Park Heights heading north on Park Heights while we wait to go through the light heading what? east? And there's another hearse to the left. People are just dying to get in, or to get out.

The rabbi also. When the person dies, he turns in his anguish, in his fear and his pain and weeping, says to his family, Help me! And his family als friends also weeping. And say that there's nothing that they can do to help him avert the evil decree. The ev not the evil de help him avert the awesome decree. So he turns to his possessions. But his possessions say the same thing, that there's nothing that they can do to help avert the awesome decree. Not all the philosophy, not all the technology, not all the science and the knowledge and the learning of human beings can avert the decree when the hour comes for the person to die. But then suddenly, what step forward are all the good deeds, the good thing the person good things the person has done in life, the compassion he or she has shown, the love, the kindness, the things that he or she has done for others. And they say, Take heart and follow us. *[almost breaking]* For we will go before you. And we will plead for you before the judge. But not even theeeyy can do anything to avert the awesome judgement. The awesome decree. They cannot keep the person alive physically. But they help to keep the person's memory and spirit alive. And the life alive through the lives of others who have been touched by the life of that person.

B has lost weight. He's lost his hair also, good bit of his hair. But he's lost weight, he's thinner. And he seems to be shorter than he was then. Just maybe it was just in my memory, in my imagination, that he was physically so much bigger than I. Maybe he wasn't quite as much bigger as I thought he was.

S said we go back so many years, and she talked about how they got married in '59. Thirty-two years ago. I remember when B and I were in school, at College Park. He used to drive into Baltimore, he to see S and me to see M. We'd drive in in his '48 Merc. I asked his son, R, if B had ever told him about the '48 Merc, and he said he doesn't usually tell them about those wild days. But I remember, it must have been '62, after I got out of the Army, and I was in Washington, B was in law school, in Georgetown. Or G W G W. And I was his witness, or the person he was defending in a moot trial. And he tried to con about having something in a book, when he really didn't, 'cause he had his finger in the book, and it really was not, and it didn't work *[laughter]* 'cause the judge caught him on it! Sniff.

I never kept up with him. I remember at one point, I remember at one point, that S had borrowed, I had loaned S my copies of *The Wall*, the Hersey novel, and *The Last of the Just* by Schwartzbart. And somehow I think, and I remember that when I went out to see them with I guess it must have been Ronny and D, this must have been in the '60s, later on, it must have been after Chuck was born, but I don't remember their kids. And she gave me back the books. And I remember thinking at the time, I remember I borrowed some money from B, like 50 bucks, and I thought I had paid him back. I wonder if I ever did, maybe I never did pay him back. Maybe I never did. And maybe, that's what she was trying to tell me then. And I remember it must have been when his sister D died, the one who was in the home. But I never went to see him, and I never sent a card. Because it was all too painful for me. I couldn't cope with death. I still have difficulty, but at least I'm here today. And going out to the cemetery. And I think he was stunned that I would be here. Maybe because he remembers that that time I was not. I don't know when F died. I don't remember that. Maybe I didn't even know. But since she was married, and her name was F S, unless someone told, had told me, I would not have known. Even had I read the obituaries, because I would have seen the name S and not have recognized her name, her married name. It was funny how I I didn't recognize N and H R right away. B said something I said something to him about how Nancy had read the obituaries over the weekend that she reads over the weekend, and he said, Well, it was our very good friend, N, and she reads them religiously. And I didn't realize that was N R. It wasn't until afterwards, when I was sitting in the the chapel where the service was being held that I suddenly realized, looking up ahead and seeing N and H, realizing suddenly that it was N and H! That the N was not just a N, a friend, but this was N R. Hadn't seen them either in years, I remember the last time I think I saw them was the early '70s, when Ronny and D came down and we went to Bud's Beer Garden. Barry got us reservations at Bud's Beer Garden. Barry. Barry Barry Barry *Belle* got us reservations at Bud's Beer Garden so we could go have crabs. And the Rs, H and N, were there then. I remember we talked about teen-age kids, and they were having some problems with their teen-age daughter. Wanting to or already being sexually act active. But it's been since then since I've seen them, and they looked so different. Although they asked right away whether I was still at Coppin. I said, Yes, my 21st year. And I'll probably be there till I retire, at this point.

B's address was 2604, my initial impulse was correct. 2604 Springhill Avenue.

And I remember today, when we talked about it, I said, his son asked if we knew each other. I told him, Yes, from the old neighborhood. I said, I said, They lived, I said, Your dad lived at 2602 or 04, and that's when B turned around and said 2604. And I said, We lived at 2614, and B said, Yes, it was they were kind of like rowhouses. Kind of "like" rowhouses? B they *were* rowhouses! N S, when I saw him once at one of the reunions, B has not been back to any of the reunions. N said that once he was in New York and, I think it was NS, and I went to see B in his office and called him B, and B said, Don't call me B. B D K. He used to sometimes use B. D K.

We're going out to the Rosedale Cemeteries the old way. Now going across what is now, we're now on Belvedere. Heading east through the city, the old way.

I remember w I remember one time when I tried to go this way, I got lost. I went through Cold Spring. Tried to get across to Erdman Avenue. And and kind of got lost. *[laughter]* Kind of got lost! I *did* get lost!

Remembering now, on this drive to the cemetery, remembering driving Raizel, not C R Bas Reb S, but Raizel Bas Reb Laybel Palevsky Macklovitch, married name, out to the cemetery to see the *troika*, what she now calls the *troika* affectionately, on the day of Ronny and Eva's wedding, that morning. And stopping to get flowers, so that she could put flowers on Aunt Freda's grave. Even though she knew we're not supposed to do that. But she did it anyhow, she wanted to do that, and that was 33 years ago, 32-and-a-half years ago. 1958. I was only 20, she must have been 30, 31, 32.

Aaannd thinking also about driving *[crying]* Nancyyyy, Cousin Nancy. Talk about your disorienting disorienting disorienting disorienting events in your life. Nancyyyyyyy!! Oh, Nancy! The day of her wedding to Dave Viaaaaaa, driving her out to the cemetery to see Uncle Morris. Sniff!! *[crying crying]* Driving her out to the cemetery to see Uncle Morris and then coming back. And she wanted to do it quietly, she said she didn't want an uproar made. She didn't wanta get Aunt Esther upset, she didn't people all in a all in an uproar about going out to the cemetery. So just the two of us went. When we came back, Uncle Layble said, if we'd'a told him, we coulda taken him, he would have come with so he could make a *Mi She-berach*. Well, we shoulda thought of it, but we didn't. But that's right, *[crying]* Nancy wanted to go see her fatherrrrr. Sniff! I told her, I said, Nance, I said, We don't have time to go see Uncle Sol and your father. But I'll take you to whichever one you wanta go to. Sniff! Sniff! Sniff! *[voice breaking and crying]* So I took'errrrr to see Uncle Morris, her fatherrrr. Sniff!

Here we are at Belvedere and Harford Road. And keeping on going across. Are we doing a cross? Yes, we're keeping on going across. Staying on Belvedere but going across Harford Road.

Belvedere has become Echodale and now we curve around to the left onto Corse Avenue C-o-r-s-e.

THE NANCY TAPES

Crossing Belair Road now, crossing Belair Road, still on Echodale. But crossed I have just crossed Belair crossed Belair Road, right. We're still on, what's? Echodale? Is it still called Echodale? Or has the name changed again? Now it's called Frankfurt Avenue. I'm sorry, not Echodale, but Frankfurt.

Hector's, just passed a place called Hector's and Ali Baba. Manny's Lunch Dinner and Pizza. On Frankford Avenue.

Turning left here on Radecke R-a-d-e-c-k-e Radecke Avenue.

The name has changed to Chesapeake, Radecke changed to Chesapeake. Crossed some other street, and suddenly the name is Chesapeake.

Making a right turn here just going over an overpass, over it looks like the Beltway, and making a right turn on Horst Avenue H-o-r-s-t, Horst.

Lotsa houses with ribbons, some of them with lots and lots of ribbons. A house with a American flag and a and a US Marine Corps flag. Hamilton Deli, passing 32nd Street.

Some trees out front of houses with just dozens, literally dozens of yellow ribbons on them.

Oh, my God! This is the back way into Rosedale! Oh, my God! Now I know where I am! And then here to the right is going to be the entrance to the *B'nai Reuven*! My God! There it is! There's the *B'nai Reuben*! We came in the back way! That's incredible! That's absolutely incredible!

I never knew how to get here this way. *[laughter]* I never came this way! This is *not* the way we came to my father's funeral. Or to Aunt Freda's. Or to Uncle Sol's. Or to anybody's ever!

Petach Tikvah Cemetery, the gate says, and *Forband* Cemetery, there're about three or four names, and there one of them is *Petach Tikvah*, the o the other one is *Forband*. It's down from my father's towards Rosedale Street Avenue to the left as you go down.

[quiet] S looks the same, essentially.

At one point, we're at the cemetery now. The rabbi threw a few shovelsful in, and B, B threw a couple shovelsful in. And then he said, Can they clear that off? Then he and S said some, he said, and B said, We said we were gonna bury her. Let's bury her. And R, B's son, got the got the shovels, and people started shoveling, rather, B, R, and S did, and the rabbi did, and then I guess a friend of the family did, and then R asked if and just handed me a shovel, and I said, Thank you. But, I still felt that somehow I was, I should back off and I did, I just stood there, and then this guy, friend of the family, took the shovel, and and then I went and got the shovel from the rabbi, and I threw in a few shovelsful, and I made sure to turn a couple upside down. And I wanted to tell them about it, but I just.

And when R threw his first couple shovelsful in with just the first one shovel, I could tell by the look on his face, the way he threw the shovelsful in, so that they clumped hard, and it was like *[breaking]* when I threw the shovelsful in *[crying]* on Nancy's coffin when she died. And I said something to Raizel then about how they had done it, Joe had done it so gently, and I hadn't, and she said, We know, we heard you, we heard it, throw it in. And R kept shoveling, and when they finally *[breaking]* decided it was time, *[crying]* R still kept shoveling. R still kept shoveling. *[under control]* R still kept shoveling. And S came S came over to me, and he said *[breaking]* that in the limousine B was talking about my being here, and how moved he was that I had come and that my mother had come to the *[crying]* funeral home. Bye, R! Bye, R! Bye, Springhill Avenue! Sniff! Goodbye! Yellow brick road. *[crying and crying and crying throughout]* Goodbye, R! Goodbye, Springhill Avenue! Goodbye, Charlie Krome! Goodbye, Freda Herlich Bulmash! Goodbye, Sol Koren! Goodbye, Morris Kanow! Sniff! I'm gonna stop and see if Eva's here. Not if Eva's here! I need to stop and see if they've if the guy fixed her stooone! Sniff! Sniff! If I can get in. I can't get in. Yes, I can. Sniff! Time out to stop this now. Go see Eva.

[subdued] S spoke with me. About how moved B was that I had come and that my mother had come. And R was just angry. He was angry about *[almost a whisper]* his aunt's death. And he tackled, he attacked the dirt mound and filling the grave. He just attacked it. Sniff!

He reminded me of Bryan, although Bryan did it so lovingly. And of Nancy, *his* aunt. R was not exactly angry, but intense, so intense.

B's shoes had mud on them, S's shoes had mud on them, R's shoes were thickly caked with mud at the bottom. It was a gesture that he gave me the shovel. I should have just gone ahead, but I stood back because I didn't want to impose on the family, on their time to do what they felt they had to do. Afterwards, it was okay.

I still do not understand how I could *not* have gone to Abe Kershman's funeral! Just don't understand how I could *not* have gone. How I or how I could have *not* gone to Abe Kershman's funeral. Just I it boggles my mind, now, it just absolutely boggles my mind.

And it staggers my imagination also, it does both, boggles my mind and staggers my imagination. It's just so incredible that I just can't believe it! Just just incredible how I can't believe it!

B is so much a part of my youth and my childhood and my growing up. I know, even before, even before Maryland and driving in to see to see our "babies," as we used to put it, with him coming in to see S and me coming in to see M. Even before that, in high school, and even before in high school, I remember we used to drive down in his car, go down to the Lombard Street, and go down to Jake's and eat corn beef sandwiches, and stand around eat corn beef sandwiches and pickles out of the barrel. I remember that. I remember that. I remember helping him wash his car one time, one time, maybe more than once. *[singing]* B is the boy for me-ee. Always kneeewww that he would be-ee. That was the song. B is the boy for me-ee. Always kneeewww that he would be-ee. Then one day he came my way, having only this to say, B, you're the boy for me-ee!

TUESDAY, MARCH 5, 1991

"You belong to meeeeee" "I'll be so" Can you hear that? "so alone" This song "alone and with" for Sidney Krome and A "out" from PS 49 "you" the Robert E. Lee Junior High School. "Maybe" Jo Stafford. "you'll be" *"You Belong to Me."* "lonesome too and blue" Haven't told you today's date yet, have I, Gentlemen? It'sss Tuesdaaayyy, March the 5th, "Fly the ocean" 1991, 9:40 AM. "in a silver plane, See the jungle when it's wet with" 38 years ago today "rain" Joseph Stalin died. "but remember, darling, till you're home again" You belong to me, A. "you" W-C-B-M. "belong" A Saturday afternoon "to me" out on the porch. I was not yet 14 actually, it was the year befooorre Stalin died.

The rabbi also said of R that she loved to travel. That she went to Mexico and Spain and Israel and Africa. That she loved beauty, not only things of beauty but beauty of the spirit. How many things do we *not* know about people we do not know that we think we do not know that we do not know? How many yeeeeaaarrsss has it been since I've seen B and S? Or even thought of them?

Just crossed Royce Avenue, just passed Royce Avenue. Coming down here on on Reisterstown Road PARK AND SHOP/PARK LANE/FREE PARKING. Am I ever gonna take a picture of that?! Whoo the hell knooows!?

[radio-male vocalist but not enough to tell who or what song] Another one of my Number 1 songs **TAPE ENDS**

TAPE NUMBER 13B

TUESDAY, MARCH 5, 1991 CONT.
Tape ran out already. Another one of my favorite songs, *You Don't Remember Me, But I Remember You.* "tears on my pillow"

Shades of the early '60s "Everybody's talkin' 'bout a new way of walkin'" and E B Kaayyyy. Do you wanta loo-oose "Do you wanta loo-oose your mind? Walk right in, sit ri-ight down, Daddy, let your mind roll on"

"from your lonesome past keeps us so far apart, why can't I free your doubtful mind and melt your cold" Now it's 4:20 P.m.. "cold heart?" Tuesday, March the 5th, 1991, "I never thought" on my way home. Tony Bennett, *Cold, Cold Heart.* "made your heart sad and blue" Something clicks in my mind, "and you're" that this song was big when I was fourteen? "unclear" B K! "for things I" B P "didn't do" Who lived down on Cole Street. "In anger" Good ol' B. You like me, don't you, Sid? she said, when we were necking, on the big chair in our living room. "that makes the teardrops start. Why"

B K, B P Where are both of you now? Or either one of you? *Ubi nunc? Ubi Nunc? Ubi nunc?* Youbi nunc!

"there" Is that a name of another character? *Ubi nunc?* "was a time when I believed that you belonged to me" There was a time when I believed that you belonged to me. Ha-Ha! "but now I know your heart is shackled"

"and melt your cold, cold heart"

THURSDAY, MARCH 7, 1991
"On W-I-T-H," You just missed "and *I'll Walk Alone.* Eight minutes before" at 7:51 AM. On Wednesday, March the, No!, today's Thursday, March the 7th, 19-hundred-and-91. I will come back to speak in a few moments, but I've got this big thing of hot coffee. Cheh-cheh-cheh! Pardon me. Right in front of me. Sniff! Cheh-cheh! Pardon me. Cheh! Gentlemen.

And right now it's the Beatles, *The Long and Winding Road.* Thinking of that not, of course, in the traditional romantic sense, "the long and winding road leads to this dri right to your door, you left me standing here a long long time ago" "Don't keep me waiting here, Lead me to your door, the long and winding road" The light is out. "Good morning, little past eight o'clock. This is S R." Anyhow. The light is out on this thing. What's that? Somebody else's car. I've got the lid up in this thing.

But anyhow, Tuesday, I wanted to put this in. Gentlemen, Good Morning. It's now 8:01, Mr. Mr. Phelps, Lieutenant Kirk, Captain Picard. Captain Kirk! Captain Picard. Tuesday night at the *shivah* house, B's cousin, when I went where they were sitting *shivah* for R, and S, B and S's daughter, *[subdued]* asked me what I remembered. Any stories about her aunt. And I was so touched. And so moved by that quiet and simple request. Not stories about B when he was young or about the car or any stuff like that, but stories about her aunt. And I said, I said, that I I have a memory of her speaking. I said, I can see her speaking. And S said, I can hear her. And I said, I can hear her also. I can hear her speaking. But I don't remember what she was speaking about. I said, I know that she was very soft-spoken, very soft-voiced. Her quiet voice speaking, and that she looks like B, or B looks like her now. They both look like their father. S K. C R Bas Reb S.

And at one point, S started talking about Eva's funeral. And how ashen she and B were after the funeral. And she and and N were talking about what a devastatingly difficult day it was for them to get through, or the worst day of their lives, to get through Eva's funeral. And S said she was so upset with her mother, because she didn't wanta hear what her mother had to say, when she walked in the house, and her mother said something about how, yes, she did feel sorry for Ron. She understood how he was grieving. But that eventually, he would get his life back in order, and he would get things back together, and he would go on. But, S's mother said, the one she felt sorry for was Eva's mother.

And here I think now also of Aunt Esther and anyhow, also what S said about R made me think of of Mindy and and Bryan and Craig and and Nancy who was their aunt. *[voice breaks]* And myself *[cracks into crying]* and Aunt Freda! *[loud]* Lo! Lo! Lo! These over 36 years agooo! Now. It's over 36 years ago. December of 19-aught-and-54. And thinking also of Joe and Aunt Esther, and and thinking how for for Ruthie it was so devastating, and for Aunt Esther so devastating, to lose your child, *[voice louder breaking into crying]* to lose your chi-ild! to lose your chi-ild! How devastating that was. They talked about Eva's death and Eva's funeral. And S said that when Ron went back to Detroit, they never heard from him again, and it was like he had cut himself off from them. Whoops! Hold on here, Guys, hold on, time out.

S *[voice breaks]* and R! And here we come *[crying]* to Royce Avenuuuue! And Hi, Aunt Freda! Up at 3316 MOhawk 4-2448! MOhawk 4-2448. MOhawk 4-2448. *[loud and breaking]* There are phone numbers that you never forget. REgent 7-7512. 4-1-5-7 Braille in Montreaaaalll. And she said, S said, It was like he h'd cut himself off, and *[breaking]* they never heard from him again. And that B, B was so upset and so sad by it, because our family had been, we had been like brothers, and my mother had been like a mother to him and, and although we may have not realized it, we helped him get through such a very very difficult point in his life, time in his life. And I thought to myself, *[breaking]* Oh, I understand that. How you cut yourself off what was before. You respond to death, *[breaks]* *I* respond to death. *I*, and Ronny, we both did. Responded by cutting ourselves off from what was before. Sniff! Oooh, dear! Ooh dear! Cutting ourselves off from what was before. Time o

SIDNEY KROME

Do you know how tough it is to drive a car with your right hand holding a microcassette recorder and your left hand holding a coffee mug, coffee, one of those car coffee cups? Mr. Goodwrench. Heritage Chevrolet. 11234 Reisterstown Road Owings Mills, Maryland 21117. Whoops! 301 356 2-2-hundred. That's what it says in white on this blue cup-like thing.

And they talked about, N talked about what they did for dinner before Ron and Eva left to go to Detroit, and how they went from, they went to B and S's hoouuse, and then they came to N's house, and it was like a round-robin dinner. And and and how much, how they used to have to go over used to go over they used to have listen to tapes of they'd listen to tapes of Redd Foxx, Redd Foxx and Redd Foxx and Shelley Berman, because Ron and and Eva really liked Redd Foxx, and they and Shelley Berman, they were so big on Shelley Berman and Shelley Berman *[voice hysterical and loud]* and Shelley Berman! *[crying]* Zalman! His routine about Zalman d deciding to be an actor, to go into show business. And Zalman Krome, my great-grandfather. Zalman! Zalmanesser. Oh, Lordy, Lordy, Lordy, Lordy, Lordy! Here we are, PS 59. Sniff. Cutting one's self off. Cutting one's self off. That's what I did all right.

Ruthie's book work gonna work with Ruthie on her book and thinking about. How many friends did I cut myself off from. There was, well, basically two. There was A. And there was M. Just cut myself off. Sniff. Oh, dear, have to call Jewish National Fund. And I have to call the JCC today, both of them.

The question is, where does the long and winding road lead to? Where does it start from? Where does it end? What kind of what kind of "wooo-wooo" what kind of, what kind of a countryside? What kind of a geography does it go through? Where is it going through? That's the question. What kind of places are there along the way, the long and winding road? Maybe that's what that's what that's what that's what Samuel Beckett was talking about in his novels, in *Molloy*. We just travel along this, and and in and in and in and in the play in the play, what was the play called? What was the play called?! *Waiting for Godot*. Not just waiting, but we're also traveling along a road. Along a long and winding road. Let it be, let it be. "Hey, Jude." "A long and winding road," and "let it be" "a long and winding road" and "let it be." And that Billy Joel song the Billy Joel song the Billy Joel song, what's called?! Billy Joel sooonng. Watch it, lady!!

I remember this song also. *Do Right, Like Some Other Men Do*. Git geh get outa heah "Get outa heah and get me some money too. Why don'tcha do right" Do ri-iight. "like some other men dooo" Like some other men dooo. "like some other men doooo" Why don't you do right like some other men do? get outa here and get yourself some whatevers!

Right, that was Peggy Lee as he said, Peggy Lee. Ooo-waah. "If your sweetheart" Oohh! And Johnny Ray, man! Oh, listen to this! Dig 'is Johnny Ray!

THE NANCY TAPES

"sends a letter of goodbye" Johnny Ray and *Cry*! Remember him on the Ed Solomon Show? Hah-hah! Ed Sullivan Sullivan! "it's no secret" Go ahead, get some big green apples. "you'll feel better" Add to the "if you cry" God! When was this?! Was I a senior in high school? A junior in high school? It was back in the '50s, those golden moldy-oldy '50s. "When waking" When waking from a bad dream. "from a bad dream" Listen to that line: when waking from a bad dream "don't you" don't you sometimes think it's real? "sometimes think it's real?" But also when you're in the middle of reality, don't you sometimes think it's a bad dream? "But it's only false" Don't you think that? When waking from a bad dream dream "emotions" don't you sometimes think it's real? When waking from a reality, don't you sometimes think it's a bad dream? "that you feel" What was that? That book in Paul's class? "if your" I've got that someplace on one of the tapes. "heartaches" All right, time out, man. In here for apples. "seem to"

"sunshine" Remember sunshine can be found. "can be found behind a cloudy" Behind a cloudy sky. "sky" So let your hair down "so let your hair down" and go right on "and go on and cry" on and cry. Hear that, go on and cry. Dipstick!

[metal and glass clinking sound] [footsteps] [car door opening] [scraping][goes on for a while][footsteps] [like broken record going over and over needle stuck in crack] [wind] [music] [sounds quieten down] [music] [other sounds very quiet now] [radio voices singing-unclear song-goes on for a while] [clicking] [footstep sounds get louder again, like broken record playing over and over stuck in crack] [song continues unintelligible] [footstep type sound continues- or broken record type sound] **[NOTE: These are the sounds I refer to in the beginning of SIDE A, when I taped on 03/07/91 over the originally taped 03/04/91 recording; when I talk about having left the recorder on in my pocket; I was going to record over them, but decided to leave them on the tape as part of the "melange of the chaos factor, the chaos potpourri"; recorded when I got out of the car and went into the FARM FRESH to get apples.]** These sounds continue. Beeping sound at one point. Radio voices singing. Scraping. Crinkling. Zipper-type sound. Banging of some kind. Singing voices. Zipper type sound. And again. Male voice--mine? They're good, aren't they?

Beeping sound-ah, that's the computer price scanner! Scanner beeps. Voices singing. My voice but unintelligible. Speaking to the woman who worked the cash register when I went to get apples. She says something. Then I say, Have a good day. She says, You, too. Loud sound of bag being picked up and carried. Voices singing still. Scraping of bag? Motor type sound. Footsteps walking with bags; goes on for a bit, pulsed, rhythmic. Car door opening. Bags put into car. Door slammed. Seat belt bell rings. Dong dong dong dong dong. Scraping sounds. Things quieten down. Male radio voice but unintelligible. Radio music-voices and music-gets intelligible-"will you ??? me in the middle, will you oooooo, bay-bay"

Radio dj male voice-"And I'm your first *unintelligible*. Well, of course, you do. How could I unintelligible. Carolyn?" Female voice, "Yes." Male voice, "Of course, you have them. How do you get them? Well, at 9:30 this morning, we will draw from among all these *[some scraping sounds--as of clothing rubbing together]* fax entries we've gotten so far." *[loud scrape-shuffle]*

"Keep adding to the uh ... fifty ways you might leave your lover. *[clothes or paper scraping]* Asking for originality here, not necessarily just the actual lyrics of the song, but this is certainly an interesting entry: My way to leave your lover: about one AM I told him we needed to talk. *[buzzing and humming]* I picked him up, *[metallic or plastic scraping]* went for a ride, all the time him telling me, quote 'Anything, you name it.' end quote. *[buzzing]* Well, when we got this long dark road, I pulled over and said, 'Anything? Get out!' I went home. True story of how I left my lover." Signed, Dee Trouble *[?]* Come on!"

Female voice--"Want to lose weight? *[loud scraping] [voice unintelligible under scraping sound]* "once you drop a few pounds. *[more unintelligible under scraping]* "The Diet Workshop is offering super savings. *[voice unintelligible-"If you vee-you"]* "I'm the friend, the very best program at the very best price. Choose it[?]" *[abrupt shift of voices-change of station?--probably pushing the SEEK button for ongoing station changes]*

[music voices singing] [Male voice dj] "Caroline that was" *[abrupt shift-change of station?]* Male voice--"from outside the courthouse" *[abrupt shift] [change of station] [voices singing] [another shift]* Male voice "*unintelligible--* Saint Paul" "sight"? *[another male dj voice]* "A high of 55, fair and cool tonight, low of 30. Partly cloudy and cool tomorrow with a high of 45. *[paper scraping] [buzzing]* And fair and cool over the weekend with a high of 40. 47 degrees out at the airport right now, B-W-I. In downtown we're in at 51." *[buzzing and scraping] [very loud male voice-commercial]* "Here's some news about *[very loud scraping over-words unintelligible]* one of our best values in retirement living to be found in this area today. *[low level buzzing]* Harmony Hall in Columbia. This is *[unintelligible-loud scraping]* I wish *[unclear] [louder scraping]* and before I even entered the facility, I was impressed with its *[scraping over]* well-kept grounds. *[unclear]* plenty of them as well as a gazebo and a *[unclear]* added a perfect *[loud scraping] [unclear]* to this pastoral setting. *[chime-seat belt chime?]* Inside I was especially impressed with the enthusiasm and the sincerity of the staff. *[loud abrupt scrape or door closing?]* It was genuine. *[low level buzzing and scraping]* Their relations" *[abrupt end]*

[signal clicking] [some very loud scraping and knocking] [car revving and passing] [my voice but unintelligible] I take a part in[??] I left the *[parket??]* book. *[loud scraping] [cars passing] [loud scraping-sounds like walking through leaves] [clicking] [more scraping continuous] [paper scraping] [clicking] [scraping]*

THE NANCY TAPES

[sound almost as of walking] [louder clicking] [door closing??] [voice quickly in bg] [loud scraping] [sounds as of walking] [my voice muffled and unintelligible] [sounds as of footsteps] [low level beeping sound] [loud scraping]

[female] "Good morning." *[more walking type sounds--aha! as of paper bag scraping or swinging on leg while walking] [my voice]* "Hi, Mr. Roberts." *[?] [more loud walking and bag swinging and scraping sounds] [my voice]* "How're you? You didn't recognize me under this hat, did you?" Laughter: Ha-Ha-Ha--Ha!" *[other male]* "No, I didn't. *[unclear]*" *[loud scraping] [my voice]* "Fine, thanks. How you doin'?" *[other voice unclear] [my voice]* "I'm goin' around foolin' people today." *[loud scraping] [other voice]* "unclear." *[more loud scraping and bag swinging against leg sounds] [my voice]* "I walked in the library the other day, and they thought I was comin' here to represent the Mafia." *[loud scraping] [other voice]* Laughing, but words unintelligible. *[my voice]* "Who's that gangster? Oooh-oooh-oooh-oooh, wind's gonna blow it off!" *[very loud scraping]* "Who's that gangster comin' through the door?" *[other voice]* "Thank you." *[My voice]* "Thank you, too." *[very very loud scraping and bag scraping swinging against leg with walking rhythmic sound-goes on for a long long while] [strange burping-grinding kind of sound] [louder and sharper scraping also for a long while with the other sound still going on] [thumping sound] [then sudden quietening after one last hard scrape] [now quiet humming and buzzing]*

[My voice] "What the heh-hell was that? *[loud scraping again] [walking and swinging bag scraping sounds and footstep sounds continue for a while] [sounds quieten down] [music??] [very very loud scraping sounds] [female voice?] [very loud scraping sounds] [my voice-muffled]* "Good morning." *[other voices-kind of mechanical?] [very loud scraping sounds and sounds of bag scraping against leg while walking] [some thumping sounds-footsteps] [my voice]* "Good morning." *[very very loud scraping rhythmic sounds continuing] [some kind of mechanical sound--elevator door and elevator?] [sounds quieten and scraping stops] [my voice]* Heavy breath exhale. *[quiet buzzing and humming] [mechanical sounds-elevator stopping and door opening?] [loud scraping and bag swinging and scraping while walking sounds-continue for a long while-slow down after a while] [footsteps] [swinging bag scraping sounds quieten down] [scraping sounds-sounds as of bags being slid on a table??] [then quiet] [tinkling-keys??] [door opening] [loud scraping of bags being slid on floor??] [my voice]* "What's that?" *[very very loud scraping and a knocking and more scraping] [sound of coat being taken off-cloth on cloth??]*

[scraping quietens and disappears] [creaking and knocking] [quietish buzzing and humming and creaking and knocking] [sound of zipper] [very very loud scraping of paper of bags-goes on for a while] [voice-radio?-unintelligible, barely barely audible] [more scraping, then quietish humming and buzzing and

quietish scraping] [metallic clanking] [very loud scraping-several times] [more metallic clanking-cabinet door opening? hangars clanking? but kind of quietly] [quiet humming and kind of hissing] [door of cabinet? closing] [quiet clicking and quiet hissing and humming] [soft metallic clanking] [quiet clicking and hissing continue] [a few more metallic clanks and bangs as of door] [quiet clicking--is that a clock sound?] [quiet buzzing] [loud metallic clank as of something falling with loud clattering] [very loud scraping goes on for a bit] [more scraping as of bag swinging and scraping against leg] [rhythmic scraping-as of footsteps going on for a while] [then suddenly very loud such scraping and stepping continues] [metallic squeaking and grinding] [more scraping and footstep type sounds-going on for a while]

[voices but unclear] [female] "Yeah." [another female] [unclear] "turn it off and check for uh" [more loud scraping] [female] "Hi, Dr. Krome." [very loud banging and scraping] [female unintelligible] "you gonna need some help." [more scraping then metallic clattering] [scraping footstep type sounds] [female voices unintelligible] [more scraping footstep type sounds] [music??] [very very loud footstep type scraping sounds] [thump] [very loud buzzing sound-mechanical?] [more scraping footstep type sounds] [very loud mechanical buzzing droning continues] [more loud scraping footstep type sounds] [and buzzing] [loud zipper type sound] [scraping and clattering and footstep type sounds and loud mechanical droning sound] [mechanical droning gets louder] [footstep type sounds continue] [droning sound slowly quietens down and disappears while footstep type sounds continue] [kind of cloth on cloth type rhythmic scraping type sound]

[voices-unintelligible] [my voice] "I'm a bit"[?] [footsteps] [voice but unintelligible] [footstep type sounds continue] [voice unclear and unintelligible] [male] "Morning." [my voice] "Morning, Joe, how are you?" [footsteps] [other voice-barely audible] "Good morning." [my voice] "Morning. [footsteps] "Fine, thanks." [more loud footstep type scraping sounds] [loudish buzzing humming] [some kind of clattering sound-door opening?] [more footstep type sounds] [more clattering sounds with a bang] [very very loud scraping burst] [more footstep type sounds] [loud rhythmic scraping sounds like the footsteps, but more rapid] [voices-female? radio?] [loud footstep type scraping and swinging sounds-quieten down but still rhythmic-go on for a long while-steady paced and steady volumed] **TAPE ENDS**

> *NOTE:* **THE FOLLOWING PAGES WERE ORIGINALLY THE OPENING PAGES OF TAPE 910304A.001 [TAPE013A]; THEY WERE THE OVER-RECORDING OVER THE ORIGINAL ORIGINAL BEGINNING OF 03/04/91. BECAUSE OF THE**

THE NANCY TAPES

OVER-RECORDING, THEY ACTUALLY BELONG HERE, AT THE END OF TAPE 910304B.001 [TAPE013B].

THURSDAY, MARCH 7, 1991 (CONT.)

Good morning, Gentlemen. It's 10:52. I suddenly discovered at 10:48 this morning, I'm on my way to the Red Cross for a hemapheresis donation. But I suddenly discovered at 10:48 this morning on my way when I took out the recorder, this c microcassette recorder to microcassette record little things here, I suddenly discovered that it was on, it was on RECORD, it had been on on RECORD in my pocket, probably since since I put it back in my pocket early this morning roughly at about, Cheez! I don't know, 8:15 8:20 when I went to the went to the the the the the FOOD FRESH at Mondawmin to get some apples. I started to rewind and record over what I had, the noises accidental noises I had recorded. And then I decided, No, that I would not do that, that I would simply leave these noises on there. These are accidental noises, obviously, 'cause I did not intend to record them. Go head, go right through the reyed light! Look at that! Right through the red light, didn't even blink! And these are accidental noises, but I'm gonna leave them on so they can become part of the melange of the chaos factor as as MD refers to it. That will become pum suh part of the potpourri, the chaos potpourri, the chaos factor for you, Gentlemen, Mr. Phelps, Captain Kirk, Captain Picard, to review for purposes of finding meaning.

Actually, and also today I had in the mail was a card from EA of Towson Maryland Writer Proj Writing Project to whom I had given a a copy of *THE LIFE of a STAR*. And the card, on Maryland Writing Project card paper, says, March 4, 1991, Dear Sydney spelled with a y, Thank you ... dot dot dot How lovely. Come read with us at the Writing Project sometime. Especially I love the quote "Dark Cloud and the Blue Giant " unquote and the quote "Black Hole" unquote. And then a quotation from "Star Stuff," "That which we were/which we thought we were/which we throught [sic] we were with an r/which we thought/and which were were [sic]/we are not now nor will be again." And then she says, I'm wondering now where memory is: colon and then a quotation. "The whole process is a lie unless crowned by excess, it break forcefully crowned by excess it break forcefully one way or another from its confine [ment] or find a deeper well." Quotation from William Carlos Williams. I appreciate the quotation. Very good. I have to, that becomes part of the part of the part of the potpourri mix of the chaos factoring. Over and out. Going now to Red Cross for hemapheresis donation.

It's it's 1:41. Of course, what I just realized is that all that stuff was taped over, recorded over stuff that I had previously recorded, so I've lost stuff from March the 4th. What a dipstick!

[NOTE: AT THIS POINT THE MARCH 4 RECORDING CONTINUED, WHICH I HAD RECORDED OVER. THAT IS NOW THE BEGINNING OF TAPE013A.]

THE NANCY TAPES

TAPE NUMBER 14A

FRIDAY, MARCH 8, 1991

[*Johnny Mathis*] "where or when" Who knows where or when. "wheeennnn" Today is, what's today? Friday, March the 8th, it's 8:12 am, we're here at Henry G. Parks, Jr. Circle. Not Park Circle anymore, but Henry G. Parks, Jr. Circle. Who knows where or when?

MONDAY, MARCH 11, 1991

"Memories are made of this" Dean Martin. Tryin' to remember what year? Memories are made of this. "Don't forget a small" Good morning, Gentlemen. It's 7:51, Monday, March the 11th, 1991. I'm out in front of the "fold it lightly" Giant where I've just dropped off some newspaper for recycling. "Sweet sweet, y' can't beat the memories you gave me" "your lips and mine, Two sips" What year was that? I don't know. I have some things to tell you, Gentlemen, but I'll be just a few minutes "memories are" once I get myself started "made of this" and get out on the highway.

Good morning, Gentlemen. It's now 7:55. I'm taking a different route *[rowt]* route *[root]* route *[rowt]* route *[root]* route route *[rowt rowt]* route *[root]* route *[rowt]* this morning. I'm heading up Reisterstown Road now up to the Owings Mills Boulevard entrance to 795, to ride down 795. Do a little do a little cruisin' this morning. I don't know. Hell, it's 7:55 already. Well, what the heck! I better hold off while I turn around here. Time out.

Two things to add to the add-dendum for today. Yesterday evening, we had Mother and Lou over for dinner. Cheh-cheh Pardon me. Pardon me. Cheh-cheh Mother and Lou over for dinner. And in the course of, Mother was talking about Aunt Esther, how she cries every night about Nancy, and that she told Mother that she sees Nancy every night, and Mother said she told her, Of course, you see her every night, you won't let her go, you don't let her rest, you don't give her soul any peace, any rest. That's why you always see her, 'cause you won't let her go. If you stop giving her, if you would only let her go, then she would have peace, and you would have peace. And then she asked me if that was right. And I said, I don't know, Mother. She said, I said, But I know do know that Aunt Esther will not have any peace unless she's willing to let Nancy go. I said, Whether Nancy is still walking around, whether Nancy is without rest and without peace, I don't know. But, Aunt Esther is without rest and without peace. I don't know about Nancy, herself, being without peace or having peace or being without peace. Curiously refreshing ca

The other thing had to do with some news reports, I guess it was on CNN last night, about plane crash that went down someplace. I can't remember where, and it went down with 20 people and 5 crew and they were all killed, and they said it went down so fast and so hard. And just just almost no pieces, no identifiable pieces of an airplane, it just kind of disintegrated. And a couple of the people commenting on it, a couple witnesses, one kid, I caught the last part of it, and apparently from where he was standing he could see it going past him, and he said something about the people beating on the windows. People beating on the windows. People beating on the windows. Just incredible, awesome, frightening! Beating on the windows. And somebody else said that that when it went past, it actually went low enough that it scraped scraped a part of of an apartment building, and then it showed f where a few bricks had come off, just barely had tipped it. And they said that apparently the pilot had tried to bring it down between the buildings so it wouldn't hit any buildings, which he successfully did. So he would not kill the, so that the crash would not kill more people on the ground than in the plane itself. But the people beating on the windows. And the woman who said that about the plane scraping the building also said that when she looked up she saw the man a man waving a red flag, and it was as though he was just wanted to let people know that that he couldn't do anything, and that that was it, he just had to bring it h it just was coming down, and nothing, I don't know about so the if he was waving the red flag to warn people away from in front of them. Who whom could he have warned away? And and how could they have gotten away? A disaster.

People beating on the windows. Nancy, did you beat on the windows? Beating on the windows.

[radio-piano] Now what was this one? Now what was this one called? It's still Monday, March the 11th. Just arriving at Coppin. Here's this song on W-I-T-H, this song on W-I-T-H.

TUESDAY, MARCH 12, 1991

"And you" Okay, here's that Billy Joel song, *And So It Goes*. Good morning, Gentlemen. It's 7:20 AM, what the hell is today? Tuesday, March the 12th. I'm on my way down to the Dawn Patrol b N-C-C-J Dawn Patrol, and I've just missed the damn light! And I'm gonna sit here, sit here and sit here and sit here and dawdle and dawdle and dawdle! I ain't never gonna get nothin' done in my life! Just sit around and piddle around all the damn time! Damn it! "you're the only one who knows" Look at that.

Anyhow. I guess it was Saturday or Sunday, Sunday, after we had Mother and Lou over, my mother and Lou. I may have said this before, I don't know. Sophie picked up the picture of her mother and Thea and Uncle Mike and and and

Theo Nick. And she looked at it, and she burst into tears and said, *[whispered]* I want her back. I want her back. I want her back.

I want her back, she said. And she cried, and I held her. She said, I want her back. And she said, I wanta cook dinner for her. I want her back. God, do I know that feeling! I want my father back! I want them all back! Want Aunt Freda back! And Uncle Sol, and Uncle Morris *[voice breaking and getting louder]* and Eva! I want them aaallll baaack! Want them all back. And Nancy. Want them aaall baaack! But they can't ever come back!

That's why Aunt Esther doesn't wanta let Nancy gooo! That's why she sees her every night! She doesn't wanta let her goo, she doesn't wanta let her gooo, she doesn't wanta let her gooo! She wants her back, she doesn't wanta let her gooo!

THURSDAY, MARCH 14, 1991

Good morning, Gentlemen. It is 8:04 AM.

Good morning, Gentlemen. It's 8:04 AM, 8:05 now, I'm heading down Reisterstown Road, it's it's Thursday, March the 14th. It's ice raining or something like that. There is snow and ice on the cars, and I just the the ice that covered the snow just flipped up and came smashing into the windshield. Not smashing! It just broke against the windshield and for a momentarily instant there I couldn't see. But basically, essentially, the point is, here's the probably the last snow storm of the of the winter. Paul was looking forward to the expectation that this would be our big blizzard, that we'd really get hammered. He said, Every 4 years we had a big blizzard, '79, '83, '87. He was expecting one this year. Unfortunately, it turned out, this has turned out thus far not to be the big dump that the weathermen and we all thought it would be. They had said at one point 4 to 6 or 8 inches even, but basically it's a 1 to 3, and the roads are pretty clear, and essentially it means that no school day or anything, although I just heard on the radio that they're expecting another big dump coming up this way between 9 and 10, it's due to hit Washington about now, and then will hit here in about an hour from then. We'll wait and see what happens.

Listening now on the radio to the cassette recording not the radio cassette recording, the copy I made of the 1938 Benny Goodman Carnegie Hall Jazz Concert. *[Krupa's drums] Sing Sing Sing.* At one point there before it was at the end of it, I was listening to the piano solo, I have to find out who played the piano because of the crystal clarity of the piano, tinkling on the ivories. Great! Marvelous! Wonderful! Jubilation!

[Sing Sing Sing brass]

Here comes the piano part, I want you to listen to this, guys, listen to this *[piano solo]* real well!

THE NANCY TAPES

Get ready, get ready! Passing Royce Avenue! Get ready for this one now! Get ready! *[pause for piano--clarinet high-pitched--crowd cheering--Krupa's drums]*

Here it comes! Listen to that piano, man! *[long pause again for piano solo]* Who's that piano man? *[whispers urgently]* The piano man! Who's the piano man!? Go back and read the jacket! *[long piano solo]* Who's the piano man on Benny Goodman's *"Sing Sing Sing"* from 1938?!

Who was that piano man? The piano man! The piano man! Need to find out who wuuzzz the piano man!

MONDAY, MARCH 18, 1991

Good morning, Gentlemen. It's 8:03 AM, Monday, March the 18th. And here I am on Seven Mile Lane. Seven Mile Lane. Is that what this is? Seven Mile Lane. Seven Mile Lane and Slade Avenue. Going on Seven Mile Lane, heading towards Park Heights. And then eventually down Park Heights to Coppin, to my job. Curiously refreshing. It's pouring out. And, of course, you understand why I'm here, don't you? Weeelll, because you don't, because I'll have to tell you. Because I had to take Paul took Paul to drop him off at school today. Because of the pouring rain.

Ye-es. Refreshingly curious. And there was something else I was gonna say but, of course, I can't remember what I was going to say. Did I say how about how last Sunday after my mother and Lou left, Sophie looked at the picture of her mother and Thea and Uncle Mike and Theo Nick and said, started crying and said, I want her back, I want her back. I wanta cook dinner for her. She wanted her mother back. She wants her mother back. I told her I understand the feeling, and then in the car when we were coming back from, was it coming back from or going to Ocean City? She said the same thing, and she said, Can you understand that? She said, Was it like that for you with your father? I said, *[whisper]* Yes, Sophia, it's always like that. You always want them back. Always want them back.

[rain on car] When I dropped Paul off, right before I dropped him off, he looked over and he said, Oh, there's B. And he went to stand with the grandson of Barney, of Kessler's Delicatessen on Park Heights and Violet Avenue. Isn't it curiously refreshing, refreshingly curious, that he's friends with Sam and Barney's grandson?

It's 8:11, I've just passed the old Pimlico and now passing the old Uptown Theatre, Kingdom Hall of Jehovah's Witnesses. And here we are at at past also past also past also past also Spaulding Avenue. And here's traffic line-up here. Past Spaulding Avenue where Ronnie and D *[sic]* lived used to live lived lived. Okay, watch out here. Traffic traffic. Hold on and off now!

SIDNEY KROME

In the in the in the pouring rain, in the pouring rain. In the pouring rain. In the car before talking with Paul about how looks like chance of the blizzard he was expecting is over and then I, he said, Nope, he's holding out. And then I told him about the article by Jacques Kelly 'bout the great blizzard of '58, 2 feet of snow, snowflakes almost 2 inches across. And I said to Soph, after I read the article, that was the one where we had the big beer blast with the Theta Chis. When we were all trapped at College Park in the in the, and classes were canceled for about 2 days. Ah, yes, I re dismember it well, I remember it well when someone else reminds me. But frankly my own memory is not real great about remembering things like that that I could remember in terms of dates. Sophie said something about remembering the blizzard of '54 in Steubenville. Just incredible. I can't remember those things. I remember the blizzard of '66. I remember my motorcycle was almost completely covered out in front of the University Hills Apartments. Yeeehhhsss, my Ducati. Heh-heh-heh-heh! What a dipstick!

Now at the corner of, where am I? At the corner of Park Heights and Cold Spring Lane, and to the right Park Lane. Now what used to be READ'S now REVCO LIMITED. And I remember the Hobby Shop down on Cold Spring Lane, down there. Time out for more driving here. If I can.

Shirley Avenue, just crossed Shirley Avenue, to the left was what used to be SIDLEN'S pharmacy. Now coming up here is Keyworth. Ready noooowww, Keyworth Avenue, down to the right is PS 59, Alcott Place now, and up to the left was down to the right was that up to the left was Enoch Pratt Branch 16 Keyworth Avenue. Now, Springhill Avenue, down to the right JAKE'S Tailor Shop. Up to the left 2612 2614 2604. Ooohh God! All those wonderful addresses and those houses. And now to the left right here now, just passing Violet Avenue, there on the corner was what is now a townhouse, a rowhouse. What used to be what used to be what used to be KESSLER'S. Here Robinson's Variety Store what used to be on the corner of Ulman Avenue what used to be what used to be SUSSMAN'S Drugstore. And now coming up down here at Hilldale what used to be ROLAND'S Barber Shop and what used to be, what was that? The *Agudas Achim*, the *Shaarei Zion Shule* down here on Park Heights Avenue. Lower Judea. Here we come now, coming down towards coming down towards now coming down towards nooww Park Circle which is now the Henry G. Parks, Jr. Circle instead of Park Circle. Over and out, out and over.

CARLIN'S PARK used to be up to the right. CARLIN'S PARK. CARLIN'S PARK. I remember listening to the, I could hear from my bedroom from my bedroom at night with the window open, sleeping with my head down at the foot of the bed so that whatever breeze there was would come over me. Hearing the hearing the sound of the the laughing clown, the mechanical clown. And the sound of the riiides. And the sounds of the shooting gallery. The popping of gunshot, of b-b shot, of shot.

[very quiet] I remember that well. I remember that well. That I remember well. *[Classical music quietly throughout, and the sound of chirping also]* Well I remember that. Well I remember that. That I remember well. I remember that well. Three different ways to say the same sentence. Well I remember that. Well, *[comma]* I remember that. Or, *well* I remember that. As an adverb. Or, *that* I remember well. Or, I remember *that* well. I remember that well. Remember that I well. No, I can't do it with "remember" first, but I can do it with "I," with "that," and with "well." Sniff. That's intriguing. But I get four different versions, because "well" can have a comma after it as a kind of expletive. Or "well" can *not* have the comma after it, and it stays as the adverb, how telling how I remember that. Huh! How 'bout that!

And now to the left, as we pass through, have passed through Park Circle. To the left was where the to the left was where the old reservoir used to be. It was cut down years ago, even when I was a kid into ballfields. And the old aquarium. Sniff. How well I remember that. I remember that well. *That* I remember well. Well? I remember that! Over and out now. Too much traffic and rain and slippery roads. Here we go, over and out. Now!

Good evening, Gentlemen. It's now 5:44 P.m., Monday, March the 18th. Up Reisterstown Road now coming home. And I saw as I got on the Beltway from Liberty Road the sun dripped dropping out from under the clouds. And now it's well below the clouds. And it reminds me of the day that I drove to Steubenville with the boys and saw the sun, a molten glowing droplet. Then there was more haze in the sky, so there was more of a hazy molten golden. Now it's more of a droplet, now it's more round, it's more clear. You can see the sun. Although there is kind of a white haze behind it. A hazy haze. A hazed hazing haze. *[progressively louder over next three hazes]* Haze! Haze!! Haze!!!

TUESDAY, MARCH 19, 1991

Good morning, Gentlemen. It is now 9:11 in the morning. I have just come from the Weis. I'm on my way down to school. And I was in Weis I g saw GC. And I have on my shades and my hat and my trenchcoat, and she said, Oh, she said, you look like, I said I think she maybe didn't recognize me in *[Clouseau-ish]* my new disguise. And she said, Aw, she said she's she said, You look like a private detect Ch-ah. You look like a private detective. And, of course, *[Clouseau-ish]* as I realized, Gentlemen, that is precisely the look that I'm looking for, the leeuuk. Partially between Clouseau, actually the Clouseau look, I have a modified Clouseau hat on, actually, a walk not really exactly a Clouseau hat, a trenchcoat. And it's funny that the other day CM told me that I looked like Clouseau. And someone else said Sherlock Holmes. I am trying to ferret out the mystery of all this chaos, what's the meaning in all this chaotic disorder, this disorderly chaos. The mystery. Trying to find out the mystery. Somebody said something the other day, I think I recorded it on one of these tapes but I'm not sure, about about accepting the mystery of life.

Understanding what it's oh was it was something from Goethe. From Goetheehh. It was a an epigraph on a program on tv on PBS. And I think that, I think that I did did put it in here, about about knowing the knowable and accepting the mysterious. Accepting mystery. Accepting the mysterious mystery.

Yeeeess. That got wiped off. Yeeess.

Heading now at the traffic light here at Reisterstown and Keyworth. Stopped at the red light. The Louisa May Alcott School, PS 59, The Alcott Place to my left. And I see they have, they have planted some some shrubs, some bushes along the front of Alcott Place, that is, along the the Reisterstown Road side. And the wind is coming right down Reisterstown Road. And the ones aw to the as you face the door to the right of the door, the wind is pushing them so that they're already they're tilting over slightly to the right. And that struck me. That they're pushed over to the right in the wind. They're already not upright.

WEDNESDAY, MARCH 20, 1991

Good morning, Gentlemen. It is now 8:50 A.M. on Wednesday, March the 20th, 1991. Had my father lived, he would be 81 today. Today is his birthday, March the 20th, 1910. Happy Birthday, Daddy. Happy Birthday, Daddy. Put that in your smoke and pipe it, Gentlemen. Mr. Kirk, no, Mr. Phelps, Captain Kirk, Captain Picard. Gentlemen!

Last night, Sophie and I were gonna just drop Paul off at his what we thought was just his last basketball night, and then go get a cuppa coffee. It turned out it was he fin he told us that it was his awards night. Get off my tail, you idiot! That it was his awards night. So we went in, and in the end he got he got three awards. He got one award for his team, for the majors, winning first place in the majors. There were four teams in the majors, two in the in the clinic. We also learned last night that he was the captain of his team. They had a super-shooter contest, and Paul won the super-shooter contest in his age group, so he got a second trophy. And then at the end as as we were getting ready to leave, C called us came ov came over and he came over, C came over, and he pulled out a slip of paper. And he had talked earlier about the CW Award. C was the the referee, the old guy, the referee who refereed for like over 20 years in the in the Rec Council. C was he I don't know if he's still ali I think he's still alive, I don't think he's dead, but he's just a marvelous person, and and he really liked Paul and Paul liked him. And anyhow they gave to the clinic, one of the clinic kids, a little girl, a CW, they established award in in honor of C, 'cause he was such a committed and dedicated person. And

Paul got one also. He told C told us at the end right before we were leaving. And so and we talked we just it was just absolutely delightful, and and I thanked C for 10 years of helping take care of our kids and and thanked K, the basketball coach for helping to take care of our kids, especially Paul 'cause he didn't know Charlie. He talked about how much he liked Paul and what a special kid Paul was, and and it's just absolutely marvelous. And then later I called K aside, after we were all leaving, *[very quiet]* I went back in and pulled K aside and thanked him again, especially for that phone call last January when he called Paul. It just saved Paul so much. And the the just the general depression of of *Giagia's* death. And I almost cried, and I could tell that Paul almost cried last night when he was leaving. 'Cause it was really it was his last night of rec council basketball, the whole part of his life was was over, a part that he loved, that he enjoyed, that helped him to grow. And it's over. And I know he was almost ready to cry, I could tell. *I* was almost ready to cry. At one point, K asked him if he was gonna be back next year, and and he said, Not if I make the team. 'Cause he was going out for the OM High School basketball team, and K and C both said to him, Well, here's hoping we don't see you next year! Sniff! *[almost breaking]* And we almost would have missed this night if he hadn't told us about it. *[voice cracking]* And it was so beautiful. It was so beautiful. He's such an incredible kid. I wanted to cry, I wanted to cry. I feel like crying now. And I know how Charlie feels about not having his high school anymore, he really missed that. He misses that. He missed it last fall, and he misses it even now, I know. Even with his rugby. Rugby is not quite the same for him.

But Soph wished Paul *si haritiria kai stanotera*. At one point he said, There are that's enough *si haritirias*. *[laughing]* And he just didn't seem to want any this morning when I said something to him. I don't know. I'm not sure I understand it. That's the way he is.

THURSDAY, MARCH 21, 1991

Good morning, Gentlemen, it's 8:26 AM, Thursday, March the 21st, 1991. I'm at the intersection of Reisterstown Road and Northern Parkway. And what I just heard on the radio W-B-J-C F-M 91.*[point]*5 the *Thais Meditation* by Julian Salmonet? I forgot the guy's name! Isn't that idiotic!? I wrote down the name of the piece. Beautiful violin piece, very haunting. Look at this! These dipsticks!

Add to the list of music pieces *I Vespri Siciliani, The Sicilian Vespers*. Again I missed the name of the composer. But listen to this a moment, if you can. *[music playing]*

THURSDAY, MARCH 28, 1991

Good afternoon, Gentlemen. It's 3:26 on Thursday, March the 28th. I'm driving up the Jones Falls Expressway, I've been down at school in the office. And

I've got the top off the Beretta, and I put my hand up in the wind blowing, and it made me think of that day back in aught I guess it was in May of 19 and 62 when I got out of the Army. And I went with JH and BL to the Riviera and driving around the Riviera and standing up through the roof of JH's open Volkswagen sun roof. And there's lots of smoke up ahead, looks like there might even have been a fahr, a fahr fahr.

Cheh-cheh. The smoke seems to have cleared already. Must not have been a fahr.

Maybe it was a near.

SUNDAY, MARCH 31, 1991

Good day, Gentlemen, it's 12:12 on Sunday, March the 31st, 12:12 afternoon, sunny bright day, I'm on my way down to the *Taverna Athena* to meet Soph and the boys and Eleni and Stelio to have a Palm Sunday lunch. Today's also the second day of Passover. Last night was the second *seder* at Mother's. Today today today today today today today, yes, I was shifting folders and stuff around from my office at home, and there written on a folder, a student had written, I think, on a student folder, I told you this would happen. I told you this would happen, it said. And then when I was getting stuff to write it my stuff together to put in my pocket, to getting dressed, and I put this cas microcassette recorder in my pocket, I suddenly discovered and the *yahmokuh*, and I suddenly discovered that the little piece of tombstone was gone! That little piece of granite or marble, whatever it was. I don't know where it is! I'll have to look for it, have to remember to look for it, *[rapidly run together]* look for that piece of granite, look for that piece of marble, looking for a piece of tombstone! Dumb-heyed!

Also rediscovered that arts exhibition from Rhode Island, I guess it was when I was at Brown University in Providence. *To Bid Farewell. To Bid Farewell.* Representations of Death in Ancient Art, something like that. But it was To Bid Farewell To Bid Farewell. To Bid Farewell.

12:12 on Sunday three-thirte, 3/31/91. 12:12 12:14 actually, 12:14.

THURSDAY, APRIL 4, 1991

Good morning, Gentlemen, it's 7:36 AM. Thursday, April the 4th, 1991. Today's the twenty- twenty- twenty-23rd Anniversary of the Assassination of Martin Luther King, since 1968. 23rd Anniversary. Had another one of those absolutely experiences, absolutely disorienting experiences, one of those orie experiences that it just my *sukiyaki* has been devastated again. Looking at the paper early this morning about 6:30 6:20 6:25-ish, page 4C of the "MARYLAND" section of *The Morning Sun*. RCS. And I **TAPE ENDS**

THE NANCY TAPES

TAPE NUMBER 14B

THURSDAY, APRIL 4, 1991

Good morning. Good good good morning again, Gentlemen. It's now 7:37 AM, Thursday, April the 4th, 1991, the 23rd Anniversary of the Assassination of Martin Luther King, Jr.

As I said at the end of the last tape this morning, I had one another one of those devastating one of those disorienting experiences, one of those experiences that simply again devastated my *sukiyaki*. Reading the morning paper at about uh 6:20 6:25, page 4C of the M "MARYLAND" section of *The Sun* today, under the "OBITUARIES," RCS. And I saw the name S, and I thought, I read it because I thought, Gee, I wonder if this is any relation to AS whom I had known d then when I was at College Park and worked in the parks that summer. And as I read into it, she had died in Esconcito or someplace like that in California. She was 46, died of cancer. She had And then I saw that she had owned the M Limited, the boutique in Pikesville until 1987 when she moved, and that's when I real what a second! Wait a second! The M Limited was RK's place! Son-of-a-bitch! It was RK who had died at 46 of cancer! Just just incredible, I couldn't believe it! Couldn't believe it! Devastated my *sukiyaki*, totally disoriented. RK? I don't remember when M died. Don't remember knowing about her funeral, but I remember that I missed Abe's funeral. How did I miss Abe's funeral? 'Cause I was busy, I had work to do, *et cetera*, that kinda bullshit! I remember I saw Abe on *Yom Kipper* I guess, or *Rosh Hashanah*, or sometime, at the what they call the Gucci Gucci Giant in Pikesville, on Old Court. Still had all his hair, but it was all white. Man looked fantastic for a man of his age. Seventy-something. And I debated whether or not to call M Nancy, and, of course, I realized I had to call Nancy, I had to let her know. So I waited 'till almost 7:30, right before leaving. And I called her, and she was kind of devastated, but I told her, I said, Nancy, I said, I'm sorry to be the bearer of bad tidings this early in the morning, but I had to tell you, I had to give you the opportunity, if you wanted, to go to the funeral, you had to know about it, the funeral's at four o'clock at Sol Levinson, and she said, There's nobody left except H. I said, 'Cause the last time I'd seen him after aught so many years, since the old neighborhood, I I saw him again what in '88? At the at the JCC at the Fitness Club Pro-Fitness at the JCC. Cheh-cheh. That's when I discovered he was a triathlete. Triathlon athlete. RK. And then the last time I'd seen her was was in the '80's? Or the '70's? I saw her once when my mother was in the hospital. She was there with M to visit somebody, to see M? I don't remember exactly. I know she and M came by, no, M was in the hospital, and she was there to see M, and they came by Mother's room. That's what it was. But the last time before that I had seen R was at S's office, when I went down about my nose. And she was in S's office also.

She recognized me before I recogn I didn't recognize her at all. She recognized me. Course, after she told me who she was, I reco realized who she was, but RK, she died Tuesday, actually, which was April the 2nd, the article said. My *sukiyaki* is again devastated. And the name was spelled K! Then I looked it up to try to find f H's address so I could send him a, plant trees in her name. Sniff. But I couldn't believe that it was k. I always it was k. But I could not find a listing for H under either under k- k-k-k. I don't think I looked k. But anyhow I could not find a listing. Hmmm!

7:42, down P Park Heigh Pa Pa Pa Pa Reisterstown Road through Pikesville. Coming down now toward the old Milford Mill Road Avenue. Thinking. In what? six months? October November December January February March. It's under six months that's the second young woman from the old neighborhood to go in less than six months. First Nancy Kanow Via Simpson. Then RC *[very rapid for rest of name]* K-S. And years and years and years before, I remember, Ruth's good friend AC died. I think she died of cancer also. Oh, they're devastating my *sukiyakis*! Absolutely devastating my *sukiyakis*! My *sukiyakis* are devastated! I am disoriented. Sniff.

Where did I see that, another article, one of those events that suddenly happens? There is no before, and there is no after. No nonono and there's no explanation. Sniff. There's no expectation, and there's no explanation of why. Oh, that was, I think, in that write-up about that family in the Midwest, TIME MAGAZINE, the this tha the the young kid, the guy R, not young, he was an an adult in his '20's who came home Christmas and blew his family away, just automatic weapon, just killed them all sitting around the the table. And then blew his head off with a shotgun. And there was so much blood that it dripped through into the basement, the article said. Seven people in the family, I guess. Devastating. Devastating. Devastating. Devastating. Devastating.

Something has happened to the speed mechanism on this thing. All of a sudden, at the normal it sounds fast, and at the slow it sounds real slow.

Must be a battery problem. I'm gonna have to change the battery as soon as I get a chance.

All right. I am testing this now. It's 7:49 AM, coming down Reisterstown Road, passing the church that was across the street from the block where where *Maar* Lesser's house was where I went for my *Bar Mitzvah* lessons. Coming down Reisterstown Road now passing Beehler. Who lived on Beehler? Somebody lived on Beehler. Was that MA? Lucille Avenue. And here's Woodland Avenue! Coming down coming down coming down Reisterstown Road op through the yeller light! Moving down faster farther farther down Reisterstown Road. Virginia Avenue. Coming down coming down coming down. There's a street with no name. And here is Royce Avenue! Royce Avenue Royce Avenue 3316 Royce Avenue

Mohawk 4-4 2448. Aunt Freda was another one who died early, another one of the old neighborhood girls to die early, Aunt Freda Herlich Bulmash at the age of 37 in 1954. And here we come to Park Circle. Not Park Circle! Park Lane Shopping Center.

Well, okay, now, that obviously was clear that it was the batteries that were going, and I should've realized that because that's why the light was out that the bat now the light is now that I've gotten fresh batteries in there, the light is nice and bright.

Coming down closer now into the old neighborhood, down to pass past Shirley Avenue. And now here we come to Keyworth, and to the left, to the left to the left PS 59 Louisa May Alcott now Alcott Place, to the right the old G's Drugstore, to the left now M's Salon which used to be P's LP's, to the right along here, PO used to live along here, PO. And here we come to Springhill Avenue! Springhill Avenue, Ladies and Gentlemen! Up to the left, Jake the Tailor's and *way up* to the left, the 26-hundred block of Springhill Avenue, where the Ks also lived. That's Kanows and K, now. Cheez! No, I shouldn't say there was only two, that was actually three! in less than a year because just a scant month ago R RRK RK and RK, 2604 and 2606. 'Course RK was not a young girl, I mean, but she was one of the old Baltimore girls from from the Springhill Avenue neighborhood. RK. So that's actually three. Kanow. Nancy Kanow. Nancy Kanow. October the 30th. RK. March the March the March the March the 3rd, was it? Sunday, March the 3rd? Or was it Saturday, March the 2nd? I think she died in Ma on March the 2nd. Aaaannd RK ooonn April the 2nd. So we have a Kanow, a K, and a K. We Three Kings of Orient Are. Good Lord! That is three.

SUNDAY, APRIL 7, 1991

Good morning, Gentlemen. It's 11:37 AM Eastern Daylight Time on Sunday, April the 7th, in Steubenville. Last night, Easter Saturday night into Easter Sunday morning, while I was in the house, and Sophie and everybody was in church except for Dad, who was sleeping, I turned the tv around and channel selector and came upon the middle of a movie called, *Weapons of the Spirit*, about *LeChambon* in France where they helped to save the Jews. And at one point Bill Moyers was interviewing, Pierre Sauvage was the name of the guy who put the movie together. He was from *LeChambon*, his Jew who was born there, actually, he was not oh, his family was not from *LeChambon*, but they got refuge there.

And he not Pierre Bill Moyers but he, Sauvage, was interviewing one of the women who talked about who was saved there, and how her, I guess her s brother and sister-in-law or brothers and sisters-in-law and cousins and aunts and uncles, everybody were deported, and asked her how many came back, and her response was, *Aucun.* Not one. *Aucun.* Not one. Not one. I have to see if I can get hold of that or watch, see when it's gonna be on tv again. And and record it.

And also the other day, I guess it was Saturday? Friday. Thursday night, Dad said the reason he didn't go to church was because there was too much bullshit there. And Friday he said it was because he, it hurt too much to see other men there with their wives and since his wife, Maria, my mother-in-law, my o Mother was was gone, he it just hurt him too much, and he talked about all the pain of it, and I said, Well, you have to think about the good things. And he said, Yes, but even when you think about the good things that hurts. And that's true. It hurts.

MONDAY, APRIL 15, 1991

Good morning, Gentlemen. Has been a while. It's 8:45 AM, Monday, April the 15th, income tax day, the Ides of April. How are you guys this morning? It's a little bit later than usual, but I've just gotten a haircut with Louis. Lazars Sonntag, the barber at Gentlemen's Quarterly.

Last night we had dinner with at at Suburban House. Mother took everybody out because it was Lou's 85th birthday. Who was there? Lou and Mother and Bertha and Mother's friend Sylvia and Sophie and Paul and me and Nancy and Jon and Riva and Al and Aunt Esther, and Joe was there because Joe had. Oh, nice move, buddy! Because Joe had been in to spend ti day with Aunt Esther so he came along to have dinner with us. And Aunt Esther talked about how she keeps seeing Nancy and and that Nancy keeps saying she wants to come back. And she asked if I thought it was just her imagination. And I said, Yes, Aunt Esther, I said, you want to have her back, I said, but, unfortunately, you can't. I said, The only place you can have her is in your love and your memories, in your heart, but you can't ever get her back the way she was *[cracks and breaks on "before"]* befoorrrre. *[crying]* You can't ever get her baaaaaaccck the way she was befoooooorrrrre! Sniiiiffff! Uuuoooooooohhh! Lordy, Lordy, Lordy! And she talked about how Joe criiied, and how she cried, and and Joe was talking about how i because he ev eh eh Esther cries all the time because she sits in that hoouuse, and all she does is look at Nancy's pictures, she has nothing to do, no place to go. Sniff. No wonder she cries so much.

And then later last night, Sophie told meeee thaaaaaaaat that Joe had said that he had met somebodyyyy. And she's a lot of fun, she's fun to be around, and just talking companionship right now, and that's all it is. And I said, Well, I said, Ronny got married, what? a year, 14 months after Eva died, he was married again, so, what's the difference? I mean, not what's the difference? But, what's the, you know, it's not surprising. I mean, listen, nobody, I said, I certainly didn't expect Joe to stay unmarried, I said, he's a young man! He's only 48 years old. What's he gonna do? Stay unmarried the rest of his life?

SIDNEY KROME

Oh, look at the traffic on the Beltway all jammed up already underneath this Reisterstown Road. And yesterday was the Holocaust program, and today I talked with Louis. And yesterday during the Holocaust Program, what made me really want to cry finally and not finally but what it was was seeing this one woman, I c I her name's L L L? I can't remember her name, but it's in the program as she lit the candle for the Russian Jews and the Polish Jews. Aaannd when the cantor was chanting the *El Molay Rachamim*, she was *[breaks into crying]* standing there crying, I could see her on the stage. With her handkerchiefff, and then rocking and shaking and crying. And afterwards Rabbi Schiffer said, *Nur auf simchas*, as they say. And I said, *Nur auf simchas*. And I told him about *bescherteh sach*, about Riva's about Estelle's cousin, and it turns out that Riva and Al were saying last night that that they are back in Leningrad. Actually, they're Soviet, I thought that they had left and gone to Israel. They were just visiting in New York. But they're back in Leningrad, and they speak Hebrew so apparently, they're gonna be going to Israel sometime soon.

Saw Jonathan and Nancy, and then they left. And there's STAPLES. And thinking about how detached I've been from the family. How detached I've been. From the family. Of course, Sophie would say it's a two-way street, and it certainly is. But I have not done very much on my part to initiate any contacts. And thinking also about the Kurds. *[loud]* What the hell have I done?! I sit and bitch and moan, but I haven't even sent in a dollar to anybody. For Kurdish relief. Let alone call anybody or do anything or protest or complain. Nothing. Do nothing. Don't do anything. Except bitch and moan. Ah, man, and I I don't know, I'd like to be more Jewish, I'd like to be in the family, l like to be this, and like to do that, but all I do is sit. Those who agonize don't act. Who said that? Oh that was Pierre Sauvage talking with Bill Moyers about *LeChambon, LaChambon,* that town where they saved the Jews, the town where where Albert Camus lived while he wrote *The Plague.*

I agonize. He his point was making was that what you see in the literature, characters who agonize and then decide to do do the right thing, he said that basically, in real life what happens is people don't agonize, they they they simply do what the right thing is. They don't, but they don't agonize about it, they go ahead and do it. Unlike me, I sit and agonize. And then there was what was it? in that in in a in a calendar, one of those pocket calendars, it may have been the one that that BW gave me from from the bookstore. You know where, you know those calendars that have quotations from famous people. Had a quotation from Yogi Berra! And what did the quotation say? It said, You can't bat and think at the same time. And that's one way of putting what Sauvage said about people, you can't agonize and act, those who agonize don't act, those who act don't agonize. You do! You do, you simply do. And me? I don't do, I just sit around and piddle around.

THE NANCY TAPES

I'm the greatest fucking dawdler in the world! Moral dawdler. Practical dawdler. Do dawdler. Dawdle dawdle dawdle. I mean, like last night, it was, after all that, the whole day and then I just couldn't take it anymore, to sit down and have to do the Jesus! You asshole! And have to do the have to do the the notes for tonight to be. That guy made a right turn and stopped! right in the middle of the road! Have to do my notes for the for being MC for the thing for for Father C. tonight.

I'm sitting here *[almost crying]* at 9:02 in the morning on this rainy Monday morning of April the 15th driving down Reisterstown Road. Sniff! I've passed Royce Avenue. And I can see PS 59 down there. Sniff! *[still crying]* And all I could think of was that Monday night in the hospital. And Ronny looking at Ruthie and saying, *[crying]* She's going to die, we're losing her, she's going to diiieee! Sniff! It's Aunt Freda all over again! She's going to die! It was 36 years. Sniff! And here we come up to Springhill Avenue. Crossing Springhill Avenue. Sniff! ts Crossing Delancy Street. Crossing Springhill Avenue. Oh, dear, she's going to diiieeee! Sniff! I'm sitting here and tears are running down my cheeks. And I'm crying. And it's raining. Sniff. Ooohh! If I had known Amy was gonna take so long to print that thing, I would've added the thing about Nancy. Sniff! But I didn't know that. I didn't know that. Sniff! That should've been in there, and I'm sorry, Nancy. I was trying to keep it short. Sniff! And it was Ruthie who wanted to add all the other things.

It was like, what finally happened last night, with talking to ET oohh, there's a funeral getting ready t Mount Lebanon Baptist Church down here on Reisterstown Road. What the heck is this?! UTILITY WORK AHEAD, okay. Okay, just kinda droned on and on, and I just couldn't take it. *[loud and angry]* Oh, stop that noise! And then I had to call Di, and then so much time on the phone and so, what happened to the day? I went to church with Sophie and helped with that. Then I went to the Holo came home and then went down to the Holocaust Program, and then I came home and barely had a few minutes to rest, and Mother called, and it was time and had to go to dinner, and we came home, and then I had to call ET, and then after that talk to T then I had to talk to D. And so instead of being able to work from eight to, it was 8:30 20 to 9 8:30 or after 8:30, by the time I got done on the phone, and I just couldn't take it. And the tension, the pressure. Always so much to do. It was like I, as I said to H years ago, All I ever wanted to do was to teach and to write. Once I got into JP JAP's English Lit class in senior year at City, and I decided I wanted to be a teacher and I wanted to be a teacher and a writer. And I've just kind of fucked around! and dawdled and piddled and dipsh dipsticked! And done everything except write. Always managed to find an excuse. I remember when I was teen-hager, I talked about being irresponsible. Sniff. And Raizel said something about, Enjoy your irre time of irresponsibility. Dawdle around and dawdle around and dawdle around and why am I not spending all this time sniff writing and putting together these novels and these poems and all the stuff that I wanta write? Oh, hell! I said now I'm gonna become Vice President for Academic Affairs, and TW said, she was delighted, she was so happy, she said, Is this what you what you want? And I said, Actually, no, I said, what I really want is to teach and to write, but this is an offer I can't refuse. Actually, I could've refused it, but now I don't think I can. Sniff. I just don't know. There's just so much, there's just so much to do. I'd be the academic "white shadow" at Coppin State College. I don't know. I need to work on my work on my work on my work, and I'm not gonna have time for all the stuff, I'm just gonna have. Oh Lord! Retirement, retirement, when? From this. Sniff. I figure I figure. What do I figure? I have to work what? Nine more years? Four years at and five years of four five nine years of before I can retire would be in 19 90 9 in the year 2000. I'll be 62. Come on, lady! Come on, mister, move! Be 62. The year 2000, that will give me 30 years with Coppin plus 3 years military plus the 3 years be 33.

FRIDAY, APRIL 19, 1991

Good afternoon, Gentlemen. Surprise Surprise. It's 5:09 P.m. on Friday, April the 19th, 1991. Today is birthday of of of PM's birthday. PM's birthday is today. I did it. Cheez! Where am I goin'? PM's birthday. PM's birthday today.

Surprise, it's Friday afternoon, and here I am preparing to tell you that RE died, RE of the Criminal Justice Department of Coppin State College! Who died who died who died at the What is this?! This is a dead-end also! Why why don't they tell you this?! You try to take a short-cut and all you do is get lost, Sidney! Cheez! National NAACP Headquarters. Anyhow. He died Wednesday night had a cerebral aneurysm. Fell out, as they say, while he was giving a report to the Fellows of the Maryland Center for Thinking Studies. Aaaannndd took him to Liberty Hospital. Where they kept him on a machine, and they transferred him to transferred him to University for organ harvesting as they say. His, Where am I going?! His sister said later that by the time it that some cousin had obviously auth had authorized and by the time she found out about it, it was too late to do anything, and she wouldn't stop them because there was a team coming in to get his liver also. Let me stop a minute.

Then I had to help his sister go into go into get into his office. And get into his office and somebody, JA, was saying that R's office 5 835 was saying that that was also LJ's office, LJ, who also died of the Criminal Justice Department 'bout 4 years ago. Coronary, I think, not not really not cerebral aneurysm, but he died also, a heav overweight black and late '40's, early '50's died of not died of but was overw heavy and a smoker, *et cetera.* And then today when I was there in the office, today on Friday again, his niece, R's niece, was looking through his stuff looking through the no, that was was that his niece? Or was that TW? One of those students was looking through his stuff and found the funeral program from LJ. Is that incredible or is that incredible? Oh, dear. And his sister, A, said today that she really felt it when the funeral director told her she would have to pick out a casket.

Yesterday, LR said something about, we were talking about how quickly R went, R said something about, I said something about how it makes you feel your mortality. And she said something about how it makes you feel insignificant. And I I just didn't feel like challenging that at the time so I let it go. But no, not insignificant, insignificant compared to what? the universe? But R made a difference in his life. People who make a difference are not insignificant. That's significant, that they are *not* insignificant. And there was something else, something else about significance and insignificance. My mind is going going going going going. I have to stop a minute.

Ah, yes. EG and two students stopped me today at noon and that CB in in had said something about. EG had asked for lists of the students, Criminal Justice. And said it would be ready about noon, so she sent the students over at noon. The students said that what what B said was something about how G wants them to drop everything.

And when today I went to get him to print out the press release for the for WJZ and asked if he could tell me something in confidence. So I closed the door, and he told me how disappointed he was in my colleagues, 'cause the fact that they were there Wednesday night when R had his attack, he said, and that *he* had to go to the hospital with R because nobody else would. I couldn't believe it. That they let him go with R to the hospital instead of one of them going with him. Just incredible!

Happened with R was another one of those disorienting sudden and shocking and jolting and disorienting experiences. Y' don't expect it, you go to a class, you go to a lecture by a colleague, and he *diiies* in front of you practically! And here now here's an accident on Liberty Road. Cheh-cheh! Disorienting experience, and they're there trying to get someone into an ambula into an ambulance onto a stretcher. Onto a stretcher and into an ambulance.

When I got to the Red Cross my blood pressure was 140 over 84. I was so rushed I was just going crazy trying to get there in time. And when I lay down on the couch for the pheresing, I practically fell asleep. It all just drained on out of me, and even one of the nurses said something about how I looked at ha as though I had just let it all go out. And I had.

FRIDAY, APRIL 26, 1991

Good afternoon, Gentlemen. I don't know how long this thing is going to last right now, it's 1:37 P.M. on Friday, April the 26th. Coming up Garrison Forest Avenue on the way to Forest Road on the way to the Veterans Cemetery to bury RE.

And just passed other cars going in the opposite direction which also had the yellow the orange stickers with the black lettering FUNERAL going in the opposite direction, just leaving there. Like funerals pass in the day, ships that pass in the night. At the funeral service, the minister, Psalm 91 and Romans Romans I didn't catch which chapter, but verses 35 to about 37 or 39. Over and out. And at the funeral, CM said she had met a cousin cousin of a cousin who had, young cousin who had passed recently, turned out it w LW. She had met LW. Very interesting.
TAPE ENDS

THE NANCY TAPES

TAPE NUMBER 15A

TUESDAY, APRIL 30, 1991

Good morning, Gentlemen. Welcome to a brand new tape, I think. I can't remember if I recorded anything on here or not before. It's 7:50 AM, Tuesday, April the 30th. And I'm crying in the car as I as I came around the Beltway towards Liberty Road and I'm now co coming down Liberty Road. And I suddenly realized it's six months to the day since Nancy died on October 30th, 1990. A Tuesday, also a Tuesday, also a Tuesday. Sniff.

And I was in the car, driving, and yesterday I had gotten a card from TS, he was back in Bad Aibling again on his way to Budapest and Prague, and I I don't remember what he does that he travels so much. And the card said something like, Hi, I'm your annual card from from *Deutschland.* Just something about just to remind you how merciless time is. And that popped into my mind as I was driving. And I kept thinking, it's ending. Sniff. I have, even in the best of possible estimates, even if I make it, let's say, to 85, which is roughly let's say this is 1991, I'll be 53, that would be 32 years. Even if I were to make it that long, which is to 85, that's 32 years. I have less time to go than I've already had. Sniff. And I was thinking about all the things that are undonnne, that have not been done. And I was thinking, it's endinnnggg. There's so many things to do. Sniff.

Oh, JAP! When I went to him, when I was 16, for a letter of reference for a scholarship. Sniff. And he said, Aren't you the young man who had so much potential? Had, in the past tense, that I didn't live up to. And that's the way I feel, there are so many things that I could have done, that I ought to have done that I didn't dooooo.

Talking to P last night, and he asked me a personal question, he said, about how it is to to be married to someone of a different faith, a different culture. Sniff. And there I was thinking of how I regret not having allowed myself or encouraged myself to be more Jewish. Sniff. Unfortunately, I think, that my mother was right 23 years ago or so on just more when she said to Soph as Soph told me that that she felt that being Jewish meant more to me than I wanted to admit to myself then. And she was right, but I didn't want to admit that she was right. *Dominez, dominezi, domineaza.* It was her constant attempts to dominate. Sniff.

Oh, Lord. Oh, Lord. It's coming to an end. Do you hear that, Kirk? Do you hear that, do you hear that, Phelps? Do you hear that, Kirk? Do you hear that, Picard? Do you hear that, Mike Barnett, with 2 t's? The Man Against Crime? Do you hear that? Over. It's going to be over. And out.

It's now 7:59 AM. I'm now heading down Hillsdale, turned off of Liberty. I felt earlier that I just wanted to go to Uncle Morris's grave, to the cemetery. And I wasn't sure whether I was gonna go or not. Part of me just wanted to go ahead and go to work 'cause I have work to do. Get back to the wooorrrld or stay in the world. But then I decided, no, I just I just I'm gonna do this, I'm gonna do this. There is neither rhyme nor reasonnn. It was 8:35! *[almost crying]* On the morning of October 22nd. Annndd I was ready to leave the cemetery, and I was in the car. And I I backed up 'cause I had this sudden real impulse that I had to go back to Uncle Morris's graaaave. I told you this befoorre. Sniff. And then later I found out that it was exactly at that time. Joe said it was at 8:35 that the surgeon began the surgery, the operation, on Nancy. Sniff. Sniff. Ssshhhit! Ssshhhit! Ssshhit!

Faaalling apart agaaaiiin. That famous song by Marlene Dietrich. In *The Blue Angel*. Faalling apart agaaaiiin, agaaaiiin a-faalll apaaart. And *sonst gaaarr niiichchchts!*

Here I am heading along Windsor Mill Road to Uncle Morris's cemetery. And I think back to that day in July, whatever the date was, in 1964. When Nancy and Dave got married. They were And and she wanted to go to the cemetery, and I said, Nance, I said, We don't have time to go to both places. Do you wanta see your father or Uncle Sol? *[crying]* And she wanted to see her father! Sniff. And I took her out here. Sniff. Sniff. Sniff. I took her out here. Sniff.

Good morning. It's 8:16. I'm sitting I'm sitting in the car. Ready to leave. I've just left Uncle Morris's grave. The three guys mowing the lawn, one in mowing the lawn mowing the grass on the graves, one in a power driver and the other in, y'know, the kind that you drive, the tractor mower, and the other push mowers. Powered power-driven. Self-propelled.

And there were a lot of stones on Uncle Morris's stone stone stones. And I said I hoped he had been able to help Nancy's passing be a little bit more easy than it would have been without his help. And I criiiiiied and I said I wanta go baaack. And I thought of the only words I could think of him saying, standing on the porch at 2616 Springhill Avenue, looking down and saying, Hey, boy, get off the lawn. And I remember Aunt Esther, I was standing on the porch and Aunt Esther screaming from inside the house, Mor-ess! Mor-ess! Mor-ess! And I was terrified and afraid to go in. And FW went in and came out and she said, I don't know, but her father's lying in there on the floor. And I was too terrified to move. There goes the window going up. And I have these memories, dim memories, of his grocery store, near the old Oriole Park, I think. Oh, my goodnessss.

[quieter and quieter] And the student at Coppin, yesterday. Talking about Native American women writers. And Thomas Wolfe and s and book and saying, He's wrong, you can go home again, and you have to go home again to your roots. But then in response to a question, she said, You can't *really* go home again, because things change, you can't go back to what it was, you we grow and we develop. And I remember thinking that when I said that about Beryl in 19-ought-and-78, when I went up for one of his daughters' weddings. You go back in your

memories. And I stood there at Uncle Morris's grave, crying, and thinking ultimately, There's no consolation. But thinking also of EG at the funeral for RE, how she stood up and, of course, the and the first thing she said was, I believe in the resurrection. And that reminded me that at that memorial service for Sam Jones at the church in Mount Vernon, when someone, was it BC or me? said something about no consolation. And she got up, and she talked about the resurrection. And how she expected one day to see Sam again. The resurrection. It must be consoling. At least in some way. To the Christians who believe in it. It must be consoling. It must be consoling to those who believe in heaven now. That their loved ones go to heaven. Oh, they weep, most of them, as much as we do who do not believe in it. How could it not offer some consolation? *[softer and softer, quieter and quieter]* I don't have that consolation. I don't think that consolation is real. As much as people believe it, I don't think it's, it's *real* in the sense that it consoles them. But I don't think it shows, I don't think it connects with a a let's say a reality of a heaven. All I wanta do is sit here and cry. But I can't. Falling apart again. I stood leaning on Uncle Morris's stone, and I criiied and I criiied. And I felt like I was going to just break down and just break down, and if I'd had a page if I'd had a phone in my hands, I would've tried to reach S and see if I could come in. But I will muddle throuough. Muddle through.

What I really want to do is teach and write. Although part of me *does* want does want does want to take this job as Vice President for Academic Affairs, part of me just want, there're so many things I want to write. She'd'a been good woman if there'da been someone there t'kill her every minute of her life. From Flannery O'Connor's story, "The Misfit." Ultimately, the presence of death really sharpens our vision.

Do I really wanta take this job? I don't know. I remember when I told TW, she jumped up and hugged me and said, Oh, congratulations! Is this what you really want? No, T, it's not what I *really* want. I need the killer instinct, the firmness, to go after what I really want. But I do partly want this. I can make a difference at that school. With those teachers, with those students. But if I were to die in three years, is that what I want to die having done? *[louder and louder]* I need to do my writing! I need to do my writing! I need to work with Ruthie on that book! And not just talk about it! And not just think about it! Just do it!! Dammit! Do it! Dammit!

I'm on my way out, Uncle Morris. I asked myself, standing, leaning against his stone, leaning on his stone and crying, what was I doing there? And I guess it was Nancy. *[softer and softer]* It was Nancy it was Nancy it was Nancy it was our youth it was our childhood. I can't *[very loud]* believe that *[crying]* Nancy's dead! *[sobbing and crying]* Jesus, I don't believe it! God dammit! God dammit!

THE NANCY TAPES

[crying voice] George Sherman was the first of the cousins to die. The husband of a cousin. But he was older, he was already around 60 or in his 60's when he died. But also, and isn't this funny? It's like Ruth Sherman said to me in 1967. Sniff. *[crying]* She said she couldn't talk to him, he was her husband, she'd been married to him 20 years, and she couldn't talk to him! Because he wasn't family! I was family. I was family. But he wasn't family. It's hysterical! *[crying hard and loud]* Nancy's deaead! Deaead! God dammit!

8:27 AM. Mostly we just muddle through. JP, where are you now that I need you? Oh, God, that was 19-ought-and-62. TS. I had this fellowship to go back to this assistantship at George Washington University. Haagh! Stay a year, try it out, see what it's like. No, I had to get back. No, I had to get back and get on with my life. I have that picture of TS, up on the hillside at *Ma'ayan Tzvi* overlooking the Mediterranean. The night before I left. Ssshhit! What an asshole! Not necessarily her, but Israel. Oh, well. What will happen to these tapes? What will happen to all my stuff? It'll get aaalll pitch-ed out-ed. *[singing]* It'll get aaall pitch-ed out. It'll get aaall pitch-ed out. It'll be part of the bonfire of the van-uh-tyy. My van-uh-ty. That I think I could do something. That I think I could do something. But if I don't do anything. Yes, it's me, and I did it myself. Ba-bom-ba-bomp!

WEDNESDAY, MAY 1, 1991

Good morning, Gentlemen. It's 8:04 AM on Wednesday, May 1st, Mayday! Mayday! Mayday! and that's the caaall now, hasn't it been in all these long months that I've been doing these tapes? Mayday! Mayday! Mayday! Mayday! Just turning off the Beltway onto off 695 onto the Liberty Road here on my way to school this morning and was listening to to to to to to the tape of *Orfeu Negru*, *Black Orpheus*, the opening song, *Manha de Carnaval* and heard the phrase, "*por un momento di sol*," for a moment of sun, a moment of sun, and that's an idea for a novel, a book, a movie, not a movie, a novel, a book, a poem. One moment of sun. Well, well, well. One moment of sun. Over and out, Gentlemen.

Just heard the line, "*Serafina, ha wa ya, chi bella essa! chi bella essa!*" "How beautiful it is! *Un momento di sol!*"

8:13 AM, coming down Liberty Heightsss, it's still Mayday. *Orfeu Negru* playing in the background. *[accordion O Nosso Amor-loud as mike held up]* You can probably hear it. And I just thought, I'm sitting here, I'm gonna cry *[crying]* again. And I'm longing for the dead. I have such longing for the dead. For those who are dead. And I was thinking again about our dead young or our young dead. I guess I didn't really realize when it started until I was at Uncle Morris's grave yesterday. And suddenly realized that he was only 50 when he died. He was only 50. It seems to run in the family. Death runs in the family.

SIDNEY KROME

[O Nosso Back on.] Death at an early age runs in the family. It runs in the family. It runs in the family. That's another poem. Death runs in the family.

It does not skip a generation. As they say about some things that are inherited. *[O Nosso]* It goes from generation to generation. *[crying]* And I'm so sad. I can't stand it.

How did T put it in his card that I mentioned yesterday? I am here to remind you how merciless time is. And I suddenly realize now that 30 years ago this year 1961 in June, Ruth and Dave *[voice breaking]* got married. And in August the 16th, *["Manha"]* Eva died. And the family reunion, I don't think Nancy realized it, I don't know, maybe she did and just didn't say anything. *[crying]* The family reunion, it's gonna be held on the weekend, the 15th and 16th and 17th, the 30th Anniversary of Eva's death. Sniffing sob. Oh, God! *["Manha"]* And 30 years ago, we saw, I saw *Black Orpheus* when I was in the Army in Germany. Sniff. 'Cause I remember buying the album and carrying the album back with me. From from here back to Germany. When I came back for Eva's funeral. *["Manha"]*

There was some song on the radio yesterday that made me think of A. Clome, let me cutch thee, he said. Clome, let me cutch thee.

A bumper-sticker 8:18 AM on a car here in the gas station. STOP THE TEARS. I can't stop the tears.

All right, I'm continuing this at 8:33, just stopped at Farm Fresh for apples and coffee. So there I was, out in the bivouac area at night eatin' black olives and drinking vodka I think we were, with EK and S. And then someone came looking for Krome, Where is Krome? Where is Krome? An emergency call, had a phone call, emergency call. And Ruthie was on the phone. And Ruthie was on the phone. And told me that Eva had died. *[loud and breaking]* That Eva had died! That Eva had died! That Eva had died! So I told her to call the Red Cross to confirm, and that I would begin processing to see if I could get leave to come home. But because it was not imme what they call immediate family, not a blood relative, I could not get emergency leave. And so I had to use my own leave time. And I took off, I came home. And missed the funeral. Missed the funeral. And there was Ron on the porch. Let's see, who picked my up? EK? And was it Ruth? Or Nancy? It must have been Ruth. Picked me up at the airport in DC, Washington National. And I had my tie off, my tie under the epaulet strap. And a GI came up and told me that I would get gigged, picked up by the MP's for being out of uniform, that they were really strict around DC, and so I fixed my tie. And I guess it was Ruth and Dave and EK came to pick me up.

And we pulled up at the house at Glen Avenue, and my mother was standing out on the sidewalk wait came down to the sidewalk. Other people were up on the porch, including Ronny I think. And somebody said, *[breaks into crying]* Is this the brother everybody was worried about? *[crying again and loud]* Oh, dammit! Dammit!

[voice still broken] And that was almost 30 years agoooo. We have May, we have June, we have July to get through, and half of August. In three-and-a-half months, it'll have been 30 years.

THURSDAY, MAY 2, 1991

Good morning, Gentlemen. It's Thursday, May the 2nd, 1991, 9:50 AM. Perhaps in the background you can hear the Overture to *Porgy and Bess*. Today is, Cheez! what is it? 22 years, 22 years today, the 22nd Anniversary of the death of Solomon B. Levin. Lordy Lordy Lordy. Time flies when you're havin' fun! I am here to remind you how merciless time is. Did you ever forget that? Sometimes, you do. Don't ever forget that! D'you hear me? Phelps, Kirk, and Picard? Don't forget that. I am here to remind you how merciless time is.

"and the livin' is easy" Remember Aunt Freda? Remember Sonny? And why he sings this song? "fish are" He didn't know why. "jumpin'" Till I told him in my piece about *Porgy and Bess* "and the cotton is" by sending him a copy of it. "high" "Oh, your daddy's rich, and your ma is good-lookin'" Punch it tunchra! "So hush little baby doon't you cry-y"

Good afternoon, Gentlemen, it's 6 good evening 6:14 P.m.. What the heck's today's date? Thursday, May the 2nd. Yes, the 22nd Anniversary of Sol's death. And went to LL's class today because he invited me because MO was there. And in the course of his talk, O was talking about different jobs and things, and and how he had started at WJZ, and a student said, Well, God forbid if I, she said, I don't wish something happened to you, but if something *[My Man's Gone Now]* did happen to you, would your position still be there? And he said, Well, and he kinda laughed, and he said something about and he said something like I'm only 46, I hope to be around for a while. "Aaaaaahhhhh" *[My Man's Gone Now]* And, of course, the irony, which lodged deep in my brain at the moment, "aaaaahhhhh" stays there still, is that, of course, RE was 46. *[My Man's Gone Now]* and hoped to be around for a while also. Hoped to be around also but he's not.

I I'm here to remind you how merciless time is. Merciless merciless. Time, sometimes it's not even time, it's life, it's death that's merciless. Death comes like a thief in the night even during the daytime. Yes. Yes yes yes. And here I am wearing two watches, Sol's watch which managed to keep 'bout ten minutes time today off and on and my and the watch that that Mother gave for Charlie which Charlie wouldn't wear so I wear so I could tell time. Yes, two watches. Why am I wearing two watches? That's why.

FRIDAY, MAY 3, 1991

Good morning, Gentlemen, it's 7:52 AM, on Friday, May the 3rd, 1991, I just turned off Reisterstown Road onto the Beltway ramp going to work in the morning. Mr. Phelps, Captain Kirk, Captain Picard. Couple days ago I saw, maybe yesterday maybe the day before, in one of the cracks in one of the mortar in in the brick stepway to our house, a dead baby baby baby bird. Naked without feathers, and dead. Pinkish bluish. Then this morning coming out, I don't know if it was the same one that someone had skushed down there or another one, but down on the sidewalk, the walk part leading to our house, down towards where the cross where the main sidewalk is, there was another one lying out there spread-eagled. Another dead bird, baby baby baby bird, baby baby baby baby baby baker bir bir bird bird bird bird bird bububir bubir bir bubirbir bubir bird. Made me think of how when I was walking back in December of '88, around after the time hearing of LS's son's death, and I was walking, and coming out of a drain, sewer drain not a dr sewer a drain pipe, under from under the ground into the gutter, there were two dead bababy baby baby drowned baby birds there. And then today the also the pink of the bodies of the birds. And reading the paper and over a hundred thousand dead in a cyclone in in Bangladesh. And also seeing the thousands and thousands and thousands of petals of blossoms of pink blossoms from the trees. I think they were magnolias, but I'm not sure, pink dogwood, pink dogwood, pink dogwood, like the hundreds of thousands hundred thousands bodies of people and animals floating floating back onto the shores of Bangladesh after they had been washed out and drowned and floating back. The dead birds, the dead people, the dead animals, the dead, the petals floating, swirling in the wind, the petals swirling, in the breeze, and the people floating, floating back, their bodies bloated, bodies bloated bodies bodies bloated floating back, floated bloating bodies floating back bodies bloating floated back.

Borealis Wind Quintet doing *Overture to Porgy and Bess*. The Wind Quintet Quartet. Quartet of winds. Listen to this. *[mike held to speaker]* It's now 8:00 AM 8:00 AM, Friday, May the 3rd, 19-hundred-and-91 years.

[loud music still-Wind Quartet-continues for a long time]

MONDAY, MAY 6, 1991

Good morning, Gentlemen. It's 8:17 AM, Monday, May the 6th. In the background you can hear *Sinbad Sinbad Scheherezade [violin]* playing in the background. In the background *Schehere* **TAPE ENDS**

THE NANCY TAPES

TAPE NUMBER 15B

MONDAY, MAY 6, 1991

Good morning again, Gentlemen. 8:18 now. You can still hear *Scheherezade Scheherezade* playing in the back ground on this foggy grey rainy misty Monday morning, May the 6th. On my way down to work I went up and went to response and went to the Giant, dropped off newspapers, then decided I'd come around, came round 795 and down. I started to get off on Beltway towards Liberty Road, then decided what the heck? I wanted to listen to *Scheherezade* to *Scheherezade* so I came round the Beltway towards, I-83. Pardon me. But there was such a traffic jam already on the Beltway that but fortunately I was able to get off in at Reisterstown Road, now I'm coming down Reisterstown Road down Reisterstown Road Reisterstown Road.

Yesterday met Ron and Di and Amy at the hotel for brunch, and Mother and Lou and Aunt Esther and Nancy and Cheryl came and Jon, and at one point I could hear Cheryl talking to Ronny, and Cheryl asked him something, I didn't quite catch what, probably how he could take Mother's nudging of him. And he was saying, Cheryl, I've lived long enough, and I know now that I've got one life to live and it's my life, and it's tough enough living it, and I don't listen to what other people tell me to do. He said, I no longer I don't even I don't tell my kids what to do anymore, I, do they live their lives, I live my life. And that's the way it is. Or words to that effect.

And whose life am I living? I accepted this pending appointment as Vice President for Academic Affairs, but all along I had been thinking, Do I really wanta do this? Do I really wanta stay in administration? All I really want to is teach and write. When I said that to Soph at one point, she said, Well, but you have other talents as well, you can do other things. Bum-ba-bum! Ba-ba-ba-ba-bum-ba-bum! *[louder Scheherezade]* Bum-ba-bum! Bum-ba-bum!

8:29 8:29 Just passed Royce Avenue. 8:29 AM, just passed Royce Avenue. Royce Avenue passed. Made it past Royce Avenue. 3316 Mohawk 4-2448. Over and out.

Cold Spring Lane and Reisterstown Road. Reisterstown Road and Cold Spring Lane. Reyed light, got the reyed light. Stop now. Over and out. 8:30 AM 8:30 AM Over and out. At Reisterstown and Cold Spring Lane.

[Scheherezade] 8:31 Just passed Keyworth Avenue and PS 59. Coming up now on Springhill Avenue. Here we go just passed Springhill Avenue right now! Over and out. Out and over. Out and under. Over in and under. Under and in. Now here's Violet Avenue, Violet Avenue nnaow! To the left, Kessler's, the former Kessler's.

THE NANCY TAPES

TUESDAY, MAY 7, 1991

Good morning, Gentlemen. It's 7:36, Tuesday, May the 7th, 1991, heading down Liberty Heights, Liberty Road Liberty Heights. Just crossing the WELCOME TO BALTIMORE sign at Northern Parkway. On my way to work this morning early 'cause of the budget meeting. Budget meeting.

When I came out to get the paper this morning, came out to put my stuff in the car, saw the and I noticed that yesterday evening when I got home, all the white blossoms, the sepals from the white blossoms on our white dogwood tree, were scattered on the lawn, and on our sidewalk, in swirls and eddies where they had been swirled and eddied by the wind, the storm that went through Maryland yesterday afternoon. With in some places winds up to 70 miles an hour. It was so bad Paul said that he ran home from the playground, ran home from the basketball court where he was hoopin' with his buddies, and he said they hated to leave 'cause they were having such a good time, but I guess it got so bad that he had to come home. And he ran home.

The white sepals from the white blossoms from the white dogwood. Lay in swirls and eddies where the wind had whipped them and swirled them. The wind and the rain flattened them out. Like the bodies of the dead in Bangladesh. And there was a report this morning on the news that some children, the bodies of children were found tied to the branches of trees where their parents had tied them in hopes of keeping them from being swept out to sea by the terrible winds of the cyclone. What was that book? I have to read that book that I just got from the Jewish Book Club, *God and Evil.*

The music, Gentlemen, that you might have been hearing in the background, although I turned the volume down, was Debussy's *La Merrr, La Merrr,* the tape I made and playing in the car from the album and I can't read the writing 'cause it's it's it's it's on the same record with Ibert *The Ports of Call Port of Call.* But the album number I can't read, this is too small. Print is too small. Print is too small, and I have the shades on. Let me stop this a second.

It's the Boston Symphony with I guess it's Charles Munch, the conductor. RCA Album Number, God, I can't read this handwriting. This stuff's so small. One second, let me stop this for a second now.

Yes, it looks like LM Lunar Monday LM Number 22111 LM Number 22111.

WEDNESDAY, MAY 8, 1991

Good morning. 7:30, Wednesday, May the 8th, 1991. 46 years after VE-Day. In the cool sunshine of a morning in middle. In the cool sunshine of a mid-spring morning early in May. The white sepals, petals of blossoms of the ou dogwood tree, litter the lawn in our front yard. Some will lay where they fell, having floated through the air to the grass below. Others, blown by the winds of the storm that swept through two days ago, scattered on the sidewalk, on our neighbor's on my neighbor's lawn, on the main sidewalk, in the gutter, while I listen here to classical music, a piece whose name I do not even know. And the women walkers, in their jogging suits, in their shorts, in their sweatshirts, in their jackets and hats and caps and slacks, sneakers of many colors on their feet, walk through the development, and the dead in Bangladesh, putrefied from days in the sea, fall apart at the touch, and no one wants to touch them.

WEDNESDAY, MAY 22, 1991

Good morning, Gentlemen. It's 8:15 AM, Wednesday, May 22nd. I'm heading west on in on Route 31 towards New Windsor, and just past the Babylon Vault Company. Is that incredible?! Babylon Vault Company. Dozens upon dozens upon dozens of concrete burial vaults, stacked and stacked in stacks and stacks and stacked in stacks like the apartment buildings in New York. Stack after stack after stack after stack. "Lovely Rita meta maid" In the background.

TUESDAY, JUNE 4, 1991

Good morning, Gentlemen. *[long pause for Benny Goodman clarinet]* Good morning, Gentlemen, it's 7:50 AM, on Tuesday, June the 4th, 19-hundred-and-91. In the background, Benny Goodman *Sing Sing Sing* from the *1938 Carnegie Hall Jazz Concert*. Bop bop-bop-bop 53 years old today! In my prime! In my prime! Here we go, listen to this. *[longish pause for piano solo]* Must find out who the piano solo is by. The other day so of course, I'm going down, I'm heading down Reisterstown Road now, but I'm gonna cut over at Hooks Lane. To go down Park Heights. Go down Park Heights Avenue. Go past Springhill. I need to get those pictures of 2614 and 2616 mounted and framed. Bam-be-dam-bam-bam-be-dam-bam-bam-bam. The other day when I was walking, thinking about BK, BK! Nobody ever got hurt in my memories. Like the time B ran up, we were playing guerrillas? World War II Japanese and the Americans in the jungles. Listen to this piano. *[longish pause for piano]* Uh-oh! I think the batteries are gone!

The light does not stay on all the time, it must mean the batteries are getting weak. But anyhow yes the light's off now. Okay. BK, BE was spread-eagled, tied down by the hands, by the wrists and ankles. B came by with a hunting knife, *["applause"]* and said, Don't worry, B, I'll get you free, to cut the rope, and cut B's wrists. *["stomping right into Krupa's drums"]* But but I don't remember that, and I don't remember the blo I mean I remember that, the concept of it, *["brass-Sing Sing Sing Sing"]* but I don't remember the blood. I don't remember the pain, the anguish, I don't remember, must not have been very bad, either that or I just don't remember it very well. And somebody sat on BE while we were wrestling. Was it B? And he puked. Just sat on his stomach and up come the up-chuck.

THE NANCY TAPES

Time to rewind and go back to *Bei Mir Bist Du Ch'rayn. Bei Mir Bist Du Shayn*. I used to say, *Bei Mir Bist Du Ch'rayn*. And so they didn't get hurt.

And today when I was out walking my walk and walking my walk, I looked up and there was the moon, the waning moon was down to half. The waning moon was already high in the sky, the southwestern sky. But by the time I got back and even by the time I had gone out, it had already begun its slide down the western slope of the sky in the morning. It'd already begun its western slide. Unlike roughly a week ago.

Today's the second anniversary of Tienanmen Square. I remember the poem I wrote two years ago. Haven't written a poem, haven't written a piece for the s paper, even for B, for *The Sun* in two years since October, almost two years. Since October of '89. Wow!

In any case, when I was out last week, I was heading north, the full moon was on my left, just barely up above the horizon. Sniff. And the sun was rising to my left to my right. I remember at 5:18, the sun moon was very low, setting, the setting moon was very low, and the rising sun was still below the horizon, it had not yet risen above the horizon, it was only 5:18. The rising sun below the horizon, the setting sun [*sic*] above the horizon. Opposite each other. That was the day I saw that black cat with the golden eyes. The black cat with golden eyes. The black and white cat. And when I came up from Fitzharding Lane. Better watch this here. Watch it, bitch!

And here's the tape now back to the beginning with *Bei Mir Bist Du Shayn* [*singing*] *Bei mir bist du shayn*. [*longish pause for bei mir*] *Bist du shayn* means that you're grand. Ba-dat-n-dat-n-du-dat-n-da-da. Baaa-ba-ba-baaa.

When I came up from Fitzharding Lane, up Wimbledon around the con street part, between Fitzharding and Countess Drive, [*"bei mir"*] the moon was directly behind me. And then I came around the curve of Wimbledon Lane, when I looked back the moon wasn't there. And it was around to the right. As I curved around to my right, I had to look back, and it was back to the right. The angle had changed because my position my position relative to the moon had changed. Now this had come up before, I remember talking about this. How the moon seems to change its position, but it's actually my position relative to the moon that changes, that seems to change the moon's position. Changing change. "*bist du shayn*"

Thinking about the cards from TS. "please let me explain" The one from Bad Aibling, actually *Mietraching Flughafen*, "means that you're" *Flughafen Mietraching* that's the word, *Flughafen*. "grand" Something Annual spring card. "again I'll explain, it means" To remind you how merciless "you're the fairest" time is, and then one later from *Kishkunfelegihaza*, so this year I got two from him. "I could say *bella bella*" The *Kishkunfelegihazas* of our past. "even say *wunderbar*, each language" How merciless time is, but also how merciful time can be because *Kishkunfelegihazas* sometimes stop being that, and they become simply towns. "I've tried to explain" "*bei mir bist du shayn*" And sometimes they get worse. "so kiss me and say you under" I'm thinking "stand" about Nancy Kanow Via Simpson. And Eva Mae Hirsch Krome. And all our young dead. What was Rose Rosie Krome's maiden name? I have no idea. I need to find that out too. I need to get back down to the Hall of Records in Annapolis and do some research on on the family, birth dates and death dates. I need to get Charlie Krome's birth certificate. "*bei mir*"

8:03. Just crossed Rogers Avenue and Park Heights. *Stompin' at the Savoy.* *[music loud and voice low]* There was A to Z Arthur Kravetz used to be there. Bam-bam-bu-bam-bu-bam-bu-bam-bu-bam-bu-bam-bam-bam

["stompin'"] McDonald's to the left coming Hayward Avenue where the old Pimlico Hotel used to be. *Ava shahlum*, as they used to say, *ava shahlum*.

Ava shahlum. Somebody said that. Was it MW one year? Said that CH had had to have an arterial graft in his leg? Came close to dying.

Passing the old Pimlico Theatre and passing *[voice louder]* Spaulding Avenuuue where Ron and Di [*sic*] used to live *["stompin'"]* many moons ago tha, 30 years ago, Jack! 30 years ago. He graduated from University of Maryland Medical School and moved up into the big Dee-troit. Bam-bam Detroit! Where shortly thereafter in August of 193061 [*sic*]. Not D, Eva. Eva. He lived there with Eva, Eva Mae Hirsch Krome. In August in 1961, Eva died. Bam-bu-dam-bam-bu-dam bam-bu-dam bam bam-bu-dam bam bam bam-bu-dam bam *["stompin'"]* bam bam. Coming down Park Heights Avenue here.

Coming up to the right now St. Ambrose Catholic Church, remember good old St. Ambrose, the Fs used to go there. And to left, to the left someplace over here was place where we had, TEP had a fraternity party, and I took HL. Yes, I remember that. I remember it well. *["Stompin'"]* And passing Wylie Avenue, in the back in there behind St. Ambrose, of course, is, 'cause there's no intersection here with Park Heights, is Royce Avenue 3316 Royce Avenue MOhawk 4-2448. Calling Aunt Freda. Calling Aunt Freda. Or, I can call Raizel REgent 7-7512. 4-1-5-7 Braille. 4-1-5-7 Braille. It's gone. They ain' no more Braille. There Braille. But they ain't no more Raizel and Kenny there. And to the right here Park Lane Shopping Center. I remember Park Lane Shopping Center. Used to walk up here, go to the hobby shop around the corner on Cold Spring Lane. Yeees, coming up. Here now coming up to the corner now, intersection of Cold Spring Lane and Reis and Park Heights Avenue. REVCO which used to be READ'S. And, of course, right across the street is RITE-AID DISCOUNT PHARMACY. How bright!

["Stompin'"] Moving right along, crossing Cold Spring Lane now. And there the fishmarket, I remember that used to be remember the kid S, the kid who was mute, deaf mute. Yes, I remember him from Carlin's Park, and there was a

write-up in the paper about him not too long ago. And the old Avalon Theatre with the marquee all blackened. To the left the what was this? The *Agudas Achim* Synagogue with the and there was the, there was the park here now on the right where R's Hardware used to be. And next door to the synagogue was the that clothing store, the haberdashery where I bought that jacket and my mother made me take it back. And out in front of there the *Agudas Achim* one day, one Saturday, I was walking up it was JS and AA. And one of them said something about not going to *shule*, and that's only for Jews, and making some snide remark, and the other one said something about, Leave him alone, all the good stuff that he does with the kids down at the at the Isaac Davidson Hebrew School, Isaac Davidson Hebrew School Saturday services. And here's coming up now on Shirley Avenue, hey, there's a traffic light on Shirley Avenue. There didn't used to was one. And there was a gas station where there's now the lit little park, Shirley Avenue Street Park, sort of thing. AL'S CUT-RATE LIQUORS which used to be SIDLEN'S PHARMACY. SIDLEN'S. Well, I'm stuck here at the light now for a while. But that's all right. Just kinda hangin' loose. Hangin' loose, hangin', hangin' loose, loose hangin'. And to the right, is a t Shirley Avenue Street Park, but to the right, where Shirley Avenue used to go through to Par Reisterstown Road, there used to be a Time out.

There used to be the playground behind fips PS 59, which is down to the right as I'm coming up here now onto Keyworth Avenue. And that's where W and who else was it? A couple other guys and I we kind of felt up D. Up to the left on Park H on Keyworth Avenue is is is Enoch Pratt Free Library Branch 16. Down to the right was PS 59. *["Stompin'" ends]* Coming up now on, here's Springhill Avenue Spring, we lived up to the left on Springhill Avenue 2614 2616. There it is, and right here, right on the corner, was the Fs, and we passed to the left it was B, D, N. And to the left on the corner was the Gs, H and F and B and their son H. But now I also passed, Cheez! I'm goin' too fast! passed what used to be Kessler's Delicatessen, now passing Sussman's Drugstore at Ulman Avenue. Sussman's Drugstore. Remember the story about C and J. Who knows if it's true? And here's the and what *shule* was this here on Hilldale? And probably was This this was the old *Shaarei Zion* to the right was Roland's Barber Shop Roland E. I used to come down here, and the women useta women useta women useta, when I'd get my hair cut short. And here's *"Sing Sing Sing"* sing. Women useta talk about how I'd get my hair cut short and all my curls, how much they liked my curls. Yeeeaahh, Babe. Ba-da-da-da-da-daaaa-da-da-daaaa. Okay, here we go. Movin' right along here. Comin' down into Park Circle, Henry G. Parks, Jr. Circle now and, of course, Carlin's Park is all gone. It's Parks Sausage now. It's taken over the place. And down to the left now, I'm just here at the traffic light at Park Heights Reisterstown Road coming into the right. To the left is the old reservoir where the reservoir used to be, and we used to go, we used to, we used to go sled riding down the hill of the down the hill of the down the hill of the down the hill of the, used to go sled riding down the hill of the what? down the hill of the reservoir, and one time Ronny went down, there was this car coming and he just couldn't stop and he, he made it past before the car came by. We thought he was a goner. And then they lopped off the reservoir and we used to play softball on the fields there. In high school days, *in illo timpo, ston gero*, that was 40 years ago, Man! No, almost 40. So it was like 1953. So it was 38 years ago. I was like 15, 16, 17, 14, fift 15, 16, and 17. The old Cavaliers. And on the other side of the reservoir there used to be the little flat field where we would play football. And then over on the other side of that across the street was Three Sisters. *[Sing Sing Sing]*

[Sing Sing Sing] Comin' down Reisterstown Road now past Park Circle, to the left is the cutoff, and there the up through Auchentoroly Terrace there's the Auchentoroly Terrace *shule*. Still up there. Still a *shule*. And coming down now. There's that Mount Lebanon Baptist Church, I remember when they were building it. They had to stop for a while. But here we are coming down towards Liberty Heights and Mondawmin. Left here is the old Superintendent of Parks house, I don't think it's in use for anything at all.

And here's the slope of the hill, the little slope, the little the little slope where AS and I had to cut grass with sickles one y that year that I was working in in the parks. And I got that awful awful case of of what? of watchacallit? of poison ivy on my forearms, my two forearms, my four twoarms. *[next number on tape-saxophone]* And I remember, fell asleep holding my arms above my head, lying at the foot of the bed with the in front of the open window and then the moonlight came through during the night, and I woke up looking up at my arms down over my f hanging over my face, with the calamine lotion on them glowing in the moonlight, and scared the shit outta myself. *[sax]* I remember that, do you remember that? What am I doing up here? Oh, yes, I'm coming up here to get some apples maybe. Yes. Okay. Over and out.

DAY AND DATE NOT GIVEN

[strange unclear sounds, almost as though in a train station] [voice like PA system announcement] Good morning.

MONDAY, JUNE 10, 1991

Good morning, Gentlemen. It's 7:54 AM, on Monday, June the 10th, 1991. C News note, last Tuesday on my birthday I got the I got the got the got the got the written confirmation, finally in writing about my new position, even though it will not officially be announced until later this month. In any case in any case in any case, this morning, when I out went walking.

THE NANCY TAPES

Okay, from the other day, last Friday, thinking about the moon, how it's waning we wane watching the waning moon, how it crescents in, verb form, it crescents in, hollows out, the crenscet crescent slims while the hollow bulges, moving in from right to left. So that the horns of the moooon point west! Point in the direction of the setting moon. This morning I came out, and and the moon was high enough in the western sky when I got out, and that part of the sky was still a darkish blue, very dark, and as the as the sky lightened, with the lightening of the sky, the moon also paled and pastelled a little bit. And eventually the the shadows and hollows and the *mares* and the craters of the moon lightened also, and instead of being a dark grey became a pale blue grey, like the sky around the moon so that it appeared that all those things were kind of hooles in the moon, and the sky showed through. The the waning moon was sliding down the western setting s its its the western sky, its setting sky. While the light from the sun was coming up on the eastern sky, the 18th of, was it 5/18? No. It was 5:18 in the morning, that Wednesday. That's what it was. The Wednesday before, which would have been, let's say the the the 1st, 31st, the 29th of May. Okay. It was a half moon and and, full moon, a half moon, and it's essentially this, it is crescented, crescented, crescented in, and this morning, it was a just a very slim sliver, the crescent had crescented in so far that the moon had actually slivered and was a pale a g a not pale, it was a a glowing white thin sliver of a moon. But, of all places, it was in the eastern sky, the southeastern sky. It had not yet gone up to its zenith, to its high point. And and even as it did so, the the, as it was there in the eastern sky, the eastern sky burst, the clouds burst into blossoms of color mostly mostly magenta, bright vivid rich magenta, and here we come coming up on a traffic tie-up. Why didn't I pay attention to the fact that they said it was backing up to Liberty Road? Well, here now it's backing up to 795. So here I am on the Beltway and things are slowing down. Anyhow, magenta. And it slowly pastelled. The s clouds pastelled into a mauve and then pastelled into a white and then finally at the end at about 5:45, when the sun, according to the schedule, had already risen, but I couldn't see the risen sun because of the *[laughs]* Couldn't see the risen sun! Oh, what a pun! Because of the trees on the horizon, but although the clouds higher up had pastelled, verb, note the verb form, pastelled, the clouds had pastelled into a white from a from a magenta into a a pastel mauve, pale mauve, into a a very fine white-orange orange-white which is what they were also last week, and then finally into just a glowing white down at the by the horizon, the clouds were still turned a darker orange and ma richer magenta and purple, just very very rich blossoming colors of, of the clouds the clouds blossomed in colors. But up above, the moon eventually as it as it paled, as the sun rose and as the sky lightened, when I remember it was in the eastern sky, so it the sky was not dark the way it had been previously, but as the as the the sun light came up and as the sky paled to a almost a almost a white a bluish white, the moon also pastelled and faded, and eventually it it almost got lost, and eventually it did get lost behind this big reverse crescent cloud just i a very big cloud but hazy thin fine cloud that looked almost quite literally like a painter's brush stroke, so much so that you could almost see the lines. I could almost see the lines made by the individual hairs on the brush-stroke. That kind of a of a swirl of a painter's brush-stroke on a canvas. And I I just needed to make the mention of that before I forgot. Okay, I think over and out.

And okay, back to 5 it was 5:18 in the morning the moon rise oh, the cats, did I mention the cats from last week? Oh, good grief! Is this an old Edsel? On the right? The cats. Black cat with bright orange-yellow eyes. It is an Edsel! A cat with bright orange-yellow eyes, black cat, very very black so that the eyes just kind of stared right out, came right out so brightly.

And then a black and white cat. With white spots, black cat with white spots. What else? The chipmunks. Oohh, that the birds chirping, the birds chirping. I wish I could remember **TAPE ENDS**

THE NANCY TAPES

TAPE NUMBER 16A

MONDAY, JUNE 10, 1991
[NOTE: On August 12, 1991, I inadvertently over-recorded over the first four pages of material originally recorded on June 10, 1991. When I got to the end of SIDE B, I mistakenly simply turned the tape over and began re-recording on SIDE A; thus, I recorded material from August 12, 1991, over the first four pages of the original June 10, 1991, recording. Those first pages from June 10, 1991, are thus irrevocably and irretrievably lost. I have put the first four pages on this side, i.e., pages actually recorded on August 12, 1991, at the end of TAPE016B.ED1 (NOW TAPE016B.ED2) where they belong.]

[abrupt opening, like something cut off] [Paul] said, Does this mean you have to work all summer? And I said, Yes, and he said, What a bummer! He said, You have to go to work every day? And I said, Yes. What a bummer! And that suddenly put a different perspective on it. Oohh, dear. Oh, dear, oh, dear, oh, dear. And let's say that I put four years in. My acting year and three years on a contract, that's four years. By then, he'll be graduating from high school. And he won't have the summers free. There we go. *[voice breaking]* And there we gooooo! *[crying]* Daaaddyyyyyyyyy! Oooohhhh, dammit! I never had the summers with my father! Sniff! Sniff. Daddy! Daddy, Daddy, Daddy, Daddy Daddy Daddy Daddy Daddy Daddy! Sniff. Come baaaaaccckkk! Come baaacckk!

"Buzzard, keep on flyin' over" It's now 7:56. "Ain't no" Passing Woodland Avenue "body dead" coming down Reisterstown Road "this morning" past Woodland. "living's just" Passing now Virginia. Coming down towards Royce Avenue! Royce! Avenue! "Two is strong where one is" Passing now St. Ambrose Avenue. "feeble" And now, there's the sign! On the left! "unclear" Royce Avenue! 34-hundred block, Royce Avenue, 3316, Mohawk 4-2448. Hi, Aunt Freda! "sharin' grief and" *[crying]* Hi, Aunt Freda. "sharin' laaauughter" Hi, Aunt Freda. "laaaauuughter" Goodbye, Aunt Freda. "and love like"

Comin' down, comin' down Reisterstown Road farther and farther down Reisterstown Road approaching the area the area the place the street the spot the house or the houses, 7:58 am. To the left now, there's Shirley Avenue and the Shirley Avenue Street Park and the I - D - H - S I Do Hate School Isaac Davidson Hebrew School. "pack your things and" And what used to be the playground for PS 59 "fly from here" Louisa May Alcott School. "carry grief and" And there's PS 59 Louisa May Alcott School which is now Alcott Place. And to the right, the remains the remnants the former "two folks livin'" G's Pharmacy and to the left, "in this" the P's Family "shelter" Place, and there to the right was PO's house. Coming up now on "singing" Springhill Avenue, Springhill Avenue, crossing Springhill now, there it is, up there was Jake the Tailor and past there 2614 and 2616, the Kromes and the Kanows. *[mike directed to radio]* "and Porgie's young" Forest 7-3756 "aaaaaa" Mohawk 4-1014 "gaaaiiii" Po'gie's young again. "aaaaaiiiinn" On past Violet where Kessler's used to be, "keep on flyin'" and Ulman Avenue now, Sussman's "Po'gie's" Drugstore. "young" Kessler's. Paul Krome, one of his best friends, "agaaaaaiii" the grandson of Barney Kessler, "aaaiiiinnnnn" Sam and Barney Kessler, owners of Kessler's Delicatessen.

    Coming down now towards Park Circle which is now which is now which is now which is now which is now Henry G. Parks, Jr. Circle. And past where there was, where once used to be Carlin's Park. With Carlin's Pool. Carlin's Pool and the ice rink, and the skating rink. And the amusement park. And the clown's laughter carrying through the night "Bess" up to the house "you is" on Springhill Avenue "my woman now" where the open window where I lay in my bed "you is" with the window open, "you is" my my head at the foot of the bed, "you must laugh" listening to the sound of the laughter of the clown "two instead of oooonnne" *[voice starting to break]* coming through the windoooowww *[almost crying]* coming through the windooooww. "want no"

    And to the left now, the old Reptile House and the remains of the old reservoir cut down years ago even when we still lived in the neighborhood to make ball fields where we used to play ball and before that we used to we used to do what? We used to we used to do what? We used to come down "if you" the "you hear me sayin'" the slope of the reservoir on our sleds. "with you I'm stayin'" And Ronny came down, and I tell this over and over and over and over again. "Po'giiiieeee" Ronny came down, and there was a car coming and we thought he'd had it but he didn't have it because he made it, he got across before the car got there. "IIIIII's your" Fort-u-nate-ly, fort-u-nate-ly, fort-u-nate-ly. Coming down now towards the intersection with Liberty Heights. All right, lady, go by. Coming now to the intersection of Liberty Heights, "Beeesss" where MF lived around the corner on on Liberty Heights. MMF died in, was it his first year medical school, second year medical school cancer of the testiculars testicular cancer. "gie I's" Sshhit!! *[yelled]* Sshhit!! *[yelled]* Sshhit!! "'cept you shall go too" D, his sister, and B, his brother. "there's no wrinkle on my brow"?

DAY AND DATE UNCERTAIN, JUNE ??, 1991

    Good morning, Gentlemen. 7:52 AM Coming down Park heights Avenue towards Old Court Road. Ahead of me as I came down was a crow eating carrion, some animal had been hit by a car and skushed and mashed, and there was gush on the road, and there was the crow eating the carrion. "love you and mourn you" And he flew away and flew away an I oh not away, but left the carrion when the car approached. Reminded me that last night *The Birds* was on tv and there was attack on the on the heroine in the house when she went into a room she should not have gone into. An and this morning also when I was out walking, something happened at 5:26 I made a mental note of, "she'll shame ya and she'll blame ya" but I can't remember what it was. But anyhow, something but I also noticed this morning that that it was ver it was clear, it was cool "a woman is a" it was calm, "soome time thiing" and even the birds that were chirping were calmly chirping, not loudly, but calmly chirping. And today as we walked out, Soph and I walked out to our cars to go to work, she said that, we were talking about Paul. "let a woman grieieve ya" And she was saying how she was trying not to get too emotional because he's finishing middle school now, and tomorrow's his last day, and she said that he said something about "'caaauuuse" and incidentally in the background is *A Woman Is a Sometime Thing* from *Porgy and Bess*.

He said something about she that they had they talking about the time passing, and and she said something about how the year had passed quickly, and he said, La Last year had passed quickly, but but this year had passed even *more* quickly. And then he said to her something like, I'm not a little kid anymore, Mom. And she said, Yes, but you'll always be my baby. And then he said something about how he didn't like growing up, he was having too much fun just being a kid. And I think that's absolutely marvelous. He doesn't wanta grow up. And I said, I know exactly how he feels. Now getting coming on is *My Man's Gone Now*. I said I know how exactly how he feels because, when I was a kid I had my father, but then when I was 16 I didn't have a father anymore! And now I don't have a father, now I am a father. Father. In any case, and I said to Soph that he never says anything like that to me, and she said, well, he does to her once and only once in a while. And I said, Yeah, I said, but he *never* says things like that to me. And she said maybe because she always calls him her baby, and stuff like that, and I don't know, maybe that's why it is, but I felt like crying because of that, too. Feel like crying because of a lot of things. But that's one of them. "loose my man"

And another is *My Man's Gone Now*. "since I loose my maaan" 'Kay. And here it is on "Ooooooooooooooo ooooooooooooo" 7:56. Getting ready to go in, I'm going to Nancy's, getting ready to make a left turn here on Smith Avenue to drop off the stuff about the about the family reunion.

Picking up a little bit later, 7:57. Reminded me how, when I told Charlie that we were going to Ocea to Florida instead of Ocean City, "my man's gone now" his head kind of rocked back and he was dis obviously disappointed that we weren't going to Ocean City. Even though he wouldn't really be going with us 'cause he's working, but might be able to get a couple days, and I know Paul was also a little disappointed when we weren't going to Ocean City, and I don't know if it's because he misses us at Ocean City or or if he just doesn't wanta go that far away or, actually I'm gonna miss Ocean City, going to the Crab House and taking Paul fishing. Taking Paul fishing. This may be the last. *[almost crying]* Last year, 1990, may have been the last time I take any of my kids fishing. *[crying] [yells]* Dammit!! Dammit!! Dammit!!

"Lookin' lean and hungry" It's 8:09, down Park Heights. "let dat buzzard keep on hangin' round my doooooor" My dooooooor. Passing now Arthur Kravitz A to Z Studios. On Park Heights Avenue coming down, passing now McDonald's. The once "Step up, brother" and not again home of the Pimlico Hotel. Yes. Yes yes. Yes. Yes yes. Yes. Yes.

Crossing Belvedere Avenue and the old Doctor Davis dental place upstairs and "What is you anyhow?" the old Pimlico Thee-aterrr. And Sssspaaauuulding Avenuuuuee Ronny and Eva Spaulding Avenue and the Uptoowwnn Theatre. U - P town Uptown "pack your things" U - P Up "and fly from here" UPS and Garrison Avenue. "carry grief" Up up up And the old Luskin's.

Just passed the St. Ambrose Church and Wylie Avenue and now in front of Park Lane, Park Lane. Lark Pane. Womp! Park Lane. Again. At 8:11 AM. Huh-huh-hyuh-huh-huh.

What used to be Read's, now REVCO. And now there's the old fishmarket what used to be Carmel's, SC. And the Avalon Theatre. "Bess, you is my woman now" And the fire station and the street park where Avalon Hardware used to be and the haberdasher next "you is" across the alley from the Alamo "and you must laugh and dance" across the alley "and sing" from the *Agudas Achim* "for two" *shule*. "instead of ooooooone" AA and JS, was it? that who it was? Yes.

"want no wrinkle on your brow" One of whom made a remark about my, about *shule* being for Jews and my not being there, and the other of whom said something about how I was helping out the kids in the I Do Hate School Isaac Davidson Hebrew School *shule* Saturday services there with GP, Mr. P's son. Okaaiiyy? Okaaiiyy. And there's the which *shule* is this that was a church became a *shule* and now it's a church again? The big old greystone building. And there where the gas station used to be at Shirley Avenue has been a little street park type area with a dooeeve. "Porgy, I's your" And to the right Shirley Avenue Street park, down to the right I Do Hate School Isaac Davidson Hebrew School, and to the left there was Sidlen's Pharmacy is now a liquor booze place. And here we come to Keyworth Avenue.

And up to the left wuz iz Enoch Pratt Free Library Branch 16, 'n' to the right is Louisa May Alcott School, PS 59. And here we come acrossing Springhill Avenue to the right Jake the Tailor's, to the left the memorial! the memorial! immemorial houses 2614 and 2616 Springhill Avenue. *Ava shahlom* as they say, and there was Violet Avenue where Kessler's used to be on the corner. Kessler's *ava shahlom* reconverted into a house, reconverted into house and passing Sussman's drugstore, where I used to go to get sundaes and comics on Friday nights. *Shaarei Zion* here at Hilldale, and there was Roland E's Roland's Barber Shop but the time that w used to at the time, but the time, the time but the time what happened? Yes, when I went down, and my mother wanted more of her Equanil, and I came down and asked him, and there was he talking to a customer. She never told me you needed a prescription! And he said, Well, you need a prescription, "Po'gie I'se" tell your mother to get the prescription filled, and I'll give her some more. Okay, thank you. "nooowww" SJ Perlman, *Under the Spreading Atrophy, or The Road to Miltown*.

At the traffic light, I'm on Park Heights, to my right is Reisterstown Road, "nooooooowwwww" at the former Park Circle, now Henry G. Parks, Jr. Circle. Parks' famous flavor sausage, the new building here. It's become a quasi-industrial park instead of the old Carlin's Park, swimming pool, roller rink, ice rink, amusement park, and I still in my mind's ear hear the laughter of the clown, the mechanical clown, at night. I know how you feel, Paul. It ain't necessarily so, Jack.

FRIDAY, JUNE 14, 1991

Good morning, Gentlemen. It's 9:31 AM, Friday, June 14th, Flag Day, 1991. I'm on my way back to Coppin, coming from the Triple-A building down on Mount Royal Avenue where I had gone to pick up a map to route us to Virginia Beach and also to get some   get some get some getsomeuh traveler's checks, traveler's checks, and when I walked in, they had moved! They had moved! What was in there was their corporate offices or something like that, and their automotive services, but but the touring agency had moved out to Lutherville! And now they said it had moved in March of 1990, it had been in several newsletters and all this kinda crap. But I couldn't believe it!   I c one of those disorienting, disconcerting, totally discombobulating, sukiyaki-devastating experiences. Bleeeehhhhh!

WEDNESDAY, JUNE 19, 1991

Good afternoon, Gentlemen. It's 4:51, Wednesday, June the 19th. Surprise. Mr. Phelps, Captain Kirk, Captain Picard. I'm sitting in a condo, in the master bedroom of a condo, in Sanibelll, on Sanibel Island, off the coast of Fort Myers, Florida. Howyalikethemapples?!

Couple quick comments I needed to get in here while I have the chance. We did drive down Friday afternoon, mad dash down to Virginia Beach. Mad dash up from Virginia beach on Sunday. Paul had a greeeaaat time with Stelio and Angie Nicholas. And Sunday we made a mad dash back up to Baltimore to Owings Mills, saw Charlie for a minute, packed up, headed for the airport. Well, we were already packed. Unpacked some stuff, shifted some stuff around, met Pana at the airport. Almost *mou pireh to panicko* on that plane going down before the flight even. And had a vodka and then another vodka. Paul kept telling Soph about the lights of the cities going by. What I didn't realize until they told me later was that what he was looking at was lightning, and it was just really awesome. But he didn't tell me, of course, 'cause he was afraid that I would *pireh to panicko* and I would panic and get nervous and scared and all that stuff. Which was very nice of him. He really watched out for me. So Sunday night we got to Sanibel. Monday we did a little shopping. Tuuueeesdaaayy, I went for my morning, went for a morning walk, I left at 7:20. Went past, headed east went past marker 5-and-a-half, then 5. And I wound up at marker 3-and-a-half.

And some things that I wanted to talk about. Yes, dead fish. Here and there a dead fish lies, the flies, flies of some kiind swirling above. One fish, his eyes eaten out or rotted away, lying on his side. His left side exposed. Dark and eaten away, the bones not white but dark brown. The birds. Yes oh, and thinking that, picking up the s the shells and the shells, later as I said to Soph, were cephalopods and even was thinking about that that the cephalopods, they think with their foot, I almost said think with their feet, but they only have one, think with their foot. They walk with their head. As opposed to the mollusks, which are, I guess, the bi-valve or whatever they're called. Anyhow, also yesterday I saw a yellow sign, small yellow sign that said "WARNING DO NOT DISTURB SEA TURTLE NEST something like SUBJECT TO A PENALTY OF FINE OR IMPRISONMENT OR BOTH PLEASE DO NOT PLEASE DO NOT PLACE BEACH FURNITURE DIG OR DRIVE A STAKE WITHIN 10 FEET OF THIS SIGN SUBJECT TO PENALTY OF FINE OR IMPRISONMENT OR BOTH IF YOU SEE ANYBODY DISTURBING THIS PLEASE CALL DEPARTMENT OF FLORIDA STATE DEPARTMENT FLORIDA DEPARTMENT OF NATURAL RESOURCES PHONE NUMBER

And the birds, the pelicans, pelicanspelicans. And there were some that had like white caps around their heads, the top back of the head, and they were white underneath. Most of them were grey and dark. There were two different kinds of white birds that I saw yesterday. Smaller ones, thinner ones, white with a short only slightly curved, very very slightly curved black beak and black legs and yellow toes with black talons. So they were the black-beaked, black-legged, yellow-toed, black-taloned white birds. Then there the white ones, a little bit, slightly larger, 'n' slightly off-white with a longer red beak, distinctly curved and about twice as long, and red legs and red feet, I think. Okay.

I talked about the turtle, right, the cephalopod, and the fli fish, and the flies, and the beer bottle on the beach and the k today also a red Coke can on the beach, yesterday also a red Coke can. So yesterday it was from 7:20 and I got back about 8:50. Today I got out, got up earlier, woke up, it was 6:30, and it was grey out, and by the time I got out it was 7:00 and it cleared. And I walked to the west this time. And when I went past the just past the 6 mile marker, I saw one of those yellow sea turtle signs the one I came it was about twenty yards past it. When I came back later, I noticed that there was a there were two of them actually there. I had missed the second one. And when I I went up. And at 7:25, I saw clearly the tracks, what was clearly the tracks of a sea turtle coming up from the sea, depositing its eggs, I think, although I couldn't really tell if there really eggs had really been deposited. And then gone back down, and that was, as I later measured it, approximately, I thought at the time it was twenty yards, later saw it was about fifty yards be fifty yards inside of the PUBLIC ACCESS WALKWAY NUMBER 2 sign. That was at 7:25 this morning, and when I saw that, I suddenly realized, I'm not sure how, but it made me think of why I was looking just for this particular kind of shell, what Paul called yesterday just the weird ones, conch shell type spiralled ones. And it what it made me think of was the conch shell that my father brought back from the Philippines, that Daddy brought back from the Philippines, and probably a few others, I think, but basically one from the Philippines.

And I walked on farther and at 7:45, just inside, and it turned out it was about twenty yards inside of Mile Marker, not Mile Marker, PUBLIC ACCESS WALKWAY 6, was another set of tracks coming and tracks going out of of what was apparently also again a sea turtle. And that's when also what occurred to me was, what there was about these shells, not just that but multi-chambered memory. Thinking of the chambered nautilus, that curls around and coils around itself, but this was the multi-chambered memory. What I also realized that there are multi-chambered memo*ries*, that is, each memory within a chamber had many chambers to it, and there were many different things inside those each memory, so there are memories are multi-chambered and memory itself is multi-chambered. Incidentally, reminded me also that yesterday, when I was out yesterday morning, I did see a sand carving of an octopus, and it was really just was really very good with the eight tentacles, and someone, I don't think I noticed it on the way up, but I noticed on the way back someone had actually stepped right in where the face, let's say roughly would have been in the center of the head of the octopus. Also there were a couple of sand castles built, with using cups or metal things as caps. There was another one today, also of a sand castle, a better one, one that seemed to have a whale with it.

Multi-chambered memory, multi-chambered memories. There was the what looked like perhaps an empty shell of a crab burned yellow-ish orange, lying in the sun. There was also a catfish partly eaten away. And thinking about the turtles. The first one I went past, inside PUBLIC ACCESS WALKWAY 2. The turtles bury their eggs underneath. And thinking about how some of the shells I found were on the top surface, others were partly buried, and others were only fragments lying on the top so that you thought the whole thing was buried, but when you picked one I picked it up, there was nothing else except what was on the top. And my eye eventually got pretty good at just picking out those orange-ish colored shells that that I really liked so much.

And farther on up where probably, much much farther up near where I would have been, there was a a four-part conduit looked like with the center part looking like a lighthouse with a widow's walk. And I saw what looked to be a double.

Anyhow by that grey lighthoused one, lighthouse type thing structure in the center four parts sticking out, there was like a doubled sea turtle sea turtle track. Yesterday I was thinking about how lackluster and ordinary the architecture was, and then I suddenly realized that all these shells are pretty much essentially the same, also just the way the architecture is. Okay. Over and out.

Except that there's something different about each of the shells, mainly because they come just in parts and pieces, mainly. Thinking also about Paul. We're getting ready this evening, it's now 5:05. We're gonna be taking him back up to the school to play basketball, he played on Monday from 6 to 8. He played six out of eight games with guys twenty in their 20's and 30's. And some of them maybe a couple of them in their 40's, maybe, couple. But in their 20's and 30's. And he really held his own, it was just incredibly beautiful to see him. One guy named B really kind of helped him out and gave him encouragement. Afterwards I thanked him. He asked how old Paul was, and I said he was 13. He said he thought he was 16 or 17. And it was just sooo beautiful to watch him, he w just incredible determination, he just kept going, and he held his own with those guys.

[THURSDAY?, JUNE 20?, 1991 NOTE: ALTHOUGH I ORIGINALLY TYPED THE DAY/DATE AS GIVEN, THIS IS ACTUALLY STILL WEDNESDAY JUNE 19, PER COMMENTS ON BEGINNING OF SIDE B, NOTED ON WED 11/6/96 7:41 AM]

On the beach. Billions, asss Carl Sagan would probably say it. Billions and billions of shells in many places just crunched and broken. The crunch of broken shells, just incredible quantities of them.

And this guide book at one point said be careful how you step, not to step on the new deposit, the new layer of shell each day, because they could be somebody else's treasure.

Also today, Paul and I were in the water, and we saw, or it's, actually he spotted it first and pointed it out to me, in a kind of a dog fight a big black bird with a light head, light part of the head was white. Going after a small much smaller white bird. Just wheeling and turning, both of them. Until another white bird came over, and then the black bird broke off the attack. And then it just curved and swirled looking, obviously apparently looking for food in the in the sea, in the Gulf of Mexico which is so warm, the Gulf waters are so warm. And just spiralled, more closer and closer to land, and I kept thinking of Yeats' "pern in a gyre," "pern in a gyre."

Looking at one point as though it were looking at us. As possible food. But fortunately, he did not decide to come down and try us out.

FRIDAY, JUNE 21, 1991

Good afternoon, Gentlemen. It's 4:35. Friday, June the 21st. This is the summer solstice, the longest. In Point Barrow, Alaska, they have twenty-four hours of sunshine. DC has some and I don't even remember what they have. It's in the US **TAPE ENDS**

THE NANCY TAPES

TAPE NUMBER 16B

FRIDAY, JUNE 21, 1991
    Say today. I just picked up on the other side of the tape. I don't remember what they are, I'll have to check them out. But I just wanted to get a few things down before I forget. Actually, couple days have passed, Gentlemen.
    Let's see, on Wednesday, one of the things I think I forgot to put down on tape was thinking about the beach and the shoreline, aaaallll the layers of shells and thinking the shell-encrusted shore. Or the shell-encrusted beach. And the pelican-peopled shore. Landward and seaward, pelican-peopled. Landward and seaward. Making me think of I what I thought of was Dylan Thomas "the heron-priested shore." And I want would want people to think of that "heron-priested" when I say peligan pelican-peopled and shell-encrusted. And the shell-encrusted shore, the beach. In Pana's book on shells on Sanibel, it said something about how you need to be careful stepping not to step on the newest layer of shells because they could be someone else's treasure, i.e., because of all the shell hunting, the shelling, as they call it.
    But thinking oofff the shell-encrusted shore as a barrier, a berm, like the antitank barriers and berms in Iraq. Designed to keep the sea in and people out. Or to keep people in and the sea out. Doesn't. Not working either way. The sea breaks out, comes in. Or goes in. People move out, come in to the sea or go in to the sea. It works both ways or does not work both ways.
    Yesterday, n no, Wednesday morning also, I saw this tall grey bird, one near a fisherman just kind of standing there, and Pana said les yesterday, It's what they call "Big Bird," a big heron who just stands there.
    Yesterday morning, I guess it was, Thursday morning, when we first went to try to go deep-sea fishing, a blue heron flew up, or Pana called it a blue heron, but it was smaller than that big bird but it was just an incredible blue to bluish-black color. Gleaming. Looked almost like one of those small white birds but a little bit bigger but not as big as that big bird. And then when we got to the deep-sea fishing place yesterday morning, Thursday morning, I took a picture of one of those big ones, and they had a couple of those birds, and the woman said they were blue herons. But they were different from the one that we saw flying up as we drove out of Seascape. Which was clearly blue, definitely blue, a dark blue, almost a black, but with a shine to it.
    And last night, there was a thunderstorm, actually, it was a lightning storm off to the east. And Paul and I, it was so spectacular Paul wanted to see it, so we went down onto the beach and took the camera and tried to take some pictures. And it just covered like on the eastern part of the sky, oh, maybe a third of the horizon all together. It just moved from the left to the right and back again. Great, from so far

away we we heard no thunder whatsoever, but there were huge flashes of light behind clouds that would silhouette the clouds and silhouette the trees, and there would be streaks of lightning going horizontally or j almost diagonally above the clouds or at least, not above the cloud, above the low clouds in the distance just above the horizon. Above the clouds above the horizon. Ththen in the distance at sometimes, especially towards the left, the lower left end, we would see what would appear to be just tiny bolts of lightning, but clearly they were miles and miles away, and there was a bolt of lightning coming down from a thick layer of clouds down through the air to hit the sea. And we could we could even see those. And there was about a half moon. Kind of cloudy at first-ish a bit, and then it it kind of cleared, and it was very very clear on the beach. Very clear. And we stayed out for fifteen or twenty minutes and watched some more from the deck, or the lanai, as they call it. And it was just kinda great standing out there with Paul. Watching that just amazing display of lightning. And a shift a rolling flash just moving from the right down to the left and back and a lot in the center and a lot in the more in the center and up to the right and some of the right ones were farther away up beyond the condos and we couldn't even see them. Except we could see the the fl the glow of the light behind the clouds and above some of the clouds. Just an incredible display of of pyrotechnics of lightning flashing. Just a few with the little lines of lightning that we're used to seeing. Many of them we we just saw was the glow of the air and the glow of the clouds, come probably coming off from some of those. Magnificent!

Yesterday, Thursday, also, we stopped at the Jimmy Connors Sonesta Spa Rev Resort Hotel, whatever it's called. And took the guided tour, and the guy showed us around in the tennis stadium, and pointed up to the top where there was an osprey nest, so I managed to get a picture of the osprey nest. And the BETAR bed, I didn't take a picture of the BETAR bed, but at least the guy let Paul lie in the BETAR bed. Over and out. Out and over. Over and under. Onder over.

MONDAY, JUNE 24, 1991

Good morning, Gentlemen. Good morning again, Gentlemen. It's, what the hell time is it? It's 8:36. Monday, June the 24th. I'm on my way down Reisterstown Road going to work this morning. After a week in uh Sanibel. The weekend before that in Virginia Beach.

Aaaannnd talking to Pana last night on the phone when we called to thank her for everything and she called back. And she said how lonely she was down there now that we're gone. Aaaannd she said how we talking about Paradise in in and I I think she said but it's always nice when you have *parea*, and I said, well, that sounds like the title of a good story. "Even in Paradise You Need *Parea*." Or, "There's *Parea* in Paradise."

Thinking also. Let's see. Friday night, after the fishing trip, late Friday night early Saturday morn sometime after we went to sleep, just incredible display of thunder, thunder rolling thunder rolling thunder rolling. On and on. And I remember thinking the night, two nights before, the night before when Paul and I were out on the beach but even even before then, before we went out on the beach, that time we couldn't, there was no thunder, there was no sound, it was just the lightning. But then that but I did hear a couple of good rolling thunders out on the beach, and the sound was incredible, and it reminded me of the sound of the thunder on the Aegean when I was on the boat going to Athens.

But anyhow Friday night the thunder rolled as spectacularly as the lightning h'd flashed the night before, and then Saturday night. That reminds me, incidentally, that on the flight down on Sunday, Paul kept saying to Sophie something about the lights of the city, but actually what he had been looking at was the lights of lightning displays. But he didn't want to tell me 'cause he didn't want to f scare me.

Anyhow also Saturday Saturday we went to Mucky Duck ca Captiva and had seat in the second row watching the sun set as we ate and then going outside and watched the actual sunset, and how the waitress had told Pana it was a setting at 8:24 and went out and watched it set. And in the distance at the horizon, one of the things that I decided that made it so spectacular, and it was it was it was a pastel spectacularity if one may use that kind of phrase. Because of the sheer expanse of the of the sea around it. Reminded me of watching the sunsets at Carmel where you look out into the vastness of the Pacific. Here the vastness was not as great, but you didn't know that. What what you did know was that the sea was calmer, because it was the Gulf. And not the not the Pacific. But anyhow in the far far distance, there was there was like there was a layer of clouds and a space and then there were some of those tall spiralling, towered clouds that were beyond that, and it was as though they were way beyond actually the base of them was beyond the horizon, they were sticking up above the horizon. So that the you would see them silhouetted, starting from under the sea to above the sea and under the upper layer of clouds under which the sun's cuh rays were the sunlight was coming. And it reminded me the night that Paul and I had been out watching the watching the the lightning, and how we could occasionally see tiny jiggles of lightning. Far far off at the horizon under the cloud bank between the in that tiny space between the cloud bank and the and the horizon of the sea.

Just turned around now down onto Liberty Heights Liberty Road which becomes Liberty Heights. And forgot what I was thinking this morning as I was on my walk, all of a sudden it occurred to me that it's been thirty years since Ruth and Dave got married. Was it June the 19th? Or the 16th? Or the 17th? Somewhere around there. And I missed their 30th Anniversary. I have to try to remember to call tonight. Even as I thought about before, why I always think so much about death. I thought before and put in one of these tapes a while back about how in August at the time of the family reunion it would be the 30th Anniversary of Eva's death. August 15th, 1961.

Anyhow back to Sanibel and Captiva and thinking about about a poem, how we were on our way, it was 8:30 after 8:3 but see when s watched the sunset, and it was beautiful, it was not spectacular, but it was beautiful. We didn't stay very long after the sun had set to watch what Pana later called the afterglow which we did see as we were going heading down the coast towards to go back to Sanibel. That's part of where the spectacularity lies is in the afterglow not in the setting itself. But in any case, we headed back, and as we crossed over onto Sanibel on Sanibel heading east, all of a sudden we could see more displays of lightning. And again no thunder, no sound. East, probably over Fort Myers, I guess. There was this enormous, in the darkening sky in the East there was this enormous whitish cloud, it looked very very much like the V-Ger cloud in *Star Trek The Motion Picture*. It had that strange shape, I'm not sure what it's called, I'd have to find out what it's called, look up what it's called. Almost like a mushroom cloud, the top of a mushroom cloud in a nuclear explosion. But it was whitish only, barely whitish in the darkening sky, and above was slightly more than a half moon giving off its light. When we got to Windows on the Water and looked up, and there we could see as we were walking across the parking lot, Pana want said what what is that? It was a bright star, it was Venus and Jupiter, and right next to Venus, very very tiny barely visible, in the glow from Venus was a tiny reddish dot which was Mars.

Thinking later about wri about a poem about heading east from Captiva, east from the Mucky Duck, after the sun set. That dog-leg right and left past some of the shore stores and shops, the dog-leg right and left, where there was no parking, where I pulled over to catch the afterglow and tried to take one quick picture of the afterglow. And then coming out from the, the congested, what's the word? congested not the word congested. Aaahhh Constricting congested, you know, when you feel when you've got the sensation that you hate narrow spaces. Claustrophobic, road closed in by the narrowness of the road. The narrowness of the trees and then the more openness of the road on, once you pass Blind Pass, interesting name, Blind Pass. And come across Blind Pass. See, and I never did get that book. I happened to see it one time. And I should have gotten it right then, but I didn't. Anyhow.

Blind Pass onto the road on Sanibel and suddenly there's more expanse. Of course, even Sanibel is narrow, but rel things are relative and narrowness of Captiva, the widening of of, what is it? Of Sanibel and then the wh the greater widening, of course, once you get onto the mainland. But going from the fading light of sunset over the sea, the lightning on the other side, and the moonlight and the stars above, not the stars, the planets, in that case Venus and Jupiter and Mars. It was after 8:30, and the sun had gone down and so we got in our cars and left the M car and left the Mucky Duck, left the people sitting on the beaches, on the beach, with their cameras and their video cameras and their camcorders and their drinks and their beers in their hand, their drinks, the wine and their beers in the hand and people going back across to their homes and their condos and we made the dogleg right, and there was the afterglow and then we made the dogleg left and I pulled in. And across Blind Pa took a picture and across Blind Pass and Paul tried a couple pictures that were left for the lightning. But who knows what we got, if we got anything. On that set.

    And I guess it was on the plane or was it in the car or someplace in the car, maybe on the way to the airport, talking to Sophie about, thinking about Paul and what he said about how what a bummer it would be it was going to be, that I was going to have to work all summer. Thinking how, is it worth it? And then she said, Well, of cour, yeah, she said, Well, it's professionally, for you, it is worth it. And I remember that sh she also thought I should take it, it wasn't just me. But thinking, I almost cried talking with her, and I'm not sure that she felt quite what I felt or what I wanted to say about how for years there won't be summers to spend with him anymore, because he will be graduating from high school and like Charlie he'll be getting a summer job *et cetera et cetera* and going to college, and and it just will not be the same. And she said she said that's why you have to take each day as it comes. Take each day. It's good for me professionally, but part of the reason I took it also was that I wanted to take it, but also I still I wanted just to teach and write. And it would've been great to give up being Executive Assistant to the President and be able to teach and write. And have the summers off to write and to be with the family and the kids. That's, I know, less money and maybe less satisfying in some ways, but also much more satisfying in others. Aaawww, shit, man! Get off my back, Sidney!

    Shall I give it no more than four, should I give it four years and no more than four years? I'll be 57. Or give it five years? At the most. I've given this four. I need to give this, I've given the Executive Assistant to the President four. Need to give that also maybe four at the most. And then he'll be graduating from high school, and then, of course, we'll *really* need the money. I need to start socking and socking and socking money away for him and for Charlie. Just poor planning. Very poor planning. Very poor planning. The trips. Everything else. All the spending. There it goes, man, there it goes. I think your chance of ever really just devoting yourself to teaching the way. You didn't do it before, did you? No, y 'cause you always just piddle-farted around. Oh, well.

    Okay, didn't record.

THE NANCY TAPES

MONDAY, JULY 15, 1991

Good morning, Gentlemen. It's 6:45 AM on Monday, July the 15th, 1991. I'm on my way around the Beltway to Liberty Road to go down to Coppin to pick up some stuff so I can go to my first ever Chancellor's Council Presidents' Council and Chancellor's Council meeting at which I am representing the president. It's been a looonng time since I've recorded anything, I don't remember how many weeks, I'll have to check it out sometime. One of the things that happened in between is that the I had accidentally pushed the button and it played everything out, so I rewound anyhow, so I'm picking up till now.

Now, two weeks ago today, I started as Vice President for Academic Affairs at Coppin. I was quite moved when I walked down the hall and saw the sign that said VICE PRESIDENT, ACADEMIC AFFAIRS. Very very moving, almost cried a little bit.

Today I'm probably almost gonna cry again a little bit some more 'cause today is the 37th Anniverserary, name your beneficiarary from that movie, Anniversary of Daddy's death. It was a Thursday, not a Monday. This early in the morning everybody was still sleeping. All right, is this guy gonna let me in or not? No, he's not. What an assshooolle! Okay.

Anyhow. Something I thought of over the weekend, sort of related to that is I remember when I was in Parisss after the war heh! heh! heh! Paris after the Army, and I was studying Fraanche at the *Institut Catholique*, and G from *Belgique*, *un Flemanduh*, with wheum I hung around, and the Spanish C something-or-other, I think his name was C. Could be totally wrong. But anyhow one of the things that G used to say was the French expression, *Ça m-est egal. Ça m est egal*. That is all equal, is all one to me, it doesn't really matter to me. It In other words, so that's a fourth person to add Oh, oh! Watch out, Sidney! For the truck!

All right, now I am safely onto Liberty Road after that truck did not yield, and I had to che! pardon me, wheeze, watch out for him. But anyhow, G used to say, and I picked up from him, *Ça m'est egal!* That is, It's all the same to me! It is equal to me! It is all equal t *Ça m est egal*. And I realized, of course, that in addition to Perry Neam, Ian Naow, eh-cheh! And who's the third? Perry Neam. Ian Naow. Perry Neam and Ian Naow. Who was that third one? Perry Neam. Ian Naow. And there's a third character I wanted to have as heroes of my novel. But, I can't remember who the third was, but any case, I just remembered, of course, that there has to be a fourth. And that is the famous Armenian, Sam Etegal! Perry Neam, Ian Naow, and who was the third? Perry Neam. Ian Naow. There was another one. And anyhow now comes also Sam Etegal. Sam Etegal.

37 years today. Went to Kessler's. Dad went to work. And he diiieed. He died died died died died. *Dayeinu*. Died died died *dayeinu*. It would have been enough, and it certainly was enough. Ah, nooo, 'tis not so deep as a well, no, nor

so wide as a church door, but 'tis enough. 'twill serve. That was GS, the black cook. The summer I was 19. Or was it 18? 19. Working at the Penn-Mar Hot Penn Rock Hotel in Penn-Mar, Maryland. And then I found out later, of course, that the lines were frommm *Romeo and Juliet*. And Rome-owed what Juli-et.

Sam Etegal. Sam Etegal, Perry Neam, and Ian Naow. But who was the other one? Someplace on one of these tapes I have his name. Sam Etegal, Perry Neam, Ian Naow. It's on the tip of my brain.

37 years, Dad. *[crying]* 37 years. Watch out, Jack! 37 years. I have devastated my own *sukiyaki* or Suki Tawdry. I have devastated my own *sukiyaki*. I went to *shule* yesterday. *[laughing]* That is funny! The rabbi said right away, Do you have a *yuhrtzeit*? Because people don't come, like me, I don't come now unless they have a *yuhrtzeit*. Suki Tawdry. I devastated my own *sukiyaki*. Sam Etegal. Perry Neam. Ian Naow. And

It's funny, the other day, this is still Monday, July the 15th. It's just 6:53 AM. It's funny that the other day, B said something like, I'm not really deeply religious, I'm not very mystical, he said, but I believe that God wanted you to be here. That is, to be at Coppin. With my writing abilities to help write get through this. Well, I'm not so and I said something like how there are always there are mysterious coincidences, and how I had been writing for jobs, and I told him about the letter to Bethany and that the person what it that guy, I didn't mention his name, but that he had taken the position. And that otherwise it would have been offered to me. *Ça m'est egal.* What it makes me think also of how I said once to Soph that I was born to teach and write. And she said that there were other talents that I had. But I really think now that I was born to teach and to write. And I've gotten myself off into all this other crap. Swayed and influenced. Pander myself. It's like S said that he believed that God wanted me to be Jewish. I need to call S. God wanted me to be Jewish. I think what I didn't recognize was that also that I wanted me to be Jewish, maybe that's what S meant. To be a Jewish teacher and writer. To be Jewish and to teach and to write.

Sam Etegal, Perry Neam, and Ian Naow. Who was the other one? Who was the other one? Sam Etegal, Perry Neam, Ian Naow, and who else?

WEDNESDAY, JULY 17, 1991

All right, guys. Now this may strike you as a strange time to be calling, but it's Wednesday, July the 17th, it's 22:43, that's something like about seventeen minutes to eleven at night. But I just had to call because I have to tell you that last night? or this morning, either last night before I went to bed or this morning after I shaved, I suddenly remembered the name of the other guy! It was Perry Neam, Ian Naow, now I added Sam Etegal the other day. Remember that? But the th original third one, whose name I had forgotten, *[whispers]* was Peter Burns! Remember?

THE NANCY TAPES

Don't get any on your peter 'cause it burns. Peter Burns, Ian Naow, Perry Neam, and Sam Etegal. How's that?

MONDAY, JULY 22, 1991

Hey, guys, good evening, it's 10:28 Monday night, July 22nd. Surprise, surprise! Back home tonight I watched *Pinochio*, and at the end I realized, and then I cried because I realized because I realized Pinochio saved his father's life. He went down und downie ocean down under the ocean and got into Monstro the monster whale of a whale, and he got Monstro to sneeze his father out, and he saved his father from drowning when his father was almost drowning. When his father said, Go save yourself, Heeeyy! What did Pinochio say? He said, Whoa! And he took his father and he saved Papa Gepeto and he saved his father from drowning, from Monstro the monster whale, the whale of a whale. He saved his father's life. Whoa! Shit! He saved his father's life.

That's the tv in the background up here in the room, in the bedroom. Whoa!

MONDAY, AUGUST 12, 1991

Good morning, Gentlemen. After a an incredible hiatus, I don't know how long the hiatus was, even so how can I call it incredible? Here it is Monday, August the 12th, it is 7:21 AM. Have I told you lately that I've been promoted to Vice President for Academic Affairs? I don't think I ever even mentioned that. Which the which happened what? five six weeks ago, I guess, July the 1st was my first day. Today is Monday morning, and it's a bright, it was a beautiful sunrise this morning, orange-y clouds and a pastel sky. Sniff. What a flash, bam, alakazam, wonderful you came by. Time out while I time out while I make this turn here.

In any case, good morning again, Gentlemen. Captain Mr. Phelps, Captain Kirk, Captain Picard, and actually I should have always included amongst you, Gentlemen, *[whispery]* I don't know how I left him out! Mr. Barnett, the man with 2 t's, The Man Against Crime, Ralph Bellamy Man Against Crime! Barnett with 2 t's. The light-turn signal here, Reisterstown Road and Village Queen Drive. **TAPE ENDS**

IN HERE ARE THE FIRST FOUR PAGES OF TAPE016A.ED1, PAGES WHICH I RECORDED ON AUGUST 12, 1991, OVER THE FIRST FOUR PAGES OF TEXT RECORDED ON JUNE 10, 1991.

That was the tape ending, and now the beginning in. I've made the turn, going down Reisterstown Road. Big Endians and Little Endians.

What the hell was I talking about? Aaahhh, yes, Nancy's unveiling. "You will never lose the light that shines from your eyes." The line from Darren's poem the one on her stone. Kind of a beautiful burgundy colored stone. And oh, there're so many people there and God crying crying crying crying crying crying crying crying crying *[said rapidly]*. Sophie said Kathie did not look well, she looked kind offff her face looked didn't look well. In any case, I'm glad I didn't finish and try to read that poem. Because it's the kind of poem, as it says in the beginning, it should have been written ten months ago when Nancy died and in the pain and the grief and not not it doesn't seem to try to find any, and it and doesn't seem, it does *not* find any relief from the grief. Ain' no relief how do you spell relief from the grief? There is no relief from the grief. You don't spell relief from grief, ROLAIDS. You don't spell it. I don't know how you spell it. But anyhow, I'm going down Reisterstown Road today.

Very grief poem poem. Oh, yes, and I was thinking, yesterday Bob and Shirley were here also, they everybody came over to our house afterwards. Come-ona my house, my house-a come-on-a. Rosemary Clooney. From the 50's. Aaannd thinking last night, all of a sudden, that one of the things one of the memories that I have of Nancy's death and funeral, one of the memories that I'll carry always is as we were in the car outside the funeral home, Danzansky's, and the hearse pulled away, the line started to pull away, and there was Shirley standing out on the sidewalk, Nancy's friend Shirley. *[almost crying]* And she looked so lost and alone. She was standing there talking, you could tell, I could tell, that she was saying goodbye to Nancy. And what it made me think of last night was the story of Marion Kershman told about how Abe walked into the house and said, *[voice breaks into crying]* Charlie Krome's dead. Charlie Krome's dead. Charlie Krome is dead. Friends. Friends don't let friends drive dead. Sniff. Here I am. Friends don't let friends drive dead. Pikesville Office Supply. Oh, they're not gonna open till what time? Time out.

And Ruthie on Saturday when she called back to tell me about Aunt Esther, to ask me about Aunt Esther and me having a big fight, I said, No, Ruth. And then she got on the phone, and she was crying and she said, It was so hard living with the reality when she had to listen to Aunt Esther's confabulations, and she said she was sorry, and she was apologizing. And I said, No, Ruth, you don't have ever have to apologize to me. Sniff. And what I actually meant was, of course, that I owe her an apology because I was the one who should've been watching out for Aunt Esther, I was the one who should have been calling her at least once a week. Sniff. And be going by to see her once a week. Sniff. Just to say hello and see how she was doing. But, noooooo, man, no, no no nononononononono, Sidney can't do that kind of stuff, can he? Anyhow. Over and out. Was that over and out? Or was it something else that flitted through my mind? Through my mind flitting. Flitting through the mind flit flit flit. Quick, Henry, the Flit!

[NOTE: THE ABOVE PART BEGINNING WITH "That was the tape ending....." WAS THE PART I HAD MISTAKENLY OVER-RECORDED ON SIDE A OF TAPE 16.]

TAPE NUMBER 17

NOTE: FIRST TAPE TRANSCRIPTION: TAPE WHICH BEGAN IN AUGUST 1991 AND WHICH ENDED DECEMBER 1994. THERE WAS A GAP FROM SOME TIME IN JANUARY 1992 UNTIL THE DECEMBER BEGIN AGAIN RECORDING. USED NEW TRANSCRIBER; DEC BEGIN AGAIN DATE WAS 12/10.

MONDAY, AUGUST 12, 1991

Oh, Good Morning, Gentlemen. Boy is this gonna be a screw-up!

It's 7:35 Monday, August the 12th. Listen. I did it again. On that last tape, just before this I again turned it over back to SIDE A without realizing and recorded some of today over what had been previously recorded. The second time I've done that. And it, pardon me, I need to pay attention to what I'm doing here a little bit. But coming down now, down Reisterstown Road, past Woodland, and now Virginia Avenue, cheez, I just said this into a different tape that I listened to. Virginia Avenue and what is it? Saint Ambrose Lane. Whatever it is, and then there's Royce Avenue, by God, there it is, Royce Avenue, 3316 Royce Avenue. Saw Jerry and Kathie yesterday at the unveiling for Nancy, Nancy's unveiling, the unveiling of Nancy's stone, Sunday, August the 11th, nineteen hundred and ninety-one. August, September, October, actually, it's not 10 months, Ruth, it's 9 months, 8-and-a-half, close to 9 months.

Ruth said at the graveside yesterday after the ceremony was over something about how, y y you hear people say there's always a reason. Well, this was this was a time in which she said there was no reason. And that's what you have to accept is that there was no reason. Once you can accept that, and there was no reason. And later PW sitting in our kitchen said there were two things he holds against God: one is this with Nancy, and the other was Eva. Eva Hirsch, Eva's death, Ronnie's first wife, Eva, Eva, Eva, Eva. And at one point yesterday, F asked me, she said, "Now, how old was your father when he died?" She said, "Was he 40?" And I said, "No, he was 44." She had thought he was 40, but actually he was 44. He had lived 10% longer than she had thought. Also yesterday, Ruth asked, was talking about the picture that Amy, Craig's girlfriend, had done, the pastel that she had done that she had done from the pictures I had given Ruth of of Springhill Avenue, and and oh, here we come to Keyworth Avenue, PS 59, on the left, PS 59, now the Alcott whatever they are, on the right was what used to be G's and P's, okay, and there was PO was down here on the right, and here we come to Springhill Avenue, Reisterstown Road and Springhill Avenue--Go, guy!--and up to the left is Jake's and up past there was 2614 and 2616. And I showed both the picture that, a photograph that I took, and the the pastel that Amy had done and F said something about how beautiful it was, and yes, "And it never looked that good even when we lived there." And, "It was seen as through the haze of love and memory," but really it was not what it was, it was not even, it lacks the vibrancy or something. *[sniffling]* And, cheez, I have to call remember to call S to change the appointment date from Thursday--I'll never make it by 3 o'clock, it's gonna be impossible for me to make it down there. Anyhow, and here I go and here I go and here I go, and where am I going? Yes, and the pictures. And, how what Amy put back, she put the rosebush back in front of our house, and she put the snowball bush in front of Aunt Esther's house.

Lordy, Lordy, Lordy, Lordy, Lordy, who would have thought, lo, these many years ago? Who would have thought who would have thought who would have thought? Thought the thought the thought the thought the thought.

And actually that was the basic premise of the poem that I was writing Saturday night for Nancy about the unveiling, for the unveiling, who would have thought who would have thought? I never thought I would never have thought in 1964 that we'd be taking her out to her own grave. And it was not a *Mi-she-berach*, it was an *El-molay-rachamim*, that the guy said. *El-molay-rachamim.*

THURSDAY, OCTOBER 17, 1991

"I picked up my shovel, and I walked to the mine, I loaded 16 tons o' number 9 coal, and the strawboss said, Well, a bless my soul. Y' load 16 tons, whattdaya get, another day older" In the background, it's 8:43 am, Thursday, October 17th, just coming down to EXITS 9A and B at Cold Spring Lane, a quarter mile, heading south on the Jones Falls Expressway. And they just announced that Tennessee Ernie Ford had died this morning in Reston, Virginia "Fightin' and trouble are my middle name" I remember that New Year's Eve party. "I was raised in the canebrake by an old mama lion" Oh, God, JD, what was that? "Can't no hightoned woman make me walk the line, y' load 16 tons" And MB and "and whattdaya get, another day older" Oh, God, it's been 15, what "and deeper in debt" No, 35, 36 years. "Saint Peter, don't ya call me, cause I can't go, I owe my soul to the company store--do,do,do,do dadadadaaahhh" Traffic is incredible, and raining. "If y' see" Gray, rain day, and "me comin'" Tennessee Ernie Ford is dead. "better step aside" Step aside. "a lotta men didn't, a lotta men died, one fist of iron, the other of steel, if the right one don't get y', then the left one will, y' load 16 tons, whattdaya get" Tennessee Ernie Ford, the old peapicker. "another day older and deeper in debt, Saint Peter doncha call me 'cause I can't go, I ooowe my soul to th' company store do, do, do, do dadadadaaahhh" *Radio 60, WCAO* Tennessee Ernie Ford, dead at the age of 72, Tennessee Ernie Ford. *[The dj begins to speak in the third person, of how he remembers this song. That it reminds him of his father. He speaks of how his father taught him to snap his fingers to this song, and how he thought it was the neatest thing in the world, the snapping of fingers, that sound.]*

What flashed as that announcement was being made and they were playing that song, the the white flashing lights on the WBFF TV broadcasting tower which looms up taller than the triple tower that used to be that I used to see from from the window of the bedroom on Springhill Avenue, used to be the WJZ, WAAM, then there was also the WBAL tower which I think is gone, has been gone for a while. The flashing white lights, and all the cables, the wires and the cables holding those towers upright, and I remember, that's not the one, but the old WBAL TV tower, how I started mentally in my mind mental mind to write a poem about it, and I remember once saying something to Raizel about how it would be the start once, I thought it was, would be the start of something like an urban *Leaves of Grass* which, of course, like a million other things, I never wrote.

MONDAY, JANUARY 13, 1992??

Testing 1, 2, 3. It's Monday, January 13th, 6:32, leaving Levindale. Lou said, "After this," while he was eating, he said, "After this, let's go home." And later, he said, when he was in the wheelchair, "The main thing is, I want to get to the house." And at one point he said, "I just want to be the same."

And he also said something, "Let's get out of here." And when I, he said, "Let's get outta here." And then when I tried to leave, he held my hand and wouldn't let go. And when I said, I had to go ho had to leave, he said, "Wait till he leaves." And I said, "Who, Lou?" And he said, "Him." And there was nobody there.

FRIDAY, FEBRUARY 14, 1992??

Testing 1, 2, 3, Testing 1, 2, 3.

Good morning. This truck, truck you, truck! Truck you, Truck! Good morning, guys, it's Friday morning, February the 14th, Valentime's Day, it's 8:34 am, and here I am on the Jones Interstate 97 heading towards Annapolis for another meeting, in the background you can hear Miles Davis from the CD *'58 Sessions* or '58 Miles, and this is *Fran Dance*. Let me turn it up a little and bring it to the front speaker so you can hear a little better.

Okay, guys, there's so much to talk about I don't know where to begin, let me begin by saying this, I just asked myself why am I not writing? I don't know why I'm not writing. Driving in the car and there was snow on the roof of the car, the Ford Escort. Here comes that Mack truck down the right, here he goes, here he goes, go, Big Daddy, go! And all of a sudden, the snow that had been crusted by some ice and freezing rain that fell overnight, slid down the back over the windshield, and the what was once a clear wind rear window suddenly was streaked with the water left behind by the melting snow, and it looked like it was, all of a sudden, instead of seeing clearly, I was seeing through like looking through an Impression looking at an Impressionist painting, looking at light filtered through water in lines the way iron filings would be aligned on a magnet, y' know, they used to do that, we used to do that in elementary school. And I said to myself, "Why am I not writing?" Looking at that big Mack truck, the big four big letters M-A-C-K. This S-O-B is really. Asshole, up yours too, Jack. Pardon my language there, Gentlemen. Looked up behind me so close I thought he was gonna knock off my rear bumper.

Anyhow, thinking about writing, wish I was writing, not only the terrorist one about Ocean City, and not only the one about the the plot to kill Stalin, but also about these four guys, Perry Neam, Peter Burns, Ean Now, Sam Etegal, and I thought of one, another one the other day, a fifth member of that group, Jim Gezint, Tzim Gezint Tzim Tzim Gezint, to your health, Jim Gezint, Perry Neam, Peter Burns, don't get any on your Peter cause it burns, Sam Etegal, *Ça m'est egal*, then Ian Naow, Ian Naow? yes, Ian Naow, as they say in Shakespeare, Snakes, Shakespeare, Snakeshit. But also Jim Gezint, Tzim Gezint. But anyhow, it was it is what, the way it was going to begin, what began this. In the beginning there were the four of them, and when they were together, they were really together, and when they were apart, they were never really apart. There were the 4 four them. And had they been baseball players, they would have been the all-time infield, not just Tinkers to Evers to Chance, but also the great Brooks Robinson at third. Had they been football players, they would have been the greatest backfield of all time. Oh, let's say, Y.A. Tittle, the Colts, '58 Colts, there would have been Tittle, and Ameche, and I don't remember who else was in there, Lenny Moore, I'd have to find out who else was in there. Aahhh, not the Four Horsemen of the Apo had they been evil they would have been the Four Horsemen of the Apocalypse. Had they been winds they would have been the Four Winds. And like that, sort of.

Miles Davis and *Stella By Starlight.* Whoa, careful. Now, Miles Davis now playing *Love for Sale. Love for Sale* It reminded me of back in Monterey, California, when I was at the Army Language School, HAM, M and I went into a like a gallery, I think it was in Carmel, and *Love for Sale*, and a girl was in there and she had a hi-fi playing, LP's, and she was playing, and what happened to be on as we walked in and we were walking around looking at stuff was a jazz version of *Love for Sale*, I don't think it was Miles Davis, I'm not sure who it was, but it may have been Miles Davis for all I know.

Or for all I remember. *Memento ergo sum.* I remember therefore I am.

Now playing is "Pictures at An Exhibition," this is the part I want you to hear: *[music leading to string snapping]* Almost, get ready, get ready for this. *[music string snapping]* That was it. With the fade-out. One more time, get ready. *[music string snapping]* Chekhov, *The Cherry Orchard*. The guitar string snapping in the distance. The sound of that. The end of *Scheherezade*. The end of the Beatles', what was that, wait, *Sergeant Pepper's Lonely Hearts Club Band [static all along] [music string snapping]* One more time, get ready. *[music lead into string snapping]* Is that fantastic! *[static]* Is that incredible! Chekhov's guitar string. *Scheherezade.* The Beatles. *[lots of static]* God, it makes me want to cry, it's so beautiful.

SATURDAY, DECEMBER 10, 1994:

Good morning, this is supposed to be on AVR, which means it's not supposed to be recording unless I actually talk, but it is recording, or it started recording even though even though I wasn't talking. Let me stop talking and see what happens.

Good morning, it's Saturday, December the 10th, it's 11:41 a.m., that last recording made about recording was made today. I thought there was something wrong with this thing, but actually it turns out that the only thing wrong was that I had it on pause, so it wouldn't play, I had the switch set wrong. Now, I'll have to stop it.

Actually, what I'm going to do is, I'm going to put this tape away in my collection of other tapes that have been previously recorded, and I'm going to start a new one today, December the 10th at 11:46 a.m., so this one is being closed down to be put away and I'll start a new tape.

THE NANCY TAPES

SIDNEY KROME

The last word belongs to Darren, Nancy's son, the poem he wrote for her while she was in the CSICU.

The Sun in Your Eyes
by
Darren P. Via

*As I look up to the cloudy skies
I tell myself not to cry
for I long to see
the sun in your eyes*

*I think of yesterday and
the love you gave us all
but I will not cry
'cause I long to see
the sun in your eyes*

*I can't possibly grasp
what you think or feel
at this time*

*probably not of yourself
you're probably thinking
of the ones you love and
all the strong caring ties*

*and how to shine with
the sun in your eyes*

*And I will not cry
No, I will not cry
'cause you have shown me
the deep blue sky*

*And you will never lose
the sun that shines
in your eyes*